LEGACIES SHARED SERIES   Janice Dickin, series editor   ISSN 1498-2358

The Legacies Shared series preserves the many personal histories and experiences of pioneer and immigrant life that may have disappeared or have been overlooked. The purpose of this series is to create, save, and publish voices from the heartland of the continent that might otherwise be lost to the public discourse. The manuscripts may take the form of memoirs, letters, photographs, art work, recipes or maps, works of fiction or poetry, archival documents, even oral history.

   Looking for Country: A Norwegian Immigrant's Alberta Memoir Ellenor Ranghild Merriken, edited by Janice Dickin · No. 1

   The Last Illusion: Letters from Dutch Immigrants in the "Land of Opportunity" 1924-1930 Edited and translated by Herman Ganzevoort · No. 2

   With Heart and Soul: Calgary's Italian Community Antonella Fanella, edited by Janice Dickin · No. 3

   A History of the Edmonton City Market, 1900-2000: Urban Values and Urban Culture Kathryn Chase Merrett · No. 4

   No One Awaiting Me: Two Brothers Defy Death during the Holocaust in Romania Joil Alpern · Copublished with Jewish Heritage Project · No. 5

   Unifarm: A Story of Conflict and Change Carrol Jaques, edited by Janice Dickin · No. 6

   As I Remember Them: Childhood in Quebec and Why We Came West Jeanne Elise Olsen, edited by G. Lorraine Ouellette and Ian Adam · No. 7

   Alequiers: The History of a Homestead Mike Schintz · No. 8

   Far from Home: A Memoir of a Twentieth-Century Soldier Jeffery Williams · No. 9

   To Be a Cowboy: Oliver Christensen's Story Barbara Holliday · No. 10

   Betrayal: Agricultural Politics in the 1950s Herbert Schulz · No. 11

   An Alberta Bestiary: Animals of the Rolling Hills by Zahava Hanan · No. 12

   Memories, Dreams, Nightmares: Memoirs of a Holocaust Survivor Jack Weiss · No. 13

   The Honourable Member for Vegreville: The Memoirs and Diary of Anthony Hlynka, MP Anthony Hlynka, translated by Oleh Gerus · No. 14

THE HONOURABLE MEMBER FOR VEGREVILLE

The Memoirs and diary of
ANTHONY HLYNKA, MP

INTRODUCED AND TRANSLATED BY
Oleh W. Gerus
EDITED BY
Oleh W. Gerus and Denis Hlynka
FOREWORD BY
Gerald A. Friesen

CENTRE FOR UKRAINIAN CANADIAN STUDIES
UNIVERSITY OF MANITOBA
*This project has been funded in part by the
Ukrainian Canadian Foundation of Taras Shevchenko.*

UNIVERSITY OF
CALGARY
PRESS

© 2005 Oleh Gerus and Denis Hlynka
Published by the University of Calgary Press
2500 University Drive NW Calgary, Alberta, Canada T2N 1N4
www.uofcpress.com

Ukrainian language documents © Stephanie Hlynka 1996
Antin Hlynka, Posol Federalnoho Parliamentu Kanady, 1940–49 © Stephanie Hlynka 1982
Introduction and translation © Oleh Gerus 2004

LIBRARY AND ARCHIVES CANADA CATALOGUING IN PUBLICATION

Hlynka, Anthony, 1907-1957.
   The honourable member for Vegreville : the memoirs and
diary of Anthony Hlynka, MP / introduced and translated
by Oleh W. Gerus ; edited by Oleh W. Gerus and Denis Hlynka.

(Legacies shared, ISSN 1498-2358 ; 14)
Translation in part of: Antin Hlynka, posol federalnoho parliamentu
   Kanady, 1940-1949.
Includes bibliographical references and index.
ISBN 1-55238-137-4 (pbk.) ISBN 1-55238-206-0 (bound)

   1. Hlynka, Anthony, 1907-1957. 2. Ukrainian Canadians—
Alberta—Biography. 3. Politicians—Canada—Biography.
4. Canada—Politics and government—1935-1957. 5. Vegreville
(Alta.)—Biography. I. Gerus, Oleh W., 1939- II. Hlynka, Denis
III. Title. IV. Series.

FC581.H59A3 2005   971.063'092   C2004-906773-7

No part of this publication may be reproduced, stored in a retrieval system or transmitted, in any form or by any means, without the prior written consent of the publisher or a licence from The Canadian Copyright Licensing Agency (Access Copyright). For an Access Copyright licence, visit www.accesscopyright.ca or call toll free to 1-800-893-5777. Exceptions to this restriction are extended to reviewers who may quote brief passages for inclusion in reviews. Every effort has been made to obtain permission for all third party materials.

 Canada Council for the Arts   Conseil des Arts du Canada

We acknowledge the financial support of the Government of Canada through the Book Publishing Industry Development Program (BPIDP) and the Alberta Foundation for the Arts for our publishing activities.

Cover design, page design and typesetting by Mieka West.

This book is dedicated to the memory of Anthony Hlynka. It is also dedicated to Stephanie Hlynka for keeping alive the memory of her husband. She has been the custodian of all his original diaries, unfinished memoirs, and notes. This book is based on these original materials, which remain in her possession. Without her full cooperation, this book would not exist.

TABLE OF CONTENTS

Foreword xi
Preface xv
Acknowledgments xvii
Introduction xix

part I SELECTIONS TRANSLATED FROM *Antin Hlynka, Posol Federalnoho Parliamentu Kanady, 1940–49* AND DRAFT MANUSCRIPT 1

Reflections on the Way to Ottawa 3

How I Became a Politician 17

The 1940 Election 25

The 1945 Election 41

Responsibilities of a Ukrainian Canadian Member of Parliament 47

The Ukrainian Liberation Struggle 51

For Equality of All Canadian Citizens 59

part II FROM HLYNKA'S DIARY AND NOTES 67

On the Way to London 69

Hlynka in London 73

Hlynka in Germany 97

Hlynka in Italy 123

The Return from Europe: Helping the Refugees 139

Epilogue 143

part III SELECTED SPEECHES OF ANTHONY HLYNKA 145

House of Commons: In Defence of Western Farmers *21 June 1940* 147

House of Commons: United Canada *25 November 1940* 153

What Price Freedom? *11 March 1944* 163

House of Commons: Farmers' Problems *23 May 1944* 169

House of Commons: Displaced Persons in
  Europe *26 September 1945* 171

The Problem of Ukrainian Displaced Persons *12 January 1946* 183

Immigration *5 June 1946* 187

House of Commons: 1947–48 Budget and the
  Canadian Farmer *27 May 1947* 199

Ukrainian Christmas *5 January 1948* 201

House of Commons: Displaced Persons and
  Refugees *31 May 1948* 207

Canada *28 September 1948* 219

House of Commons : The Present Position of Agriculture
  and its Outlook for the Future *7 March 1949* 221

Empire Day *24 May 1949* 225

Hlynka in Hansard 229

p art IV HLYNKA AS PORTRAYED IN THE CANADIAN PRESS 235

  Parliament *26 November 1940* 236

  Ukrainian Calls for Unity *26 November 1940* 237

  Ukrainian Hall Dedicated to Furthering War
    Effort *17 March 1941* 238

  Ukrainians in Canada Insist Mother Country Remain
    As Independent *23 May 1941* 240

  Only Ukrainian Member Is Proud of Countrymen
    Here *26 June 1941* 243

  Biography: Anthony Hlynka *November 1941* 245

  Definite Plan of Freedom Urged *2 February 1942* 248

  Anthony H. Hlynka Declares: For More Definite
    Pronouncement of Peace Aims *3 February 1942* 250

  Asks Canada Help Ukraine Regain Her
    Independence *3 February 1942* 265

A Peculiar Speech *7 February 1942* 268

Letter to the Editor *16 February 1942* 270

Group of Ukrainian Critics Communist, M.P.
    Charges *21 February 1942* 273

Crowded Theatre Hears Ukrainian M.P. *23 March 1942* 276

End of Race Prejudice Foreseen by Alberta M.P. *15 April 1942* 279

Mr. Hlynka Will Vote "Yes" *27 April 1942* 281

Editorial *29 April 1942* 283

Parliamentary Personalities: Anthony Hlynka, Social
    Credit, Vegreville, Alberta *March 1943* 285

Urge Ukrainians Boost Enlistments to Forces and
    Further War Drives *17 March 1943* 288

Charges People to Throw Whole Effort into War *24 March 1943* 291

Independent Ukrainian State is Urged in Brief
    to Ottawa *31 March 1943* 293

Ukrainians Play Big Role in Canadian War Forces *3 April 1943* 295

Extract from Maclean's Magazine *1 August 1943* 297

Vegreville's M.P. Married in Toronto *1 December 1943* 299

Hlynka Worries about Ukraine *27 March 1945* 300

Editorial *28 March 1945* 302

Vegreville M.P. Thanks Electors *12 July 1945* 304

Hlynka Urges Stop Pressure on Repatriates *25 September 1945* 306

Socred M.P. Slams Reds *26 September 1945* 307

Hlynka Protests Moving Ukrainians *25 January 1946* 309

Protests Patriot Betrayal to Russian Persecution *26 January 1946* 310

People Weep, Raise $5,000 as Hlynka Pleads
    for Refugees *28 January 1946* 312

'Cross Town with Cross *20 March 1946* 315

Warns against Fifth Column Work of Reds *20 May 1946* 317

All-Canada Ukrainian Congress An Eye-Opener *7 June 1946* 319

Lakehead Ukrainians Hear Anthony Hlynka; M.P. *8 June 1946* 321

Sees Red Voting Immigration Bar *24 March 1947* 325

MP Describes Plight of Displaced Persons *28 April 1947* 327

Urges Canada to Accept Desirable Europeans *5 May 1947* 329

Hlynka Asks Immigration Relaxation *12 May 1947* 332

Merely Half of Camps for Displaced Persons Found "Fair to Good" *26 May 1947* 335

Strictly Political *12 July 1947* 337

BC Can 'Handle' 230,000 Immigrants *10 October 1947* 339

Hlynka Praises The Star's Anti-Commie Leadership *4 May 1948* 341

Hlynka Asks D.P.'s Use Idle Farms *1 June 1948* 343

Voters of Vegreville Constituency! *1949* 345

MP Claims Reds' Vote Defeated Tony Hlynka *3 October 1949* 347

APPENDICES 349

1   The Historical Significance of Ukrainian Group Settlement in Canada   351

2   The Federal Constituency of Vegreville, Alberta *1940s*   357

3   The First Ukrainian Canadian in Parliament: Michael Luchkovich   367

4   Additional Readings   377

5   Speeches to Vegreville Riding   379

NOTES 381

FOREWORD

This volume is a tribute to Anthony Hlynka, an Albertan of Ukrainian origin who played a prominent role in public life between the mid-1930s and the mid-1950s. His contributions to Canada have been allowed to disappear from public view. Given the centennial in 2005 of the grant of provincial status to Alberta and the passing of many of the people whom he helped to rescue from refugee camps after the Second World War, it is fitting that the "Legacies Shared" series should publish this volume now. Mr. Hlynka's work on behalf of the people of Ukraine, whether in their homeland, in displaced persons' camps, or in their new countries in the Americas and farther afield, deserves to be remembered. Moreover, his contribution to the principle of plural citizenship in prairie Canada, an ideal that evolved out of the thinking and practice of many ethnic and religious leaders, constitutes a significant legacy to all Canadians.

This rich set of historical documents offers many points of entry into Hlynka's story. A diary covering his travels and negotiations in postwar Europe, transcribed from the notebooks in which it was originally recorded and carefully translated by Dr. Oleh Gerus of the University of Manitoba, establishes Hlynka's claim to be the "father of the third wave" of Ukrainian immigration to Canada. Excerpts from his memoir, published in Ukrainian and now translated by Dr. Gerus, offer insights into the politics of north-central Alberta during the 1930s and 1940s. Newspaper articles and speeches document the public life of a forceful representative of Canada's Ukrainian community at the height of his influence.

Anthony Hlynka was as much a conservative, an anti-Communist, and a Ukrainian nationalist as he was an apostle of Social Credit philosophy, but because of these other loyalties, he fit very well within Alberta's Social Credit movement between 1935 and 1950. He entered politics in prairie Canada at a moment when the electoral battles between the Communist, Liberal, Co-operative Commonwealth (CCF), Conservative, and Social Credit parties offered an extraordinary range of ideologies from which to choose. The very range of options both offered an opening to Hlynka in the 1940 federal election and then cut short his political career in 1949. Despite his obvious gifts, he was unable to find a new role in electoral politics before his untimely death in 1957.

Dr. Oleh Gerus provides the context for these documents in a fine introduction. As a small child Professor Gerus lived in one of those displaced persons' camps and traveled with his family to Canada in the third wave of Ukrainian immigration. He writes movingly of camp life, outlines the context of Ukrainian wartime politics, and addresses the issues raised by the profound ideological clashes of the twentieth century. He explains frankly that support for the German invaders by one Ukrainian political faction led to the creation of a Ukrainian division of the German army, a force whose internment accounts for Hlynka's visit to Italy in 1947. He notes that Hlynka was struggling to save the nearly ten thousand Ukrainian soldiers from repatriation to the Soviet Union and that Canada eventually changed its policy and admitted some of these men as immigrants. I would add that as a result, the division became a source of bitter conflict in Canada in subsequent decades.

As this rich collection of documents demonstrates, Anthony Hlynka waged an unrelenting campaign to ensure that Ukraine's national status was recognized and that freedom from ethnicity-based discrimination was the norm for Canadian citizens of Ukrainian origin. A half-century later, it takes a newcomer to prairie Canada only a little while to discover that Hlynka's plural ideal has been largely realized. The newcomer will also learn that Ukrainian nationalism remains a part of the landscape and politics of the prairies. That sense of ethnic difference within Canadianness now colours the integration experience of newcomers from around the world.

Prairie ideals include the equality of all ethnic groups and accommodate the citizen's continued activity in homeland politics, at least to a degree. They assume that ethnic group members will accept continuing obligations to the group. Despite an individual's loyalty to the limited identities derived from religion and ethnic group, prairie ideals demand an equivalent commitment to party, province, region, and nation. In short, the practice of maintaining one's loyalty to an ethnic group must be matched by an equivalent loyalty to an overarching Canadian identity. This practice – Anthony Hlynka's practice – has become a prairie-wide norm. His story underlines why ethnic identity remains a force in Western Canada. It suggests, too, that Canada's multiculturalism is much more complicated than any simple model of either melting pot or mosaic can convey.

Gerald Friesen, Fellow of the Royal Society of Canada
University of Manitoba

PREFACE

The main purpose of this book is to add to the body of knowledge that informs Western Canadian history, politics, and culture. A secondary goal is to re-acquaint the Ukrainian Canadian community with one of its distinguished sons, Anthony Hlynka, the memory of whom has diminished over the years. From 1940 to 1949, Hlynka served two terms as Member of Parliament, representing the Social Credit party from the predominantly Ukrainian constituency of Vegreville in Alberta. As the only Ukrainian Canadian parliamentarian during his first term, he became the public voice of his community-at-large about whose aspirations and dynamics the general Canadian public was largely uninformed. But it was Hlynka's involvement with the post-World War II refugee crisis, particularly his efforts to end forcible repatriation of the Ukrainians to the Soviet Union and to resettle them in Canada, that distinguished his political service. The fact that thousands of Ukrainian refugees, the so-called displaced persons, were admitted to Canada and were given an opportunity to start their lives anew can be, in some part at least, attributed to the efforts of Anthony Hlynka.

This book, then, is essentially a tribute to Anthony Hlynka's memory by one of those grateful refugees. It is not a critical biography. It is based on his diary, his memoirs and his speeches as well as on Canadian press reports and draft materials that Anthony was preparing for publication when he suddenly died in 1957. It should be pointed out that Hlynka's manuscript was conceived in the Ukrainian language because he intended it to serve the former refugees who preferred their mother tongue. Hlynka wanted to explain to this "third immigration" the nature of Canada's democracy, to impress upon them the pioneering experience and the achievements of the Ukrainian settlers in opening the Canadian west, and to remind the newcomers of his own role in drawing public attention to their precarious existence in refugee camps. However, it was only in 1982 that Stephanie Hlynka, widow of the late Anthony, was able to publish parts of her husband's manuscript as *Antin Hlynka, Posol Federalnoho Parliamentu Kanady* (Anthony Hlynka, Member of Canada's Federal Parliament). Today, in view of the fact that the vast majority of Ukrainian Canadians no longer use the Ukrainian language, the present work, undertaken with Mrs. Hlynka's indispensable co-operation, is rendered in English.

The book consists of four distinct parts. The first part contains selected, edited, and translated parts of the 1982 edition, which discuss Canadian-Ukrainian issues. The second part contains passages from Hlynka's incomplete Ukrainian-language diary and includes a collection of notes in English and Ukrainian that cover his lobbying efforts in Europe on behalf of the refugees and his fact-finding tour of their camps. The third part presents some selected speeches by Hlynka, including a list that directs the reader to Hlynka's speeches and participation in the House of Commons. The fourth part presents press accounts concerning Hlynka's political activities. Since Hlynka was a high profile politician, he and the Ukrainian-related issues that he raised for the first time received extensive coverage in the mainstream Canadian press. The elevation of the Ukrainian Canadian fact from a parochial to the national level was a major achievement in itself. An appendix includes three of Hlynka's essays dealing with the Alberta scene from the twenties to the fifties.

It is hoped that this tribute to Anthony Hlynka will remind all Canadians that his contributions to Canada and the Ukrainian Canadian community specifically were indeed of historical significance.

ACKNOWLEDGMENTS

This book is the first major publishing project of the Centre for Ukrainian Canadian Studies, University of Manitoba, as a part of its mandate to create, preserve, and communicate knowledge that deals with Ukrainian Canadiana.

The editors thank the following individuals who supplied support, information and comment: David Carr (University of Manitoba Press), Dr. Donna Norrell (University of Manitoba), Dr. Peter Savaryn (former Chancellor of the University of Alberta), Myron Momryk (National Archives of Canada), James Kominowski (University of Manitoba), Jars Balan and Andrij Makukh (Ukrainian Canadian Program, Canadian Institute for Ukrainian Studies), Ken Romaniuk and Gloria Romaniuk (Ukrainian Cultural and Educational Centre), Dr. Alexandra Pawlowsky and Marina Ranenko (Centre for Ukrainian Canadian Studies), Orest Martynowych, Zoria Lytwyn and Bonnie Gerus. Members of the immediate and extended Hlynka family who provided input include Stephanie, Eugene, Gloria, Olga, Linda and Myron.

The map of the federal riding of Vegreville (1940-49) was reconstructed from original documents by Marilyn Croot (Calgary), with assistance from Radomir Bilash (Edmonton), Dan Huzyk (Vancouver) and Fr. Eugene Maximiuk (Vegreville). Dr. Ihor Stebelsky (University of Windsor) supplied the map of the displaced persons' camps.

Major funding for this book was provided by the Ukrainian Canadian Foundation of Taras Shevchenko. Additional funding was provided by the Ukrainian Studies Foundation of British Columbia, the North Winnipeg Credit Union, the Michael Sowsun (Solsun) Endowment Fund and the Dmytro Mymka Endowment Fund, University of Manitoba.

INTRODUCTION

In 1949, Anthony Hlynka, who for nine years had been a highly visible and popular Ukrainian Canadian Member of Parliament for Vegreville, Alberta, suffered an unexpected defeat in the federal general election. The Ukrainian press in Canada reacted with surprise and shock. Commenting on the event in an editorial, the *New Pathway / Novyi shliakh* (9 July 1949), which was one of the leading Ukrainian-language newspapers in the country at that time and a long-time supporter of Hlynka, attributed his defeat to "the unscrupulous Bolshevik political machine." The paper praised Hlynka's exemplary service on behalf of Western farmers, his commitment to human rights and Canada's ethnic diversity, and his courageous initiatives in acquainting Canada with Ukraine's aspirations to freedom. But above all, the *New Pathway* emphasized the importance of Hlynka's efforts not only to save wartime refugees from forcible repatriation to the Soviet Union but also to facilitate their immigration to Canada. The editorial optimistically prophesied: "We are confident that our community in Canada and the Ukrainian people in general will not forget Hlynka's advocacy on their behalf."

Alas, in its final comment the *New Pathway* was mistaken. Apart from several commemorative articles in Ukrainian newspapers, the memory of Anthony Hlynka gradually faded in the Ukrainian Canadian community. Even in scholarship his legacy has been much undervalued. Such neglect of him is undeserved, and this volume is intended to acquaint the reader with Hlynka's life and accomplishments.

In a sense, Hlynka can be said to be the victim of history itself since, as a rule, the fickle finger of fame identifies the firsts but seldom the seconds. Thus Michael Luchkovich, the first Ukrainian in Canada's Parliament, has been appropriately remembered and celebrated by the Ukrainian Canadian community while Hlynka, who was the second Ukrainian to be elected to the House of Commons, has been forgotten by many. This happened despite the fact that in his first term, 1940–45, a period of the Second World War, he was the only Ukrainian Canadian voice in Parliament. Indeed, at that time Hlynka was the only democratically elected Ukrainian parliamentarian in the world. He understood both the uniqueness and the responsibility of his position and, with a sense of mission, tried hard to be a deputy for all Ukrainians, except the communists. The last term of his distinguished parliamentary career, 1945–49, coincided with the outbreak of one of the most crucial periods in the history of the twentieth century, the Cold War. The advantages afforded by his parliamentary tenure provided Hlynka with an ideal opportunity to publicize before the government and the people of Canada issues of ethnic discrimination, the cause of Ukraine's freedom, and the plight of European refugees. He took full advantage of the unfolding situation.

Anthony Hlynka was born on 28 May 1907 in Western Ukraine, in the progressive village of Denysiv, Ternopil county, in Halychyna (Galicia), then a province of the Austro-Hungarian Empire. At that time, the Liberal government of Canada was pursuing an aggressive immigration policy with the purpose of settling and colonizing the nearly empty lands of Western Canada, and three years later the Hlynka family, like tens of thousands of other Ukrainians, was lured to Canada by the attraction of free land.

An estimated 700,000 Ukrainians emigrated from the Austro-Hungarian empire to North and South America before 1914. Some 170,000 chose Canada, the majority coming from Halychyna. Austrian agrarian policies and a high birth rate had created an acute land shortage, and emigration oversees seemed the most obvious remedy to escalating peasant poverty. It should be noted, however, that the Ukrainians of Austro-Hungary, a constitutional monarchy, had educational facilities in their own language, a vigorous political life and parliamentary representation, and community organizations. In fact, Austrian Ukrainians had the basis of a modern society. They were poor but they were not the stereotypical illiterate masses in sheepskin coats. At the same time, the Ukrainians in the autocratic Russian empire, in sharp contrast to their cousins in Austro-Hungary, endured systematic national repression; even the Ukrainian language was banned.

The goal of most Ukrainian immigrants was land, and the Canadian homestead policy, which offered 160 acres of land for a $10.00 fee, seemed like a bonanza to those accustomed to subsistence plots in Halychyna and Bukovyna. Even though Ukrainians were latecomers to the land scramble for prairie homesteads, and thus much of the best agricultural land was already gone, they preferred the wooded land for timber and fuel. Most of the immigrants to Western Canada settled in a wide arc along the southern edge of the Canadian Shield, from the rock-strewn Stuartburn area of southeastern Manitoba through the scrublands of the Interlake to the Yorkton-Saskatoon district and along the valley of the North Saskatchewan River to Vegreville, east of Edmonton. Not surprisingly, they settled in close-knit communities (blocs) to give each other material and psychological support in this new and inhospitable land. Indeed, there was no "welcome wagon." But the pioneer generation met the demanding challenges with hard work and tenacity, and in the process, made a major economic contribution into the opening of the Canadian West, a legacy of nation-building which its descendants remember with justifiable pride.

Although farmland was the initial objective of the Ukrainian immigrants, a significant number of men found employment in resource industries and with the railroads. Some remained in the ethnic, working-class North End of Winnipeg ("The Gateway to the West") or found their way to similar districts that soon appeared in Saskatoon and Edmonton. Here, just as in the rural areas, the urban immigrants clung to each other for support, and East and Central European ethnic neighbourhoods – Ukrainian, Polish, Jewish, and German – sprang up in towns and cities across the Canadian West.

The Hlynkas homesteaded in Delph, Alberta, which Anthony Hlynka describes in his reminiscences, in today's ecomuseum called Kalyna Country, a region east and north of Edmonton. Pioneering hardships notwithstanding, education was valued and encouraged in the Hlynka household. Anthony, the eldest boy, was a big, bright, inquisitive youngster who graduated from Alberta College, a technical high school in Edmonton. To his everlasting disappointment, however, he could not afford to go on to university, as would his two younger brothers. On the other hand, it appears that he more than made up for his lack of university education by his inherent intelligence and insatiable appetite for reading. This passion for Ukrainian and English political literature reinforced in him his Ukrainian national consciousness while at the same time developing a powerful sense of loyalty to Canada and the British Empire. Young Anthony would come to consider himself a Ukrainian Canadian, a prototype of cultural duality not yet well understood during the pioneer period.

Hlynka was aware that Ukrainians, unlike North Europeans, did not have the proper ethnic profile and did not blend immediately into their host society. The distinctiveness of their language, religion, and culture made them noticeably different, and these obvious differences caused apprehension on the part of the Anglo-Canadian majority, which was accustomed to social uniformity and feared diversity. It was believed at that time that such desirable national homogeneity could be achieved in Western Canada by assimilating Ukrainians and other East Europeans with the British majority.

The assimilationist drive and rampant discrimination had intensified at the outbreak of the First World War in August 1914. The negative image of Ukrainians was reinforced by groundless suspicions of disloyalty, simply because they had come from the Austro-Hungarian Empire, which was at war with the British Empire. All those Ukrainians in Canada who were not yet naturalized automatically became "enemy aliens" when Canada entered the war. Under the emergency powers of the War Measures Act, the federal government began to register and intern enemy aliens suspected of being anything other than peaceful and loyal residents of Canada. Over 80,000 were compelled to register, and more than 8,000 male enemy aliens, the vast majority of whom were Ukrainians, were interned in twenty-four detention camps, located largely in Canada's wilderness. In addition to this flagrant miscarriage of justice, those who were unemployed could also be interned and those who attempted to enlist in Canada's Armed Forces were generally rejected as untrustworthy.

The First World War had cut off further overseas immigration to Canada. The severe economic slump after the war and the prevailing discriminatory attitude prompted a major revision of Canadian immigration policy. The vagueness of the Immigration Act of 1910 allowed the federal government to satisfy the public demand for immigration restrictions. The world was divided into "preferred" and "non-preferred" countries as a source of future immigrants. Needless to say, Ukrainians fell into the second category. It was only in 1925 that the federal government responded to the labour needs of the expanding railroads and allowed the railroad companies to recruit workers in Eastern Europe.

In the post-World War I restructuring of European borders, the bulk of the Ukrainian territory had been incorporated into the new Soviet Union while Bukovyna found itself under Romania, and Halychyna and Volhynia had become part of the revived Poland. As Polish–Ukrainian relations were tense and economic conditions severe, the majority of the estimated 68,000 Ukrainian immigrant-labourers who entered Canada between 1925 and 1930 came from Halychyna. This interwar immigration, or the "second wave," was more politicized, having been exposed to modern Ukrainian nationalism and socialism.

In the 1930s, the Ukrainian Canadian community, the single largest Slavic group in the country and a predominantly Western rural one, was in a state of flux. The community's internal dynamics produced a highly energetic organizational life, which was characterized by intense rivalry and conflicts along religious and political lines. The traditional Greek Catholic and Orthodox churches enjoyed the allegiance of the majority of the Ukrainian people while the minority embraced a variety of forms of Canadian Protestantism and even atheism. On the Ukrainian political front, a fundamental and irreconcilable line of division existed between the so-called progressive or politically left camp and the democratic-nationalist movement. The left was represented by the well-organized Ukrainian Labour and Farmer Temple Association (ULFTA), later renamed as the Association of United Ukrainian Canadians (AUUC), which was pro-communist, defended the interests of Ukrainian workers and favoured Soviet Ukraine, then part of the Russian-dominated Soviet Union. The ULFTA, which had branches throughout Canada, including Vegreville, also acted as a front for the Canadian Communist party. The more popular democratic-nationalist side, reinforced by the brief interwar immigration, saw itself as the true defender of the Ukrainian nation, both in Ukraine and in Canada. It consisted of feuding liberal, conservative, and nationalistic blocs, all of which considered civic equality and retention of the Ukrainian language crucial for community integrity. All Ukrainian organizations, including pro-communist, promoted full integration of Ukrainians into Canadian society but they firmly opposed assimilation because they believed that it threatened their cherished ethnocultural identity.

Among the democratic-nationalist groups, the two most influential organizations with Canada-wide affiliates were the Ukrainian Self-Reliance League (USRL) and the Ukrainian National Federation (UNF). The USRL was a Canadian-focused community alliance closely associated with the Ukrainian Orthodox church, while the UNF was a strictly secular organization allied with the European-based Organization of Ukrainian Nationalists (OUN). These two bodies competed vigorously with each other for consolidation and domination of the fragmented community. Attracted by the ideals of Ukrainian nationalism, Anthony Hlynka joined the emerging UNF and earned the wrath of the Alberta USRL, whose leading members had close links to the Liberal party.

Slurs against minorities were still quite acceptable in Canadian society in the 1930s and 1940s. As Canada's largest unassimilated minority (306,000 in 1941), the Ukrainians were an easy "foreign" target of Anglo-Canadian discrimination and bigotry, particularly during the acute economic dislocation and widespread unemployment caused by the global depression of the 1930s. Throughout Canada, right- and left-wing ideologies offered various solutions to the prevailing economic and social problems and struggled for public support. In Alberta, the political right prevailed in the form of Social Credit, while next door in Saskatchewan the political left in the form of the democratic socialist Co-operative Commonwealth Federation, or CCF, preached economic justice and redistribution of wealth. The CCF won power in Saskatchewan in 1940.

Anthony Hlynka's evolving political outlook, as indicated in his writings and speeches, was multidimensional. To Hlynka, British parliamentary democracy and the new British Commonwealth of Nations represented the ideal of freedom, dignity, and mutual respect. His political philosophy abhorred the socio-economic and political power of big business. Yet he embraced compassionate capitalism with socially responsible and just government. Brought up in a patriotic Ukrainian household, Hlynka was an ardent anti-communist who saw Russian communism as the brutal oppressor of Ukraine and a threat to Canada. Above all, he loved his Canada and desperately wanted Canada to respect his Ukrainian people as equals.

From his student days in Edmonton, Hlynka had been a politician-in-waiting. He had been actively involved in a number of Ukrainian cultural organizations, where he developed a reputation as a forceful and entertaining public speaker. A founding member of the Ukrainian National Federation in 1932, Hlynka helped with the organization of its locals and with subscription drives for its official publication, *Novyi shliakh* (*New Pathway*). In 1935 he turned to publication and launched a short-lived periodical, *Klych* (*The Call*) in which he waged an ideological war against communism. On economic and social issues, Hlynka embraced the controversial monetary theory of the new Western Canadian protest movement, the Social Credit, which seemed to offer a simple solution to a complex economic situation.

In 1935 the Social Credit swept to power in Alberta under the leadership of a radio evangelist, William Aberhart ("Bible Bill"), on the promise of direct money payments to all Alberta citizens, protection of the impoverished homesteads from bank foreclosure, and observance of high ethical standards. Although most of its monetary reforms would be ruled unconstitutional, the Social Credit managed to retain control of the province for thirty-six years. Ukrainians in Alberta's bloc settlements enthusiastically supported the new party and succeeded in electing several Ukrainian Social Credit candidates to the provincial legislature. However, the first Ukrainian cabinet appointment in Alberta had to wait until 1962.

Ukrainians in the Prairie provinces had had consistent, albeit politically diverse, legislative representation since 1913 but there was no Ukrainian federal presence following the defeat of Michael Luchkovich (1926–35). Hlynka, disturbed by the economic plight of western farmers, a sector that included the majority of Ukrainian Canadians, and impressed by Aberhart's legendary oratory, became a member of the Social Credit party in 1937. With the collapse of *Klych*,

Hlynka edited the party's Ukrainian-language newspaper, *Suspilnyi kredyt* (*The Social Credit*). Then in 1939, driven by the conviction that it was essential for the Ukrainian Canadian community to have its own voice in the House of Commons and encouraged by growing public support, he contested and won the Social Credit federal nomination for the rural Vegreville riding. With its overwhelmingly Ukrainian population, the riding was the former parliamentary seat of Luchkovich, who had served under the United Farmers of Alberta banner and whom young Hlynka much admired as a champion of ethnic civic equality in Canada. During the wartime election of 1940, Hlynka took the riding from the Liberal incumbent to become the second Ukrainian Canadian Member of Parliament and, at the age of 33, one of the youngest MPs.

Though a powerhouse in Alberta, in Ottawa the federal Social Credit (also known briefly as New Democracy) constituted a loosely united party of ten members, about whom Hlynka makes no comment in his recollections. Hlynka rapidly distinguished himself as an articulate advocate of the western farm sector and as a passionate Canadian patriot who unreservedly supported Canada's unity and war effort. The influential journal *Canadian Business* (see p. 285) described him as "one of the most remarkable men in the House of Commons." Hlynka's quick and thorough grasp of issues, coupled with his pleasant personality, earned him respect from many MPs outside his Social Credit caucus. In fact, on Ukrainian issues, one of his allies was a prominent Liberal member from Saskatchewan, Walter Tucker.

As the only Ukrainian in the House, Hlynka immediately drew the attention of the curious press, and the young MP quickly capitalized on this unexpected celebrity status. A former journalist himself, he keenly appreciated the power of the press, the main source of news and information in that pre-television era, to influence public opinion and government policy. Now he was in a position to acquaint Central and Eastern Canada, which knew little and cared less, about Ukrainian Canadian issues. To do so, he cultivated amicable relations with those Ottawa reporters who covered Parliament. Newspapermen found "Tony" Hlynka, who was built like a football player, to be an engaging advocate of Prairie and ethnic grievances, one with a simple name that they could easily spell and pronounce. His popularity with the mainstream press was further enhanced by his open admiration of British culture and parliamentary democracy. During his nine-year tenure in Parliament, the Canadian press came to identify him as the authoritative voice for the Ukrainian Canadian community and as the quintessential ethnic politician who was Ukrainian Canadian first and Social Creditor second. Equally, many of Hlynka's fellow Ukrainians looked up to him for leadership. Herein lies his fundamental significance in the history of Ukrainians in Canada.

As far as can be determined, the degree of attention that Hlynka and, by association, Ukrainian issues were given by the English-language press during his tenure was unprecedented and has not been equalled until Ukraine's "Orange Revolution" of 2004. Thanks to Hlynka, Ukrainian Canadians, whose community life had elicited little interest or attention from the Canadian media, were no longer a marginal factor in Canadian life. As indicated in the House of Commons official record of debates, the *Hansard*, Hlynka spoke more than ninety times. He was a frequent participant in parliamentary debates on a variety of issues – agriculture, transportation, banking, old age pensions, and Canada's foreign policy. Hlynka's presentations reflected his common-sense approach, balancing his partisanship with constructive criticism and even occasional praise of government bills, a practice no longer current in today's highly partisan Parliament. As an authoritative spokesman of the Ukrainian Canadian community, Hlynka condemned ethnic ("racial") discrimination and defamation of Ukrainians, and argued for civil equality for all Canadians, regardless of their origins.

What distinguishes Hlynka's parliamentary service, however, was his persistent advocacy of the complex subject of Ukraine, a virtual enigma for the general Canadian public. After World War II he focused on the urgent subject of Ukrainian refugees who faced forcible repatriation to the Soviet Union. Hlynka spoke thirteen times in the House of Commons about the plight of refugees, urging the federal government to resettle them in Canada. Much of what he said in the House was reported in the Canadian press, often as front-page news, and it frequently elicited editorial commentary.

The outbreak of World War II in 1939 compelled the main Ukrainian nationalist organizations to present a united patriotic front to the Canadian public and government. Bitter memories of blatant anti-Ukrainian discrimination and internment during the First World War ensured that the community would indeed consolidate itself around Canada's war effort. The formation of the Ukrainian Canadian Committee (now the Ukrainian Canadian Congress) with Ottawa's assistance in 1940 gave the Ukrainian community, for the first time, a coordinating and representative body. Since then, the UCC gradually became the officially recognized voice of all Ukrainians except the left, whose activities were banned during the first part of the war. It was the UCC that in the 1960s developed Hlynka's ideal of civic equality into the radical political concept of Canada as a multicultural nation, one only later embraced by other Canadian ethnic groups. As a Member of Parliament, Hlynka maintained close links with the UCC and facilitated its presentations to the federal government.

During the course of the war, nearly 10% of Canada's Ukrainian population – that is, more than 35,000 young Ukrainian Canadian men and women – enlisted in Canada's Armed Forces. A combination of personal patriotism, a sense of adventure, community appeals, and a desire to escape the depression-ridden prairies was responsible for such a disproportionately large enlistment. This public demonstration of Canadian patriotism on the part of the Ukrainian community was warmly welcomed by the press. The 1942 conscription vote, however, was the only wartime embarrassment to the UCC and Hlynka. Wishing to free itself from its earlier pledge not to introduce military conscription, which was strenuously opposed in Quebec, the Canadian government called a national plebiscite on 28 April 1942. Despite an intensive pro-conscription campaign by the UCC and Hlynka, a number of Ukrainian-populated ridings, especially around Winnipeg, rejected conscription in the face of overwhelming approval by the rest of English-speaking Canada. In an atmosphere of war hysteria and super-patriotism, the scattered Ukrainian opposition was severely criticized, with the *Winnipeg Free Press* particularly strident. The UCC blamed the negative Ukrainian vote, in part, as an expression of protest against alleged discrimination in the Armed Forces. For his part, Hlynka pointed out in Parliament that Canadian officers of Ukrainian descent did face subtle discrimination, for they remained frozen in the junior ranks. Nonetheless, the strong

Ukrainian presence in the Armed Forces, notably the formation of the Ukrainian Canadian Servicemen's Association in England, would facilitate the very important initial contacts with Ukrainian refugees after the war. These servicemen first alerted Canadians to the unfolding but little-known drama of the forced repatriation to the Soviet Union of Ukrainian refugees in Germany and Austria.

In February 1942 Hlynka opened in Parliament and in the Canadian press the first wide-ranging political discussion about the unresolved question of Ukraine, which had formerly been under Soviet control but was then occupied and being ravaged by Nazi Germany. The subject of Ukraine had become politically sensitive in Canada after the Soviet Union, Germany's partner until June 1941, joined the Allies. In a major speech, Hlynka argued that on the basis of the Atlantic Charter, the Ukrainian nation had the right to self-determination and that an independent Ukrainian state would help to ensure post-war stability in Europe. The reaction was immediate and widespread. *The Edmonton Bulletin* printed his entire speech. The Ukrainian press applauded him. But the Liberal government of Mackenzie King, which preferred to avoid the thorny Ukrainian problem altogether, was not at all pleased to have Hlynka advocate the independence of Ukraine at a time when the Soviet Union was Canada's wartime ally and was enjoying a high degree of public sympathy for its dogged struggle against Germany. Pro-communist groups were in an uproar and viciously attacked Hlynka for his proposal, while several Canadian editorials criticized Hlynka's apparently divided loyalties between Canada and Ukraine.

This wave of criticism did not deter Hlynka from his public concern for Ukraine. In March 1945, when the end of the war in Europe was in sight, he made an unusual proposal during the House debate on the formation of the United Nations Organization. Hlynka argued that in view of the fact that Ukraine was a Russian colony, Canada should support the participation of the Ukrainian Canadian Committee and of its American equivalent as Ukraine's democratic proxy at the founding meeting of the United Nations in San Francisco. This proposal raised many eyebrows and again generated considerable discussion in the press, the tone of which was mainly sceptical and critical. The *Calgary Albertan*, for instance, scolded Hlynka for involving Canada in the ethnic political feuds of Eastern Europe. What Hlynka did not know at the time of his presentation was that the February 1945 Yalta Conference, whose proceedings were confidential, had in fact granted separate United Nations representation to the two Soviet republics, Ukraine and Belorussia, as a recognition of their horrendous wartime suffering, both human and material. Soviet Ukraine thus became one of the original members of the UN. However, the ambivalent international status of Ukraine – technically sovereign but in reality a Russian colony – created a degree of confusion and dissension among Ukrainian Canadians, since even some nationalists began to assume that Ukraine could, in fact, attain sovereign statehood within the Soviet system.

When the war finally ended in Europe in April 1945, much of that continent lay in ruins. Allied-occupied Germany and Austria were inundated with unprecedented millions of uprooted and desperate refugees, mostly from Eastern Europe. Among them were between two and three million Ukrainians. These consisted largely of young men and women, mainly the conscripts of German slave labour, and surviving Ukrainian inmates of the dreaded concentration camps. Others were refugees from communism who chose to leave their homeland in the face of the impending Soviet occupation. The mind-boggling complex logistics of the refugee situation initially overwhelmed the Allied military authorities and their United Nations Relief and Rehabilitation Administration (UNRRA). At the historic Yalta Conference, President Roosevelt of the United States, Prime Minister Winston Churchill of Great Britain, and Josef Stalin of the Soviet Union had agreed to the mutual repatriation of citizens found in their respective zones of occupation. Special multi-party repatriation commissions were established to process the refugees, who were placed in temporary camps administered by the UNRRA. Most of the East European refugees succumbed to communist propaganda and to homesickness and returned home voluntarily. However, a significant number refused to be repatriated, mainly for political reasons. These "refuseniks" were branded as traitors to the Soviet fatherland. Having experienced communism first-hand, however, these refugees expected severe retribution, even execution, were they to return home. Soviet repatriation commissions, operating freely in the British and American zones of occupation, used force, generally provided by the unwitting British and American soldiers, to repatriate many of the unwilling refugees. The fact that thousands of Soviet Ukrainians were able to escape repatriation was due in large part to the confusion surrounding the meaning of citizenship, nationality, and ethnicity. Since Western Ukrainians (Halychany and Volhynians) had Polish citizenship prior to the outbreak of the war, they were generally classified as Poles and as such were not liable for compulsory repatriation; consequently, many from Soviet Ukraine passed themselves off as Western Ukrainians.

The human tragedy of compulsory repatriation, which was further dramatized by occasional suicides, drew the attention of the American and British press and appalled the Western world. In Canada, the Ukrainian Canadian Committee protested against forced repatriation. But it was Hlynka's fact-finding tour of the camps in Germany, Austria, and Italy, undertaken because, as he said, "realizing that had not my parents emigrated to Canada and had taken me along with them, today I could have been one of the unfortunates in the displaced persons' camps," that truly energized his campaign to halt repatriation and resettle the refugees in Canada. His passionate speeches in Parliament, on the radio, and at mass rallies throughout Canada in defence of the human rights of the refugees and his scathing condemnation of communism captured the attention of the public and the Canadian government. Other Members of Parliament also began demanding the relaxation of Canada's stringent immigration laws.

International political circumstances were also changing in favour of admitting the refugees. The Cold War began with the imposition of communism in Soviet-occupied Eastern Europe. In Canada the wartime friendship between this country and the Soviet Union had been shattered by the highly publicized Gouzenko espionage affair. In 1945 Igor Gouzenko, a code clerk in the Soviet embassy in Ottawa, had defected, taking with him evidence of a major Soviet espionage ring in Canada with connections to the United States and Britain. In the aftermath of this scandal, a dozen Canadian citizens were convicted as spies. This episode and the Sovietization of Eastern Europe shifted public mood in support of Hlynka's hardline anti-communism and into greater humanitarian concern for the plight of the refugees. The AUUC and the reinvented Communist party, the Labour Progressive party, responded to the Hlynka challenge by launching a vicious smear campaign. Their goal was to remove him from Parliament and thus silence him. Although they failed badly in the 1945 election, as Hlynka swept to victory, they persisted with their strategy and would finally succeed in ousting him four years later.

The East European refugees who refused repatriation, a little less than a million, were placed under the care of the UNRRA and designated as Displaced Persons, informally referred to as DPs. Of these around 200,000 were Ukrainians. The precise number, however, is impossible to determine because some Ukrainians claimed Polish or Romanian citizenship in order to avoid repatriation. The UNRRA organized the DP camps into national categories. Initially there were around 200 Ukrainian camps in West Germany and Austria, largely in the American zone. The camps ranged in size from several hundred to nearly five thousand inhabitants (Regensburg). Admission to these camps was governed by the UNRRA screening process, which rejected many refugees as DPs. The UNRRA provided shelter, food rations, used clothing, and rudimentary medical services. Those outside the camps had to rely on their own resources or on the not-so-compassionate assistance of the bitter Germans.

Except in the initial stages, the Ukrainian DPs in general did not conform to the popular television image of modern-day refugees filled with hopelessness and despair. The Ukrainian DPs consisted primarily of political refugees from communism in their homeland. With a disproportionately large intelligentsia, Ukrainian DPs regarded themselves as a nation-in-exile, and they categorically rejected repatriation in favour of emigration overseas, with the United States and Canada as preferred destinations. Having successfully endured the ravages and trauma of the war, they now developed a group survival strategy based on a tight organization of their camp communities. The degree of organized life in the camps varied, but on the whole it was structured and orderly. While American and British military commanders were in charge, internal camp administration, including security, was in the hands of its residents. The Organization of

Ukrainian Nationalists (OUN) tended to monopolize camp authority. Individual camps were coordinated and represented by the Central Representation of the Ukrainian Immigration.

As with any political emigration, party politics dominated camp life. More fundamental to the well-being of the DPs, however, was the role played in the camp by church, school, and press.

It is a given that one's sense of faith always intensifies during times of crisis. Represented by Catholic, Orthodox, and Baptist churches, religion flourished in the atmosphere of anxiety that characterized the early days in the camps. As the majority of refugees were from predominantly Catholic Halychyna, the well-organized Ukrainian Greek Catholic Church was the largest constituency. The Ukrainian Autocephalous Orthodox Church had emigrated from Ukraine with its entire hierarchy and a number of clergy. That church, too, established parishes throughout the camp system. The churches, in addition to fulfilling their traditional spiritual functions, acted as national institutions with recognized moral authority. In contrast to the sad history of interdenominational strife in the Ukrainian homeland, religious life in the camps was a model of mutual respect and ecumenism. In a number of camps, the faithful even shared the same chapels, which they had built together.

Although single persons predominated in camps, there were many families with children. The organization of camp schools was rather spontaneous. The initiative came from parents, teachers, and the clergy. After a rough beginning frustrated by a shortage of books and school supplies, the educational situation improved appreciably with the UNRRA's assistance and donations from Canadian and American charitable societies. By 1947 a network of Ukrainian schools, with a primary and secondary enrolment of over 10,000 students and a standardized curriculum, functioned throughout the camp system. Considering the acute abnormality and the transitional nature of camp life, the DP educational experiment was a marvellous success story.

Another remarkable achievement of the DP experience was the camp press. The birth of camp journalism was hindered not only by technical difficulties but by the fact that the UNRRA did not recognize Ukrainian nationality until the summer of 1947. This meant that the early camp publications were seriously impeded by restrictions and censorship. But beginning with a typewritten sheet, *Nashe zhyttia* (*Our Life*), in the Austrian camp at Augsburg, camp journalism was born and flourished. An amazing number of 327 periodicals, many of high literary and intellectual quality, appeared in those few camp years. For a historian, the camp press offers a vital means of access to an understanding of the DP experience.

Of course, living conditions in the camps were Spartan, but they were for the most part tolerable. Munster Lager, located in the British zone, not far from the city of Bremen in Northern Saxony, with 1,600 Ukrainians, was a typical DP camp. Situated in a pine forest, it was a former German military facility with an adjacent Allied prisoner-of-war compound separated from the military area by barbed wire and land mines. In May 1945, the freed Allied POWs had been replaced with German prisoners. The land mines would remain a constant danger until 1948, however, when the DPs were transferred to other camps. But for those three years, Munster Lager was home to both Western and Eastern Ukrainians, people who for ages had been divided by geopolitics and were now thrown together by circumstances. For many residents, the camp experience proved to be a vehicle for socialization, as regional stereotypical images and attitudes were either reinforced or purged. For instance, the Easterners perceived the Halychany as arrogant and patronizing super-nationalists, while the Halychany considered the Easterners to be overly Russified and Sovietized. The Bukovynians, on the other hand, were admired for their business acumen in the important black market. Such differences of perception notwithstanding, there emerged a prevailing sense of national solidarity. The internal power structure at Munster Lager was controlled by the members of the OUN. However, the Easterners, many of whom had had the benefit of Soviet technical training, ensured that the camp infrastructure – water, power, and sanitation – would function more or less satisfactorily. The latter group also excelled at improvisation, turning the discarded military equipment that littered the camp into much needed cook stoves, bread ovens, and heaters.

Meals in Munster Lager were provided by the UNRRA soup kitchen. Additional food rations consisted of powdered eggs, canned meat and fish, turnips, and potatoes. Children were given condensed milk and cod liver oil. Adults also received American cigarettes, which were used as currency until the new German marks were issued. In terms of its organizational life, Munster Lager had a church shared by the Orthodox and the Catholics, a primary school, a secondary school or "gimnasiia," a trade school, and a community hall, which was the centre of the camp's political, cultural, social, and sport activities. Health care, including periodic fumigation of the barracks, was provided by an infirmary staffed by several camp doctors and nurses. Indeed, Munster Lager, like many other camps, was a lively and structured, albeit somewhat stressed, community.

Back in Canada, the cautious Liberal government was uncertain as to whether or not the economic boom that Canada was enjoying would continue after the war. As a result, Ottawa maintained a policy of very limited immigration despite demands in Parliament to relax restrictions and admit some refugees. When the Senate began to hold public hearings on post-war immigration in 1946, the Ukrainian Canadian Committee and its pro-communist rival, the Association of United Ukrainian Canadians, appeared before the Senate committee with conflicting recommendations. Anthony Hlynka introduced the UCC delegation, which argued in favour of admitting the Ukrainian DPs and characterized them as a major potential asset for Canada. The AUUC, on the other hand, opposed their entry, denouncing them as Nazi collaborators; in reality, the Communist objections were based on their awareness that any influx of people who had experienced the Soviet system would undermine Canadian communism. Indeed, history proved this fear justified. The Senate committee, informally briefed by Hlynka in advance, openly sympathized with the UCC.

Anthony Hlynka responded to hundreds of letters from concerned and worried Ukrainian Canadians across the country by undertaking a private and self-financed fact-finding mission to Europe. His stated objectives for the mission were to ensure fair treatment for the Ukrainian DPs on the part of international relief agencies, to safeguard them against forcible repatriation, and to lobby the London diplomats of potential host countries to resettle the refugees as quickly as possible. Hlynka's diary record of the mission covers the period between November 1946 and February 1947. This period was the formative and thus the most unsettling time of the DP experience, when camp conditions varied from satisfactory to intolerable. Hlynka's diary also establishes the important fact that in international diplomatic and military circles, his status as a Member of Canada's Parliament opened many doors that were closed to all other Ukrainian representatives and lobbyists. Hlynka used this unprecedented political access to advance at every opportunity the cause of Ukrainian DPs, about whom there was much misinformation among members of the UNRRA and the Western occupation authorities. It is quite likely that Hlynka's intervention, in combination with that of other critics of compulsory repatriation and with the worsening relations between the West and the Soviet Union, led to the termination of repatriation in 1947.

Hlynka's underlying objective, however, was the relaxation of Canadian immigration policy in favour of the refugees, and he persisted in raising that issue throughout the country. Between 1945 and 1947 immigration controls remained tight, limiting admission to sponsored close family members and to cases involving special economic considerations. While the government was deciding what to do, Hlynka, upon his return from Europe, initiated the Resettlement Fund, the purpose of which was to help those Ukrainian refugees who were excluded from the DP camps and from the critical assistance of the UNRRA. Between parliamentary sessions, he energetically campaigned on behalf of Ukrainian as well as other East European refugees, and he fundraised throughout Canada. The money he collected supplemented the general Ukrainian Canadian Relief Fund administered by the UCC, which provided much-needed aid in the British zone.

Finally, in May 1947, under pressure from Members of Parliament, the UCC, other Canadian ethnic groups, and those of Canada's resource industries who were experiencing serious labour shortages, Prime Minister Mackenzie King announced a policy of European-oriented selective immigration. Able-bodied DPs were now eligible for admission to Canada. In the meantime, other countries – among them Australia, Brazil, and Argentina – had already agreed to resettle most of the DPs. The United States, which provided the largest share of funding for the project, also accepted the largest number. By the time the UNRRA's successor, the International Relief Organization (IRO), ended the resettlement program and closed the camps in 1952, Canada had accepted nearly 190,000 DPs and refugees, of whom more than 34,000 were Ukrainians. The arrival of these highly nationalistic and ambitious Ukrainian immigrants would have a profound, if not always positive, impact on the nature of the Ukrainian Canadian community.

One aspect of the immigration issue with which Hlynka was involved concerned a Ukrainian unit in the German army interned by the British in Italy. This was the Galicia division, whose formation needs an explanation. During the German occupation of Ukraine from 1941 to 1944, the much-suffering population had exchanged Stalinist terror for Nazi genocide. The war inflicted unspeakable devastation on Ukraine and its people. Casualties were in the millions; perhaps as many as fourteen million inhabitants of Ukraine (including those serving in the Soviet Armed Forces) perished. The German objective for Ukraine was totally exploitative. Ukraine's specific function was to supply food, raw material, and slave labour for the German war machine and to serve as a base for German expansion eastward. Nazi atrocities provoked Ukrainian resistance to the Germans, which turned into large-scale partisan warfare (Ukrainian Insurgent Army) under the leadership of the Ukrainian nationalists. Throughout the war, the OUN maintained an uncompromising opposition to both Nazism and communism. The Ukrainian resistance to Soviet power was finally crushed in the 1950s.

Given the brutality of the German occupation, why would some Ukrainians willingly serve in the German army? In 1943 Germany began replenishing its huge military losses to the Red Army with foreign volunteers who were formed into combat divisions. The initiative for organizing a Ukrainian division came from the governor of Halychyna, which was under separate German administration from the rest of Ukraine. His proposal found support in the Ukrainian Central Committee, the only officially sanctioned Ukrainian community organization under German occupation, but was strongly opposed by the underground Organization of Ukrainian Nationalists. The strategy for the establishment of a Ukrainian unit within the

German army was based on a popular, but as it turned out, wholly unrealistic view of the post-war scenario of Eastern Europe. According to this view, Germany would certainly be defeated while the devastated Soviet Union would be totally exhausted. It was assumed that the ensuing power vacuum in Eastern Europe would then create favourable conditions for the Ukrainian struggle for independence, the success of which would depend on the existence of a well-trained professional army. The proposed Ukrainian division in the German army was thus envisaged by Ukrainian patriots as the nucleus of a national army of post-war liberation.

The idea of creating a national Ukrainian army had powerful appeal in Halychyna. Over 80,000 Ukrainian volunteers, inspired by patriotism and by reluctance to become German slave labour, registered for the proposed division. Of these, however, only 27,000 were found physically fit for military service, a fact that reflects the sorry state of the Ukrainian people under German domination; only 19,000 were finally enlisted. Furthermore, German authorities would not allow the division to have Ukrainian command and to display an obviously Ukrainian character; rather, they imposed upon it the regional label Galicia (Galizien). The division did obtain the important commitment that it would be used exclusively against Soviet forces and not against the West. The Galicia division became operational in 1944 and quickly suffered disastrous losses trying to halt the Soviet advance. Regrouped, the division was posted to Slovakia against communist partisans. Just before the war ended, in a patriotic but futile gesture, Galicia renamed itself the First Division of the Ukrainian National Army and surrendered to the British.

The nearly 10,000 Ukrainians were interned in northern Italy at Camp Rimini. There the soldiers were screened by British intelligence, UNRRA officials, and a reparation commission. Their fate, however, remained dubious as they were under constant threat of forced repatriation to the Soviet Union. Like many Ukrainians, Anthony Hlynka considered the Galicia division to be an organization of Ukrainian patriots who, in the given circumstances of the time, had no other choice but do what they had done. He paid a visit to Rimini, which was a major morale booster for the internees, and lobbied for the removal of the division from Italy, as he believed that the fragile Italian government would cede to Soviet demands. The fate of Galicia was ultimately settled by the emerging Cold War triggered by Soviet expansionism in Eastern Europe. As relations between the West and Moscow worsened, the division was moved to Britain, where the Ukrainian POWs helped in the reconstruction of the country. Subsequently released, the Ukrainian veterans lobbied to emigrate to North America. But when the question of their possible immigration to Canada arose, a communist-led campaign was launched to deny them entry. However, persistent Ukrainian Canadian pressure on Ottawa and the intensification of the Cold War led in 1950 to the lifting of the ban on German military personnel, and this allowed a substantial number of the Galicia to enter Canada as individual immigrants. In response to strident attacks on the division by communist and Jewish groups, in 1985 the federal government appointed the Deschenes Commission, which exonerated the division of all allegations of wrongdoing during the war. Nonetheless, unwarranted attacks on the division have had serious consequences. They stigmatized the Ukrainian Canadian community, distorted the realities of Ukraine's wartime conditions, forced Ukrainians into a defensive position, and compromised Ukrainian-Jewish relations in Canada.

While Anthony Hlynka was winning praise throughout Canada for his refugee crusade, trouble was brewing in the Vegreville riding. In the 1949 federal election, the communists skilfully twisted the facts of the refugee issue against Hlynka. Although Canada's postwar economy was booming, the legacy of the Depression was still fresh in Alberta and the Communists exploited the inherent fear of unemployment that open immigration posed. ("Bringing in the DPs by the thousands only means that our own sons and daughters won't be able to get jobs.") While fear-mongering probably had some effect, it was the Communist strategy not to nominate a party candidate that actually played a decisive role in the outcome of the election. In the elections of 1940 and 1945, Vegreville had had a four-party race: Social Credit, Liberal, CCF, and Labour Progressive (communist). In 1949 the Liberals finally nominated a Ukrainian candidate, John Decore, a local lawyer active in the Ukrainian Self-Reliance League. Decore was one of those Ukrainian Canadians who believed that a Ukrainian MP on the government side could accomplish more for the community than could Hlynka, who belonged to a minority party. Traditionally, both federal Liberals and the Communists had a solid base in the Vegreville riding but had not been able to unseat Hlynka because of the split vote. When the weak CCF decided not to field their candidate, the Communists seized the opportunity to avenge themselves on Hlynka. They formed an anti-Hlynka coalition around Decore's candidacy. For the first time in Canada, the contest was between two Ukrainians, thus ensuring the continuity of Ukrainian representation in Parliament but seriously threatening Hlynka's re-election. The Ukrainian press in Canada, notably the Edmonton *Ukrainian News* and the Winnipeg *New Pathway*, waged a vigorous publicity campaign, urging the Vegreville voters to support Hlynka, and it warned against a Communist conspiracy. In the end, however, Hlynka lost to Decore 8,872 votes to 7,117; that is, Hlynka received only 31 fewer votes than he had in the 1945 victory.

The anticipated political benefits to the Ukrainian community from having a member in the ruling Liberal party did not materialize. Nevertheless, since the 1949 election there has been a continuum of Ukrainian Canadian MPs, mainly from the Progressive Conservative party. In politics, representation symbolizes recognition and influence, if not power. For the Ukrainian Canadian community, consistent parliamentary representation, including federal cabinet appointments, signified the achievement of full integration into the Canadian political mainstream. Yet it is noteworthy that not one of the dozens of Ukrainian Canadian MPs since 1949 has demonstrated a degree of competence and commitment to Ukrainian Canadian issues comparable to that of Hlynka. It would take Paul Yuzyk (1963–86), a Progressive Conservative Senator and an historian from the University of Manitoba, to become Hlynka's worthy successor as a parliamentary advocate for multi-ethnic equality in Canada and for Ukraine's freedom.

Hlynka took his political defeat hard. He was disappointed and hurt by the fact that his home constituency had rejected him at the very time that Ukrainian Canadians throughout the country seemed so understanding and appreciative of his political activities beyond the Vegreville constituency. His sense of betrayal was compounded by emerging health problems and personal financial difficulties. In 1949 retiring or defeated members of Parliament had to serve a full ten years in order to receive a parliamentary pension. Hlynka had served only nine years and thus did not qualify for a pension. After the exhausting election campaign, Hlynka was left with little money and a family of three to support. His return to the insurance business, in which he had been involved during the 1930s, was disappointing. It appears odd that in view of Hlynka's stature and lengthy service to the Social Credit Party, a position could not have been offered to him with the Alberta Social Credit administration. Hlynka, a proud man, would not lobby for an appointment. In the fall of 1949, Hlynka refused to campaign in Manitoba's provincial election against a fellow Ukrainian and the respected Liberal Speaker of the Legislature, Nicholas Bachynsky. It was believed by some that the Social Credit leadership did not appreciate Hlynka's decision, and this may have precluded his chances of gaining a post with the government of Alberta. Still, despite his defeat Hlynka remained for a time a celebrity among the Ukrainians, appearing throughout Canada as guest speaker at numerous community functions, and for a time the press still paid heed to the words of the former Member of Parliament for Vegreville, Alberta.

The last period of Hlynka's life is difficult to define. He remained involved in politics and ran as the Social Credit candidate in the 1953 election but lost again to Decore, who conducted a well-organized campaign. This time, in addition to Decore, three other Ukrainian MPs were elected, one each from the CCF, Social Credit, and Progressive Conservative parties. Hlynka's friends urged him to enter provincial politics, but here Hlynka was faced with an ethical dilemma. The provincial constituencies in which Hlynka was well known were represented by sitting Ukrainian Social Credit members of the legislature who had campaigned for him in the past. A principled man, Anthony Hlynka would not challenge a colleague for nomination.

In his involuntary political retirement, Hlynka recognized the unfolding historical significance of the post-war or "third immigration," notably its direct impact on the social and political dynamics of the Ukrainian Canadian community and its indirect one on the fabric of the broader Canadian society itself. Hlynka had mixed feelings about the former DPs. On the one hand, he was pleased that their uncompromising anti-communism began to erode the Ukrainian left. On the other hand, he was disappointed in the failure of the newcomers to integrate themselves into existing community organizations that needed new blood. Instead, they formed new and strictly Ukraine-focused organizations, threatening the fragile unity of the Ukrainian Canadian Committee. It appeared to Hlynka that the third immigration group did not have a proper appreciation of Canada and notably of the contributions of Ukrainian Canadians either to their new homeland or to the cause of Ukraine. With this in mind he began to write, in the Ukrainian language, an autobiographical introduction to Canadian politics and major Ukrainian Canadian issues.

Sadly, on 25 April 1957, a month before his fiftieth birthday, Anthony Hlynka, who had been battling hypertension, died suddenly in Edmonton and the manuscript remained unfinished. The Ukrainian press was full of elegant eulogies, praising Hlynka's remarkable courage to speak out on Ukrainian issues and lamenting his premature demise. His funeral and burial at St. Michael's cemetery in Edmonton was a demonstration of the esteem and respect that he still enjoyed. An appropriate memorial, made possible by public subscription, was subsequently erected on his grave. Then Stephanie Hlynka, Anthony's indispensable helpmate since 1943, decided to move with her two young children back to Toronto to live with her recently widowed mother.

What does Anthony Hlynka represent in the context of the century-old Ukrainian Canadian experience? Essentially, Hlynka's political career signals a major turning point in the evolution of the Anglo-Canadian perception of the Ukrainian Canadian community, from a foreign and even threatening one to a loyal and positive one. There is no question that Hlynka's parliamentary and community service, his high visibility, and his tireless humanitarian work on behalf of the refugees strongly contributed to the new image. In the broad Canadian picture, recognition and grudging acceptance of the Ukrainian fact into the Canadian mainstream made possible a new ethnocultural concept of Canada that in 1971 officially became multiculturalism.

If he had lived, Anthony Hlynka would have been pleased with the phenomenon of this new Canada and the Ukrainian place in it. He would have been especially delighted with the appointment of a fellow Ukrainian Canadian, Ramon Hnatyshyn of Saskatchewan, as Governor-General of Canada (1990–95), a symbolic crowning touch in his community's long and tough struggle for acceptance.

On the other side of the world, the ideal of Ukrainian independence, which Hlynka so devotedly advocated, came to fruition in 1991. Desperate efforts to save the failed communist system through a series of reforms actually brought about the opposite – the unexpected and rapid collapse of the Soviet Union. The disintegration process of the world's largest empire was accelerated by the declaration of independence made by Ukraine's Soviet parliament in August 1991 and subsequently overwhelmingly ratified by popular referendum. While the startled world hesitated in its response, Canada won the distinction of being the first Western nation to recognize Ukraine as an independent state. Anthony Hlynka would have found much satisfaction in this event as well, for it meant that two of his major dreams, one national and one international, to the realization of which he had so long and so unselfishly devoted his time and his energy, had at last come into being.

Oleh W. Gerus
University of Manitoba

part I

SELECTIONS TRANSLATED FROM
Antin Hlynka, Posol Federalnoho Parliamentu Kanady, 1940–49
AND DRAFT MANUSCRIPT

REFLECTIONS ON THE WAY to OTTAWA

Several weeks after the general election of 1940, Prime Minister W. L. Mackenzie King announced the opening session of Parliament for 16 May. Since this would be the first full wartime session, its importance could not be underestimated. For me personally, the importance of this session lay not only in the fact that I would be taking my first steps in Parliament but also because in this critical period of the war I would be the only Ukrainian Canadian representative in the House of Commons. It meant that my responsibilities would be most challenging. Furthermore, together with other novice Members of Parliament I had to learn parliamentary procedures as well as the rules and regulations of our highest legislative body. Notwithstanding these foreseeable difficulties, I anxiously anticipated my departure for Ottawa.

On Monday, 6 May, I left from the CNR Station in Edmonton. My family and a few friends saw me off. They wished me much success and promised to follow my activities in the press. I bade them goodbye and entered my car. In a few minutes the train began to move and I was on my way to Ottawa. Sitting by the window, I watched as Edmonton's lights slowly disappeared into the distance. As the train's speed increased, so did the clicking noise of the wheels on the rails. The passengers in the observation car were either engaged in conversation or reading magazines. I, too, tried to read but for some reason I could not concentrate. After about an hour, I went to my berth.

Still I could not fall asleep. The noise of the wheels and the swaying of the train engendered in me a thoughtful mood. Salient images of the past began to rise up in my mind, born of memories from my childhood as well as from later years.

As though in a dream, I remembered how, in the early days, my parents with four children moved in 1910 to our own unfinished house on a homestead in the Delph district, some 18 miles northeast of Lamont. I don't know why this image of the first day on our farm remained in my memory. Perhaps it had something to do with my experience of the thunderstorm of that first night, which flooded us in our unfinished and still roofless house. Father did everything he could to cover at least part of the roof with sticks and branches, and to plug the walls with moss and grass. As we had no beds, we slept on freshly cut hay piled on the dirt floor.

In the next few days, Father and Mother managed to build a primitive roof made of saplings and covered with flat pieces of wood. Later, the walls of the house were plastered with clay and a log floor was installed, which in time was levelled with clay.

During the summer Father worked in a brick plant in Edmonton. Mother too was obliged to earn money by working for the earlier settlers, some ten miles from home at Peno or even farther away in the Wostok region. In order not to leave four children unattended, our parents placed us under the temporary care of Nicholas Shpachynsky in Peno, which already had a post office. Our neighbour, Jacob Kurylo, gave us a ride on his ox wagon for the first two miles, but we had to cover the other eight miles on foot. Mother carried my one-year-old brother, Isydore, on her back, while father carried me, then three years old. My two older sisters, Evdokia (age 8) and Sofia (age 5), walked the entire distance themselves. A mile from the Mykhalchuk homestead, Grandmother Mykhalchuk, a kind old lady, met us with bread and milk. The next day we reached Shpachynsky's place, where we children stayed till fall.

Around the middle of October, Father returned from work and we moved back to our farm. This time we got a ride from Nicholas Maliovany. That same fall, Father installed a proper floor with boards, while Mother whitewashed the house. We lived in that pioneer house for more than ten years.

I also remembered from those early days how thick the woods were in our district. Father often marked trees with his axe so that he would not lose his way to the house from the bush.

In spring and early summer my parents worked the farm, clearing the land of trees and preparing the soil for cultivation. For the rest of the summer and during the fall, Father worked at various jobs in Edmonton or more locally as a farm hand. Mother also worked on neighbouring farms, doing gardening or fieldwork. Every fall Father would return home with essential goods for the family. One year he brought a prayer book for each child.

I remembered best the winter days and evenings. Neighbours would often visit in order to talk or to listen as Father read from various books. Sometimes they borrowed our books. Our house always had many books because Father imported them from the Old Country, from Bukovyna and Halychyna. As soon as Ukrainian newspapers began to appear in Canada, Father became a subscriber. On occasion he even contributed articles to some of them. During winter evenings, Father and Mother liked to read books and newspapers out loud well into the night.

For several winters, the neighbours requested Father to teach their children to read and write Ukrainian. At that time there was no school in the district. As a result, Father taught several boys every winter. Although I was younger than his pupils, I paid close attention to the lessons and in this way learned to read and write Ukrainian.

The Delph district had been opened up for settlement only a few years before our arrival. The school had yet to be built. In 1916 Father contacted Michael Milinsky in Edmonton, a provincial government official whom he knew. Together they approached the Department of Education with a request for a school to be built in Delph. As a result, inspector R. Fletcher was sent to the district. After his inspection, Fletcher recommended the establishment of a school, which was built on our farm. When Father again visited Milinsky, the latter suggested that the school be named Sheptytsky[1] in honour of the archbishop of the Ukrainian Greek-Catholic Church in Galicia, and the department accepted the name. It is interesting that the name of this distinguished churchman and community leader was selected before he became one of the major figures of the Ukrainian nation.

At first, Delph also lacked a church. Visiting priests conducted services in the larger homes of the district. When I attended services and took communion, the district was served by a priest who later became Archbishop Basil Ladyka.[2] Several Basilian fathers also visited. A Ukrainian Catholic church was finally erected in 1918. From that time on, church services became important festive events in the district, for the people came together from miles around.

In the summer of 1917, the Sheptytsky public school began its first year of classes. However, boys and girls fourteen years of age or more were not allowed to attend, for they were considered too old. This group of children grew up without any formal grounding in the English language. I was almost eleven then, and attended Sheptytsky for less than four years, but at least I got the basics.

My parents valued education highly and encouraged me to continue my schooling, and in the fall of 1922 they sent me to school in Edmonton. They advised me to stay with my married sister, Evdokia Marchyshyn, as this arrangement would facilitate my schooling. My sister and her husband operated a restaurant, a grocery store, and a boarding house for permanent residents as well as for farmers in transit on their way to do business in Edmonton.

My sister and her husband often took me along to concerts, theatrical events, and lectures put on by the local Ukrainian clubs and societies. Once, when we attended a lecture given by a student, who later became a doctor, my sister and brother-in-law suggested that I should get involved in Ukrainian affairs so that someday I too could speak to the public.

That school year ended in the spring of 1923. Father was then in Edmonton, as he was working on the railroad close to the city. In order for me to return to school the next fall, I had to earn money for my clothing and books. Father took me to the Alberta Brick Yard, nine miles from Edmonton, where I got a job. He also asked Dmytro Keywan, a farmer from our district who was working at the brickyard, to look after me because I was then only sixteen. Keywan gladly agreed to do so but doubted whether I could survive nine, ten, eleven, or even more hours of hard physical labour each day. However, I had no choice.

Indeed, at the beginning the work was very hard for a boy my age. In fact, toward the end of the first day Keywan had to help me. The bricks moved on a wide assembly line and I had to unload them without dropping any bricks. On the first day of work I could hardly walk to the lunchroom. Still, once I had survived that very difficult first week, I grew accustomed to the routine and worked until the middle of November.

I attended Alberta College, a technical high school, which offered a mixed technical and academic curriculum from grade seven to twelve.

That year, 1923, my parents moved from the farm to Edmonton so as to give the rest of the children better educational opportunities. Now I lived at home again. Father worked at a lumberyard where he never earned more than $70.00 per month. This income had to cover house payments, heat, light, water, food, clothing, and books for six children. In those days the regular working day was nine hours, but Father worked two hours of overtime whenever possible.

Winters were cold in Edmonton, with occasional freezing temperatures between −40 and −60 degrees Fahrenheit, and daily outdoor work was not easy. To help Father, I substituted for him after school hours and on Saturdays. Those were the circumstances in which our family lived during that time while the six kids went to school.

The next spring I went back to the brickyard. In Kennel there was a second brick factory, the Acme Brick Yard, where my uncle William Kryvaniuk was a foreman. For six summers, while attending school, I worked at one or the other of the two brickyards.

In the fall of 1926, several newly arrived Ukrainians asked me to teach them English. This request gave rise to the establishment of an evening English language school in Edmonton. For five winters I taught English four months a year, three hours an evening, three times a week. During the first two years I was still a student myself. Every year I had more than fifty students, so I could not complain about my income.

That same year I was elected president of the student body of my technical high school. For the first time, I had to give a public speech, a short introduction to the annual school concert. Although the hall was not hot, I had sweat on my forehead, while my knees knocked loudly against each other. After surviving this initial moment of terror, I found subsequent public appearances much easier.

I should add here that the attitude of my teachers toward students of other than Anglo-Saxon heritage was non-discriminatory and positive. Moreover, these teachers made a special effort to assist in developing our self-confidence. I probably did not appreciate this fully at the time, but later I understood the positive impact it had on my friends and me. I remember several immigrant Ukrainian students who had limited knowledge of English. When school concerts were held, the teachers asked these students to take part by singing Ukrainian songs. These teachers encouraged the Ukrainian boys to be proud of their native culture and origin.

In 1926 I also became more involved in Edmonton's Ukrainian community life. I joined a choir and a dancing troupe; I attended various lectures and I read Ukrainian books. My passion for Ukrainian culture was enhanced by Leo Snaichuk, who was a student at the time but later became an artist-painter. He lived in the Michael Hrushevsky Institute in Edmonton and was deeply influenced by several leading Ukrainians. I often listened attentively as Snaichuk spoke with knowledge and intelligence on Ukrainian issues. These experiences awoke in me a strong desire to enhance my understanding of Ukrainian literature and history and, at the same time, to commit myself to community service.

I completed my schooling in 1928, graduating from Alberta College in Edmonton. I decided to work for several years to earn money for further education. For two months I worked at the brickyard, but I was laid off because of declining orders. I then found a job with the Grand Trunk Railroad, loading rail ties. There I worked until late fall.

In November 1928 I again began teaching evening English language courses for newcomers. Now that I had plenty of free time, I immersed myself in English and Ukrainian books. That fall I delivered my first public lecture in Ukrainian on the positive and negative aspects of Ukrainian life in Canada, which I gave at the Ukrainian National Home in Edmonton.

In the spring of 1929 I joined an insurance company, Western Life, where I worked with P. I. Svityk, who had just become the manager of its Calgary branch. Svityk was probably the first Ukrainian to reach such a high position in the insurance industry. The nature of my work demanded constant travel through the entire province. This gave me an opportunity to meet people, to attend various community functions, and to give lectures in Calgary and Edmonton. In 1929 life was good for me, but hints of a looming economic crisis were on the horizon.

Gregory Hlynka with three sons (l to r) Isydore, Anthony, and Kassian.

In 1930 the full impact of the economic crash could be felt. The ensuing depression was first felt among workers and farmers, especially those of Ukrainian background, on whom my livelihood largely depended. I was barely able to earn enough to cover my expenses, and so in the fall of 1931 I quit the insurance business and continued with the evening language school.

In 1931 I devoted much time to two Ukrainian organizations. One was a small drama club, Kobzar (The Minstrel), whose activities included staging concerts, commemorative occasions, theatrical performances, lectures, and similar events. There was also a newly organized Ukrainian Economic Society, whose main function was to keep abreast of economic matters in order to assist Ukrainian merchants and businessmen. Ukrainian merchants in Edmonton and other Alberta towns had already formed an association, the United Merchants of Alberta. That association later gave birth to the Independent Wholesale, which was the first Ukrainian wholesale distributor of household items in North America. I was then secretary of the Ukrainian Economic Society, which worked closely with the United Merchants of Alberta. It should be remembered that during the Depression, many merchants and professionals suffered significant material losses.

The newly established weekly, the *New Pathway* (*Novyi shliakh*), provided wide coverage for all these organizations. Founded and published by Michael Pohorecky,[3] editor, and John Solianych, printer, it began publication in Edmonton on 30 October 1930. My association with the paper began with my reports on activities of the Ukrainian Economic Society and the Society Kobzar. I became a supporter of the paper because it promoted Ukrainian nationalism, whose ideology I had accepted after reading other nationalist publications, such as *Revival of a Nation* (*Rozbudova natsii*), *Independent Thought* (*Samostiina dumka*) and *The Bugle* (*Surma*). When, on 17 November 1931, the publication company was restructured, I was elected to the provisional board of directors. My function was to solicit advertising for the paper. I did this work until May 1933, when the *New Pathway* was transferred to Saskatoon.

The new Ukrainian immigration of the 1920s enriched Ukrainian Canadian life in many ways. Its influence was especially important in

Anthony Hlynka trying out his brother Kassian's 1929 Harley

the urban centres, where the majority of the newcomers settled. At the outset, the more active Ukrainian immigrants joined the existing community organizations and in this way revived and energized them. A considerable number of new immigrants were veterans of the Ukrainian wars of independence (1917–21). In January 1928, they organized the Ukrainian War Veterans Association (*Ukrainska striletska hromada – USH*), which adopted the nationalist ideology of the European-based Ukrainian Military Organization (*Ukrainska viiskova organizatsiia – UVO*).[4] These were people in whose minds the Ukrainian liberation struggle remained very much alive, and it is quite understandable that the issue of liberating the Ukrainian nation from foreign domination was more vital to them than to the Ukrainian pioneers. Their psychology and their attitude differed appreciably from those of the pre-war Ukrainian settlers and even more from those Ukrainians born in Canada. Nevertheless, at the beginning, groups of war veterans were given accommodations in the existing Ukrainian halls. But it was only a matter of time before these dynamic and committed clubs would create a Canada-wide mass nationalist organization, for during the interwar period, Ukrainian nationalism would become a powerful political force in Europe.

On 17 July 1932 supporters of the Ukrainian nationalist movement and members of the War Veterans Association held a mass rally at the Hrushevsky Institute in Edmonton. There they formed the first branch of the new national organization, the Ukrainian National Federation of Canada (*Ukrainske natsionalne obiednannia*).[5] A number of the earlier immigrants and Canadian-born Ukrainians also joined the UNF. Among the original members were teachers A. Gregorovich, W. Kupchenko and K. Magera, lawyer N. Romaniuk, A. Shewchuk, W. Dorosh, S. Waskan, and myself.

I was interested in the Ukrainian nationalist movement for several reasons. The movement's principal goal was the establishment of a united independent Ukrainian state on the traditional lands of the Ukrainian people. In this process, Ukrainian Canadians had a definite missionary role to play. The movement was based on a program of sovereign national statehood. It rejected any form of compromise with those who over the centuries had betrayed the Ukrainian people. The nationalist movement psychologically empowered the Ukrainian people by removing their deeply ingrained inferiority complex. Over the years, this movement had suffered many casualties on behalf of the liberation struggle. But where there was blood and sacrifice, there was a commitment to an ideal for which people had been long prepared to pay a heavy price. Furthermore, the nationalist movement was dynamic, full of energy and action, direct in approach, and clearly defined. Those who read nationalist literature could not help but be attracted to its ideology. That is why the nationalist movement had such a positive impact on the Ukrainian Canadian community.

Fascinated with the Ukrainian nationalist movement, I became deeply committed to the *New Pathway* and the UNF. In addition to soliciting advertising and contributing reports and articles to the paper, my friends and I visited Ukrainian communities, giving lectures and helping to organize the UNF locals. At about the same time I was elected acting General Secretary of the National Executive of the UNF, which was then based in Edmonton. Thus, until the summer of 1934, when the first national Canadian conference was held in Saskatoon (26–28 July), I worked for the UNF and the *New Pathway*. Those were the years of the deepest economic depression and I hardly managed to survive. However, I gained a great deal of practical experience that helped me later. During those years I read extensively in my free time.

From the fall of 1930, Stepan Waskan had been one of my closest friends, despite the wide age gap between us. Waskan was a tall well-built man with the appearance of a Swedish aristocrat. He had come from Bukovyna, arriving in Canada at the age of seventeen. Almost immediately he had been persuaded to join the Ukrainian socialists. During World War I, that socialist organization had become communist. For a time, Waskan worked for the communists as an organizer, and he was one of their leading and most gifted members. In time, however, he realized that the communist movement had stopped being a workers' organization and had become a tool of Soviet Russia. He left the communists in 1923.

Waskan had extraordinary talents. He was without doubt one of the best Ukrainian orators in Canada. Although he was self-taught, his intelligence and his natural abilities were quite remarkable. Once he read something, he would remember it for years. He was a master of critique, using original satirical arguments to vanquish his debating opponents. A decent and good-natured man, he was a passionate Ukrainian Canadian patriot.

Stepan Waskan was intrigued with my youthful enthusiasm and optimism, while his clear logic and occasional pessimism appealed to me. He wrote two booklets, his English language *Behind the Green House*, which was about alcoholism, and a Ukrainian drama, *Danylyshyn and Bilas*. While these booklets do not fully demonstrate Waskan's talents, they do provide glimpses of his special gifts. Of course, he had his faults. He always said what was on his mind and this upset many people.

I found work in the grocery store far from satisfying. In the fall of 1934, Stepan Waskan, William Dorosh, and I decided to launch a monthly Ukrainian publication named *Klych* (*The Call*). It had two main objectives: to wage a vigorous struggle against communism and to promote community unity among Ukrainian Canadians by emphasizing the power of united action.[6] Each of us was obliged to solicit advertising and to contribute articles to the journal. The first issue of *Klych* appeared in January 1935. But by then, Waskan was no longer in our partnership, as financial difficulties had compelled him to seek another job. Shortly after publication of the first issue, Dorosh, too, left *Klych* to earn his living as an electrician. I remained alone with the paper.

The first issue failed to produce enough revenue to cover the costs of publication. Yet the paper stimulated serious public interest. It was obvious that the success of my monthly journal would depend on increased readership and advertising. Thus, after working each day in the store, I would spend all my free time promoting *Klych*, preparing publication material, and selling advertisements in Edmonton, rural Alberta, and beyond. In my editorial effort, I was assisted by a man who knew the Ukrainian language well. After his departure, I would edit myself as best as I could.

From time to time during the winter of 1935, I gave lectures at Ukrainian settlements. My main subject was Bolshevism and Ukraine. This topic interested not only the nationally conscious Ukrainians but the communists as well. My lectures were well attended and many listeners even bought subscriptions to *Klych*. Presentations were followed by questions in which the communists naturally expressed their displeasure at my criticism of communism. Nationalistically inclined Ukrainians responded positively to me. In one community, I was asked to return and to help stamp out their local communism.

My most interesting adventure during the course of all those visits occurred in a largely communist district, frequented exclusively by communist speakers. A teacher whom I knew arranged a public meeting for me. Until that time, I had not realized that the title of my topic had a double meaning. Some thought I would speak in favour of communism while others thought I would speak against it. Hence, the hall was full of pro- and anti-communist listeners. A chairman was elected, and he called upon the audience to behave and to greet a fine young man who spared neither time nor effort to pay a visit to their community. He then invited me to speak.

I did not waste much time with an introduction but launched directly into my theme. Naturally, my speech was anti-communist.

The more arguments I advanced discrediting the communist leadership and its propaganda, the more vigorously my chairman shook his head. At first, I did not notice what was wrong. But after half an hour, the chairman got up enough courage to rise and declare that he was no longer chairing the meeting because my speech did not appeal to him. Following these words, he moved back several steps and lay down on the boards that were piled on the stage. I thanked him for maintaining order, but now I had to finish the meeting on my own. I continued, while the disgusted chairman lay on his back until the end, occasionally uttering his displeasure.

In one issue of *Klych*, I wrote an article about the work of the Social Credit government in Alberta, favourably evaluating its legislation that was designed to protect the farmers in debt. As a result of this article, the young Ukrainian provincial MLA, Jim (Dmytro) Popil, paid me a visit and proposed a joint publication of *Klych* and a Social Credit biweekly in Ukrainian. I agreed and we named the paper *Suspilnyi Kredyt* (*Social Credit*). From that time on, my editorial work increased greatly and I had to quit the grocery store to devote all my time to journalism. The first issue of *Suspilnyi Kredyt* appeared on 18 February 1937. Since *Klych* failed to attract enough subscribers to pay for itself, I ended its publication in June 1937, having produced only six issues.

As Social Credit activities expanded throughout the province, Popil and I found ourselves constantly on the road, making speeches in Ukrainian communities. In 1937 alone, we traveled 37,000 miles. All this travel was quite expensive and, as many readers of *Suspilnyi Kredyt* defaulted on their subscriptions, the paper remained unprofitable for quite some time. Financial difficulties caused Popil to leave our partnership, but I continued editing the paper until 14 March 1940. By that time, twenty-five issues of *Suspilnyi Kredyt* had been published.

In the spring of 1938, I began work in the publicity department of the Social Credit Board. My salary allowed me to subsidize the publication of *Suspilnyi Kredyt* and to help cover the costs of a radio broadcast I made on 5 October, the purpose of which was to inform Ukrainian farmers about Alberta's new debt laws. I worked in the publicity department only until the fall, when it was reorganized and I was transferred to the Department of Municipal Affairs. I was employed there until the spring of 1939.

As I mentioned before, between 1936 and 1939, I traveled extensively in Alberta and Saskatchewan making political speeches. Of all the places visited, the Vegreville area, where I grew up, remained my favourite. During those four years, I gave several hundred speeches associated with *Klych* and *Suspilnyi Kredyt*. On occasion, I even walked from place to place in summer and winter, but generally I managed to get a ride.

My speeches were attended by large crowds because almost every farmer faced the threat of losing his land and property due to indebtedness to the banks. I focused on explaining those policies and legislation of the Social Credit government that were designed to safeguard the farmers. After such meetings, I was often asked to intervene with government officials on behalf of indebted farmers. I did so free of charge, and the grateful farmers urged me to seek a Social Credit nomination in the provincial riding of Victoria, which was represented by an elderly farmer, Sam Coulvert. I began to think seriously about running in that riding. But in 1939 all provincial ridings were realigned, and Victoria and Whitford were combined into a new riding, Willingdon. However, since Whitford had been represented by William Tomyn, I felt that the new riding belonged to him. There was also a new provincial riding of Vegreville, but since several other potential candidates aspired to it, I was not interested.

In the spring of 1939, I spoke in the Warwick district, north of Vegreville. After the meeting, a farmer approached me and asked why I was not seeking a candidacy in the Vegreville federal riding. Until that moment, the thought of entering federal politics had never occurred to me. The farmer continued to persuade me, arguing that I had a wonderful opportunity to win a federal seat.

Over the next several weeks, I reflected on the intriguing suggestion of the Warwick farmer, but I could not see any real possibility of success, especially since I had no money for a campaign. Nonetheless, letters started to arrive from the Vegreville-area farmers, urging me to run federally and promising assistance. Rethinking my position, I placed two of these unsolicited supporting letters in *Suspilnyi Kredyt* and began preparing for the nominating convention scheduled for Chipman on 1 September 1939.

HOW I BECAME A POLITICIAN

In the 1935 Canadian general election, Ukrainian Canadians had lost their only parliamentary representative, Michael Luchkovich, who had held the Vegreville riding. The next federal election was expected to take place toward the end of 1939. As a rule, political parties nominated their candidates well in advance in order to be ready when the government called the election. Accordingly, the executive of the Social Credit party of the Vegreville riding decided to hold its party's nominating convention on Friday, 1 September 1939 in the town of Chipman.

Although the opening of the convention was scheduled for 2:30 p.m., many delegates, expecting vigorous competition for the nomination, began arriving much earlier in order to have time to campaign for their candidates. By noon, there were already dozens of cars on Chipman's main street, with groups of delegates discussing not just the merits of their favourite candidates but also the outbreak of the Second World War, for that morning, the radio had announced the German invasion of Poland.

Chipman was a small farm town, located in one of the oldest Ukrainian pioneer areas. Its population numbered about 300 people, consisting mainly of Ukrainians, with several Polish and British families. Located adjacent to the CN railway, the town had six grain elevators, to which local farmers delivered their harvest. There were several stores, a modern hotel, a poolroom, a bowling alley, a restaurant, a dairy and a public school. There were also four churches: Ukrainian Catholic, Polish Roman Catholic, Russian Orthodox and Anglican. The nominating convention was held in the Ukrainian Catholic hall, one of the largest halls in the district.

Proceedings began at 2:30 in the afternoon. W. M. Crockett, a lawyer, was chairman and George Chaba from Egremont was elected secretary. Present were 110 registered delegates and a similar number of guests. The first major item on the agenda was the reading of the minutes of the previous convention, which had been held

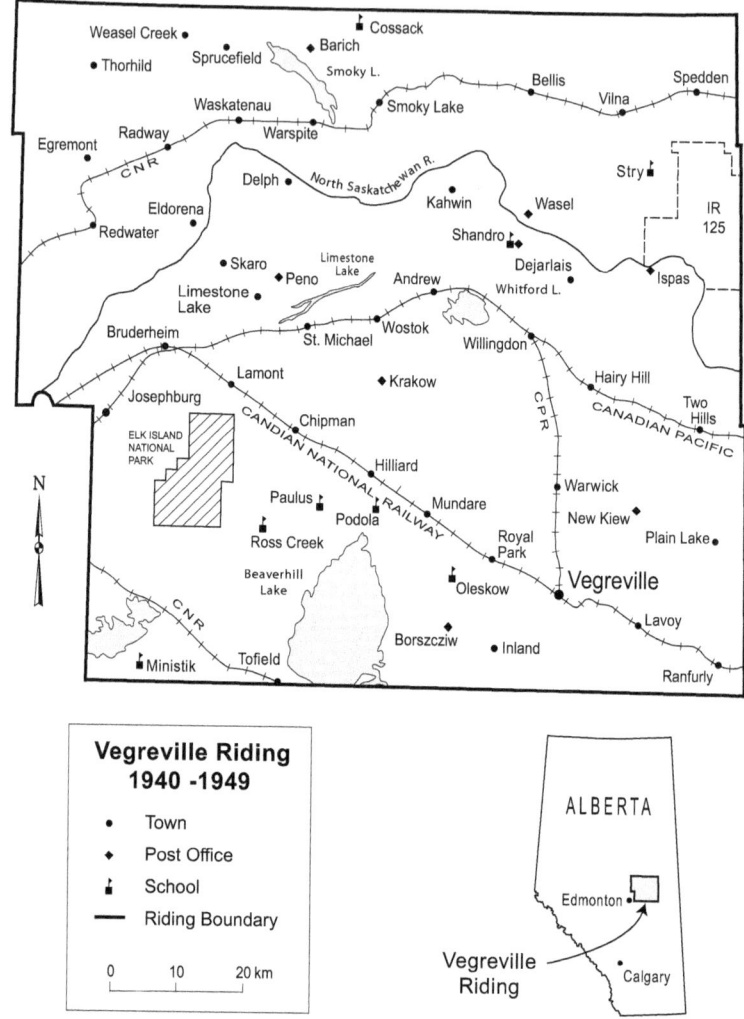

on 14 September 1935. It was noted that of the three candidates, a Ukrainian teacher, Paul Lesiuk, had received the highest number of votes, but that the Advisory Board of the Social Credit party for Vegreville had given the nomination to William Hayhurst, who had come in second.

At this point I should explain why Hayhurst had been designated the official candidate. The convention had passed a motion to have the Advisory Board make the final decision by confirming one of the three candidates nominated. Thus, when the Advisory Board named William Hayhurst, its decision was final. A large number of Ukrainian supporters of the party had, however, been outraged by this decision and had refused to vote for the official candidate.

Following the reading and acceptance of the minutes, several procedural motions were made, including a renewal of the 1935 motion to elect three candidates and to leave the final selection to the Advisory Board.

From time to time, the proceedings were interrupted by expressions of excitement and tension stimulated by the radio news of the unfolding European war. It was anticipated that Britain and France would make an early declaration of war on Germany, in response to the German invasion of Poland. Everyone at the convention understood that the newly elected Member of the House of Commons would sit in a war-time Parliament.

The convention reacted to the general public apprehension by passing a resolution in favour of military conscription in Canada. The resolution stated that sooner or later, all democratic countries would be obliged to introduce universal military conscription, as had been the case in the First World War. Accordingly, it was resolved that every citizen of Canada must make his or her maximum commitment to the war effort. The resolution also demanded the mobilization of the industrial and financial resources of the country, and it urged the imposition of fair price and wage controls in order to prevent wartime profiteering.

It was obvious from the beginning that the Ukrainian delegates to the convention were determined to have one of their own people become the official Social Credit party candidate. Despite their determination, such a goal was not easy to attain, for the unfortunate result of the 1935 convention could easily be repeated. It was assumed that William Hayhurst, as the sitting Member of Parliament, would automatically be one of the three candidates, and since the Advisory Board had the final word, it could select him once again, regardless of the number of votes the other two might receive. Furthermore, since the convention had agreed to the 1935 selection procedure, no other procedure was possible. Notwithstanding this fact, the Ukrainian delegates were quite aware that they had a unique opportunity, perhaps the only one in Canada, to elect a candidate of Ukrainian origin. No other riding even offered such a possibility at that time. As a result, they spared no effort in working to have a Ukrainian candidate receive the party nomination.

William Hayhurst had represented the Vegreville riding in the House of Commons since October 1935. By profession he was a teacher and a high school principal in Vegreville. He was polite, intelligent, and well-read. He carried out his duties as an MP quite well, but he had a difficult time representing a riding in which eighty per cent of the population was of other than British origin. This situation created serious communication problems for both Hayhurst and a large group of voters who had not as yet mastered English. Hayhurst tried to accommodate the Ukrainians by occasionally raising in the House of Commons the topic of Ukrainian national aspiration in Europe. While most Ukrainians were appreciative of his efforts, Ukrainian members of the Social Credit party urged Hayhurst to transfer his candidacy for the 1939 election to the Athabasca riding in order to leave Vegreville to the Ukrainian candidate. However, Hayhurst ignored this advice and chose to stand for nomination in the Vegreville riding.

At last, the convention reached the point of nominating the candidates. The first candidate to be nominated was Paul Lesiuk, who had been one of the unsuccessful candidates in 1935. The second nominee was William Hayhurst. Then a young farmer stood up and, after making several remarks in flawless English, declared, "I nominate Anthony Hlynka." My nomination was seconded by Fred Yurkiw from Radway. The fourth nominee was Rev. A. Khrustavka from the Ukrainian Greek-Orthodox Church. The last nominee was J. M. Lazarenko, a lawyer from the neighbouring town of Myrnam. Each candidate was required to give a five-minute presentation. The audience reacted most favourably to those candidates who spoke in both English and Ukrainian.

The vote was conducted by secret ballot. To everyone's surprise, William Hayhurst received the smallest number of votes in the first round and thus was deleted from the second ballot. In the second round, it was Rev. Khrustavka's turn to be dropped, leaving the top three candidates: A. Hlynka (99 votes), P. Lesiuk (92 votes) and J. M. Lazarenko (71 votes). This ended the formal session of the convention.

After several hours of political tension and excitement, some delegates left for home, while others stayed for lunch, which was prepared by the ladies of Chipman and surrounding region. During lunch, topics of conversation ranged from the inconclusive results of the convention to farm matters, and then to the meeting of the Advisory Board that would select and confirm the official candidate. Since the Advisory Board would meet only after the nominating process was completed in all the Alberta ridings, it seemed that the official outcome of the Vegreville nomination would not be declared for several months.

William Hayhurst and his wife were also present at the luncheon. He now regretted running for re-nomination in Vegreville. His unexpected defeat had raised in his mind serious doubts as to the advisability of participating in the forthcoming nomination process in the Athabasca riding. I tried to reassure him of my campaign support, should he win the nomination. Later, Hayhurst did win a Social Credit nomination but was defeated in the federal election. After lunch I left for Edmonton.

There I heard on the radio that the Prime Minister of Canada, Mackenzie King, had called a special session of Parliament for 7 September. The Prime Minister said that the session was necessitated by the inevitability of the British involvement in the war, and he wanted Parliament to approve a policy of close and harmonious cooperation with Britain.

On Sunday, 3 September, Britain and France declared war on Germany. That same day, members of the British Commonwealth of Nations – India, Australia, New Zealand, and South Africa – followed Britain's lead. Only Canada waited a week before its Parliament on 10 September 1939 officially declared war on Germany.

Even before the formal declaration of war, the government of Canada had resurrected the War Measures Act of 1914, which gave the government extraordinary powers to safeguard the country in time of national emergency. In his radio address to the Canadian people, Mackenzie King informed the public of the measures the government had decided to take in order to deal with the emerging crisis situation. The government created the Wartime Prices and Trade Board in an effort to control prices and the distribution of goods, and it approved the Defence of Canada Regulations, which introduced censorship of the press and surveillance of all suspicious elements in the country. All these security measures had been enacted by the Cabinet when Parliament was not in session.

The special session of Parliament lasted from 7 to 13 September. Parliament approved ten laws, all of which were directly or indirectly related to the war. On Saturday, 9 September, Parliament passed the declaration of war on Germany, and the next day the government formally declared that a state of war now existed between that country and ours. Now every Canadian household knew that Canada was at war.

Although Canadians were now becoming involved with the war effort, normal political life not only continued, but actually intensified in preparation for the forthcoming general election, the date of which was still unknown. I, too, began making speeches in my riding and started to prepare the groundwork for my election campaign. The fact that the Advisory Board had not yet met to name the official party candidate did not prevent me from undertaking organizational work. I believed that the Board would confirm my candidacy because, after all, I had received the largest number of votes at the nominating convention. In addition, I had been actively helping local farmers with their problems, as well as making pro-Social Credit speeches on the radio. I should point out that my determination to ensure a Social Credit victory in Vegreville was strongly motivated by the underlying conviction that only such a victory would guarantee the election of a Ukrainian Canadian to the House of Commons.

Prime Minister Mackenzie King finally announced that the federal election would take place on 26 March 1940. His Liberal party's platform was based on a promise not to introduce military conscription.[7] The election announcement caused all political parties to begin serious campaign work.

The Vegreville riding witnessed many instances of energetic partisan electioneering. While Liberal, CCF (moderate socialist), and communist candidates were making passionate speeches and strengthening their party organization, the Social Credit party still lacked an official candidate. In those abnormal circumstances, I saw no alternative but to continue making speeches on behalf of my party, even though my two colleagues and I all had our hands tied because not one of us was the official candidate. This frustrating situation dragged on until the end of February, leaving less than a month to campaign. Fortunately for the federal Social Credit candidates, Premier William Aberhart of Alberta had announced a provincial general election for 21 March: that is, for five days before the federal election. The federal Social Credit candidates stood to benefit from this wise strategy, as Aberhart's victory was deemed a certainty, and he believed that those voters who supported the Social Credit party provincially would also endorse it federally.

Six months had passed by the time the Vegreville Advisory Board finally met in Edmonton on 22 February to name the official candidate. Before the meeting, the three candidates promised each other to support the person selected. The Board included T. Morey, A. English, F. Appleby, W. Crockett, J. Timne and two Ukrainians, G. Chaba and G. Tomashevsky. The anomaly was obvious: the Board structure allowed for only two Ukrainian Canadian members, yet it was dealing with a riding that was overwhelmingly Ukrainian. However, Premier Aberhart, two cabinet ministers, and the secretary of the Alberta Social Credit party also joined the Board.

I was the second of the candidates to be interviewed. Board members had a list of questions from which they chose those they wished to ask. I did not feel very comfortable responding to such a wide variety of questions, most of which seemed petty, vague and irrelevant to my candidacy. During this interview, I began to think about our generous Ukrainian farmers who, with their small donations, were making it possible for me to campaign in all parts of the riding. I remembered well a young student-farmer, John Wagilek from Kahwin, who had lent me the first 100 dollars I needed to prepare for the nominating convention; during the Depression, this was a substantial sum. But I could not get one troubling thought out of my mind: if I were to become the official candidate, how would I finance my campaign? Despite this uncertainty, when Aberhart finally asked me about my ability to cover campaign expenses, I replied in the affirmative. With that, I left the boardroom.

After the last candidate's interview, we three waited impatiently for the verdict. In about ten minutes, the Board members began to leave, saying that their decision would be announced in the morning papers. But one Board member squeezed my arm as he was leaving, thereby signaling to me that I was the official candidate. Much later I learned that the Board had given Paul Lesiuk three votes and me four. Still, my troubles were not over. In the hall, someone whispered to me that should I win, my candidacy would be officially protested. After all this, my status still remained ambiguous.

I stayed in Edmonton for several days. Two days after the Board meeting, I received a phone call from the party secretary asking me to appear at the Legislative Building to meet with a delegation from Vegreville that was challenging my selection.

On the steps of the Legislature, I met Paul Lesiuk. He argued that he deserved to be chosen because of the injustice that had been done to him in 1935 with the selection of Hayhurst. I understood Lesiuk's frustration and even felt sorry for him, but I could not agree that there should be any connection between 1935 and the present. We soon entered a conference room filled with more than twenty delegates from different parts of the riding. Premier Aberhart sat at the head table, surrounded by his ministers and the party secretary.

Aberhart first called upon Paul Lesiuk to explain his grievance: then he asked the delegates for their views. Lesiuk and several delegates argued that he and not I should be the party candidate. After a lengthy discussion, Aberhart and his ministers unanimously reaffirmed the decision of the Board. Their action finally ended the challenge to my candidacy. As the Vegreville delegates were leaving, many assured me of their support. Naturally, I was quite pleased. After so many difficulties and obstacles, I was finally an official candidate of the Social Credit.

THE 1940 ELECTION

Four candidates ran in the Vegreville riding during the federal general election, which was called for 26 March 1940. The Liberal party candidate was Dr. A. E. Archer, who had been nominated at the Liberal convention held at Mundare on 2 December 1938. There he had defeated Peter Lazarowich,[8] a Ukrainian lawyer from Edmonton, by six votes: 110 to 104.

Dr. Archer's reputation in the Vegreville district, both as a physician and as a community activist, was impressive. Born and raised in Ontario, he completed his medical studies at the University of Toronto. In 1903 he moved to the Star-Lamont region of Alberta at a time of massive Ukrainian immigration into the province. One pioneer doctor, B. T. Rush, who was already there, joined forces with Archer. As we know, at the beginning of settlement, there were only primitive dirt roads in Alberta. Dr. Archer fulfilled his medical duties traveling on horseback. In 1911 Archer and Rush convinced the Methodist Mission, now part of the United Church, to build a fifteen-bed hospital at Lamont. Today [1950s] this hospital has greatly increased in size and enjoys a first rate reputation in the province. This meant that Dr. Archer had many admirers, not only in the Liberal party but among other parties as well. All this indicated strong support during the election.

The second candidate in the Vegreville riding was Herbert Boutillier, representing the socialist CCF. He was the son of the former Progressive Member of Parliament, P. A. Boutillier, who had represented the riding in 1925–26. A farmer himself, he was actively involved in farm organizations. He was a formidable candidate because he spoke Ukrainian quite satisfactorily, having learned the language while living in a district with a Ukrainian majority.

The third candidate was William Halina, a communist.

I was the fourth candidate and represented the Social Credit party. All three of my opponents had already been campaigning for several months when I entered the race. However, the campaign began to exhibit serious intensity a month before the election. The people who were well acquainted with political currents in the riding considered the main battle to be between Dr. Archer and myself, and in fact, it turned out to be so.

The Social Credit party enjoyed tremendous popularity among the farmers and as a result could count on massive support from that sector. This popularity was due to the fact that the Social Credit government of Alberta had over the years forcefully defended farmers from bankruptcy at a time when financial institutions were demanding repayment of loans, which was impossible during the Great Depression. At the same time, farm commodity prices were below the cost of production. In short, the Social Credit government of Alberta was a watchdog for farmers' interests.

The public image of Dr. Archer's admirable record of service as a physician was strengthened by the power of the Liberal party, which possessed a large organizational machine and substantial funds. He also enjoyed the support of the local Liberal weekly, the *Vegreville Observer*. A number of politically active professionals and businessmen from both the riding and Edmonton threw their support behind him as well. Several prominent Ukrainian Canadians also participated in Archer's election campaign. They included lawyers P. Miskiw and P. Lazarowich from Edmonton, lawyer John Decore from Vegreville, Dr. H. Holubitsky[9] from Radway, P. Zvarich[10] from Vegreville, pharmacist C. Chicha from Willingdon, Andrew Shandro from Edmonton, J. Palanych from Edmonton, and G. Shkwarok, a lawyer from Mundare.

Since the provincial election campaign was taking place at the same time as the federal campaign, provincial Social Credit candidates were able to be involved in the federal contest. At times, it was even possible to hold joint federal-provincial meetings. In this way, provincial candidates Peter Mitenko and William Dorosh supported me while I tried to help them.

However, the most urgent problem for me was the lack of campaign funds. The Social Credit party did not finance its candidates for the simple reason that the party had no money. This was so because the party deliberately did not solicit corporate donations in order to be free from influence of financial institutions, whose economic power over the people it was trying to break. The Social Credit party accepted only small donations from its supporters, with no return of obligation or patronage implied. The party used these petty funds to cover general election expenses. That is why every Social Credit candidate had to rely on his own financial resources.

In 1940 I had no money. I had to depend on personal loans and fundraising. My campaign found some financial assistance in the Ukrainian community, as well as among friends and relatives. Although our farmers had not yet recovered from the ten-year depression, they understood my situation and during election meetings collected small amounts of money on my behalf. Thus I was largely on my own against the wealthy Liberal party, which generously provided its candidates with funds to cover election expenses.

My campaign manager, Nicholas Shewchuk, a businessman from Willingdon, was one of those tenacious people who would never back away from a difficult situation. That winter the snowfall was exceptionally heavy and prairie roads were covered with deep snow. Shewchuk faced an almost impossible task, but he made sure that I never missed a meeting.

I also received support from three major Ukrainian Canadian newspapers – the *New Pathway*, the *Canadian Farmer* (*Kanadiisky farmer*),[11] and the *Ukrainian Worker* (*Ukrainskyi robitnyk*).[12] Although these papers did not have a large readership in the Vegreville district, I certainly appreciated their unsolicited support. They endorsed my candidacy despite the fact that their political outlook was different from mine.

There was no respite during the election campaign. The CCF and its candidate, Boutillier, waged an aggressive fight. The communist candidate fomented his party's typical election agitation, focusing mainly on propaganda and on attacking me personally. The Liberal party towered above all in terms of its publicity and the scope of its campaign organization.

Despite my organizational and financial shortcomings, I was convinced that the Social Credit party would win the Vegreville riding. I had two reasons for this conviction. First, the Social Credit party enjoyed unquestionable strong support among Alberta farmers, and my riding was predominantly agricultural. This popularity lay in the party's sincere struggle on behalf of farmers as well as in its efforts to help others who suffered from the decade-long economic crisis. Even during the 1940 election campaign, revenue from farm commodities remained below the cost of production. During the fiscal year ending on 31 March 1940, the average price for wheat was 52 cents a bushel; for oats, 28 cents a bushel; and for rye, 38 cents a bushel. Other farm produce was selling for equally low prices, when it found any market at all. It was obvious that farm income was inadequate, not only for operating the farm but even for sustaining a household. In western Canada, very few farmers could keep up with their mortgage payments and most could not even repay the interest on their loans. The banks, however, ignored these desperate conditions and insisted on the repayment of farm loans. When farmers failed to comply, banks resorted to the courts and through foreclosures took away ownership of the farm.

Everything the farmer and his family had acquired by long hard work could vanish as in a prairie fire. During the 1930s one could often see fear on the faces of farmers who had just lost their property. It was very painful to watch formerly successful homesteaders, now pleading, cap in hand, with bank agents, lawyers, and officials in an attempt to extend their debt payments. They were visibly shaken by the real possibility of losing everything and of finding themselves and their families on the street. This situation prevailed during the Liberal and Conservative administrations in Ottawa. Although the Conservatives did pass the Farmers' Creditors Arrangement Act in 1931, this federal law did little to alleviate the critical situation in western Canada, and farmers continued to lose their farms. The result was that there were very few well-off farmers to vote for the old parties. The fundamental economic question in Alberta was one of survival, not of prosperity. As a consequence, the Social Credit government of Alberta passed a series of laws to save the farmers. Unfortunately, the federal government nullified most of them as unconstitutional. In the 1930s, the main public service provided by the Social Credit party was its effort to protect farmers from the clutches of the financial institutions.

The 1940 election provided Ukrainians with an excellent opportunity to elect their own Member of Parliament from the ranks of the Social Credit party. Such an opportunity was unavailable to the Liberals, who in this election, as in previous ones, did not put forward even one Ukrainian candidate. The Conservative party did have one Ukrainian candidate, lawyer John Hnatyshyn,[13] in the Yorkton riding of Saskatchewan. An independent Ukrainian candidate, H. N. Podolsky, ran in the Provencher riding of Manitoba. It was apparent that the majority of Ukrainian voters in the Vegreville riding would reject Liberal politics, which sought Ukrainian support while denying them their own candidate. During the final weeks of the campaign, all signs pointed to a steady increase in support for Social Credit.

Among Ukrainian Canadians, two opposing views concerning our community participation in the federal election were prevalent. One view maintained that Ukrainian Canadians should participate fully in national party politics and vote for the party platform rather than for the specific interests of their ethnic community. The proponents of this view argued that only total loyalty to Canadian political parties could help the Ukrainians to win the all-important trust of those parties. Such trust would then open the door to influence and patronage: for instance, appointment of judges and senators. For the same reasons supporters of this approach also insisted that Ukrainian Canadians were obliged to vote for the candidates of the party in power. However, in provincial politics they deviated from this practice, unless the party happened to be Liberal, and so they ran candidates in opposition to provincial governments. It is clear that the argument favouring "the government party" was purely opportunistic as reflected in the Liberal slogan in Vegreville "go with the flow" – a slogan that negates traditional political principles. To vote for a party just because it might win the election has nothing to do with political principles or party loyalty.

The opposite approach also implies full political participation and party loyalty but with one important proviso. It was held that in those ridings where Ukrainian Canadians constitute a majority of the population, party candidates should be of Ukrainian origin. Any political party rejecting this condition would thereby also reject the interests of the Ukrainian community. Such a party would not deserve Ukrainian support. Only those parties that treated Ukrainians seriously and with dignity should be supported.

This latter approach reflected the attitude of the majority of voters of Ukrainian origin in the Vegreville riding in 1940. They believed that at least one Member of Parliament out of 245 should be Ukrainian. Given the settlement pattern, one could not deny that the aspirations of the Ukrainian Canadians were just. The voters of the Vegreville riding were convinced that the federal Liberal party was giving the 300,000-plus Canadians of Ukrainian origin a slap in the face by denying them even one Ukrainian candidate. For this reason alone, Ukrainian voters felt that the Liberal party did not deserve their support, especially in the Vegreville riding where Ukrainian Canadians constituted seventy per cent of the population. For the sake of Canada's democracy, and even of the country itself, it was essential that there be expressed in the federal parliament the perspective of an ethnic group as important as the Ukrainian Canadians. This was especially crucial during wartime, when the closest possible cooperation and harmony among all sectors of Canada's population were crucial.

Although these two diverse attitudes about participation in Canadian politics dominated Ukrainian thinking, Ukrainians generally viewed all parties, all candidates and all speakers with measured tolerance. They understood that in a democratic society every person has the privilege of belonging to and working on behalf of any political party that, in their opinion, deserved support. They did not expect Ukrainians to break from their party only because another party had a candidate of Ukrainian origin. In short, the Ukrainians had a tolerant attitude toward all political parties. They frequented political meetings and listened attentively to the arguments. It should be noted, moreover, that even now the political attitude of Ukrainian Canadians is characterized by their thoughtful toleration of all political parties. This was already the attitude of the Ukrainian voters in 1940 toward all candidates in the Vegreville riding.

The Liberal candidate, Dr. Archer, behaved very correctly during the campaign, as one would expect of a distinguished citizen. He spoke with moderation about his party, its program, and his own ambitions for Ottawa, should he be elected. However, Dr. Archer and several other moderate speakers were the exception. The majority of Alberta's Ukrainian Liberals brought their party's campaign to a new low as they concentrated on making personal attacks on me. When they finally realized the futility of their tactics with the voters, they resorted to false allegations and feeble distortions of the truth. Perhaps the most unfortunate outcome of their behaviour was a public demonstration of their complete lack of political professionalism. In fact, their conduct aroused serious indignation and a backlash among the voters. Farmers, teachers, merchants, and the youth, including the large Ukrainian Canadian Youth Association, not only objected to the debased level of Liberal campaign speeches but began protesting against the speakers themselves. Speakers were reminded about their past efforts to support Ukrainian candidates so that the Ukrainian Canadian community could win political recognition. In short, the voters reacted against the baseness of this political agitation as well as against the candidate's unclear position or, more precisely, the absence of any political position.

To illustrate this point, it suffices to cite two excerpts from letters to the editors of the Ukrainian press. In the *Ukrainian Voice* (*Ukrainskyi holos*)[14] (10 April 1940), Gregory Faryna from Elk Point noted the following:

> In the press and at the meetings our [Liberal] agitators urge us to vote for a non-Ukrainian [Archer] because he would be able to accomplish more for us in Ottawa and London than our [Ukrainian] candidate.... Our leaders have always and everywhere argued that Ukrainian interests in Canada demand that Ukrainians support each other.... But here, in the Vegreville riding, all of a sudden, we are told not to vote for our candidate because he represents a party which is not acceptable.

Michael Melnyk from Weasel Creek wrote the following in the *New Pathway* (25 March 1940):

> Archer was accompanied by the leaders of the Ukrainian Self-Reliance League – lawyers, doctors, teachers – who campaign on his behalf.... It was painful and embarrassing to listen to them. Last year some of these gentlemen sang a different tune. At that time, Dr. Holubitsky from Radway was a school trustee candidate

running against Scott. At those meetings our gentlemen, some of whom are now denouncing Hlynka, appealed for support on the grounds that only our Ukrainian candidate knows and understands our people best.

It is obvious that every thoughtful individual, when reflecting on the level of agitation that occurred in 1940, would have a difficult time understanding what drives our community leaders to indulge in such a campaign, especially in a riding that had a realistic chance of electing a Ukrainian MP. Yet there were tangible reasons for this. First, there were envy and deception as factors. Secondly, there was blind party loyalty. Thirdly, there were the personal motives of several individuals who wanted to ingratiate themselves with the Liberal party in order to reap rewards in the form of political appointments and patronage. There were those who believed that Dr. Archer himself, once elected, would shortly receive a senate appointment or some other important post and thereby relinquish his seat to one of his loyal supporters. But if I were to win, then it would perhaps take at least two terms to remove me from office before they could personally benefit. In the opinion of that self-styled elite, I had no right to get involved in politics without their blessing. They always considered every person who did not subordinate himself to them as incompetent and unworthy.

My opposition did have several strong arguments against me. One argument ran as follows: Ukrainian voters in the Vegreville riding should vote for a candidate from "the government party" and not for "some opposition candidate." Proponents of this argument insisted that it was essential for Vegreville, with its majority of voters of Ukrainian origin, to elect a government candidate. To do otherwise would convince the government that Ukrainians are opposed to it. They concluded their argument with a veiled threat, saying that whenever in the future there might be the need to appeal directly to the Prime Minister, the latter could say: "I'll give you what you gave me. Whom did you elect?" Another assertion held that "even a non-Ukrainian from the government party could do more for the Ukrainian cause than a Ukrainian, because all doors will be open to him." By the way, the argument about the value of having a government candidate with accessibility to power had been used in the past by the same people against Luchkovich.

The final argument against my candidacy in the 1940 election was intended to belittle and humiliate me in the eyes of the voters. It was said that Ukrainian Canadians should elect a candidate who would not embarrass them. The desired Member of Parliament had to be an educated person who would make all Ukrainian Canadians proud of him. In their eyes, I was clearly not such a person. Proponents of this outlook did everything possible to warn the voters of the Vegreville riding that they should not make the serious error of electing me.

I should note here that the majority of my Ukrainian opponents who went to such extremes to defeat me consisted primarily of the leaders of the Ukrainian Self-Reliance League. However, I should add that not all USRL members in Edmonton or in my electoral riding were opposed to my candidacy. They did not share the prevalent sentiment of their organization, and these exceptional individuals – among them John Danylchuk,[15] B. A. Chumer,[16] and A. Gordey – even placed appeals in the *Ukrainian Voice*, urging the riding to elect me. Furthermore, the majority of the Ukrainian community – farmers, teachers, small businessmen, and the youth, including the followers of the USRL and its affiliate, the Ukrainian Canadian Youth Association – did not bow to the leadership of the USRL and supported me. Some of them were even Liberals.

As far as the official publication of the USRL, the *Ukrainian Voice*, was concerned, the paper did not adopt a clear policy toward the three Ukrainian candidates running in this general election. This lack of editorial clarity was perhaps due to political pressure and internal confusion. Thus in an editorial of 20 March 1940, editor Myroslav Stechishin[17] was probably expressing his personal opinion when he wrote: "Party connections of the candidates are of secondary importance. One more or less member in parliament makes little difference to any party. But for Ukrainians a parliamentarian of Ukrainian origin, regardless of his party affiliation, is worth his weight in gold."

Five days before the federal election, Alberta held a provincial election. The Social Credit party was re-elected with thirty-five out of fifty-seven seats. This victory was a positive sign for the federal Social Credit candidates. In the provincial ridings that were part of the Vegreville federal riding, all Social Credit candidates won. Among them were three Ukrainians: William Tomyn, Jim Popil, and George Wojtkiw. Their election indicated that my chances were good. However, it was difficult to gauge the public mood on several specific federal issues. The most controversial issue was that of compulsory military service. The Liberal party, fairly confident of its victory, promised not to introduce conscription but to maintain its policy of voluntary enlistment. This promise had a definite impact on the voting.

I spent the night before the election in a Mundare hotel. That night, as on the previous two or three days, there was a heavy snowfall. When I looked out the window and saw how the wind-blown snow had covered the roads, for the first time in this campaign I began to have doubts about the result of the election. I realized how difficult it would be for the farmers to travel over this deep snow to the polls, and I recalled that urban voters generally supported the old-line parties. Moreover, I could not afford to lease cars or sleighs to transport the voters, especially the elderly, to the polls.

In the morning when I looked out again, the snow had reached the top of the fence. Seeing this, I lost all hope of winning. Who but the most courageous voters would venture out on such a day?

I remained in Mundare until noon. Here I saw several cars and sleighs delivering voters for my opponents. My supporters walked to the polls. But when one of my friends arrived around noon, he tried to convince me that among the voters being driven by the agents of my opponents to the polls, they were unknowingly also transporting some of my supporters. He said that he overheard several elderly voters with impaired eyesight saying that they were voting for Social Credit.

In the afternoon, Nicholas Lakusta and Peter Melnyk, both from Edmonton, were driving to Vegreville and took me along. Although it is only fifteen miles from Mundare to Vegreville, they had to stop at Royal Park for gas. I remained in the car while they stepped out. We noticed a sleigh being driven in a ditch along the gravel road by a farmer in a heavy buffalo fur coat. The snow was so deep that the horses were sinking. The farmer finally reached the store and tied up his team. One of my friends asked him whether he had been delivering voters to the polling stations "in order to prevent Hlynka from winning the election." Then my friend added, "Surely Hlynka does not belong in Parliament. We need an MP from the government party so that he might have influence in Ottawa and London. What do you say?" The farmer could not decide whether my friends were being serious or not. Then he responded, "What is the matter with you people? What's wrong with Hlynka? After all, he is our own man. When will we learn to act sensibly?" I was in the car and he did not see me. The farmer continued: "You gentlemen do what you think is right, but I have been driving people to vote for Hlynka since morning and will continue until nightfall. Nobody hired me to do this. I see this as my duty. You can be sure that there are many more like me. You'll see. We'll elect Hlynka. The snow will not stop us."

I was deeply moved by this farmer and I saw in him that special Ukrainian man that regardless of adversity has always maintained the dignity of his people. Lakusta and Melnyk admitted that they were just provoking the farmer, who smiled and entered the store without noticing me. Later I was told that he was William Hawryliuk from Royal Park, a man I had never met before.

At Vegreville my electoral headquarters were small. Here we spent the rest of the day with voters. In spite of the snow, the town was quite busy. Election results started to arrive in the evening by telephone and radio. At the beginning, I was eight hundred votes behind Dr. Archer. An hour later the gap widened to seventeen hundred votes. Each radio announcement placed me further behind, and by nine o'clock neither I nor the majority of my supporters saw how I could possibly catch up to Archer, who was two thousand votes ahead. However, several political observers familiar with the riding argued that Archer's votes were from the local towns where the Liberals traditionally had support. In their opinion, the farm vote would determine the outcome.

Around ten o'clock the radio announced that the gap between Archer and myself was narrowing. First the difference was twelve hundred and then it was eight hundred votes. While the results were encouraging, it was still difficult to project a Social Credit victory. However, after returning from a break to our small quarters, I was less than two hundred votes behind. The radio was now contemplating the possibility of a Social Credit win. The vote counting ended around midnight, with several farm polls to be reported the next day. It was assumed that these polls were supportive of me and that the victory would go to Social Credit. As the people drifted home from my headquarters, I and about thirty Vegreville residents spent two hours at Fedorkiw's house in happy conversation. When I returned to Mundare, a large number of my friends and supporters who had campaigned so hard for Social Credit were waiting. Here we ended the day in an optimistic mood.

By the time I awoke the next day, the radio had announced a Social Credit victory in the Vegreville riding: I won by 478 votes. However, on the national level the Liberal party was returned to power, winning 178 seats, while the Conservatives took 39; Social Credit, 10 (all from Alberta); the CCF, 8; and several independents were also elected. That day I returned to Edmonton.

A week later, a victory banquet was held at the Corona Hotel in Edmonton. A large crowd was in attendance, representing the different parts of my riding as well as Edmonton. My parents and family were present. Mother explained that neither she nor Father knew about my victory until a car arrived to take them to the banquet. Michael Luchkovich was one of the guests. He delivered a short congratulatory speech, wishing me much success. Members of the provincial legislature, William Tomyn and George Wojtkiw, also spoke, as did George Chaba and my father. Chaba's speech made a deep impression on those present as he most vividly depicted the role played by farmers, especially Ukrainian farmers, in achieving the Social Credit victory in the Vegreville riding. The master of ceremonies for the evening was George Bayrak from Edmonton, and Maria Shewchuk and the Holowach brothers provided the musical entertainment.

A few days later, I visited Premier Aberhart. Those who knew him will recall his civility. Although I had become acquainted with him before the election, he nevertheless made a deep impression upon me. He got up from his desk and greeted me in the doorway. His conduct was, as always, that of an eminent and gracious gentleman.

Over the next several weeks, before leaving for Ottawa, I visited all areas of my riding and organized my affairs. War was raging in Europe and people were following the news with great interest.

During my lengthy meditations on the Ottawa-bound train, I searched for those threads of my past that had contributed to my election as a Member of Parliament. Not only did I feel deep gratitude towards farmers, small merchants, teachers, and young people, I also owed a great deal to my parents, who had encouraged me to enjoy reading. Two other people had also contributed to my success. My sister Evdokia and my brother-in-law William Marchyshyn, with whom I had lived for ten years, had looked after me as if I was their son. I had tried to reimburse people for all the financial help I had received over the years, but I could never repay the non-material assistance they had given me.

By the time I stopped reliving the past, it was five in the morning and the train was nearing Saskatoon. Here I was going to interrupt my trip for one day. Despite the early hour, my friends met me at the station. They took me to a hotel, where I caught up on my sleep.

At ten o'clock, I met with my Saskatoon friends and later visited the editorial office of the *New Pathway* and the national executive office of the Ukrainian National Federation. At noon there was a hotel luncheon attended by representatives of all the Ukrainian organizations in the city. Of course, there were speeches. A meeting followed the luncheon and then I had the rest of the day for visiting.

At dawn of the next day I resumed my journey east, arriving in Winnipeg in the evening. My youngest brother, Kassian, met me at the station. He was a researcher at the Board of Grain Commissioners, a department of the federal Ministry of Trade and Commerce. I spent several days in Winnipeg visiting with Kassian, some friends, and several Ukrainian organizations. In addition, the Social Credit party of Manitoba asked me to make several speeches there. On 23 May 1940 the *New Pathway* carried the following account of my visit to Winnipeg:

> Mr. Hlynka, accompanied by Mr. D. Gerych,[18] paid a visit to His Eminence Bishop Ladyka, the hierarch of Ukrainian Catholics, as well as to Dr. T. Datskiw, editor of the Canadian Farmer.[19] Later

he went alone to see Mr. Stechishin, editor of the Ukrainian Voice. In the evening, he attended a political rally at Steinbach, 40 miles from Winnipeg, and then accepted the invitation of Mr. N. Marian to the silver jubilee celebrations of his brother G. Marian, where ... he greeted the celebrants and about 500 guests. Here he made the acquaintance of Bachynsky,[20] Ferley,[21] ... and other distinguished guests.... On Sunday, 12 May he attended Mother's Day at the UNF hall on Main St., which was organized by the Ukrainian Women's Organization and the Young Ukrainian Nationalists. In the evening, he went to a similar function at the Ukrainian Orthodox Cathedral. On both occasions, he extended greetings and thanked the groups for their generous hospitality.

On Monday evening, I left by CPR for Ottawa. It would take me two nights and one day to reach my destination. I arrived in Ottawa on Wednesday, 14 May at 6:30 in the morning. My brother Isydore[22] met me. At this time, he was working as a chemist, researching dairy products in the federal Department of Agriculture. As we traveled to his place by streetcar, he pointed out government buildings, including the Parliament Building. According to Isydore, there were only about six hundred Ukrainians living in Ottawa. They belonged to two churches, the Ukrainian Catholic and the Bukovynian Ruthenian Orthodox. There were no other Ukrainian organizations.

After visiting with Isydore for two hours, I took the streetcar in the direction of the Parliament. In about twenty minutes, I got out and passed through the gate of an iron fence, which surrounded the parliament grounds. In front of me was the tall tower of the Parliament Building, from which flew the Canadian flag. Just then, for the first time I heard the sound of the large clock on the tower: it was striking ten o'clock. Each stroke of the clock made a strange impression on me, as though it was the living voice of the entire Canadian nation. Each step that I took towards the building deepened my awareness of the responsibilities I bore to the people who had sent me here. I have always believed that community service is one of the highest privileges a citizen can have. Yet at the same time, I did not forget that it is also one of the most difficult and important responsibilities. Thus, deep in my soul, I reaffirmed my determination to assure the trust of my constituents by doing my best.

At the entrance to the Parliament Building, I identified myself and was directed to room 611 on the sixth floor. I shared the office with my Social Credit colleague, F. D. Shaw from Red Deer, Alberta. Our nameplates were already on the door. Later I learned that Michael Luchkovich had occupied this same office five years earlier. After the 1945 election, I was moved to another office, and Fred Zaplitny, a newly elected Ukrainian Canadian CCF MP from Dauphin, Manitoba, moved into number 611.

My office was like all other parliamentary offices. It contained two large desks, one for Shaw and one for me, a telephone that sat on a table in the middle of the room, and several filing cabinets. Each office also had a washroom with hot and cold water and clean towels, which were replaced daily. Offices of the MPs differed from those of the senators only by the colour of the carpets, red for the appointed senators and a variety of other colours for the MPs.

While Shaw and I were settling in, several Social Credit colleagues paid us a visit. These were seasoned parliamentarians, having been elected in 1935. They took us on a tour of the Parliament Buildings.

I should mention some of the privileges enjoyed by MPs and Senators. Each MP and each Senator received a travel pass, which allowed free railway transportation to anywhere in Canada. MP's expenses associated with visiting one's riding were reimbursed by the government, but those relating to other activities were not. Local bus companies usually provided free passes as well. During sessions of Parliament, all mail posted to or from Parliament was sent without postage stamps. However, MPs and Senators had to pay for air mail themselves, as well as for long-distance telephone calls and telegraph services. Finally, a pool of approximately 125 secretaries/stenographers was available to help the MPs and Senators with office duties.

In 1940 the list of parliamentary salaries contained the following information: the Governor-General received $48,666 annually; the Prime Minister, $23,000; cabinet ministers and the Leader of the Opposition, $18,000; MPs and senators, $4,000 each, with $2,000 (as of 1947) of that exempt from income tax. As far as housing in Ottawa was concerned, most MPs and Senators had rental accommodations in private homes. Only the wealthier members lived in apartments or hotels.[23]

THE 1945 ELECTION

In the fall of 1944, it was obvious that the Allied victory over Germany was virtually assured. It was only a matter of time. But no one relaxed in Canada, because no one knew what secret new weapons Germany was producing. Furthermore, Canadians were keenly aware of the imperative to continue the war against Japan after Germany's capitulation. Already in the summer of 1943, the Allies had begun to organize a number of conferences to deal with the end of the war and the problems of post-war Europe. Canadian political parties and nongovernmental organizations were also developing their own plans for the post-war period. At the same time, the press began to speculate about the dissolution of Parliament and the general election. The Vegreville Social Credit organization decided to initiate its own preparations for the forthcoming election, regardless of the date. The executive set the nomination convention for 2 September 1944 to be held in Mundare.

Since the name Mundare has been mentioned on several occasions as the site of political conventions, I should say a few words about it. Mundare [in the 1940s] was a farming community of about eight hundred inhabitants of whom more than ninety per cent were of Ukrainian ancestry. The town had nine grain elevators. The large number of elevators underscored the importance of the region's grain production and indicated the fertility of the land. It was a testimony to the success of the local farmers. Mundare had a variety of stores and shops, a hotel, a bank, two restaurants, two lumberyards, an automobile and farm implement dealership, and two schools, elementary and high school. There was also a financial agency of the provincial government, the treasury branch, which was managed by Michael Slipenky, a prominent Ukrainian Canadian. The local Ukrainian doctor was N. Strilchuk.

While the above features gave the town a sense of importance, it was well known for other reasons too. Mundare was one of the main centres of the Ukrainian Catholic order of the Basilian monks. Prime

Anthony Hlynka in the parliamentary office of Rev. E. G. Hansell, MP, Macleod, Alberta

Minister Sir Wilfrid Laurier himself had laid the cornerstone for their church on 8 August 1910. The Basilian monastery was completed in 1923 and has been training young seminarians for the priesthood. It is this religious function that gave Mundare a significant role in the lives of Ukrainian Canadians. In addition, the Ukrainian Catholic nuns operated a hospital and an orphanage. The orphanage, which educated and trained children, was maintained by individual donations and the produce of a farm managed by the Basilians.

Mundare hosted the nominating convention of the Social Credit party on 2 September 1944. The convention, attended by 162 delegates from all districts of the Vegreville riding, was held in the Ukrainian National Home. The selection procedure in 1944 was

House of Commons, 19th session. Anthony Hlynka in the House of Commons with his Social Credit colleagues. Standing in the front row, speaking, is Solon E. Low, MP, (Peace River, Alta.) the leader of the Social Credit Party. Sitting next to Mr. Low is John H. Blackmore, MP (Lethbridge Alta.). Anthony Hlynka is in upper right corner.

similar to that of 1939. First, a presidium was elected and chaired by William Matsura and George Chaba. Joseph Sawchuk, a teacher and a businessman, was the secretary. Procedural formalities were followed by speeches and resolutions. The next step was the nomination of the party candidate. I should point out that the Social Credit party had eliminated its controversial advisory boards whose function had been to confirm the official candidate from a list of three or four nominees. The new procedure called for the candidate to be elected by the majority vote of the nominating convention. Only one candidate was nominated. John Pryma moved my name and John Pysmeny seconded. I was elected by acclamation. My wife,

Anthony in Banff after parliament adjourned.

Anthony in Banff, reading – his favorite pastime.

Stephanie, thanked the delegates for their confidence in me. In the words of the *Vegreville Observer*

> Following the candidate's acceptance speech, Mrs. Anthony Hlynka pleasantly surprised the audience. She assured the delegates that she would do her best to assist her husband so that he may serve his constituency well. She received a well-deserved ovation for her brief and inspiring message which she delivered both in English and Ukrainian.[24]

The nominating convention ended with a banquet in the evening, during which provincial MLAs W. Tomyn, J. Popil, F. Baker, M. Ponich and ministers S. Low[25] and N. Tanner spoke.

The conscription crisis forced Prime Minister King to summon Parliament for a special session in November. The short session began on 28 November and ended on 7 December. The next session lasted for a month, from 15 March to 15 April, 1945. At the end of the session the Prime Minister announced a general election for 15 June.

The Vegreville riding once again had four candidates. One Ukrainian had considered running for the nomination of the Liberal party but then changed his mind and did not appear at the nominating convention. As a result Dr. Archer again received the party nomination, although it was said without much enthusiasm. The CCF party nominated a Ukrainian, Michael Tomin, while the communists [Labour Progressive party] nominated William Halina.

Although this election campaign was very competitive, it was not dirty as far as the CCF and the Liberals were concerned. This time only a small number of Ukrainian Liberal activists campaigned against me, notably the lawyers Peter Miskiw, John Decore and George Shkwarok. The communist camp agitated against me in its usual dishonest manner. However, in the 1945 campaign I enjoyed broad public support and received strong endorsement from the national Ukrainian press. The *New Pathway*, the *Ukrainian Worker* and the *Canadian Farmer* had supported me in 1940. Now these papers were joined by the *Ukrainian News*[26] and the *Ukrainian Voice*. Myroslav Stechishin, editor of the *Ukrainian Voice*, which generally favoured the Liberal party, differentiated between blind party loyalty and the election of notable individual candidates:

> Although Hlynka was elected in 1940 from the Social Credit party, he very rapidly attained the parliamentary status of a special representative of the Ukrainian people; status which he has maintained with dignity and honour. In all matters concerning Ukrainian issues, his words have been most authoritative. It would be nothing less than a catastrophe for all Ukrainians if Hlynka should lose his seat. We understand that the Liberal party has the respected Dr. Archer. But should he defeat Hlynka, then all Ukrainians, in the Vegreville riding and throughout Canada, will suffer a great harm. Ukrainian voters in Vegreville would commit a grave sin before all Ukrainians in Canada should they allow Hlynka to be defeated (30/5/1945).

I should add to the above citation the fact that from the very beginning of our acquaintance until his death in 1948, Myroslav Stechishin treated me with respect and objectivity.

The 11 June 1945 election results gave me 7,146 votes, 2,340 more than my strongest competitor, Dr. Archer. This time, Archer congratulated me and I replied by mail. In contrast to the 1940 election campaign, when I depended on personal loans and small donations, this time I received financial support from Ukrainians throughout Canada and even the United States. Donations were sent to my campaign manager, Nicholas Shewchuk, and they covered nearly half of my election expenses. While campaigning, I could not neglect my office work and continued fulfilling my duties as though there was no election. My wife, Stephanie, managed all my correspondence.

Following the election, several receptions were held in my honour in the riding and in other Ukrainian Canadian centres. In the meantime, the war in Europe had ended on 8 May 1945. It was hoped that the Japanese war would not last much longer. The Liberal party won the election and the new Parliament began its first session on 6 September. Among many new faces I met was the Ukrainian Member for Dauphin, Manitoba Fred Zaplitny from the socialist CCF party. Now for the first time there were two Ukrainian Canadian parliamentarians in Ottawa.

RESPONSIBILITIES *of a* UKRAINIAN CANADIAN MEMBER *of* PARLIAMENT

The duties and responsibilities of Canadian MPs of Ukrainian origin are much greater than those of other Canadian MPs. Besides having to take care of normal constituency matters, a Ukrainian MP has a moral responsibility to assist Ukrainian Canadians from all parts of the country, and even those Ukrainians from abroad, who make appeals to him on personal matters. Rightly or wrongly, Ukrainians see him as their "deputy," a person with whom those individuals whose English is inadequate can communicate effectively. Except during the years 1945–49, when two Ukrainian MPs – Fred Zaplitny and myself – were elected, all such work was carried out by one MP, first by Michael Luchkovich and then by myself. This sad situation testified to the fact that Ukrainian Canadians have not as yet matured politically to the point of being able to elect a number of MPs proportionate to their population.

My most demanding task was unquestionably that of attending to all those matters on which Ukrainians from every part of Canada asked for assistance. It was difficult because the issues were too vast and too complicated for one MP to handle. This aspect of my work involved making numerous phone calls, visiting various offices and departments, and answering a mountain of correspondence. Letter writing alone consumed several hours daily. The English-language correspondence was easier, as I had a stenographer who took dictation and did the typing. However, Ukrainian-language correspondence was more complicated, as I had to do my own typing. Until 1945, when the refugee issue came to dominate my mail, I managed more or less satisfactorily. But from that time on, I was obliged to sit daily at the typewriter until midnight.

It should be remembered that two years had elapsed since the end of the war before the government of Canada began to admit refugees. During those two years, both the refugees and their relatives in Canada wrote to me constantly, appealing for admission to this country.

Once limited immigration began, I was inundated with requests for information and assistance. That I managed to cope with this situation can be directly attributed to my wife, Stephanie. For five years, from the day of our marriage in November 1943, my wife helped with my correspondence. A professional secretary herself, Stephanie took care of the overload from the parliamentary stenographer and also assisted me with the Ukrainian correspondence. She was indispensable in allowing me to deal successfully with my responsibilities. For five years, she accompanied me daily to my office and worked there unpaid until we both returned home. Between parliamentary sessions, when I was on a speaking tour, she handled not only the correspondence but also the other office duties. Without my wife's help, it is quite unlikely that I would have had enough time to deal with all matters raised by Ukrainian Canadians.

In addition to making political speeches on behalf of the Social Credit party in Alberta, Saskatchewan, and Manitoba, I made dozens of speeches annually on non-party issues to various Ukrainian organizations and at Ukrainian functions throughout Canada. In my view, providing assistance to and cooperating with Ukrainian Canadian organizations, especially with the Ukrainian Canadian Committee, was one of my main duties. I was an invited guest at conventions and rallies of the Ukrainian Self-Reliance League, the Brotherhood of Ukrainian Catholics,[27] the Ukrainian National Federation, the Ukrainian Canadian Committee,[28] and the Ukrainian Canadian Youth Association, as well as at student and war veterans' clubs.[29] In some places I spoke more than once. It should be noted that I myself covered my speaking costs, with those few exceptions when my hosts reimbursed my expenses.

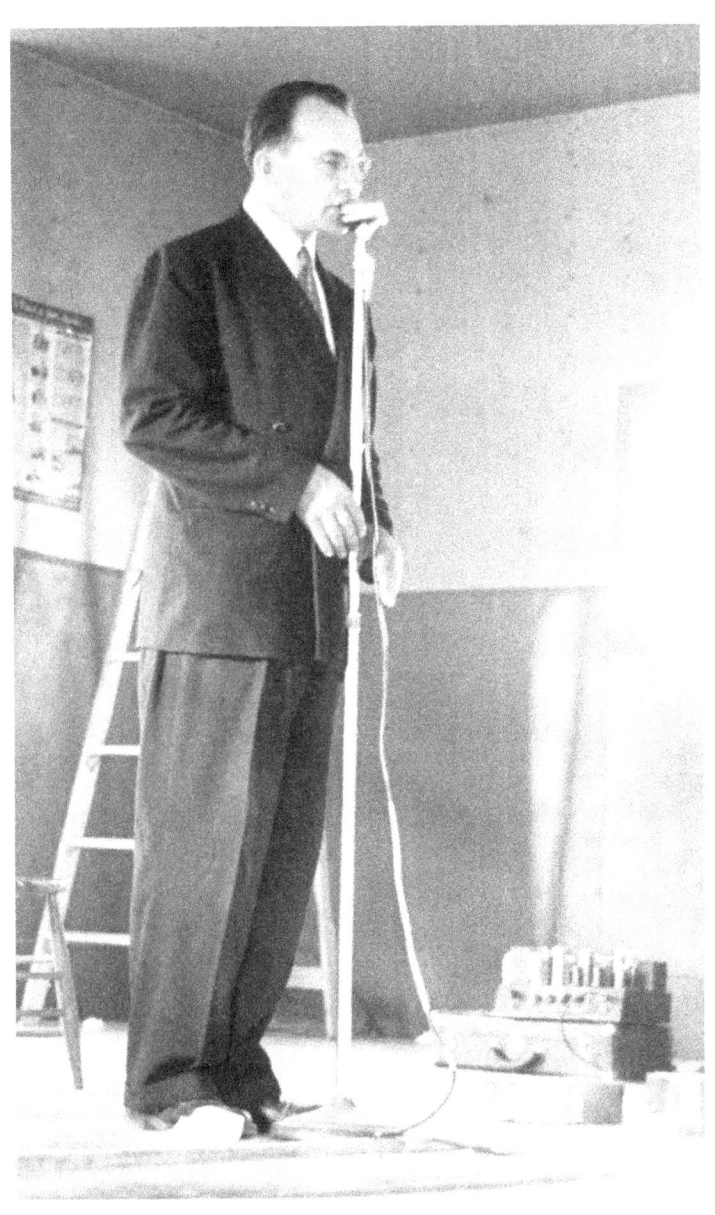

Anthony Hlynka at the mike

Stephanie Hlynka

THE UKRAINIAN LIBERATION STRUGGLE

The desire to be free is innate in all human beings. The desire of nations to be free from foreign domination, the yearning of people to govern themselves, remains one of the strongest impulses in human beings. Every nation, no matter how small, aspires to freedom so that her people can fulfill their mission in their own way by contributing to the culture, civilization, and general advancement of mankind. No person, no nation is placed on this earth to be subservient to others. Divine laws and a sense of justice are always on the side of the oppressed and not on the side of the oppressors. Unfortunately, mankind has not yet reached a moral and spiritual level that would allow it to live in accordance with Christian principles. Thus, in order to live, one must struggle for freedom. Once freedom is achieved, it must be constantly guarded. Eternal vigilance is the price of freedom.

The Ukrainian nation of more than forty million is the largest white nation without its own free state, although in the course of its more-than-one-thousand-year history, it did enjoy statehood three times. During the Middle Ages, for instance, the Kyivan State was the cultural giant of Eastern and Central Europe. However, Ukraine's neighbours – the Poles, the Lithuanians, the Tatars, the Russians, and the Austrians – were attracted by the wealth of the country and conspired to conquer and partition the land. The Ukrainian nation, the indigenous population, was subjugated.

The Russian government in particular tried hard to denationalize the Ukrainian people. Russia denied the existence of a distinctly Ukrainian nationality and ruthlessly attacked the Ukrainian language, culture, and education. Using a variety of techniques, the Russian government tried to instil in Ukrainians a sense of ethnic inferiority, thereby making a Russian identity and Russian values seem more attractive. While these Russian policies of assimilation appeared outwardly successful, the Ukrainian sense of national self-consciousness did not perish. Even during Ukraine's darkest moments, its intelligentsia managed to keep alive the idea of national freedom and independent statehood.

The First World War destroyed the Russian and Austro-Hungarian empires that had subjugated the Ukrainian people. On 22 January 1918, eastern Ukrainians proclaimed their independence and statehood. On 1 November 1918, western Ukrainians declared their statehood. On 22 January 1919, the two Ukrainian states united. Although independent Ukraine was destined to exist for only a few months, the struggle for freedom had profoundly and spiritually regenerated the Ukrainian people. They cast off their imposed psyche of subservience and re-established their sense of self-reliance, of pride, and of courage. Most importantly, they committed themselves to the ultimate realization of Ukraine's unity and independence.

Between the two wars, the Ukrainian nation continued its struggle for liberation. The four occupants of Ukrainian lands – Soviet Russia, Poland, Romania, and Czechoslovakia – understood the dynamic energy of Ukrainian nationalism and severely repressed its manifestation. Ukrainian patriots were jailed, exiled, and even executed. This repression, however, merely strengthened the Ukrainian resolve to struggle for national freedom.

During the Second World War, in its attack on the Soviet Union, Nazi Germany invaded and brutally occupied Ukraine. The Ukrainian people paid a very heavy price for the eventual Soviet victory on the eastern front; millions perished. Edgar Snow, an American journalist, drew Western attention to the destructive impact of the war on Soviet Ukraine:

> ... it was not till I came here on this sobering journey into the twilight of war that I quite realized the price which 40 million Ukrainians have paid for Soviet victory. This entire titanic struggle, which some are apt to dismiss as a Russian glory, has in all truth and in many costly ways been first of all a Ukrainian war. And greatest of this republic's sacrifices, one which can be assessed in no ordinary ledger, is the toll taken of human life. No fewer than 10 million people, I was told by a high Ukrainian official here, have been lost to Ukraine since the beginning of the war. That figure excludes men and women mobilized for the armed forces.... A relatively small

part of the Russian Soviet republic itself was actually invaded, but the whole Ukraine ... was devastated, from the Carpathian frontier to the Donets and Don rivers, where Russia proper begins. No single European country has suffered deeper wounds to its cities, its industry, its farmlands and its humanity.[30]

In August 1941 Britain and the United States proclaimed the Atlantic Charter which established a number of principles which reflected the Anglo-American vision of a better future for the post-war world. I felt it was my duty to raise in the House of Commons at the earliest opportunity the question of the Ukrainian liberation struggle in the context of the Atlantic Charter. I canvassed the opinion of several MPs and they encouraged me to speak. Parliamentary rules allow members to speak on various issues during the Throne Speech debate. I informed the Speaker of my intention and was allocated a slot at 8 p.m. on 2 February 1942.

When I took my seat in the House several minutes before the start of the evening session, I noticed that the public galleries were filled to capacity. Most members were also present.

I spoke for forty minutes on the subject of freedom of nations as the basis for a lasting peace in Europe. I spoke with passion and conviction. I endeavoured to point out that it would be in the interest of the Allied nations to see to it that the Ukrainians be granted the same privileges and sovereign rights as are being promised to other people in accordance with the principles embodied in the Atlantic Charter. I said, "In Britain, the United States and Canada, there are in existence united Ukrainian committees whose primary objective is to assist the governments of Britain, the United States and Canada in the successful prosecution of the war." And I said further, "I do suggest that, since all the Allied nations are fighting for the common cause of freedom, those Ukrainian committees to which I have referred be also invited to delegate their representative or representatives to express the view of fifty million Ukrainian people at a conference held by the Allied nations."

When I finished my speech, members of all parties sent me congratulatory cards, despite the fact that the average MP found it difficult to comprehend the issue of the Ukrainian liberation. After all, at that time the Soviet Union was our ally against Nazi Germany.

Raising the controversial question of Ukraine's freedom and its separation from the Soviet Union at the moment when pro-Soviet sentiment was powerful in Canada made my speech quite newsworthy. The Canadian press provided lengthy reports and editorial comments. The *Edmonton Bulletin*, for instance, published the entire speech. The leadership of the Canadian communist party launched an immediate protest, sending every MP, every senator, and every major newspaper a denunciation of my speech, calling it harmful to Soviet-Western relations. The Ukrainian communist leadership effectively capitalized on the prevailing amicable attitude toward Soviet Russia as the chief ally of the English-speaking countries. This pro-Soviet attitude obviously influenced a number of newspaper editors, especially those who were left-wing, for they reacted to my speech in a critical manner, as the communists wanted.

From the day of my parliamentary presentation of the Ukrainian question, in the eyes of the communist leadership I became their major enemy. Certainly the communists well knew that I had never been a sympathizer of their ideology, but in fact I had written and spoken against communism. That was why they had run their candidate against me in 1940. But when I had the courage to raise the issue of Ukraine's liberation in the House of Commons and demanded freedom for the Ukrainian nation, the communist leadership could not forgive me. From the time of my speech, they denounced me as a fascist. Curiously enough, the Canadian communists had no objection to an expression of concern for the Ukrainian people suffering during the war; the communists even tolerated disagreements with their ideology. But whenever anyone mentioned freedom for the Ukrainian people from Russian domination, the communists reacted quickly and aggressively because the idea of Ukraine's separation threatened the vital interests of their Kremlin masters.

The Soviet-sponsored Ukrainian language publications in Canada viciously attacked me for my preoccupation with the Ukrainian issue while allegedly ignoring the concerns of Canadian farmers. They spread this misinformation knowing full well that I often spoke on agricultural issues. They apparently assumed that by their attacks they could intimidate me into not making any more parliamentary speeches about Ukraine. The communists in my riding even tried to strike a deal with me. They told me that, if I stayed away from the Ukrainian question, they would organize support for me among the so-called progressive voters during the next election. They tried to convince me that the new age of Soviet power was upon us and that I, as an astute politician, should recognize the new situation and adapt to it. However, if I continued as a spokesman for free Ukraine, they threatened that they would deprive me of my parliamentary seat. My response was simple: I valued my principles and I would never compromise on the question of Ukrainian liberation.

The war ended in 1945, as first Germany and then Japan capitulated. In the last days of the war, efforts were undertaken to organize a new international peacekeeping body, the Organization of United Nations. The founding conference was announced for San Francisco, California. In Europe and North America, pro-Soviet sentiment was still widespread, although some of the more realistic politicians were beginning to express unease about the aggressive behaviour of the Soviet Union.

The debate over Canada's participation at the San Francisco conference began in the House of Commons on 26 March 1946. I saw it as my moral duty to once again raise the Ukrainian question. When I canvassed some of my parliamentary colleagues for their opinion, I discovered that while they sympathized with my objectives, they were also concerned about the possibility of alienating our wartime ally, the Soviet Union.

In my speech, I reiterated my belief in the right of all captive nations to freedom and sovereignty and to their participation in the San Francisco conference:

> In view of ... colossal sacrifices which many people of Europe have made, I submit that there should be provided a recourse to captive nations, to make it possible for them to make representations of their own cases at any and all world conferences to which free nations are invited. I am making this plea on behalf of millions who cannot speak for themselves. I believe that a similar request was made after the last war, but as far as we know no such privilege was

extended to any captive nation, which fact also contributed to the failure of the League of Nations.

With respect to the representation of the Ukrainian people, I suggest that the Ukrainian Canadian Committee and the Ukrainian Congress Committee of America be asked to send their delegation to any and all world conferences for the purpose of presenting the Ukrainian case. These organizations include the vast majority of Canadians of Ukrainian origin and Americans of Ukrainian origin and embrace all Ukrainian church bodies. These organizations have also proven their loyalty to Canada and the United States of America, their respective countries, from the first day of the war.

As expected, the Ukrainian communists launched another anti-Hlynka campaign, especially in their press. Some editorials in the Canadian press were also critical of my proposal while the Ukrainian non-communist press gave my speech a qualified support. I did not understand, however, why some people thought that the raising of the Ukrainian question at the San Francisco conference was premature.

Some of our Ukrainian "politicians" in Canada are of the opinion that the only duty of a Ukrainian Canadian MP is to serve his riding and do nothing else. They maintain this attitude even when that MP successfully and conscientiously fulfils all his obligations to his riding. Such a simplistic and isolationist approach to complex political problems cannot be morally justified. I should add here that I have never heard anywhere in Canada of attacks on MPs for being interested in and taking part in national Canadian and international affairs. On the contrary, our fellow citizens value more highly those MPs who are involved in affairs beyond the riding level. These voters believe that such an MP enhances the stature of their riding. Ukrainian "politicians," however, are different. They had campaigned against Luchkovich in 1934 because "he had gone to Europe," and against me in 1949 because I "devoted too much time saving the refugees" and was "too deeply involved in the Ukrainian liberation struggle." Ironically, these dubious attacks proved to be very harmful to me.

There are also Ukrainians who do not mind that a Ukrainian Canadian MP becomes involved in issues beyond the riding.

However, they insist that their MP must stay away from the issue of Ukraine's liberation. It is not surprising that the communists would say this, as it is their duty to frustrate all efforts to free the Ukrainian people. But this sentiment is, surprisingly, shared by some of the nationally conscious Ukrainian Canadians who consider the raising of the Ukrainian problem in Parliament as "diplomatically inappropriate." In their view, the Ukrainian question should be debated at an international level and an ordinary Canadian MP simply lacks diplomatic skills to handle it without embarrassing Canada and the Ukrainian community. It seems to me that those who lack the courage to speak out in defence of their ancestral nation hardly constitute any kind of an asset either to themselves or to their heritage.

Notwithstanding negative criticism directed at me from some sectors of the Ukrainian community, I found much encouragement, praise, and support for raising the question of Ukraine's freedom. The majority of Ukrainian Canadians properly understand and appreciate such efforts. Furthermore, I know from personal experience that MPs of British and French origin encouraged Fred Zaplitny and myself to articulate in Parliament issues relevant to Ukrainian Canadians, including the troubling question of Ukraine itself. They are of the opinion that a Ukrainian MP has not only the right but the duty to inform his colleagues about Ukrainian matters. Intelligent MPs consider speeches on the subject of Ukraine a useful service to Parliament because they help Canada to develop a better understanding of international affairs. There are also MPs who have large numbers of Ukrainian voters in their ridings and are sensitive to their special concerns and speak out in the House of Commons. Similar voices expressing concern for the Ukrainian situation in Europe have been heard in the British Parliament and the United States Congress. This fact in itself should be enough to inspire any Ukrainian Canadian parliamentarian to action on behalf of Ukraine's freedom. Every Ukrainian Canadian MP must be a defender of Ukraine. This is a difficult but the only correct approach.

FOR EQUALITY *of* ALL CANADIAN CITIZENS

It would be unjust to rank Canada among those countries that practice extreme racial discrimination against individuals or groups of "foreign" origin. Such discrimination has no place in Canada. It is, nevertheless, true that Canada is not totally free from prejudice and discrimination. Several forms of discrimination can be found in this country, but only one category of Canadian citizens is responsible for it. These are people who cannot accept the fact that not all Canadians are of the same racial or ethnic origin. Such people can be found in every region and at every level of society. But it would be an error to judge the entire Canadian nation for the faults of this one category.

Among Anglo-Canadians, one can distinguish three groups, based on their attitude toward their fellow citizens whose ethnic background is different from theirs.

The first group, though small in number, consists of enlightened people who are free of any sense of prejudice. These people are always happy to interact with their fellow citizens. They consider it almost their civic duty to be interested in the problems of other Canadians and to assist them with advice and influence. They do this because they understand that Canada is no longer a colony in which the citizens of the imperial British nation enjoy pre-eminence over other citizens. In their view, Canada is the homeland of all its citizens, regardless of their origin or their wealth. These sympathetic Canadians appear to be biased in favour of "foreigners," because they understand the difficulties of their situation. Their interest and concern are based on compassion. Such people can be found in all parts of Canada and at all social levels: in education, in journalism, in commerce, in religion, and even occasionally in politics.

The second group consists of people who mind their own business, pursue their own interests, belong to community and church organizations, and leave others alone. The majority of Canadians belong to this category. They do not interfere in the affairs of others and resent interference in their own affairs. They are convinced that in a democratic system every individual or group can do anything it wants as long as it does not interfere with others. In their view, a person can speak in whatever language he or she prefers and belong to any organization or church. These people do not impose their attitudes on others and do not wish to be imposed upon. In short, the majority of Canadians believe in a philosophy of "live and let live."

The third and last group of Anglo-Canadians is not very large, but it consists of individuals who are prejudiced against those whose origins are different from their own. These people are also found in all parts of Canada and at all levels of society. They refuse to accept other Canadians as equals. They know only one language, and that often quite poorly, but cannot suffer to hear someone speak a different language. They view with suspicion non-British organizations, about which they may know nothing. They consider all who are not of British or French origin as foreigners. These people are definitely racist and consider their fellow citizens, especially those from Eastern Europe, unworthy of being "true Canadians." During the economic depression, government officials belonging to this category expressed outrage when the so-called foreigners were obliged to seek welfare assistance. They considered these foreigners to be the major drain on society despite the fact that official statistics showed that the "foreigners" were the smallest component on the welfare rolls. These bigoted Canadians discriminate at every step. Should your name end in "chuk," "sky," "enko," "uk" or in hundreds of other endings that prove your foreign ancestry, you will be treated contemptuously.[31] In short, these impatient assimilators and the "builders of the Canadian nation" create difficulties for all Canadians and provide serious disservice to Canada. It is not surprising that ignorant people could be overcome with anti-foreign mania, but it is surprising when educated individuals, some occupying high positions, also engage in this irrational nativist hostility toward "foreigners."

One of the most notable attacks on East Europeans came in the late 1920s from a widely respected Protestant bishop, J. E. Lloyd. In a letter to his clergy, he characterized East Europeans as "dirty, ignorant, garlic-smelling, and undesirable continentalists." After a Member of Parliament, Michael Luchkovich, responded to Lloyd in the House of Commons on 28 May 1929, racist Canadians became a little more careful with their public comments. However, in 1940 three news items appeared in the Canadian press, stories that gave voice to the clearly prejudicial attitudes of Canada's government circles. This time I assumed the responsibility to answer this prejudice in my 25 November 1940 speech in the House of Commons entitled "Canadian Unity." (See page ??) In the speech, I cited directly the offending references. The first appeared in the *Edmonton Journal*, 1 November 1940.

R. L. Maitland, leader of the [Alberta] provincial Conservative Opposition, expressed strong criticism against the continuation of foreign languages and foreign attitudes in this country. Mr. Maitland expressed dissatisfaction about the teaching of foreign languages in Canada's schools.

Following my criticism of Maitland, Conservative MPs tried to explain to me that Maitland had the Japanese in mind. In my view, this did not justify his attitude.

The second quotation was also from the *Edmonton Journal* of 4 November 1940:

> War pressures make it necessary to increase the federal police force and 800 new recruits are being accepted by the RCMP. But in view of the stringent intellectual and physical requirements, the quota has not been met. Applicants must be single and of British racial origin.

The third example appeared in the *Saskatoon Star-Phoenix* on 8 October 1940. The news item concerned J. W. Parker, head of the municipal welfare in Saskatoon, who stated that "we should have two levels of assistance, one for Central-Europeans and another for the 'white people.'"

My turn to speak in the House of Commons came at eight o'clock, at the beginning of the evening session. Most members were in their seats while guests and visitors filled the galleries because debates over the Throne Speech were varied and interesting. This was my third speech but my first on the subject of discrimination. At this point in the war, a considerable number of Ukrainian Canadian servicemen were already overseas. I used that fact to attack discriminatory and unjustified attitudes toward the "foreigners." Members on both sides received my speech favourably. W. A. Tucker, member for Rosthern, Saskatchewan, agreed with my position unreservedly, although Tucker belonged to the Liberal party while I belonged to the Social Credit. From that day, he cooperated with me and often supported me on a variety of issues of common interest.

From the time I delivered my speech in defence of Canadians of "foreign origins," Tucker was not the only one who understood that, as the sole representative of Ukrainian Canadians in Parliament, I was responsible for more than my constituency and my party. I carried the daunting responsibility of representing the entire Ukrainian Canadian community. This is how many parliamentarians, ministers, officials, and the press came to view me.

My next speech on the subject of discrimination was on 8 June 1943. During the debate, I drew the attention of the Minister of the Navy and the Members of the House to the statement of Lt. Commander A. A. E. White, which appeared in the *Saskatoon Star-Phoenix* on 21 October 1943. Among others, White stated that candidates for naval officers must be "from 18 to 45 years of age and of British origin." In my short speech, I demanded that naval officer ranks be opened to non-British candidates and that all forms of discrimination be eliminated from the armed forces. In response to my protest, Angus L. Macdonald, Minister of the Navy, said that the cited incident was not authorized by his department. I was not sure whether the answer was true, but it was possible that White had expressed his personal opinion. Nonetheless, this did not exempt the department from its responsibility to rectify the blunder and to make certain that such views were not repeated. As I remember, several French-Canadian members were also angered because the quoted statement excluded French-Canadians from officer ranks in the navy.

My criticism of discrimination was also connected with the issue of radio broadcasts. During the war, beginning on 13 September 1939, all broadcasts in languages other than English and French were forbidden until further notice. However, there was an exemption for departments of the federal government and the state-run Canadian Broadcasting Corporation to sponsor minority language broadcasts. On 26 August 1940, Scottish and Welsh were exempted from restrictions.

I considered the language limits placed on radio broadcasts as a definite form of discrimination, as an indication of distrust of Canadians who spoke "foreign" languages. I have always been of the opinion that language broadcast restrictions in a democratic country like Canada was a mistake, especially at the time, when democracies were struggling against totalitarianism. Of course, the government must be careful during war. It must be careful even with the legal languages. For that purpose, we had wartime censorship and that was enough. I was determined that a democratic country should utilize all languages of its people in the pursuit of wartime objectives. It appeared to me that government advisors consisted of individuals who did not understand the diverse nature of Canada's population and its attitudes. This is why they provided the government with a simple solution: forbid broadcasts in "foreign" languages. This edict did Canada more harm than good.

Now let us turn to the matter of wartime registration of people who became Canadian citizens after 1 September 1922 and who had originated in Germany and Italy, or in the lands that were occupied by Germany and Italy at the time of the declaration of war. In the pursuit of national security, the government dealt properly with those alien residents of Canada who still maintained the citizenship of the countries with which Canada was at war by compelling them to register as enemy aliens. However, the demand to register and fingerprint Canadians, some of whom had been citizens of Canada for nearly twenty years and whose Canadian-born sons were voluntarily serving in the armed forces, was both unjust and harmful. I should note that the Defence of Canada Regulations also included the registration of Canadian residents of Japanese origins. This included not only those without Canadian citizenship but also naturalized Japanese and even those born in Canada.

To illustrate how misinformed the Canadian government and its officials were about the international situation, we have the Czechoslovakian example. Canadian citizens of Czechoslovakian origin were also required to register, despite the fact that Germany had invaded and occupied that country in 1939. Only as a result of protests from the Czech government-in-exile, were the Canadian Czechs removed from the list of enemy aliens.

Another example of Canada's poor awareness of international realities concerns the Ukrainian Canadians. Those of our people who became Canadian citizens after 1 September 1922 and who "at the time of their naturalization were citizens ... of any country or territory which from 3 September 1939 was under the sovereignty or control of the German Reich" were required to register. The government did not have even a minor official of Ukrainian origin to assist in determining to whom that unfortunate regulation pertained. Ukrainians were included for compulsory registration because their citizenship papers gave their origin as Austria, Poland, or Romania. Canadian officials were unaware that the Ukrainian homeland was occupied by the neighbouring states. And the absence of Ukraine from the map of Europe further confused the question of citizenship with that of nationality. Ukrainians in Canada loudly objected to the registration and inundated their Members of Parliament with protests and demands for exemption. During 1940 and 1941, I received numerous such letters with requests to intervene. I repeatedly contacted the Minister of Justice, Ernest Lapointe, who upon examination of individual cases, gave exemptions. Eventually, all Ukrainians were exempt from registration as enemy aliens. Those who had been registered were de-registered.

It should be noted that several Members of Parliament – J. T. Thorson and W. A. Tucker, as well as others – also worked on behalf of the Ukrainians. In addition, Orest Zherebko,[32] then a member of the Saskatchewan legislature, was actively involved in this issue.

It should not be forgotten that during the First World War, Ukrainians and other immigrants who came from enemy territories were treated very harshly by Canada.[33] The majority of Ukrainian residents were considered Austrian citizens and a large number of them were interned in concentration camps while others were compelled to work on government construction projects. Many had their citizenship certificates revoked and became disenfranchised. In addition, all Ukrainian newspapers were obliged to publish everything in English and Ukrainian. These emergency wartime regulations were removed after the war and the Ukrainians regained their citizenship and civic rights. The Conservative government of the day was responsible for all these discriminatory regulations. This was the main reason why so few Ukrainians have supported the Conservative party. The Liberal party capitalized on the Conservative mistake. During every election Liberal leaders have reminded the Ukrainian voters how the Conservatives mistreated them during the First World War. In all fairness, however, it should be said that during that war Ukrainians were still newcomers and did not have the necessary leadership to represent them effectively before the government. As a result, the government was uninformed. However, during the Second World War, the Liberal government did not have such an excuse.

part II

FROM HLYNKA'S DIARY AND NOTES

One of the most memorable events for me was the fact-finding tour of Europe. Whenever I recall those three months (November 1946 – February 1947), they seem like a dream. Since a book would be needed to describe fully my observations and significant moments, I will limit myself to a general account of the journey.

ON THE WAY *to* LONDON

Loud banging on the door, followed by calls of "Sir," awoke me around six o'clock in the morning. I jumped out of bed and opened the door. Before me stood the ship's steward dressed in white. I rubbed my eyes and asked what had happened. He replied that it was time for a hot cup of tea. As I was not yet fully alert, I could not understand why he had awakened me and was now offering tea. Nevertheless, I was in no position to resist, so I took the tea and began to sip it. After several minutes, I remembered that on a British ship everyone drinks tea, in accordance with British custom, even those who are half-asleep. However, such service did not appeal to me because I was unable to go back to sleep until breakfast time. Furthermore, the sweet tea left an unpleasant taste in my mouth. When the steward returned, I thanked him for the tea and explained that I was not used to drinking it in the morning, as Canadians prefer coffee. He was surprised that Canadians had not developed a taste for morning tea but was probably pleased that he had one less passenger to serve.

When I uncovered the porthole, I saw that our ship was sailing down the St. Lawrence. For the first four days I made no effort to get acquainted with the passengers, as I thought it would be more useful simply to observe the more interesting individuals. During this time, I read in the cabin or in the lounge. Once the ship entered the open sea, Stephanie experienced seasickness and periodically rested in the cabin.

On the fourth or fifth day I decided to get acquainted with some of the passengers. The ship carried 120 passengers, mainly representatives of various Canadian manufacturing firms and young wives with children who were returning to Britain after a failed wartime marriage. There were many causes for such failed marriages, including the wife's inability to adapt to Canada because of homesickness for family and everything British. In this context I remember a young Canadian man who worked in the office of a large Canadian firm but whose wife wanted to return to London because in her view Toronto lacked sophisticated cultural and social life. To please her, her husband was obliged to move to Britain.

We befriended four interesting people with whom we spent the entire crossing. One of them, Wilkes, was a middle-aged Canadian from Vancouver, co-owner of a paper mill in British Columbia. He was on his way to the Scandinavian countries to study the newest methods of manufacturing paper. He said that while the Scandinavian pulp and paper industry was smaller than the Canadian one, it is advanced in its methods of production. Another passenger was an Englishman named Deering, who had served as a ship's steward for eighteen years. As he intended to settle in Canada, he had come over to investigate the country. This young man was widely read, with a rich experience acquired during his travels. The third individual was a twenty-nine-year-old Englishman who had taken the advice of his parents to sell his large grain mill in Calgary and return to Britain, where he owned a similar business. The last person we befriended was a young woman, Betty, who had married a French-Canadian but who, after a year in Canada, had also decided to return to Britain. This young lady had the talent of being able to compose beautiful poetry in a matter of minutes. She was also a singer as well as a contributor to several literary journals. In addition to these four people, we became acquainted with several Canadian businessmen, especially with A. J. B. Millborne, a representative of Trust and Loan Company of Canada from Montreal, who later visited me in Ottawa.

The crossing took ten days, although the weather was so bad that even large ships like the Queen Elizabeth took eight rather than the normal four days. Despite the weather, our crossing was interesting and memorable. On December 8, just before noon, we arrived in Liverpool. Passengers were not allowed to disembark until the baggage was unloaded. This took two hours. This procedure allowed immigration authorities to process the baggage without undue confusion.

The unloading of the baggage, however, was rather curious. Since this was a small ship, it had no automatic equipment for unloading baggage onto the dock. As a result, suitcases were simply thrown down the stairs, picked up at the bottom and then carried across the gangway and arranged there for pick-up. Passengers who had bottles of Canadian spirits closed their eyes and plugged their ears so as not to see and hear their suitcases crashing down the stairs. They expected broken bottles and soaked contents. Equally odd was the absence of luggage carriers, either motorized or manual – which one finds in Canada – for moving the baggage to the customs. In Liverpool, dockworkers hauled two or three suitcases in small wheelbarrows. Baggage transfer from the ship to the customs area took a long time. Why did they lack modern equipment? It's hard to say; perhaps they were merely accustomed to doing it this way or perhaps the dock lacked sufficient space.

Once we got our suitcases, we sent a telegram to Bohdan Panchuk,[34] one of the Ukrainian Canadian representatives in London, asking him to meet us at the London railroad station. Then we boarded the train to the capital of Great Britain.

We traveled in a so-called first-class car, which is similar to a Canadian standard or parlour car. But I was curious about second- and third-class cars and visited one. It reminded me of the old Canadian coaches that we use on secondary lines in western Canada. British trains travel faster than the Canadian, averaging between seventy and eighty miles an hour. They also do not sway as much, probably because British tracks are laid over a harder and more level base.

HYLNKA IN LONDON

We arrived in London after several hours, and Bohdan Panchuk met us at the station. We immediately ordered a taxi and were taken to the Central Ukrainian Relief Bureau, which had been organized and funded by the Ukrainian Canadian Committee to help Ukrainian refugees in Germany, located at 218 Sussex Road. There we met two fellow Canadians, Rev. S. W. Sawchuk[35] and A. I. Yaremovich, as well as Danylo Skoropadsky.[36] At lunch we were joined by Ann Crepleve[37] and Mrs. Panchuk, who worked at the Relief Bureau. After lunch, we were assigned a room and went for a rest.

Monday, 9 December 1946

The day after our arrival in London, I telephoned our diplomatic representation in Great Britain, Canada House, to arrange for an appointment with Canada's High Commissioner, N. A. Robertson. We were expected at two p.m. London is a huge city, almost as big as New York, and as newcomers, we did not find it easy to orient ourselves. Nonetheless, we managed to reach Canada House before two o'clock.

First we met with the passport officer, H. W. Kember. A courteous Englishman, he had worked in Ottawa in the Department of Foreign Affairs. We applied for passports to the following countries: Germany (British and American zones of occupation), Austria (American and British zones), Italy, France, Belgium, Holland, and Switzerland. I gave Kember letters of recommendation from federal minister J. A. MacKinnon and from S. T. Wood, Commissioner of the Royal Canadian Mounted Police. In return, Kember provided an official recommendation from the High Commission to assist me when dealing with foreign diplomats, both in London and elsewhere.

As soon as we had completed visa and passport formalities, we learned that High Commissioner Robertson was already waiting. I knew him from Ottawa. He was courteous, but our conversation lacked smoothness. I explained to him the purpose of my trip: that as a Member of Parliament and being of Ukrainian origin I was interested in refugee issues, especially the problem of displaced persons (DPs). I intended to observe closely the conditions under which the displaced persons lived and to find out first-hand all I could about these people. I mentioned that their relatives in Canada were deeply concerned with the refugee problem. I gave him further details about my visit as well, including its length and my tentative itinerary.

Robertson asked me whether I knew that the Poles in Canada had agreed to work together – that is, their political left and right wings – and he inquired whether there was a possibility of Ukrainians doing the same thing. His question revealed a lack of understanding of the basic characteristics of Ukrainian politics, and I avoided replying directly by stating that I was primarily interested in those matters as a Member of Parliament and that I took little interest in the organizations themselves. I observed, however, that Ukrainians have done well by combining five organizations into one, the Ukrainian Canadian Committee, with a view of assisting Canada in the war effort.

We chatted rather informally from that point on. Robertson asked my wife whether she was of Ukrainian origin and she said yes. I congratulated him then on his appointment and said that since London was a very important political centre, he could achieve a great deal there on behalf of Canada. My congratulations seemed to please him and he invited us to tea at Canada House for the following Saturday. Finally, Robertson summed up his observations about our trip, told us more or less what would be required of us, and recommended that we ask advice from Percival T. Molson, the Third Secretary, who had just returned from a similar tour of Germany.

As we were leaving, Molson came and took us to his office. This young Canadian was from Montreal. After completion of his commercial studies, but while still studying international affairs, he began serving at the High Commission as the Third Secretary. Molson detailed his recent trip to Germany and offered us advice, especially on where to go and whom to see. He suggested that we travel to Berlin first because it was the centre for all major representatives of the countries involved in the occupation of Germany and in the resolution of the refugee problem. There was already a Canadian mission in the British sector of Berlin. Gen. Pope and his deputy, Col. Scott, headed the mission. In the meantime, Molson received a phone call from W. J. Holmes, Canada's First Secretary. He, too, wanted to meet us and proposed setting up appointments with people he felt we should meet in London.

In about half an hour we eagerly entered his office. Holmes was a young man, around thirty-two years old and seemed to be modest though quite formal. Beneath his self-effacing exterior, however, Holmes possessed a logical mind and extraordinary abilities. My positive opinion of him was confirmed when, shortly thereafter, he was appointed Canada's *charge d'affaires* in Moscow, and at the end of 1949 he replaced Gen. MacNaughton as Canada's chief representative to the Atomic Commission.

Holmes managed to arrange several meetings for us with British and American diplomats and asked me to meet with him upon the completion of my visit to Germany. He also offered further assistance, if need be.

On the way from Canada House, we stopped to see Mr. Gurton, the European head of the Colonization Department of the Canadian National Railroad. Gurton was very interested in our trip, as he was well acquainted with Ukrainians, having worked as a lawyer in Dauphin, Manitoba. He later joined the CNR and came to know such Ukrainian centres as Vegreville and Mundare in Alberta. I had one more meeting with Gurton upon my return from the continent.

We were invited for supper at the famous Westminster Stranger's Restaurant, located in the British Parliament, by Sir Howard Degville, head of the Empire Parliamentary Association, of which I was a member. I had had the pleasure of meeting Sir Howard in Ottawa, where he had been my guest for several days. Canadians of Ukrainian ancestry will remember him from his travels through Ukrainian communities in 1940 when he was entertained in Winnipeg, Saskatoon, Edmonton, and Mundare.

Sir Howard greeted us in his office. Immediately, he and another parliamentarian invited us to attend the current session of the House of Commons. It was most interesting to compare debates in the Parliaments of Canada and Britain. Here in London, they actually debate instead of simply making speeches. After the session, we enjoyed a pleasant supper at which we met many Members of Parliament and their wives. After the meal, Sir Howard took us on a tour of the historic British Parliament building. We were certainly impressed by the deep respect the British have for their heritage, a respect much greater than we had expected.

In one day we had managed to cover a great deal of territory.

Tuesday, 10 December 1946

We went to Canada House again and applied for all our permits and visas. Molson called us in and suggested that I see Sir Herbert Emerson, director of the Intergovernmental Committee for Refugees (ICR), which would become defunct on 31 December 1946; he was in charge of Nansen [stateless refugee] passports for the League of Nations. His deputy was Patrick Maline, whom I had previously met in Montreal during the conference of the United Nations Relief and Rehabilitation Agency (UNRRA). An appointment with Sir Herbert was arranged for the following day at three o'clock.

From Canada House we drove to see J. H. Moore, head of the Control Commission for Germany and Austria. This meeting was arranged by Holmes. Moore appeared to be about thirty-eight years old and impressed me very favourably. He was most courteous and briefed us on the various responsibilities of this multinational commission. He also filed an application with the occupational military authorities for permission for us to travel to Germany and Austria, especially to Berlin and Vienna. He sent the documents to Berlin and followed up with a phone call to speed up the bureaucratic process, which normally took several weeks. The next day we heard from Berlin that my military passports were approved. However, in view of the current dangers inherent in travel in war-ravaged Germany, Stephanie was not granted a military passport. It seemed that the authorities also feared that travel permission for Stephanie would have obliged them to issue passports to the wives of British parliamentarians, and this would have caused problems of housing, travel, food, and security. Thus, Stephanie, disappointed as she was, had no choice but to remain in London until my return from Germany.

Hlynka at the London (England) office of the Central Ukrainian Relief Bureau with fellow Canadians. L to r: Anthony Yaremovich, Rev. S. Sawchuk, Stephanie, and Anthony.

I also requested military passports for the representatives of the Ukrainian Central Relief Bureau, specifically for Bohdan Panchuk and Anthony Yaremovich,[38] who had been waiting approximately two months for these documents. The Rev. S. W. Sawchuk, vice-president of the Ukrainian Canadian Committee and a military chaplain, who intended to visit several refugee camps, was also waiting for a passport. The official response was that the representatives of the Ukrainian Central Relief Bureau could not be issued passports until such time as the bureau was formally recognized by the British and American authorities as a legal relief committee for Ukrainian refugees. Furthermore, the military authorities did not permit more than three Canadian representatives to travel at once. At that time there were already two other candidates. Since I had already been given travel permission back in Ottawa, I did not have long to wait. I also requested the special currency that was in circulation in the British zone of Germany. Once in the American zone, I would receive special American currency. Upon completion of all the formalities, I got my money and my military passport. I was pleased to note the important statement on the passport that the government of Canada authorized my visit to the continent.

Wednesday, 11 December 1946

From 10:30 until noon, Bohdan Panchuk and I met with Sir Herbert Emerson, director of the Intergovernmental Committee for Refugee Affairs. Sir Herbert was an elderly man, probably around seventy years of age. He was professionally expert in matters of international passports, political refugees, immigration, and aid. He had had rich experience in these areas because he had been chairing various British and League of Nations committees ever since the end of the First World War. Our discussions revolved around questions of care, repatriation, and resettlement of refugees. Sir Herbert noted that his task as head of an international committee was to speak from the perspective of this committee and not from that of the British government, notwithstanding the fact that he was an Englishman.

Sir Herbert gave a summary of the activities of the refugee committee during the war. As far as its future was concerned, the committee was to end officially on December 31 of 1946. Its functions would be taken over by a new organization, the International Refugee Organization (IRO), which was in the final stages of formation and which would assume the functions of the UNRRA. It was expected that the best and most experienced officials of the newly dissolved agencies would be transferred to the IRO.

Speaking from the perspective of the refugee committee and the IRO, Sir Herbert said that the simplest solution to the refugee problem would be their repatriation home. Consequently these two organizations would direct their resources to encouraging and convincing refugees that repatriation was the best solution to their difficulties. It was apparent, however, that a sizeable group of refugees from a variety of Central and East European countries would not accept such a solution and wanted to remain as refugees pending their permanent resettlement elsewhere. Until such resettlement occurred, they required care. This issue of care created a new problem. During the recent meetings of the Preparatory Commission of the International Refugee Organization, held in the United States to approve its constitution, certain categories of refugees were excluded from the IRO care. Should the IRO accept the Soviet interpretation of designating refugee categories, there was a possibility that 40 to 50 per cent of Ukrainian refugees would be denied IRO protection. On the basis of information available, it appeared that nearly 150,000 might be removed from DP camps and dumped on the German population without any resources for finding food and shelter.

I believe it is important to explain the three crucial clauses of the IRO exclusion, as stated in the appendix to its charter:

1. "All individuals who after the Second World War took part in any organization whose aim was a violent change of government in their homeland would be excluded from IRO care."

    It is clear from the wording of this exclusion that a large number of Ukrainian refugees would fall into this category, because almost all of the nationally conscious Ukrainians had belonged to organizations whose goal was the liberation of Ukraine from foreign occupation.

2. "All individuals who after the Second World War were leaders of movements which are in opposition to the countries of their origin or who encourage refugees not to return home are excluded from all IRO care."

    Should the majority of the IRO officials assume a pro-Soviet position, then clauses one and two of the above would not only deny IRO care to the majority of Ukrainian refugees, but it would make it impossible for them to emigrate, as only the IRO-sponsored refugees would receive visas and be allocated space aboard ships.

3. "All individuals who, during the war, in any way collaborated with the enemy are excluded from IRO care."

Under this clause, Soviet authorities included almost all refugees who found themselves in enemy territory, because the Soviets did not believe that the refugees had been taken forcibly by Germans for labour or military needs. This article included the Ukrainian personnel of the Galicia division interned after its surrender in Rimini, Italy.[39] Thus the IRO would exclude from aid everyone in the above categories as well as deserters from the Red Army and political refugees from the Soviet Union.

When I asked Sir Herbert for his comments on such a gloomy prospect for Ukrainians, he replied that the exclusion of a large number of Ukrainians and other refugees from the IRO would indeed create an acute situation for them and a serious problem in general. He added that in such circumstances the overseas Ukrainians [in Canada, the United States, Brazil, and Argentina] should be prepared to make funds available to assist with resettlement and to help those excluded from the IRO. Overseas Ukrainians also had a responsibility to lobby and to pressure their governments to allow the resettlement of the DPs. He stressed that concentration on relief aid would not resolve the problem and that it was essential to focus all attention on the question of voluntary repatriation and on finding a new home for those who refuse. With intensive commitment, the overseas Ukrainians could do a great deal toward resolving the DP problem by collecting relief funds and by persuading their governments to admit Ukrainian refugees.

While listening to Sir Herbert's comments, I decided that upon my return to Canada I would establish a resettlement fund for the purpose of providing relief for the excluded Ukrainian refugees.

As far as any action with regard to repatriation and, for that matter, any action directed at the rescuing of Ukrainian DPs was concerned, Sir Herbert stressed that nothing could be resolved with memoranda and propaganda, for these could often be interpreted in negative ways. As an example, he cited the UNRRA conference in Geneva on 14 August 1946 where he had been given a stack of political literature that appeared hostile to some of the countries present at the meeting. Such activities, in his opinion, would not help Ukrainians to receive the protection of the IRO but would actually harm those who deserved such aid. In fact, all such political propaganda strengthened the position of governments unfriendly to the refugees and weakened the hands of those who wish to help.

With respect to Ukrainians from Soviet Ukraine – that is, those who were Soviet citizens before 17 September 1939 [before Soviet occupation of Polish Western Ukraine] – Sir Herbert said that neither the IRO nor any other refugee committee offer them any assistance or are even in contact with them, since they were still considered Soviet citizens. It is in this context that we find the real reason why so many Ukrainian refugees from Soviet Ukraine changed their names: in order to hide their true identity rather than to conceal their wartime misdeeds, as had been alleged by communist agents.

Searching for reasons why, a year and a half after the war, the Canadian government would not allow immigration, I asked Sir Herbert how the British authorities viewed the possibility of refugee immigration to Canada. He replied that he could not speak on behalf of the government but personally, he was convinced that the British government would favour large-scale immigration to Canada. Responding to the question about refugee orphans, Sir Herbert explained that the official policy was to assist them to return to their country of origin. Only legally adopted orphans were not subject to repatriation. In conclusion, Sir Herbert praised the Vatican for its extensive aid to the refugees and he added that the Vatican helped not only the Catholics but all refugees, regardless of their religious beliefs. We sincerely thanked Sir Herbert for nearly two hours of such an informative meeting.

At 4 o'clock the same day we had a tea engagement with Richard Stokes, a very influential Member of Parliament whose Labour party formed the government. Stokes had invited us – that is, Stephanie, Panchuk, and myself – for dinner at the parliamentary restaurant. Having read his speeches in the British *Hansard* while in Canada, I looked forward to meeting him. I had also sent him, as well as other Members of Parliament, two of my speeches on the issue of war refugees. In his letter to me, Stokes had said that should the need arise to raise this issue in the British House of Commons, he would gladly speak out and would appreciate receiving further information from me. Indeed, on 3 March 1946 Stokes had defended in the House of Commons the head of the Ukrainian Representative Committee in the British zone of Germany. To illustrate Stokes' knowledge and determination, let me quote from the *Hansard*:

> Mr. Stokes asked the Chancellor of the Duchy of Lancaster whether he knew that the head of the Ukrainian Representative Committee

in the British zone had been arrested in Hanover on 15 January and could he explain this arrest.

Chancellor of the Duchy of Lancaster (Mr. John Hind): Dr. Lucyk was detained for questioning on suspicion of spreading anti-Soviet propaganda during and after the war.

Stokes: Is my honourable friend aware that this man has been recognized by British authorities as the de facto leader of this organization and that brutal persecution was repeated at the end of February? Forcible repatriation has remained on the daily agenda in the British zone of occupation, notwithstanding the promises of my honourable friend that this must not be done.

Hind: I am not aware of what you imply in the second part of your question. In connection with the first part of the question, it could hardly be said that police interrogation represents a gross violation of accepted norms.

Stokes: In view of the fact that this man lives in a camp, was there a need to arrest him? It is not difficult to question a man in the camp without casting a suspicion of criminality upon him. If I cannot get an answer to this question, may I ask another one?

Hind: It appears from the last part of the question that no one residing in camps should be arrested regardless of the accusations made. I cannot accept this.

Stokes: Point of order. Since I am not allowed to complete my questioning, I declare that I will raise this issue in another context.

The above debate indicates that Stokes upheld certain high moral principles, which I applaud, because not every Member of Parliament was prepared to defend a stranger. It should be remembered that Stokes had nothing to gain from intervening on behalf of Ukrainians. Indeed, he intervened on behalf of justice.

Stokes was a curious individual not only because he was prepared to continue his defence of Ukrainians, but also because he was the only Englishman we met in Europe who resembled an American, both in attitude and in character.

Having met Panchuk previously, Stokes asked what he could do to help us. We informed him that the most pressing issue was the effort to save the nine thousand soldiers of the Galicia division who were interned in a prisoner-of-war camp in Rimini, Italy. He knew that the division had not fought against Britain and the United States, but against Russia. The urgency of the Galicia matter stemmed from the fact that both the Ukrainian Central Bureau in London and myself were in possession of critical information to the effect that the Soviets were determined to get their hands on the division. In the various international negotiations then taking place, the possibility of the exchange of the Ukrainians for some political concessions on the part of the Soviet Union could not be excluded. It was thus essential to save the Ukrainian division from Moscow's claws.

But even if the division was not going to be handed over by the British or the Americans, it would remain in serious jeopardy. The British and American troops were going to evacuate Italy three months after the signing of the peace treaty with Italy, which was scheduled for 10 February 1947. This meant that should the division remain in Italy beyond the middle of May, it would find itself at the mercy of the new and weak Italian government. It was assumed that as soon as Italy signed the peace treaty, it would begin negotiations with Yugoslavia for the return of Italian prisoners-of-war. It was quite likely that the Ukrainians could be offered as an item of exchange. Communist Yugoslavia would then transfer the division into Moscow's hands.

Once he understood the precarious situation of the Galicia division, Stokes expressed his surprise at not being informed earlier of their plight. He said that despite the shortage of ships, there was no time to waste in transferring the Ukrainian internees. The problem was, however, to find a country that would accept them.

We also briefed Stokes on the latest methods used by Soviet repatriation missions in their attempts at forced repatriation. Stokes had frequently spoken in Parliament on the subject of compulsory repatriation, urging the government to end it once and for all. Although acts of forceful repatriation had become less frequent, they still occurred. Collusion between some camp administrators and the Soviet missions allowed the latter to make surprise raids in order to hunt down Ukrainian refugees on the pretext that they were war criminals. Soviet repatriation commissions were supplied with camp documents and names of Soviet Ukrainian refugees by their agents living in the camps.

Stokes was well aware of many such cases, as he traveled extensively throughout Germany and Austria, keeping his eyes open to abuses. Later we discovered that on the refugee issue, the British government feared no one more than it did Stokes because he was so well informed and so outspoken. He did not hesitate to defend those who could not defend themselves. Such a commitment required a person with high moral standards, and the Member of Parliament, Richard Stokes, was such a champion.

Thursday, 12 December 1946

That morning we heard further disturbing news from Italy about the vulnerable situation of the Galicia division. As well, letters had arrived from different parts of Germany and Austria raising concerns about the current screening procedures of refugees and their exclusion from DP camps. In view of these developments, it became urgent to facilitate as quickly as possible the emigration of the Galicia division as well as the resettlement of the general refugees. We heard rumours that South American countries were prepared to accept a large number of refugees. I therefore telephoned the various South American legations in London, explaining that as a Canadian parliamentarian I wanted to meet with their chief immigration officials. Appointments were fixed. At the same time, Canada House arranged for me to meet with several relevant British departments.

At two o'clock Panchuk and I arrived at the Uruguayan consulate. We entered a small, one-room office occupied by only two officials: the secretary of the consulate and his assistant. Their consul had gone to New York, and his assistant was sick in bed. Both officials spoke satisfactory English. To one of my questions they responded with pride that Uruguay had a population of two-and-a-half million. They gave us several English language brochures to acquaint us better with their country. With respect to immigration to Paraguay, they advised us to get in touch with their government and they provided us with the pertinent address. Should the Uruguayan government agree to accept the Galicia division, the subsequent details could be worked out with the Uruguayan consul in Rome, whose name and address they gave us.

I should add here that while we understood the unsuitability of climatic and other Paraguayan conditions for Ukrainian immigrants, the urgency of the Galicia situation was such that it was essential to accept any suitable option.

There was one European country, which I am not at liberty to identify, that was prepared to give the Galicia personnel a temporary refuge for several years. However, this country demanded guarantees that another nation would provide the division with a permanent home. While another country was ready to help, it was unwilling to complicate its relations with the Soviet Union because of fear that Moscow could destabilize it through communist agents and the "fifth column." Given this unfavourable situation, we had to find a quick solution to our dilemma.

At Australia House we had a more than two-hour meeting with the director of immigration to Australia, T. M. Nulty. The main purpose of our meeting was to find a way to involve the Australian government in Ukrainian immigration, especially of the Galicia division and of the Ukrainian refugees in Austria because the situation there was similar to that of Italy: they faced repatriation. It was assumed that Austria would also shortly sign a peace treaty with the Allies and that three months later, British and American armed forces would leave the country, thus putting the Ukrainian refugees at the mercy of the Austrian government. Since there were Austrian prisoners-of-war in Soviet hands, one could not exclude the possibility of Austria's willingness to exchange Ukrainian refugees for its people held in the Soviet Union.

Nulty was an experienced and long-serving Australian diplomat. He had been a delegate to various international conferences and was familiar with many countries. He was anxious to see us because he had been to Ottawa, knew Canada, and had had dealings with Ukrainian Canadians. He told us that between 1935 and 1939 a number of Ukrainians from Manchuria had arrived in Australia on Chinese passports. It had been his responsibility to establish them as peanut farmers in a tropical zone. They were a good type of settler and the

Australian government was more pleased with them than with other Slavic immigrants, who were a comparatively small group.

As far as immigration to Australia was concerned, Nulty noted that his government would like to double its population. There were only seven million Australians and the war demonstrated that such a thinly populated nation is vulnerable. However, at the moment Nulty was authorized to encourage only British immigration. Such immigrants were being generously subsidized by the Australian government, for it would cover the majority of their transportation costs. As far as the multi-ethnic European refugees were concerned, initial plans suggested permitting immigration only of those refugees who had relatives in Australia. On the question of Ukrainian immigration, Nulty proposed that we prepare and send him an appropriate memorandum. He would gladly append it to his own recommendation and would forward it to the Australian government for examination. He indicated that in the meantime, individuals could apply to emigrate and their acceptance would be decided on a case-by-case basis. He added that his government has always been ready to accept professional people.

For our part, we briefed Nulty on the achievements of Ukrainians in Canada and the United States, and provided some data about the Ukrainian refugees. It appeared from our visit that our initiative and personal contacts could produce satisfactory results only in a year or two. Before we left, Nulty asked his secretary to bring in tea and sweets. Over tea, we had pleasant discussions on a variety of subjects. At our departure, Nulty promised to visit me when he returned to Ottawa.

On the main floor of the handsome stone building that was Australia House, we again looked at pictures and information brochures about Australia, the purpose of which was to promote extensive British immigration to that country. Two captions caught my attention. One read "Complete factories with their workers can be transferred from Great Britain to Australia." The other caption was "Australia is a member of the British Commonwealth of Nations and therefore a free and independent nation. A common allegiance to the Crown unites her with other members with whom she shares similar institutions of government and ideals of liberty. Being autonomous, she occupies a separate place among the nations of the world, to whose general welfare she is anxious to make her proper contribution."

As I was reading these captions, it occurred to me that Ukrainians should demonstrate a similar unity and a similar mutual support as does the highly cultured British nation.

Friday, 13 December 1946

At ten o'clock in the morning, Panchuk and I had a meeting with the senior officials of the Argentine embassy. We were greeted by Señor Ricardo Siri, one of the chief functionaries of the embassy and its *charge d'affaires.*

Our purpose here was the same as at the other legations. We wanted to ascertain what prospects there were for Ukrainian refugee immigration to Argentina as well as for the resettlement of the personnel of the Galicia division. Señor Siri spoke English quite well, as a result of working as a journalist in the United States and other English-speaking countries. First, he delivered a general overview of Argentina. He said that the population of Argentina was around fifteen million while the land area was approximately one-third of Canada's. According to him, Argentina had a plan to accept around four million new immigrants, but understandably, most of them would be Latins, mainly from overpopulated Italy. If Argentinian plans were realized, then around thirty thousand immigrants would be admitted every month. He believed that for humanitarian reasons Argentina would accept a large number of DPs. The current delay was due to finances. First of all, the Argentinian government wanted to help the orphans by bringing over a substantial number of them. Furthermore, the government was not interested in single immigrants but in families, even families with one disabled member. This concern with orphans and families certainly interested us because most states, while recognizing that it was their Christian responsibility to help orphans, were refusing to admit them.

While most host countries were also interested in entire families, they preferred healthy and physically fit immigrants. Men with strong muscles would have priority. By the way, this was also the position of the Canadian government. At this point it was useful to contrast Argentina's position on orphans and disabled family members to that of Canada. The Canadian position was and still is that one unwell family member would result in the refusal of entry to the entire family. The acceptance of orphans was deemed too risky, and Canada did not even want to talk about them. This policy did not mean that the Canadian people lacked humanitarianism, because they had, on the contrary, already demonstrated their humanitarian concerns. But immigration officials, who decided such matters and for whose actions government must be held responsible, did not display any humanitarian sentiment toward the war refugees. One detected there no sentimentalism whatsoever.

Siri explained to us that the Argentinian government had dispatched a special immigration mission to Europe, headed by Father Jose Clemente Silva, whose status equalled that of a minister with full powers to decide immigration matters. At the moment the mission was in Paris, on its way to its headquarters in Rome. Siri urged us to seek an audience with the mission as soon as it settled in Rome. He anticipated a positive outcome to the Ukrainian immigration problem since Argentina was planning to admit four million immigrants.[40]

Upon leaving the Argentine embassy, we quickly found a taxi to take us to our next appointment. Because of the distance, the driver wanted a pound ($4.00). We agreed without any argument, and although we were fifteen minutes late, we arrived at the Apostolic Legation at 11:15 to meet with his Eminence, Archbishop William Godfrey.

We entered the papal legate's residence. Shortly afterwards, he came into the reception room, greeted us cordially, and asked us to sit down. We apologized for being late. He said he was glad to see us and that he had already met several Ukrainian Canadians: the Rev. Dr. Wasyl Kushnir,[41] Stanley Frolick,[42] and Anthony Yaremovich.

We gave the archbishop the disturbing information about the possibility of forcible repatriation to the Soviet Union of the Galicia division and briefed him about our meetings with diplomatic representatives. We told him we were doing everything within our power to find countries that would accept the division. We requested that he ask the Holy See to issue them visas. Archbishop Godfrey promised to do everything possible to help for humanitarian reasons.

I had with me several copies of my speech on the subject of Ukrainian displaced persons, which I had delivered in Parliament on 25 March 1946, and so I gave him one. I drew his attention to the fact that I gave considerable credit to the Vatican for its refugee assistance. He was pleased with that and added that the Holy See had been doing a great deal of relief work but that this was not known by the general public. Consequently, he was delighted that I gave the Vatican proper recognition in Canada's Parliament. We thanked the papal nuncio for his sympathetic attitude to our concern and departed.

We next rushed to Canada House where Sir George Randall, one of the most important functionaries in the British Foreign Office, was to meet us at 12:15. When, the previous day, I had been informed that an appointment was being arranged with Sir George, I had considered postponing it until after my return from the continent but had decided, out of courtesy, to keep it. The meeting proved to be one of the most interesting and important appointments of all.

With his dignified appearance and manner and his elegant attire, Sir George immediately made a positive impression on me. Without waiting for us to explain the purpose of our visit, he began discussing the issues that gave us concern. His deep understanding of critical Ukrainian refugee problems certainly surprised us. I immediately compared this professional British diplomat with other high officials with whom I had dealt and to whom I had had to outline the issue several times before they could grasp it. In his opening statement, Sir George noted the following, "We gladly would like to contribute to the resolution of the refugee problem, but at the same time, we must remember that the Soviet Union is our ally and we cannot do anything that may be interpreted as an unfriendly position or act toward the Soviet Union."

Sir George said that the four thousand Ukrainians who were in the British zone of Austria were the most immediate problem and that it would be very helpful if some Canadians of Ukrainian origin could go to Austria to assist in determining how many of these refugees had relatives in Canada or the United States. This could then lead to family sponsorship of the refugees. He said that international protection was being sought for Ukrainians in Italy, but they could not be transferred to the British zone of Germany because it was already overcrowded. He noted that some countries would accept the Ukrainians from Italy but only on condition that the IRO would guarantee that in two years they would be resettled elsewhere. Belgium and France had made this offer. He assured us that the officials responsible for the Galicia division were continuing their search for a solution.

Sir George continued: "We have to be careful in British zones not to give Russians any reason for criticism. They have already alleged that the British and Canadians sent agents to camps in Germany to work against the USSR. We must be careful because such people as Norwegians and Latin Americans are undecided in their stand on some of these matters and could perhaps be swayed by the Russians. Ukrainians make it difficult for us by hanging out their national flags on DP camps and conducting anti-Russian agitation."

He added that the British government was well informed about the Ukrainian situation and that it was not necessary, indeed even harmful, to combine humanitarian rescue operations with politics. The British government would not allow any activity that would deepen misunderstanding with the Soviet Union. He noted examples of Ukrainian spokesmen who had minimized the humanitarian, Christian, and cultural aspects of life, but instead had emphasized the political side. Such presentations were harmful to rescue operations, he stressed.

Sir George advised us to work out the details with his assistant, S. J. Edmonds. We made an appointment for the next day.

Saturday, 14 December 1946

In the morning Panchuk and I met with S. J. Edmonds, Sir George Randall's deputy. On the question of the quick resolution of the refugee dilemma, Edmonds displayed less optimism than had Sir George. He stressed that it was desirable to have a large-scale voluntary repatriation because that would help to resolve the refugee problem. He added that if large numbers of refugee workers and peasants would agree to return home, then it would be much easier to resettle the intelligentsia remaining. He was of the opinion that ordinary workers and peasants were less endangered by the consequences of repatriation than were political activists. However, I pointed out that current immigration practices made it much easier for agriculturists and labourers to gain entry overseas than it was for professionals.

Edmunds cited statistical data on the refugees in the British zones of Germany, Austria, and Italy. The dubious data listed Ukrainians from Western Ukraine as "Polish Ukrainians" (2,573 inside camps and 1,300 outside) and those from Eastern Ukraine as "Soviet Russians" or as "undesignated" (1,214 in camps, 3,952 outside).

Concerning the Galicia division (9,000 men), he expressed doubt whether they, as surrendered enemy personnel, would receive any aid, because international bodies can function only on the principle of compromise and in this case it was likely that there would be strong opposition from the Soviet side. Still, there was a possibility that at least some Ukrainians could receive the necessary aid. While Edmund was speaking, I was stricken with apprehension that many Ukrainian soldiers would be handed over to the Soviets as a gesture of good will and only a few would be saved. I was upset because I wanted to save all the soldiers of the Ukrainian division. After all, their only choices under German occupation of Ukraine were execution, slave labour, or military service. More importantly, they had not fought against the West but only against the Soviet invaders of Ukrainian lands.

I asked Edmunds what would happen to the Ukrainians in Italy and Austria after the impending peace treaties. He reiterated that which we had heard before: namely, that following the peace treaties, the future of Ukrainians would depend on the governments of Italy and Austria. Then I asked him whether he would assist with visas and ships for the refugees should we find a country or countries prepared to accept them. He replied that finding a host country could resolve half the problem, but he had doubts about finding available ships. As far as the cost was concerned, the post-war treasuries of most countries were nearly empty, and he did not foresee an easy solution to this dilemma. We thanked him for the consultation and left.

That evening Stephanie and I were entertained at the residence of N. A. Robertson, Canada's High Commissioner in London. There we met Mrs. Robertson. The Robertsons had two very charming young daughters: one a well brought up and pleasant university student and the other an inquisitive five-year-old. Both girls helped their parents to welcome the guests. We became acquainted, among others, with Lt. Col. J. J. Robertson, who at one time had lived in Regina, Saskatchewan. Now he was Canada's agricultural commissioner in Britain. He invited me to contact him after my return from the continent because he wanted to introduce me to the major international commercial representatives in London and to brief me on issues of international trade so that I could raise them in the Canadian Parliament. We were also pleased to encounter Col. Chambers, who had been a member of the Canadian Parliament and my colleague from 1940 to 1945. Chambers was head of the Canadian Veterans' Affairs Bureau in Great Britain. He, too, wanted to see us after our trip so that he could establish some contacts for me and show us around London. I promised to call him as soon as I had time.

In general, we were quite pleased with that evening because all present expressed serious interest in the refugee issue and in our fact-finding mission. Mrs. Robertson, who had just visited her relatives in Norway and Sweden, was especially curious about our trip. We became aware for the first time that Mrs. Robertson was of Scandinavian ancestry. As we were leaving, Robertson invited us to see him after our return and to share our impressions.

Sunday, 15 December 1946

We spent the entire day at the Central Ukrainian Relief Bureau (CURB), except for two hours during which Rev. Sawchuk, Stephanie, and I went to Hyde Park to listen to speeches. This is a world-famous public forum where orators stand on benches or wooden boxes and deliver pronouncements on a variety of political, religious, and other topics. No one interferes with their freedom of speech, a freedom that continued to be exercised during both world wars. That is why this park has become a symbol of liberty in Britain. We were told that at one time even Churchill sharpened his oratorical skills there.

That Sunday, five speakers were addressing the public at the same time in different parts of the park. Onlookers listened to those that appealed to them, often moving from speaker to speaker. For me the most interesting orator was a clergyman who spoke about "peace and those who undermine it." He severely castigated the "veto" by which the Soviets make peace impossible, and he strongly criticized the nature and direction of Soviet foreign policy. During his delivery, he was questioned and heckled by communists but his skilful and witty responses deflected comments and provoked loud laughter. This cleric was unusual in that on this cold winter day he was dressed only in his black clerical coat with no hat or gloves, while most other people were shivering from the cold; even those who were heavily dressed shivered from the cold. In his conclusion, he invited listeners to his church, where he was to continue his talk that evening.

Another noticeable speaker was a young dark-skinned Indian or African man. Speaking in precise English, he castigated the British for their intolerance toward his people. He demanded better treatment for them because in his view, they had made a significant contribution to the British war effort. Young sailors joked with him and asked questions, to which he responded quite wittily.

In other parts of the park, more speakers awaited their turn. Regardless of what a speaker says, he or she is never arrested at Hyde Park. The British government believes that such speech-making is therapeutic for the presenters.

This is how Rev. Sawchuk, Stephanie, and I witnessed the world's largest forum for freedom of speech and democracy.

The rest of the time we spent at the Central Bureau, taking photographs and talking with long-time Ukrainian residents of London as well as with the more recent arrivals. Among them, we met Danylo Skoropadsky, son of the late Hetman Pavlo and the leader of the Ukrainian monarchist movement, as well as Dr. Korostovets, a Ukrainian activist who had lived in Britain for twenty or thirty years, and his wife, who had just returned from the displaced persons' camps. The newcomers included Dr. Dmytro Dontsov,[43] the well-known theoretician of Ukrainian nationalism, and Mr. [Mykyta] Bura, head of the Association of Ukrainians in Great Britain. These two later settled in [Toronto] Canada.

Monday, 16 December 1946

This morning I met with William J. Ford, the Third Secretary of the American embassy, to discuss the matter of emigration to the United States. He said that the American policy was to adhere to the existing complicated quota system without any exceptions. I requested visas for several Ukrainians and he gave me a number of application forms. I thanked him and left.

Having been granted a special pass, Stephanie, Rev. Sawchuk, and I went at 2:30 to the sixth plenary session of the Intergovernmental Committee on Refugees and Displaced Persons Affairs, which took place in a large church not far from the Parliament Building.

Sir Herbert Emerson, director of the committee, delivered his opening address, which Stephanie recorded in shorthand. Sir Herbert captivated the entire audience with his presentation. He clearly described past and present activities of his organization and sketched out possible solutions for the refugee and DP problems. After him, delegates from Switzerland, the United States, and Australia spoke. Mr. Nulty, with whom I had met several days earlier, recognized us in the gallery and greeted us warmly. Canada's representatives, Robertson and Molson, were also at the head table, around which twenty to thirty delegates were seated.

The last person to speak that afternoon was a delegate from Poland. He was a young representative of the communist government of Poland. With his opening statement, he launched an attack on the IRO, accusing it of favouring the resettlement of displaced persons rather than repatriating them to their countries of origin. He harangued the senior diplomats, arguing that for the sake of harmony and international cooperation the committee should repatriate the DPs "so that they would return home to rebuild their democratic countries." This man's entire presentation was characterized by an abrasive tone and it was difficult to listen to his crude statements at an international forum where other speakers maintained proper decorum and mutual respect. The response to his speech was muted whereas everyone applauded Sir Herbert for his deeply moral presentation.

Tuesday, 17 December 1946

Stephanie and I finalized the financial and other details of our journey to the continent. I was scheduled to depart by air on the morning of 19 December with Canadian General Morris Pope. Stephanie was going to remain in London and assist with typing at the Central Ukrainian Relief Bureau. After my return, we would travel together to Rome.

Wednesday, 18 December 1946

Before my departure for Berlin, I found time to visit the Brazilian embassy. During the visit, Yaremovich and I learned that Brazil's immigration mission was already in Europe and was collecting information about the refugees with the aim of resettling some of them in Brazil. This was a useful visit.

We also approached the Austrian legation. Our main task there was to impress upon the provisional government of Austria the fact that Canadian and American Ukrainians are keenly concerned about the fate of Ukrainian refugees and that we were working hard to facilitate their resettlement.

In the evening I received a phone call asking me to come to Canada House at 8:30 the next morning.

Thursday, 19 December 1946

When I arrived at Canada House at 8:40 in the morning with one suitcase in hand, a car was waiting to take me to the airport. A young lad from Vancouver was my chauffeur. In forty-five minutes we were at the airport. I was immediately offered a cup of hot tea to warm up. Soon other passengers arrived. The last to arrive was General Maurice Pope, head of the Canadian military mission in Germany; he was based in Berlin. He immediately asked to see the Canadian Member of Parliament and I introduced myself. While immigration officials were checking passengers' passports, Pope had another cup of tea. Finally, we all embarked and the plane took off. Altogether there were seven passengers: Pope and his ten-year-old son, a daughter of one of the senior British officers, three soldiers, and myself.

Soon Gen. Pope came to sit beside me to become better acquainted. He had praise for the Ukrainian refugees whom he had encountered in his work. After a lengthy conversation, we dozed off a bit. When I woke up, the clouds were gone and the topography of either Belgium or Holland was clearly visible. Our plane flew at 155 mph but it seemed stationary. The ground was covered with green grass as it had not snowed yet. I could see sandy-coloured fields and the red clay roofs of houses that looked like toys. Rivers and roads divided the countryside into squares.

Around noon all passengers were served lunch, coffee, chocolate bars, and candies. I ate my lunch and drank the coffee but saved the sweets for refugee children.

After lunch, the general and I continued our conversation. He explained the composition of the Canadian Military Mission, its task, and the difficulties it faced. He was pleased that I had decided to go to Berlin first, because the headquarters of the Allied occupying powers of Germany and Austria were located there. He cautioned me that occupational authorities were not overly friendly toward civilian visitors to Germany and that I should try to avoid them. Pope promised to assist me in Berlin in every possible way, both personally and officially through the office of the Canadian Military Mission. He said that a Canadian car would be provided for me for the duration of my stay in Berlin; his deputy Col. Scott would accompany me at all times. I thanked him for this offer, detecting in it the sincerity that characterized a Canadian speaking to his fellow countryman.

Later the pilot, Fl. Lt. J. Curtis of the Royal Canadian Air Force, invited me to see the flight deck. I had always been curious to know how a plane was steered and kept in the air. I had assumed that there was a steering wheel like that in a car, with the pilot sitting behind it. But here I saw that everything functioned semi-automatically and that the plane was locked into a flight position. I was introduced to the rest of the crew.

HYLNKA IN GERMANY

At 3:30 in the afternoon we arrived at the Berlin airport. Two cars met us. Gen. Pope took one to his residence. Col. J. J. McQueen from Medicine Hat, Alberta, took charge of me. On the way to the hotel, I had my first opportunity to see the famous German concrete highways and the impact of bombing. Rows of mid-sized trees flanked both sides of the road. There were virtually no vehicles other than British and American trucks. The people walked or rode bicycles. We encountered many women and old men pulling wagons loaded with branches and leaves to heat their dwellings. On both sides of wide sidewalks there were very few buildings that were not totally destroyed. Most of the city looked like the aftermath of a severe earthquake. Large buildings had been torn apart, and everywhere lay piles of concrete slabs, bricks, and twisted metal. One look was enough to confirm stories that had appeared in the Canadian and American press about the total destruction of the city of Berlin.

I was taken to the Savoy Hotel, which had been damaged but now was partly repaired. Col. McQueen showed me to my room. I would have supper in the hotel and take a rest. He promised to pick me up at nine o'clock the next morning. The room assigned to me might be called a luxury suite. At the entrance, there was a waiting room with a table and chairs for guests. The walls of the main room were covered with attractive wallpaper, while velvet drapes hung over the large window. A luxurious carpet and fine furniture greeted the eye, and the bathroom was finished in ceramic tile. There was a small towel but no soap. In short, this suite gave one an indication of what might be enjoyed by people who could afford such hotels. While the British personnel managed the hotel, its entire staff was German.

My supper consisted of soup, bread, beef, pears, and coffee. All the waiters were men. As elsewhere in large hotels, an orchestra played during the meal. All the waiters spoke English because most

Ukrainians in D.P. Camps of West Germany and Austria 1946–50. Used with permission, courtesy Dr. Ihor Stebelsky. "Ukrainians in the Displaced Persons Camps of Austria and Germany after World War II" *The Ukrainian Historian* 23, no. 3–4 (1986): 57.

of them had lived and worked in Canada or the United States but returned to Germany in the 1930s.

After supper, I requested a telephone directory to see if I could locate any Ukrainian organizations, priests, or perhaps individuals still remaining in Berlin. I was given a small book, which contained only the names of senior military officials and of various branches of the occupation authorities. A few British and American voluntary relief agencies were listed as well but no ordinary citizens were listed. When I asked about a general directory, I was told there was none.

I spent the evening in my room compiling a list of names and addresses of people I was scheduled to meet on my fact-finding mission. After I reviewed my plans, I went to sleep.

Friday, 20 December 1946

A car arrived at nine o'clock, soon after breakfast. I was taken to the large building of the Canadian Military Mission. First, I was invited to Col. McQueen's office, where I left my coat, hat, and rubbers. Then we went to the office of Col. S. M. Scott, the senior advisor to the Canadian Military Mission. After my short chat with Scott, the three of us went to see Gen. Pope. Here all four of us discussed my goals and plans. The others explained briefly the circumstances in which I would find myself. Incidentally, they wanted to know if I intended to give any speeches, and if so, on what issues. I replied that I had no such intention because first, the Canadian government had not yet formulated a concrete immigration policy and secondly, the main purpose of my trip was fact finding. They appeared satisfied with my answer and offered some very important advice, which I followed during my entire journey.

Following our lengthy discussions, Gen. Pope invited me to his place for dinner. He then left me with Col. Scott and drove home to inform his wife that I was coming. We went back to Scott's office for further discussion. Scott cautioned me that the special currency used by the British personnel in Germany and which had been given to me could not be circulated among the German population. All gratuities should be paid with cigarettes. He noted that one package of cigarettes was worth the monthly wage of a hotel or restaurant worker. He then gave me several packages of cigarettes and two bars of soap.

At noon, the general's car arrived and transported us to his house for dinner. There I met his Belgian wife, his seventeen-year-old daughter, and a wife of a senior French official, whose name I could not remember. They spoke mainly in French because the hostess had difficulty with English.

After a sumptuous meal, Gen. Pope led me to the living room where we discussed various matters until 2:30. Initially, he was especially interested in the latest news from Canada. Then we moved to other topics. As far as immigration was concerned, he was in favour of admitting a large number of refugees to Canada. He said that he always expressed this opinion when meeting with government officials and when filing his reports. While he was fairly well informed about the Ukrainian refugee situation, he asked me to elaborate on the subject, which I gladly did. The general, with his broad worldview and his extensive knowledge, made a positive impression on me. I asked him to tell me something about himself and his military career. He modestly recounted his sixteen years of service on behalf of Canada at various diplomatic posts in several countries. He admitted that his assignments were never easy because they always carried so much responsibility. I learned that Pope was a Canadian with part French heritage. He had done his university studies in Canada and Britain. Our conversation was interrupted by the arrival of the chauffeur.

Gen. Pope and I returned to the offices of the Canadian mission. I was flattered when the general would not allow me to open the door but instead opened it himself, saying that I was his guest. Then Col. Scott came to take me to the British military headquarters where I had a three o'clock appointment. Pope asked me to be back by six o'clock because we had a reception at the South African Military Mission. Then Scott and I drove to the British headquarters.

There I was introduced to several high-ranking officers, but the official part of my business called for a meeting with Lt. Col. J. W. Waggan-Hughes. He and I had a forty-five-minute conversation, or rather, he spoke and I listened. From the moment of our introduction, he talked so comprehensively and quickly that I felt no need to ask other than occasional questions.

Waggan-Hughes was a most interesting and well-informed man. He was one of those rare individuals who acknowledged the mistakes the British authorities had made and was prepared to rectify them. I asked why the Central Ukrainian Relief Bureau in London had not been given permission to send its representatives to the DP camps in order to provide aid to the Ukrainian refugees, while other national groups had been given that right. He acknowledged that indeed, Ukrainians had not been treated fairly, but this was due to political complications. However, he said that this unjust treatment had been reviewed and that in a day or two CURB would be authorized to function legally in the British zone of Germany. I thanked him for the encouraging news.

To my second inquiry, as to why government documents classify Ukrainians as Poles or Russians, he said that by the time I would visit the Department of Foreign Affairs or the Control Commission, the word Ukrainian would be in use.

My third question to Waggan-Hughes concerned the troubling subject of compulsory repatriation. I told him that Ukrainian Canadians have been receiving very troubling letters and documentary evidence that instances of forced repatriation to the Soviet Union still frequently occurred despite the fact that military and official circles were insisting that the practice had been stopped. He replied that at the moment there were 114 Soviet repatriation personnel, who were allowed to visit DP camps only if accompanied by British and UNRRA officials. The Soviets had the right to appeal to the refugees to return home but were not allowed to use force. He said that there had indeed been cases of forced repatriation but that these had occurred only on occasions when the camp administration was absent. New precautions were now being taken to prevent any further repetition of such incidents.

Waggan-Hughes quickly approved my itinerary for the British zone and suggested that I could make speeches in camps if I wanted. I explained that I had decided not to do so. Before I left the office, Col. Waggan-Hughes telephoned the headquarters of the British command at the town of Lemgo in Germany and instructed them to look after me upon my arrival. As I had decided to leave that same day, he told them to meet me in the morning at Bad Oyerhausen and to provide me with transportation to Lemgo, located some forty miles from Bad Oyerhausen; at the moment there was no train connection. Waggan-Hughes also arranged to reserve a compartment for me on the train to Bad Oyerhausen.

My next appointment was at the American military headquarters to obtain permission for a tour of Berlin. Col. Scott and another officer took me through the British and American zones of the city. This was a fascinating trip, as we visited many areas of the two zones, travelling over both main and side streets. Piles of rubble were everywhere. It was impossible to distinguish where stores, restaurants, large hotels, and government buildings had previously stood. The German parliament, the Reichstag, bombed and burned, was completely destroyed. I was told that there used to be a large park beside it, but we could not find a trace of it now. In other words, there had been total devastation. However, in the suburbs one occasionally saw undamaged, or only partly damaged, houses. In these gutted buildings lived an estimated three million people. I was also told that there were still many bodies beneath the rubble.

Not many people were on the streets but those whom we saw appeared stunned, as if they had just left the morgue. Some streetcars were running and even the subway functioned to some extent.

We stopped beside the monument to the Soviet military. It had been erected in the British zone. Beside the monument two armed Soviet soldiers stood on guard. The Soviet zone of Berlin began several feet from the monument. The British officer who accompanied us asked in jest if I had a permit to proceed further. As we turned in the direction of the American headquarters, I noticed Soviet officers for the first time. Dressed in camouflage uniforms, they stared at us as their car pulled alongside ours. After a few minutes, they turned into a side street, while we continued on our way. When I asked if Soviet military personnel needed a permit to travel in British or American zones, I was told that the Russians traveled wherever they wanted. Americans and British did not exercise a reciprocal right to travel in the Russian zone, especially at night, unless such trips were prearranged, because there had been a number of incidents of American and British soldiers not returning from there.

At five o'clock we were already at the American headquarters. There I met with Lt. Col. Carney, who was responsible for the refugees and prisoners of war. The visit was mainly a courtesy call, to let them know when I intended to go to the American zone of Germany, so they could relay this information to their headquarters in Frankfurt and Heidelberg. Carney knew about me from the control office in London, where my visit to the American zone had been approved. But since the permit had arrived after my departure, Carney promised to send another one to Lemgo so that it would be there when I completed my fact-finding tour of the British zone. Carney then asked several formal questions about my trip and took notes of my answers. This ended our official meeting. But then he enquired from which part of Canada I came. When I said Edmonton, he immediately relaxed and dropped the serious official tone, as though he had found a long-lost friend. He excitedly explained that he knew Edmonton because he had been stationed there with other American soldiers during the war. He mentioned his Canadian friends there and could not restrain himself from praising the city. In the end he promised me that the Americans I would meet during my tour would treat me as courteously as the Edmontonians had treated him.

Col. Scott returned me to the hotel to pick up my luggage and to check out. My bill for the room and meals was so low that initially I thought the cashier had made a mistake. But I was told the amount shown indeed included everything.

We picked up Gen. Pope and his wife and drove to a reception at the South African Mission. The hosts, a general and his wife, were of British origin. They greeted all the guests as they arrived. In all, there were representatives from fourteen countries. The majority of them were uniformed military personnel with their spouses. They included Americans, Britons, Swedes, Swiss, Norwegians, Chinese, and others. There were only three civilians. I was told that representatives from the "Iron Curtain" countries were also invited but that they had never attended such functions.

Gen. Pope and the host introduced me to the guests already there and then to those who were arriving. Once everyone was there, we were invited to help ourselves at the buffet table. In the meantime, the ladies served appetizers to those too shy to go to the table. In addition, guests were treated to South African drinks. In such a pleasant atmosphere, guests enjoyed their food while engaged in conversation.

The central figure at the reception was a middle-aged but robust British officer of senior rank, dressed in the air force uniform. His jacket was half-covered with a variety of ribbons. This was Sir Sholto Douglas, marshal of the Royal Air Force and head of the British military government in the British zone of occupation. I was introduced to him and his wife at the beginning of the evening. During the meal his witticisms and humorous comments created a relaxed and friendly atmosphere. Eventually Sir Sholto came over to get better acquainted with me because he already knew about my intended mission, about my Ukrainian background, and about my concern for the Ukrainian refugees. In response to his question how I enjoyed the evening, I answered that I was pleased to be here and added that it was difficult for us to be truly happy when all around us were so many unfortunate people in such tragic circumstances. This statement provided me with an opening to further discussion. Sir Sholto mentioned that in the opinion of the military personnel who deal with refugees, the Baltic and Ukrainian refugees were the best liked. He added that undoubtedly there were good people among the other groups as well.

He said that his staff had been urging Canadian and Australian governments to admit large numbers of refugees. Similar discussions were taking place with South American governments. He saw no reason why Canada could not accept many of these refugees. Sir Sholto praised lavishly the intellectual resources represented by Ukrainian and other DPs. From these serious topics, we switched to the lighter subject of wartime and post-war adventures. Other officers joined us, wanting to share their personal adventures.

Later Gen. Pope asked for my opinion of Sir Sholto and added that the latter was not only a military man but also one of Britain's leading diplomats. I answered tactfully that one did not need a long conversation with Sir Sholto to conclude that he had definitely earned all the awards that decorated his chest.

Guests began to leave around 8:30. We thanked our hosts for the reception, bade farewell to those remaining, and departed. Along the way we dropped off Gen. Pope and his wife. Pope insisted that I come in for a few minutes. I took the opportunity to thank him for the frankness and sincerity he had shown toward me and to thank Mrs. Pope for a delicious dinner. I also thanked him for assigning Col. Scott to me. Pope remarked that Scott was one of Canada's top historians and had lectured for many years at American universities. I confessed that I would have never guessed it because he was so modest and unpretentious. The general wished me a safe trip and we left.

Before catching my train, I spent the next two hours visiting the quarters of the Canadian military mission. There I met several Canadians, of whom James MacCordick was the most interesting. This young man had just recently completed a two-year service at the Canadian embassy in Moscow. MacCordick gave me five packages of cigarettes, which should last a week. I bade goodbye to Scott and, accompanied by young MacCordick, went to the railroad station.

MacCordick knew some German and was able to find my train quickly. He took me to the ticket office to show my permit, which gave me the right to travel on military trains. As we approached the train with MacCordick carrying my suitcase, the conductor came running to us and breathlessly explained that it was his duty to take me to my compartment and to look after me. I thanked MacCordick and, accompanied by the conductor, settled into my compartment. In a few minutes the train began to move.

I read for the first hour before going to bed. As I heard people complaining about overcrowding in the train, I expected someone to occupy the empty berth in my compartment. But the conductor assured me that I would not be disturbed. I locked the door as a protection against young thieves and went to bed. In the meantime, the train was speeding across the Soviet zone to Bad Oyerhausen.

Saturday, 21 December 1946

I woke up at six o'clock. I got dressed and stared out of the window at strange sights. Occasionally the train stopped for a few minutes at one of the larger stations. At every station there were hundreds of people with bundles and parcels waiting to catch the train, but our train was so packed that it had no room for new passengers. It was cold outside and the conductor said that many people wait for hours or even days to find a place on the train. Our train was to arrive at Bad Oyerhausen in the British zone at 7:15 a.m., but because of the heavy snow and sharp frost, we finally reached the station only at noon.

I was met there by a British air force officer, Phillip Howard-Trip, who was an official in the department in charge of prisoners-of-war and refugees. He had been waiting for the train since five o'clock and was almost blue from the cold. He recognized me by my Canadian clothes and suitcase, while I recognized him by his British appearance. In a few minutes he warmed up his tiny car, which was probably even smaller than the popular British Austin. It was so low that during the ride I felt like I was being dragged on the road. For most of the trip we traveled on the Autobahn, the superhighway built in the 1930s. Howard-Trip explained that this was one of the best roads in Europe and it stretched across the whole of Germany.

In an hour and fifteen minutes we arrived in Lemgo. This was a small but important town, as it was the base of the British military government for occupied Germany, of the headquarters of the UNRRA, and of the Intergovernmental Commission for Refugees (IGCR). The British had chosen this town because it contained a large number of undamaged barracks and other military buildings. Having no vital industries, Lemgo had not been bombed during the war. The British had designated this town for their use before the end of the war.

Howard-Trip took me to the officers' mess No. 2. There he introduced me to several officials from the aforementioned organizations, and there we had lunch. I was then taken to a concrete building, which was clean but cold as ice, and where a room had been reserved for my use. I shared this facility with one officer. I was given a key and asked to return to the officers' mess at 4:00 p.m.

Anthony at a displaced persons' camp, Germany.

Anthony visiting a displaced persons' camp, Germany

Oleh Gerus, translator and co-editor of this book, standing in front of Munster Lager camp, Germany, 1947. (See page xxiv)

Camp inspection

Camp sick bay

Speaking with refugees

More meetings with DP camp personnel in Germany...

When I returned to the mess, I was immediately invited to tea. Here I met Brig. Kenchington; Col. Todd, who was deputy head of the refugee commission; Col. Pulverment, who was also involved with the refugees; and Col. Brian Buckingham, deputy and later head of the Intergovernmental Commission for the British zone.

After dinner, we moved to the main room and began our discussions. My hosts wanted to know my itinerary: how long I planned to be in Germany, which camps I intended to visit, etc. When this part of our discussion was finished, I asked for a clear explanation of the structure and functions of the three organizations with which I would be dealing. I considered this information to be crucial for my mission. As they were giving their explanation, I drew up an appropriate structural diagram. I asked for detailed information on Ukrainian DPs, as it was important to find out what these men thought about them, specifically about their rights: their postal rights; their right to publish and receive newspapers; and their access to food, shelter, and clothing. I also raised the question of forced repatriation. I needed this information in order to be able to compare objectively the official perception of the refugee situation with the reality that I would see in the camps. Should there be any disparity, I would certainly draw that to their attention. They responded tactfully yet openly.

I was informed that during my stay in the British zone, I would have a car and a chauffeur at my disposal, as well as the services of Col. Buckingham. His responsibilities included accompanying me throughout my mission, arranging for meals and housing, organizing visits to the DP camps, and making certain that there would be reliable transport. I was naturally pleased with this arrangement as I knew neither the German language nor Germany. Having a guide and a chauffeur certainly resolved this problem. It appeared that the British military government took my presence quite seriously.

Following the meeting, I was invited for supper at the officers' mess No. 1. During the evening, I met more senior officials from the occupational authorities and the humanitarian relief agencies. Among those present was a young official by the name of Derek Grey. Unaware of the purpose of my mission and of my views, and perhaps trying to impress me, he began to tell me that a Polish lawyer had told him that the Ukrainians were excluded from receiving aid from

UNRRA, from the military government, and from relief agencies. At that time the British zone contained 122 DP camps composed of refugees of different nationalities. Seventy-six camps were under the UNRRA, 35 under the military government and 11 under relief agencies. Asked whether he considered this disturbing Polish information reliable, he assured me that it indeed was, since the lawyer in question knew Ukrainian DPs well, having once been a prosecutor in Poland where had he dealt with Ukrainian political crimes against the Polish state. While listening to this naïve individual, I realized that any further exclusion of Ukrainians from humanitarian relief would certainly help his career with the new International Refugee Organization (IRO), which would shortly assume control over all DP camps. At the end of our conversation, I said to him that in his place I would not listen to reports of prejudiced people and asked if his superiors knew the source of his information. When he said no, I suggested that they be informed.

At eleven o'clock Col. Buckingham took me to my quarters. Before going to bed, I jotted down the gist of my discussion with the young official about the exclusion of Ukrainians from DP camps and noted his anti-Ukrainian prejudice. I intended to forward this information to Derek Grey's superiors upon the completion of my mission.

Sunday, 22 December 1946

After breakfast, I spent the entire morning typing letters to my wife, Stephanie, who had to remain in London, and to my relatives in Canada. After lunch, I met with Col. Buckingham. I was most interested in hearing about the Ukrainian DP camps that he had visited in the middle of November. He spoke very positively about the Ukrainians and could not stop praising their cleanliness and adaptability. He had been struck by the way they had repaired damaged barracks, garages, and barns, and had converted them into acceptable living space. At four o'clock we went to the officers' mess for tea.

This time Buckingham introduced me to a highly intelligent Pole by the name of Alexander Dehn. He was born in Poland, received his university education in Britain, and conducted business in the United States and later in Poland. His wife and a young daughter now lived in a DP camp in the American zone while he was employed by UNRRA headquarters in Lemgo.

Monday, 23 December 1946

Just before noon, I was taken to the building that housed the main offices of UNRRA, the military government, and the IGCR. My visit started with Mr. Rickford, Buckingham's immediate superior. I shook hands with Rickford, Dehn, and one woman, a social welfare officer. Her name was B. Tomlin and she was a former Winnipegger who used to be a reporter with the *Winnipeg Free Press*. Her father was a professor at the University of Manitoba. She knew many prominent Canadians, especially Paul Martin, a member of Mackenzie King's cabinet, whom she had met at a conference in Europe. It seems that these political connections allowed her to be included in the various British secretariats.

From this office we visited a number of bureaus. In one of them I got a map of the British zone, showing all the DP camps, and a similar map of Austria. I also received the latest statistical data on the camps, as well as copies of several recent reports. I noticed that the term Ukrainian was not listed as a separate nationality although nine other nationalities were. This was done despite the fact that some of the camps were totally Ukrainian. In the official reports, the Ukrainians were identified as Poles, Russians, Romanians, and "undetermined." Yet, even such small nationalities as Latvians, Lithuanians, and Estonians were listed separately. Thus I was going to visit displaced people whose national identity was not even recognized.

When I raised the issue of the non-recognition of Ukrainians as a nationality, I was told, quite correctly, that the subject was the responsibility of London. But those officials I spoke to agreed that it was illogical to deny the existence of hundreds of thousands of people, every one of whom claimed to be Ukrainian. One senior official even gave me his curious definition of a Ukrainian. "A Ukrainian is," he said, "a person who becomes indignant when called a Pole and belligerent when called a Russian." As I was taking notes of our conversation, those present seemed uncomfortable with the subject of non-recognition. One official attempted to placate me by saying that there was a positive side to non-recognition because this prevented the Soviet repatriation commission from demanding the return of Ukrainians.

I left with a heavy heart. During lunch I kept asking myself why the Ukrainians were receiving so little attention in London. How could the experienced British diplomats ignore more than forty million people? In my mind, I contrasted the Ukrainians with the small Baltic nations whom the British government protected by excluding them from forced repatriation; it even held its own officials liable for the violation of this protection. The Ukrainians, however, were being forcibly repatriated by various means, and for some reason, it was difficult to stop this practice.

Col. Buckingham was unable to accompany me on the first day of camp visitation because of pressing business. He assigned Dehn and Mrs. Tomlin to accompany me. I was urged to visit the Ukrainian Catholic monastery of St. Andrew at Antenbachen, some twenty kilometers from Lemgo. Dehn knew it well, as he had frequently delivered UNRRA provisions there.

We left at 1:30 for the monastery. Upon our arrival, we were met by a priest who invited us inside. It was a large residential house whose original occupants had perished during the war. The only survivor, a woman, donated the house for the monastery. The abbot was Johann Peters, a Ukrainian Catholic priest of German ancestry. Five priests, ten monks, and one young orphan boy lived there.

Three of the priests explained their past experiences, how they had been conscripted for slave labour in German factories and how in 1942 they found themselves in the notorious Nazi Dachau concentration camp. They were liberated by the Americans in 1945. They pointed out that of the three thousand clergymen of various nationalities interned in Dachau, only 147, including four Ukrainians, had survived.

There was also a priest from one of the DP camps, who was visiting the monastery for the Christmas celebrations. His information proved to be most fascinating because he had just returned from the western region of Ukraine to which he had been voluntarily repatriated in the winter of 1946. He had been there for six months before managing to escape to the West. He provided vivid details about what had happened to the vast majority of those Ukrainian refugees who had allowed themselves to be manipulated into returning home. He said that many of the returnees died along the way, others were imprisoned, and the rest were exiled eastward. He painted a horrendous picture of the communist repression of Ukrainian people. This repression was feeding the Ukrainian partisan movement because the only alternative to resistance was to accept genocide.

These priests also talked about other subjects, noting that while they were receiving food rations, they lacked shoes and clothing. They asked me to convey to the Ukrainian Catholic monastery in Mundare, Alberta their urgent need for religious books. They urged me to obtain for the Ukrainian DPs the right to write letters in their own language because at that time the military censors did not allow such letters, giving the lack of Ukrainian translators as their excuse. While specifically addressed Ukrainian newspapers were admitted into the camps, some camp commanders did not allow the general distribution of Ukrainian newspapers, although all forms of communist propaganda circulated there unhindered.

Before we left, we were treated to dark bread with butter, cookies, and coffee.

We returned to Lemgo, and I had supper with Col. Todd in the officers' mess No. 2. He was of the opinion that after the current security screening that was taking place throughout the DP camps, there would be further screening. This information disturbed me as it meant that in the near future many more Ukrainians could be deprived of the UNRRA humanitarian aid.

Tuesday, 24 December 1946

Col. Buckingham and I left this morning for Camp Lade, arriving there just before noon. Buckingham went to the administrative office of the UNRRA, which was headed by Col. S. Krolikewicz, a Pole by origin but now a British citizen or at least a resident of Britain. I don't know what Buckingham said to him, but he came to our car expressing dissatisfaction that we wanted to see the camps under his jurisdiction without giving prior notification. I told him that while I wanted to inspect all his camps, I was mainly interested in Ukrainian camps, as I was of Ukrainian ancestry myself. I knew he was obliged to cooperate with me, as I had authorization from headquarters. His tone gradually moderated and he quickly dispatched one of his officials to the Ukrainian camp with instructions to bring over its administration. In about fifteen minutes several young Ukrainians arrived in the director's office, and after introductions, he said to me: "You can ask them anything you want." Again I explained to him that I intended to visit the Ukrainian camp myself, not merely speak with a few people. When he saw my determination, he got into his car and we followed him to the Ukrainian area.

As we approached it, I noticed that the residential buildings consisted of old barns. We entered, accompanied by those Ukrainians who had met us earlier. After asking them several questions, I went to inspect the rooms occupied by the refugees. Opening a door at random, I encountered two young women and two babies in cradles. I looked carefully at these women. Both were around twenty years old and at that age should have been healthy and attractive. But their sunken eyes, cracked lips, and pallid appearance indicated illness. I asked whether they had enough to eat in order to breast-feed their babies, but they did not answer. I then assured them that they could confide in me because I was searching for the truth in order to protect them. One girl responded that the food was inappropriate and inadequate. When I looked into one crib, I saw a seven- or eight-month old baby. It was pale and its eyes were not bright as in a healthy child, but dull. As I uncovered it, I noticed that the infant was dressed in a patched shirt made from old diapers. To prove to myself that this was not an isolated case, I inspected the other baby and found the same dull look and the same ragged clothing. I asked if these women had received any clothing from UNRRA for their children. They replied that in the six months that they had been living in the camp, they had received no clothing at all.

In another room I encountered a thirty-two-year old woman with a young girl standing alongside. I asked several questions about their condition and she responded in the same listless way the other two had. Then she started to cry. I asked if she had been abused. She said she could not continue to live in such miserable circumstances. I turned to the girl, asking her name. But as she moved back from me, I noticed that her legs could scarcely hold her up. It was clear that she was suffering from malnutrition.

My first inspection left me very depressed, thinking that similar conditions no doubt existed in other camps. I asked to see more rooms, those occupied by single men, because I assumed that singles are usually placed anywhere. I was right. Twice as many men as space allowed were jammed into those rooms. Their rooms were inferior to those of women. Although their clothing appeared satisfactory, they complained that it was not warm enough for outdoor work, which they did from time to time. But there was one thing about these boys that uplifted me. They were not afraid to complain in the presence of UNRRA officials that they were treated worse than other nationalities who were placed in superior urban camps. They pointed out that after they had renovated their original camp, they were arbitrarily relocated to these old barns while the Polish refugees took over their camp. I left this Ukrainian camp, which proved to be the worst of all the camps I inspected during my mission, full of vivid and painful impressions and valuable information.

The camp administration invited me for lunch. During lunch, one of the officials explained to me that these four hundred Ukrainian DPs had nothing to complain about because, after all, they do receive some free aid for which they should be grateful. Then in a whisper he added: "You are from Canada and you don't realize that these people had less in their villages than they have here. There they even lacked wooden floors. You didn't know that." He further explained that the reason why the Ukrainians were transferred from better camps to their current location was to keep them together. He added that there were still many Ukrainians in Polish camps who were afraid to identify themselves lest they be relocated.

After lunch we inspected Polish camps. There everything was as it should be. That day a children's concert was being held in a large hall. Several British youngsters whose parents worked for UNRRA were there as guests. The hall was filled with refugees. Children of various ages sang Polish religious and patriotic songs and recited poetry. I was introduced to the leaders of the Polish community. There was also an Englishman by the name of Wood who was in charge of food and clothing supplies. He said that he had become so fond of these refugees that he was prepared to follow them to their new destination.

We also inspected the camp hospital staffed by Polish physicians who, judging by the condition of their patients, seemed to carry out their duties conscientiously.

We left the camp and spent the night in Hamburg. Buckingham had reserved accommodations for me in the officers' mess. Col. Bressi, the commanding officer, was a gracious host who ordered us a delicious meal and provided lodgings in comfortable large rooms. After supper, he acquainted us with the many officials of various nationalities who were there for Christmas Eve. When I eventually got to my room, I gazed at the fine furniture and the expensive paintings and noted that everything was quite luxurious. This was not an ordinary building but a castle, the property of some German who leased it to the British for the duration of the Allied occupation of Germany. As I looked around my room, it occurred to me that the German nation could never be a friend of the Ukrainian people. The Germans live in a crowded environment; they are always searching for colonies. I am sure that upon reflection every Ukrainian would reach the same conclusion.

At this point Hlynka's notebooks become a skeletal listing of his exhaustive itinerary of the DP camps that he inspected from 24 December 1946 to 9 January 1947 and a list of key Ukrainian personalities with whom he conversed. He lists the following camps with Ukrainian refugees: Braunschweig, Hanover (Camp Lysenko), Heidenau, Hamburg, Schleswig, Keil, Lubeck, Frankfurt, Augsburg, Munich, Regensburg, Innsbruck (Austria). Upon his return to London, Hlynka shared his impressions of the refugee situation on 14 January to the Association of Ukrainians in Great Britain:

I must say that in my opinion the Ukrainian refugees found in the camps that I visited represent the best people who have remained in Europe. I am saying this not because they are my brothers but because this positive opinion has been repeatedly stated by camp commanders.

Everywhere I visited our people I was struck by their efforts to maintain cleanliness and order in their daily lives. Even their most modest accommodations drew attention to cleanliness. It was obvious to me that this practice was a direct result of their innate concern with cleanliness and order.

All Ukrainian refugees distinguish themselves with outstanding organizational skills and managerial abilities. I saw a number of camps in which the entire internal administration was in the hands of Ukrainians while the camp commander exercised supervisory control. In private discussions with me, camp commanders expressed their satisfaction with Ukrainians, frequently praising their work ethic.

I witnessed a great deal of highly energetic activities of our DPs. These activities are taking place despite the fact that they know their life in camps is transitory. They could be transferred to other locations in a month or two. However, this state of uncertainty does not discourage them in their efforts to make their camps more livable. And when they are transferred, they display the same degree of commitment to the improvement of the new camp....

Ukrainian traditions of strong family life, of social involvement, and of brotherhood combined with a steely determination to maintain these important cultural traditions characterize our refugees.

I witnessed the following incident. An elderly woman was sitting and embroidering. Her old and tired eyes were filled with tears but she kept on working. To my question what she was embroidering, she said it was a gift for the camp commander's wife and it would take three months to complete. I did not ask her why she was making such a gift, but I understood her intention. With this gift she was trying to win the commander's sympathy for all refugees in the camp. That elderly lady undertook this difficult and lengthy project in order to help improve the condition of all her people!

I was also interested in the composition of the camp supervisory personnel, that is, the various non-Ukrainian officials. I discovered a variety of individuals. Among senior officials, I met good people who understood the value of Ukrainian refugees and treated them with kindness and sympathy. Among lesser officials, there were also good people with strong humanitarian instincts who carried out their duties with almost religious fervour. Such was one Australian lady and such were the two British women who, during one incident of forcible repatriation, screened the refugees with their own bodies from machine guns, declaring that should arms be used they would have to be shot first.... But I also found mean-spirited lower officials. They constitute a serious problem because it is they who are in direct daily contact with the refugees and have caused them considerable harm. I find it impossible to explain their meanness towards the refugees.

I will give you one example of this attitude. In one camp, our refugees managed to establish two chapels which the authorities located on the fourth floor of a large building. In that camp there are many elderly people who have difficulty in walking, even on level ground. How can they climb to the fourth floor? These old people, however, are so religious and so devoted to their church that they struggle with the stairs to get to the chapel. There is no need to give you more examples, although I have many. You do not need them but I do.

The following image always stands before me: It could have been that my father had not immigrated to Canada but had remained in the Old Country. It could have been that instead, someone among the current refugees would have immigrated to Canada, and his son became a Member of Parliament and today has visited a refugee camp in which I was a refugee. I know what I would want from my Ukrainian parliamentarian in such circumstances....

This is the reason why I made no speeches in camps and led no demonstrations. I know very well what the refugees need. I wanted to see as much as possible and indeed I have.... The problem of our refugees is a problem for all Ukrainians....

America (PHILADELPHIA) 11 FEBRUARY 1947 AND *Nashe Zhyttia / Our Life* (AUGSBURG) 18 MARCH 1947.

HYLNKA IN ITALY

Thursday, 16 January 1947 (London)

Stephanie and I awoke at 4:40 in the morning and got ready to leave for Rome. After breakfast, we walked to Paddington Station and, after some difficulties, reached the airport. There we cleared passport and customs inspections and boarded the plane. At noon we landed near Marseilles, in France, to refuel. Here we had lunch and then proceeded to Rome, flying over the rugged part of France. I noticed that half of the seats were empty although I had a difficult time trying to reserve a seat for my wife. Perhaps this was due to the Allied restrictions placed on travel to Italy.

We arrived at Rome airport at 3:30 p.m. as expected. All passengers boarded a bus that took us to the hotel, Albergo Flora. When we tried to register, we were told that the hotel was full. Then I asked the clerk to find me a telephone number of the Ukrainian Relief Committee. He could not find it. As he spoke some English, I asked him to find the number of the Basilian Fathers, among whom was Fr. M. Kohut from Canada. This search was also futile. Then I remembered that Professor Yevhen Onatsky,[44] a frequent contributor to a Ukrainian Canadian paper, the *New Pathway*, lived in Rome. To my surprise, his name was in the phone book and so I called him. Mrs. Onatsky answered the phone. When I explained to her who I was, she called her husband. I was delighted to hear Onatsky speak in such excellent Ukrainian. He invited us to stay with them and immediately dispatched a man who took us from the hotel to his residence not far away.

It was a pleasure to make the acquaintance of the Onatskys, who provided us with a large comfortable room. We were soon called to the dining room, where the regular Thursday meeting of the Ukrainian community in Rome was being held. Onatsky called upon me to say a few words to the twenty people gathered there. I gladly obliged him. My brief talk about my mission was followed by questions focusing on Canada's restrictive immigration policy and on the Ukrainian Canadian community in general. For instance, they wanted to know what the Ukrainian Canadians were doing to help the refugees in the matter of resettlement. I pointed out some of the current immigration complications and the necessity to change in Canada the negative public opinion about the refugees. I also said that while Canadians and Americans of Ukrainian origin were perhaps falling short of what was expected of them by the refugees, they nonetheless were trying to help.

Among those present, we met Mrs. Konovalets, widow of the assassinated Ukrainian nationalist leader,[45] and Mykola Azovsky, a famous Ukrainian artist who had just completed portraits of Cardinal Tisserant and other distinguished personages. We were told that Azovsky was one of the most gifted artists in Ukraine; he had painted Soviet leaders, including Stalin.

When the meeting ended and the guests left, we had supper. Here we had an opportunity to get to know the Onatskys better. We learned that Mrs. Konovalets was a permanent resident of Rome and was supported by the generosity of the Sawchuk and Hultay families in Canada. We also learned that since her husband's assassination in 1938, some Ukrainians have kept away from her.

That evening I telephoned Fr. Kohut. He had already been notified about my pending arrival but didn't know when. He recognized my voice and promised to see us the next morning.

After a long chat with the Onatskys, we retired to our room. Onatsky told us of his imprisonment by the Germans during the war [1943–44]. When he returned to Rome, he was in such dreadful condition that his wife did not recognize him. The Onatskys had been living in Italy for 27 years. Onatsky was a delightful person with a hearty laugh.

Friday, 17 January 1947

The first thing in the morning, I phoned the British embassy. I said that I wanted to contact the various British and American officials involved with the Ukrainian refugees. I was told to come to the embassy and someone would discuss the matter with me.

Father Kohut arrived at the Onatsky residence and took us to the British embassy. There we were met by Mr. Oliver, a young man of about thirty, who told us that he could spare us only five minutes as he had another appointment. He suggested that we call on Col. Tomlin of the IGCR. He also said that he would be glad if something could be done to get the non-Italians out of the country, as Italy suffered from overpopulation and unemployment. I asked him if he could get someone else to discuss the matter with us, seeing that he had to leave. However, he felt that the embassy could be of little real assistance as the Allied Control Commission and the IGCR were handling the entire refugee problem and would be in a better position to help us. He also mentioned Mr. Manion, the Canadian trade representative in Rome.

We went to see Col. Tomlin of the IGCR. As we were being led into his office, he jumped to his feet and in an inexcusably rude manner told us that he had another appointment. When I asked him when we could see him, he suggested next week. I told him rather firmly that I did not intend to stay in Rome for more than a few days. He then relented and said we could come between three and five o'clock that afternoon. We returned to the Onatskys for lunch.

Shortly after three p.m., we returned to see Col. Tomlin. We waited outside his office for a few minutes until his secretary took my card to Tomlin and asked us to enter. Col. Tomlin immediately apologized for not being able to see us in the morning. When I raised the subject of the Ukrainian DPs, he said that there were indeed some Ukrainians in Italy "and many of them fought for the Germans." He seemed to be reminding me of this fact. Then he said:

> We have done our best but these people are under military control and the military will not release them. We are now bound by the provisions of the IRO and we can only deal with such people as defined by them. We can help a refugee who does not wish to go back, who was a slave labourer. It is our task to repatriate all of them, except those who for valid reasons should not be repatriated. We are faced with decisions which may have political implications, but it is for us to decide whether the stand is right or wrong. We say a Soviet citizen is a person who lived in the Soviet Union in 1939.

We will not deal with them. The people who are definitely and entirely excluded from aid are war criminals, collaborators, traitors, dissenters, and those who carry on subversive activities.

He added that any person who had done something in the interest of the Allies fell into the category of those entitled to assistance.

I asked him about forced repatriation and he said: "Of course, we have no forced repatriation, as Allied soldiers would not carry out such an order." He also said, "Our job is to look after any person who is not looked after by anyone else. If a person came to us with a visa, we would help him. But we cannot do anything for these people until they obtain visas." He was, however, inclined to think that there could be a danger of renewed forced repatriation after the peace treaty with Italy was signed. He then telephoned Maj. Simcock and we left for the Allied Control Commission Headquarters.

Maj. Simcock was rather cordial. He immediately agreed to issue an authorization for Stephanie and myself to visit the camps at Rimini (Riccione), Reggio Emilia, and Bagnoli. But he cautioned us not to raise false hopes. He wrote out the authorization in pencil and asked us to pick it up on Monday. It was to cover me, Stephanie, and a driver. He was sorry that they did not have a suitable car to take us around, for even he had to travel by truck the next day. He invited us to go with him, but we finally decided not to go. The major also offered to make plane reservations for us, but we opted for car travel.

In the course of our amicable discussion, he showed me a copy of a letter written to the Soviet representatives. The major pointed out that someone had made a mistake in telling the Soviets that among the DPs in Italy there were between five hundred and six hundred Soviet citizens. In fact, only one Soviet citizen had expressed a willingness to be repatriated. Two more wanted to return in 1947, while twelve others who were Soviet citizens in 1939 were undergoing the second screening. Their intentions would be known shortly. He reminded the Soviet authorities of the British-American policy not to apply force and expressed regret that someone had tried to mislead Soviet citizens among the DPs.

Maj. Simcock also mentioned a Canadian who had spent $4,500 to purchase a farm for his eighteen-year-old relative interned at Rimini. But the Canadian immigration authorities had refused to grant the boy permission to enter Canada. I would try to get particulars on this case later. The major pointed out that the boy had only been fifteen when he was taken into the German army and so was immature. Besides, what other choice did some of these people have? They were forced to go at gunpoint. The difficulty here seemed to be that the military authorities would not release these people from detention camps.

The major promised me access to some of his files, which contained complete and concrete information on the cases of people who were "victims of circumstances." We thanked him and promised to see him after returning to Rome from our inspection.

At 5:00 p.m., we had an appointment with Lt. Col. James P. Manion, the Canadian Trade Commissioner. He was the son of the late Dr. R. J. Manion. Col. Manion pointed out that Canada had never had an embassy in Rome but said that we ought to have one, even if it served only as a listening post, since Yugoslavia was so near and the Soviet Union was next to Yugoslavia. He also said that having an embassy was important from a commercial point of view but that a mere trade representative would not be enough.

Col. Manion mentioned that he had met Mr. N. E. Tanner in Paris and had been very much impressed by him. He was of the opinion that the Alberta Social Credit government was one of the best provincial governments in Canada and that its record had been recognized as such. Col. Manion had been on active service during the war. He invited us to lunch on Saturday, 18 January.

In the evening we returned to Mr. and Mrs. Onatsky's residence. We had supper and sat at the table, talking until nearly midnight. I told the Onatskys what I had seen in Germany, what conditions were like in Canada, and something about the life of Ukrainians there. They, in turn, shared with us the trials they had gone through, especially of Yevhen Onatsky's arrest by the Nazis and of his two-year imprisonment. In the course of our discussions, Onatsky ironically observed how "odd it was for Ukrainians to perish in German prisons from American bombs." We were shown a Ukrainian-Italian dictionary that Onatsky had published, as well as a book on Italian-Ukrainian grammar and a short history of Ukraine in Italian. Most of these works had been published with money earned by Mrs. Nina Onatsky, who operated a boarding house (pensione). She was a university graduate but did this mundane job in order to raise money for her husband's publications. Mrs. Onatsky was a very noble and refined lady.

In the course of our conversation she informed us that many Yugoslavian soldiers in Rome were actually Russians in disguise. Some of them had presumed her to be Italian and had spoken Russian among themselves while she was chatting in Italian.

Saturday, 18 January 1947

I visited the Ukrainian Catholic Seminary of St. Josephat. Ukrainians acquired the seminary in 1931 but moved into it only in 1932. The cost of the building, about $500,000, was financed by the Vatican. Metropolitan Sheptytsky was instrumental in the building's acquisition. It was a Basilian centre, with twelve priests and thirty-one students. Fr. Joseph Zayachkivsky was rector and referred to the seminary as a Ukrainian embassy in Italy.

This is how Fr. Zayachkivsky talked about the refugee situation: "These people had fine homes, land, orchards, and much more. They left everything behind and now endure the difficult life in DP camps. They want freedom. Should the conditions in their homeland change even partly, all these people would walk back. Our people would even walk to Canada, if it were not across the ocean."

He also commented on the situation on the new Ukrainian-Polish frontier, where population exchanges were taking place. Voluntary resettlement was being accompanied by the forced expulsion of long-time Polish residents from Soviet Ukraine and of Ukrainians from Poland. "Polish communists are expelling Ukrainians from the Lemko region." He said, "Oh, how those people cried and how they kissed the ground. The Poles said they would not force the Ukrainians to leave but they set their villages on fire. People moved as though they were going to a funeral. Some went mad from this trauma. Ukrainian nuns were robbed and exiled. Their houses were looted. In Christianopole one nun was shot. In Peremeshyl about forty children were left without care when the local priest was exiled."

It appears that at the end of 1946 there was a total of fourteen thousand Ukrainian refugees and surrendered military personnel of the Galicia division in Italy. Nearly eleven thousand of them were in camps. A further five thousand Ukrainians were serving with the free Polish army stationed there.

Monday, 20 January 1947

Fr. Kohut, Stephanie, and I returned to the Allied Control Commission to pick up our gasoline vouchers as well as an authorization to travel in Italy and to visit DP camps. In Maj. Simcock's office we met Col. C. B. Findlay, director of Displaced Persons' Division. Col. Findlay seemed to be going out of his way to make sure that our authorization was correct. He walked into Maj. Martin's office, bringing with him Lady Barbara Simmons, whom he introduced to us. He invited us to come for supper to their mess in the Victoria Hotel. We accepted.

He then took us to their statistical office. There he showed us the current classification of the DPs by category. There was no Ukrainian category, but there were Polish and Russian. When this was pointed out, the colonel said he was shocked that Ukrainians were listed as Russians.

When I asked him who would be responsible for setting the Allied policy with respect to Ukrainians from the Soviet Union, he replied that both the British and the Americans would be. The foreign offices of both countries would have to agree on policy. When asked whether the British and the Americans alone constituted the Allied Control for Italy, he said yes, but added that the Soviet Union, France, Greece, and Yugoslavia each had advisory membership on the Control Commission. However, he emphasized that the latter countries did not interfere in the handling of the DP problem.

When asked what he thought of the Ukrainians, he replied that there were among them, especially at Rimini, many fine people, including youngsters who had been conscripted into the German army. He believed that those Ukrainians who had no guilt-blood on their hands had nothing to fear.

The Director of Rimini camp, accompanying Stephanie and Anthony

On the road in Italy. Anthony,
Stephanie and driver Ivan
Hirny, pausing for a photo.

Tuesday, 21 January 1947

Fr. Kohut, Stephanie, and I set out early in the morning for Rimini. Our driver, Ivan Hirny, who was with us throughout our visit in Italy, picked us up. By night-time we had reached Ricione, after a somewhat harrowing experience of driving through a thick fog along the Aegean Sea coast. Maj. Carrigher kindly accommodated us in a hotel.

Wednesday, 22 January 1947

I inspected the camp at Reggio Emilia with its 1,422 internees, of whom 165 were Ukrainians. Capt. A. Simpson, the officer in charge, reported that the Ukrainians in the DP camps already had been screened by the Allied Commission. The records of their screening were in Rome. The important food situation in the DP camps was as follows: each resident received 2,200 calories a day. Extra rations were provided for young children, the sick and pregnant women. Meat was served once a day. Rations were drawn from British and Canadian military supplies.

We left toward the evening expecting to attend a concert at Rimini, where the personnel of the Galician division were interned, commemorating the proclamation of Ukraine's independence in 1918. However, the roads were so bad and it was so foggy that we did not arrive until about ten o'clock at night when the concert was over. We were asked to come back the next day for the repeat performance of the concert, just for our benefit.

Thursday, 23 January 1947

We arrived for the second time in Rimini about noon and had lunch with the senior officers, both British and Ukrainian. After lunch we took some pictures outside and toured the camp.

The winter of 1946–47 was exceptionally severe, both in England and on the continent. It was shortly after the war and there was a shortage of fuel and of food. Snow covered the ground and it was very cold in the camp, which consisted mainly of tents. As we walked about viewing the camp, we were immensely impressed by the

Pausing for a photo, Italy

Returning to Rome from Rimini. Heavy snowfall. Anthony, Stephanie and driver, Ivan Hirny.

In Rome

Visit to Rome Wednesday, 22 January 1947

Ukrainian commanding officers and men, who had managed to convert the primitive camp into a community. They established churches [Catholic and Orthodox] in metal quonset huts. They turned some of the huts into workshops, where they created beautiful articles out of whatever materials they were able to find. They presented us with some of their creations, which we brought to Canada. Stephanie arranged with Eaton's store in Montreal to have these articles displayed prominently in their department store window, and later she donated the articles to various Ukrainian institutions in Canada.

After the tour we attended a meeting with the leaders of the camp. They were very anxious about their future. They asked what decisions had been reached one way or another so that they would not be kept in the dark and treated like children.

There were about fifteen hundred young men in the auditorium, and the rest listened to the concert in their tents through the loudspeaker system, which the boys had made themselves. It was extremely cold in the auditorium, but the talented young men gave a superb performance of a musical concert and a play. We were deeply moved.

[According to the camp publication, *Rimini, 1945–47*, Hlynka's visit was a major morale booster for the hungry and apprehensive Ukrainian soldiers, classified as surrendered enemy personnel. The following is an excerpt from the camp publication.]

> "On 23 January extraordinary guests visited the camp, namely, a member of Canada's Federal Parliament Anthony Hlynka and his wife Stephanie. Already at their entry to the camp one could notice the special attention paid the Canadian visitors by the senior British officers.... After a brief reception in the commandant's office, the British departed and the guests began inspecting the camp, accompanied by the Ukrainian camp commander, Major Yaskevych, and Fr. Kohut and Fr. Korduba. But something strange happened. Rather than following the official tour itinerary of the camp – school, chapel, theatre, and workshops – they wanted to see the tents of the common soldiers, shake hands with the inmates, sit on their miserable beds and inquire into their personal lives. Even before they visited two or three tents, the news spread throughout the camp

that these guests really want to understand the actual living conditions of the ordinary Ukrainian soldiers.

After the concert, the commandant invited Hlynka to address the audience. Hlynka thanked the British guests, those protectors of the camp, for the understanding and humane treatment of people in their care, people who had lost their homeland. He stressed the fact that his Ukrainian electors with relatives in this camp, as well as the Canadian government, have definite interests in the fate of Rimini camp. They delegated him to inspect and assess the situation in the camp and assist the inmates in their difficult predicament. It was with this objective in mind that Ukrainian Canadians had earlier dispatched Fr. Kohut to Rome and now they sent Hlynka. Then the Member of Parliament delivered special greetings from relatives in Canada. Hlynka declared that while he is a Canadian politician, his blood is the same as ours. His parents left the village of Denysiv for Canada in 1910 while his wife was born in Ulucz, Halychyna and these facts made our concerns their concern. Hlynka promised to do everything possible to resolve our dilemma quickly and positively."

Friday, 24 January 1947

The return trip to Rome took us a whole day. It began to snow very heavily. With each hour, the roads were becoming more treacherous. We worried that we would not get back for Saturday, the day we were to have an audience with the Pope. We were lucky to be able to get out of ruts and after fifty miles of snow-covered roads, we came to better roads and eventually to no snow. We stopped at Jesy for gasoline. An American-Italian officer was in command of the camp there and asked us in for tea. While waiting for tea, I noticed that an elderly woman was crying in the office. When I asked the man in charge what was wrong, he told me that he had been ordered to transfer the woman's father and son to a transit camp, from which the two were taken to Yugoslavia. The woman had just learned that both were shot as soon as they had crossed the border. He said that he was under military orders and could not refuse sending them back. We reached Rome late that evening.

Saturday, 25 January 1947

Back in Rome, we were informed that our audience with the Pope was scheduled for Monday, 27 January at noon. Fr. Kohut, who had arranged it, bought a black tie for me, while Stephanie got her shawl and proper clothing for the audience.

Monday, 27 January 1947

Our private visit with Pope Pius XII was one of our most memorable experiences in Rome. Before becoming Pope, Pius XII had represented the Church in the United States and now he spoke English with us. I raised the issue of the plight of the DPs and he listened intently while asking a few questions. The Pope was curious about our nationality and I explained that both Stephanie and I were born in Ukraine ,but now we were Ukrainian Canadians. The Pope blessed us and a crystal rosary, which Stephanie had bought for her mother. He then asked if Stephanie would like to have one of his rosaries, which, he said, was not as beautiful as hers. Of course, she accepted it.

Tuesday, 28 January 1947

I visited the Argentine Immigration Mission at the Grand Hotel. Unfortunately, Fr. Silva, who received me, could not understand English and I did not understand his French. The dilemma was resolved when he called upon the Minister to talk to me. Adolpho Schilingo was a former newspaperman who had worked in the United States both as a journalist and a diplomat. After I discussed the need to resettle Ukrainian refugees, he asked me to inform the Ukrainian committee in Rome to submit a list of people who want to immigrate to Argentina, and he would approve it. Later that day I saw Maj. Simcock and reported on our trip.

Saturday, 1 February 1947

We left Rome for Paris by train and arrived there on Monday. There we met Mr. Sozontiw, a Ukrainian émigré who had lived in Paris for some time and was a successful businessman there. While in Paris, we stayed at his place. I visited the Canadian Embassy and later met with some of the leading Ukrainians, including Bishop Mstyslav Skrypnyk[46] of the Ukrainian Orthodox Church.

Thursday, 6 February 1947

We left for London by train and crossed the English Channel by ferry.

Friday, 7 February – Wednesday, 12 February 1947

I held a series of meetings with my Ukrainian Canadian colleagues (Sawchuk, Yaremovich, Panchuk) and Canadian and British officials on the subject of refugees and emigration.

Thursday, 13 February 1947

We left by train for Southampton where we boarded the celebrated liner, Queen Elizabeth, and sailed home by way of New York.

THE RETURN FROM EUROPE: HELPING THE REFUGEES

My wife and I returned from Europe in the middle of February 1947. We boarded Queen Elizabeth on 13 February and disembarked in New York on 18 February. We took the train to Montreal, from where we hurried to Ottawa as the parliamentary session had already begun.

In Ottawa, hundreds of letters, which had arrived during my absence, awaited me. The bulk of the mail, which came from all parts of Canada, expressed deep concern about the fate of refugee relatives in Europe. Till that time, the Canadian government had given permission to a handful of DPs to enter this country. By the end of December 1948, only 114 Ukrainian and Polish refugees had been admitted. During the two years after the war, Ukrainian Canadians not only had been appealing for admission of their relatives but were also demanding a clear explanation of the legal procedures required for the sponsorship of the displaced refugees. Thus when our community learned that I had returned to Ottawa, the volume of mail almost doubled. In addition, my European correspondence also increased. In order to cope with so much work, I began my workday at 7:00 a.m. and usually ended around midnight. Only with the assistance of my wife and a full-time secretary was I able to answer all letters.

In addition to my correspondence, I had to carry out my parliamentary and constituency responsibilities. I worked at this hectic pace for the remainder of the parliamentary term – that is, until the announcement of the general election in June 1949. However, my correspondence could not resolve the immigration problem because the government continued to approach this matter with reluctance and ambivalence. It often delayed the necessary administrative orders necessary to facilitate large-scale refugee immigration. In these circumstances, greater pressure had to be exerted on the government in the House of Commons. Several members from different parties agreed to raise the issue of post-war immigration. Walter

Tucker, David Croll, and Leslie Mutch spoke from the Liberal party. Lawrence Skey and Cyril Merritt frequently spoke from the Conservative party. Fred Zaplitny and Ross Thatcher represented the CCF. In the Social Credit party, the entire responsibility for immigration fell on me. Before my trip to Europe I had spoken in the House seven times about the need to open Canada to European refugees. Upon my return I made six more speeches in favour of immigration. In all, between 1945 and 1949, I delivered thirteen speeches in the House of Commons on the controversial subject of immigration and resettlement.

In addition to my involvement in parliamentary debates, in lobbying the government, and in answering letters of my constituents, I realized that the refugee dilemma required direct contact with our community. Every weekend, when the House of Commons was not in session, I visited Ukrainian communities to talk about my inspection and assessment of DP camps. These public rallies had three objectives:

1. To inform the people about the refugee situation in Europe and about its possible resolution;
2. To publicize the rallies in the Canadian and Ukrainian press in order to sharpen public awareness and generate support; and
3. To move beyond simply feeling sorry for the plight of the DPs and do something practical to alleviate their condition.

On my part, I initiated the Resettlement Fund. The purpose of this fund was to provide money for visas and for transport of those Ukrainian refugees who were excluded from the UNRRA and IRO camps and assistance. Those refugees who were already in camps had at least some hope of eventual resettlement, once they passed medical and security screening. But those who were denied shelter and food in the camps found themselves in a precarious situation. Even those who had the opportunity to emigrate to South America could not do so because they lacked money for visas and transport, and they had no relatives overseas. They were in a hopeless situation, facing forced repatriation to the Soviet Union. It was with such people in mind that I launched the Resettlement Fund.

I appealed for donations at twenty-two public rallies held in all parts of Canada, from Montreal to Vancouver. My presentations about Europe and Ukrainian refugees generally lasted two hours. Another two hours were needed to collect funds and read out the names of donors. Contributions were made to the local Ukrainian Canadian Committee. In places without the UCC, special committees were formed. Collected funds were sent to the Relief Fund at the central UCC office in Winnipeg. Costs relating to hall rentals and publicity were covered by separate collections in order not to deplete the Resettlement Fund. I raised funds in Toronto, Montreal, Hamilton, Vancouver, Vegreville, Mundare, Winnipeg, Edmonton, Calgary, Saskatoon, Radway, Willingdon, Andrew, Smoky Lake, Winona, Grimsby, St. Catharines, Sudbury, and Ottawa. At these rallies Ukrainians contributed $28,500. The Relief Fund held this money in a separate account. I was determined that every last cent should go for its designated purpose.

As far as my personal expenses for the European tour and fundraising were concerned, they were covered by borrowed money. I always explained my situation to the audience and encouraged them to help defray my costs with their donations. My fellow Ukrainians managed to provide $3,000, while my actual expenses stood at $4,600. However, I never violated the trust of the people. Once a significant amount of money was collected, I would meet with the board of the Relief Fund to make certain that the money was spent properly and was accounted for.

In time we learned that many of the refugees from beyond the camps had finally been accepted into the DP camps. This meant that their need of our assistance diminished. However, I rejected efforts to divert funds for administrative costs and insisted that the resettlement of the refugees remain our prime objective.

I believed so passionately in the refugee cause that I gave it as much energy and time as I could. To my surprise, I began receiving letters from my Ukrainian friends in the riding urging me to drop the refugee issue because it had provoked a serious anti-Hlynka campaign at home. I could not bring myself to believe this, especially since other MPs who spoke on behalf of the refugees were being showered with praise for this humanitarian activity. At any rate, fundraising stopped as it was becoming physically impossible for one person to cope with the amount of work that came my way. To continue, I needed at least one more person to help with the office work.

At this point, the broad narrative of Anthony Hlynka's notes and unfinished manuscript comes to an end.

Anthony Hlynka's memorial service

EPILOGUE

Two years after Anthony Hlynka's death, the Ukrainian Canadian community unveiled a memorial at his gravesite at St. Michael's cemetery. On Sunday, 10 May 1959, Peter Savaryn,[47] distinguished community leader, delivered the following eulogy.

The Second Anniversary of Our Great Loss

Many years have passed since the end of the war. But who among us – those former numerous refugees, the so-called DPs, and now free and prosperous citizens of the United States, Canada, and other countries – does not remember those frightening times, when in accordance with the agreement of the great allied powers at Yalta, we were forcibly dragged "home"? People were jumping from buildings, some were slashing their wrists, others went insane, and all the while, the world calmly watched this unfolding tragedy.

But very few people know that the man who courageously defended those refugees, the man who in large part was responsible not only for the termination of compulsory repatriation but also for the opening of immigration doors to Canada and the United States, left us two years ago. That man was the former Member of Canada's Parliament, Anthony Hlynka.

One has only to recall his speeches made in Parliament, especially the six presentations made between 1942 and 1948, to appreciate what a tremendous loss the Ukrainian community in the free world suffered in the passing of Anthony Hlynka. In parliamentary debates of 24–26 September 1945, Hlynka demanded in the name of humanity and Christianity the end to forcible repatriation, which was sending people to certain death. He gave examples of refugee camps at Manheim and Ingolstadt, he cited accounts of eyewitnesses, he read letters, and he quoted philosophers. Above all, he had, personally and at his own expense, made a fact-finding tour of the camps to determine the reality of the situation. He reminded the public of the

Yalta agreement and pleaded for assistance for those for whom there was no apparent help coming from anyone. And all this was taking place at the time that the Soviet Union was still an ally, at the time when it seemed that violence would prevail. But thanks to Hlynka and others like him, it was justice that prevailed and today we live like normal human beings.

Furthermore, Anthony Hlynka had the courage to demand that the Ukrainian Canadian Committee and the Ukrainian Congress Committee of America be admitted to the San Francisco Conference, which was finalizing the formation of the United Nations Organization to present the Ukrainian case. Hlynka stressed that no country had suffered more casualties and destruction during the war than Ukraine did and, in the name of justice, demanded that Ukraine should be given her independence, notwithstanding the fact that the Soviet Union was an ally. When speaking on the subject of the San Francisco Conference, Hlynka said with an almost prophetic sense: "I am in complete agreement in regard to the sending of a Canadian delegation to the conference, but I consider the principles forecast, upon which the future world structure is to be organized, as unsound and contrary to the democratic concept of life and prejudicial to the sovereignty of many small nations and people." He correctly believed that the growing influence of the Soviet Union would bring terrible calamity for the world.

Member of Parliament Anthony Hlynka absolutely believed in what he said and did that what he believed. And he worked and worked, ignoring his personal health and his material security. Quite likely this is why he departed for eternity so prematurely, as he was not even fifty years old when he died. With his passing, we lost one of the best sons of the Ukrainian people. He was a community leader and a politician whom our current members of parliament should hold up as a role model.

The grateful citizens of Edmonton and surrounding areas erected on his grave this modest monument, which was blessed today by the bishop of Edmonton, His Eminence Nil Savaryn, with assistance of eight priests. Let the earth under which he rests be always light and let this monument be a recognition and tribute to his life, which he had so totally devoted to Canada and the Ukrainian community in the free world.

part III

SELECTED SPEECHES OF ANTHONY HLYNKA

IN DEFENCE *of* WESTERN FARMERS

House of Commons
21 June 1940

MR. HLYNKA: In my opinion, what the group in this corner of the house is asking for may be boiled down to the three fundamental things of life – food, clothing and shelter. For the past three days we have been engaged in discussing what is probably the most important bill of the present session, that relating to conscription. The agricultural assistance bill, it seems to me, is at least next in importance. Considering the plight of our farmers in western Canada, we sometimes wonder whether this government realizes its obligations towards these people. It seems to me that, for some reason or other, this government has a grudge against the people, at least those of western Canada, and that it is trying to revenge itself upon the farmers of the west. Every hon. member will admit, I am sure, that during the past ten years our western farmers and workers have had no assurance that they would get three meals a day, along with clothing and shelter. When these three fundamentals of life are denied to our humblest and poorest, it is about time for this government to shake off its sleepy mood and proceed to give assistance to our people.

Last September, when the leader of this group, the hon. member for Lethbridge, came home from the session, his little boy asked him a question.

Mr. MacNICOL: Not about finance, I hope?

MR. HLYNKA: He said, "Daddy, do you think that you will keep up with this line of work?" My leader replied, "Why not?" "Well," said the boy, "it surprises me, Dad, that according to the press you are always wrong and the Prime Minister is always right. How is it? Is the Prime Minister such a brilliant man, much more so than you are?" The leader of the New Democracy group answered his little son in this way: "Well, son, some people may think to-day that the Prime Minister is right, but there will come a time when the people will realize that we are right and have been right all along. And I am sure that that time is not far off."

As a new member, I have been astonished at the readiness with which government supporters, when the views of our group were propounded, have taken offence or tried to distort anything we have suggested. The government at this time should be only too glad to receive suggestions from every corner of the house. I do not see any special evidence of wisdom in any one particular section of the house and therefore I suggest that we should try, at this critical moment, to work together as one family for the purpose of solving our problems. Our people are entitled to food, clothing and shelter. The two old-line parties have denied the Canadian people these three fundamental necessities of life in the last ten years. We must have these things to begin with if we are to exist at all. Napoleon on one occasion said that an army travels on its stomach. I say that a nation exists and fights on its stomach, and you cannot expect the Canadian people to carry on unless they are given adequate care, unless they have the assurance that conditions will make it possible for them at least to exist, to say nothing of getting a real living.

I disagree with some members in our group on one point. Many of them have stated on the floor of this house that the present government gives no privileges to the underdog, no privileges to western farmers and workers in the economic sense. I disagree with that, because our farmers and workers enjoy one privilege, a privilege which is exclusively theirs, or almost exclusively – the privilege of paying taxes. They are never asked to express their opinion as to whether they can bear the burden of taxation that is being piled up on their shoulders. Now, at this critical time, when our farmers in the west need assistance as never before, what do we find? This government invests $750,000, three-quarters of a million, in a building in this city, the Jackson building, to be used for war purposes. Should the government do this, if it is sincere, as I hope it is? Should it invest three-quarters of a million dollars in a building of this sort – a dead investment – at a time when we need this money for our people and to further our war effort? After passing the important bill that was put through yesterday, the government could take possession of that building without paying three-quarters of a million dollars. They could have had the use of that building for the duration of the war. If we are going to have equality of sacrifice, if we are going to conscript wealth and industry, that would be the right place to begin at this time. It is inexcusable to spend three-quarters of a million dollars for this purpose, and I suggest that we are justified in saying to the government that they are hindering our war effort by sinking money in an investment of this kind, an investment that is as dead as a doornail.

A few days ago I received a copy of a magazine with beautiful pictures in which suggestions are given as to where one can go for a holiday. I am sure some of the members of this house, and especially government supporters, must have forgotten that the people in western Canada especially do not know what a holiday means. It is about time that we thought of giving them a chance at least to exist. Recently I read a book with the strange title "How to Live on Nothing a Day," written presumably by a liberal. It is an attempt to force a philosophy upon the people of Canada that it is possible to exist and enjoy life, not on a dollar a day, not on a dollar a year, but on nothing a day. Why should anyone suggest such a thing? We should try to help people along.

We have often heard from the government side the statement that this is war-time and that their obligations are exceptionally heavy. Of course, they will offer a whole lot of such excuses. But great men, any number of great men working together, never shun their responsibilities or look for excuses; they rise to the occasion. If they are really big men they can cope with any situation, no matter how serious it may be, and excuses of that sort are nothing but admissions that the government is incapable of dealing with the problems of the day. Until the poorest and the humblest in our country are provided with food, clothing and shelter, neither this nor any other government in Canada can pride itself upon having discharged its obligations to the people.

I do not know how many of us have ever stopped to consider the implications of what is called interest. We in western Canada have had a little more to do with interest than some of the people in the eastern part of the country, and I have been wondering why the federal government in the past has never concerned itself with the fact that our people have paid interest rates ranging from one to fourteen per cent. May I point out something in simple arithmetic? One dollar at three per cent compound interest gives us a total in one hundred years of $19.22 – using one hundred years as a round figure. One dollar compounded at the rate of eight per cent gives a total of $2,199.76, and one dollar at ten per cent gives a total of $13,780.00 – and mind you, our people have had to pay at the rate of $13,780 for the use of one dollar; at least, that is what it would amount to over a period of one hundred years. But we have never heard of any supporter of the government getting up on the floor of this house and telling the government that this is going a little too far, that this burden should be taken off the shoulders of the people. They have allowed our people to pay this rate of interest and to-day they wonder why the morale of the Canadian people and of the people of the British Empire is not as strong as it should be. That is the real reason.

Who invented this compound interest? I should like to know who gets the benefit of it. Surely not the poor people in western Canada, not the producer, not the worker. What would this government say if our farmers in western Canada refused to produce wheat on the assurance that they would get five per cent above the cost of production? They would say it was sabotage. Some of the manufacturing concerns have refused to put in tenders in time of war because they were not allowed more than five per cent profit. I say to you, Mr. Chairman, that this is real sabotage. If the farmers of western Canada were assured of five per cent above the cost of production I am sure they would be satisfied; and on behalf of those farmers I ask that this government consider at least the question of the cost of production.

Mr. MAYHEW: Will the hon. gentleman permit a question?

MR. HLYNKA: When I get through.

Mr. GARDINER: What has this to do with the bill?

MR. HLYNKA: I am trying to point out to hon. members that the farmers of the west must receive greater assistance than they have received in the past. I have pointed out on other occasions that they did not need charity but only what was coming to them.

Mr. GARDINER: Assistance to the farmers of western Canada, about which the hon. gentleman is talking, has been carried on under another bill.

MR. HLYNKA: Section 3 of the bill reads:

3. The governor in council may enter into agreements:
(a) with any of the provinces respecting the alleviation of unemployment conditions and of agricultural distress therein and to assist those in need;

I believe that settles it.

Mr. GARDINER: Assistance to farmers in connection with feed and fodder, and the relief given in farm homes, has been given through the Department of Agriculture under another arrangement in the most difficult years. This measure has to do with the lending of money and making grants in aid to the provinces to carry on the work of relief.

MR. HLYNKA: I still maintain that this is agricultural assistance. Our problem is one of distribution; our farmers and workers must have more purchasing power placed in their hands. This government has absolutely failed to show us how it can place that purchasing power in the hands of our people, and it has absolutely failed to show me how it is going to wipe out unemployment. It seems to me that the government is just dragging on from day to day, and you know that at five per cent compound interest any sum of money doubles itself in fifteen years. If this government carries on its present policy for fifteen years it will simply mean that our farmers will have to repay the money lenders twice the amount originally received.

I am not going to speak at any great length –

Some hon. MEMBERS: Hear, hear.

MR. HLYNKA: I know the hon. members on the government side are anxious that no one else should express his opinion, but no one party has a monopoly on the desire to help our people. We all want to do our bit in that direction. I happen to represent over fifty thousand people, and I do not think any member of this house will suggest that we should not have the privilege of saying what we have to say.

We in western Canada are not so much interested in theories or in the wording of bills. We have been fed with all that sort of thing for the past seventy years or so, and our people find themselves in distress to-day. We are interested in the results that are achieved by putting the bills into operation. In most of the totalitarian states they have resorted to the production of synthetic bread. We do not need to do that. Canada produces ample supplies to feed not only Canada but the whole British Empire. All our farmers ask is a fair price for their wheat and a little assistance when they really need it. If they get that, believe me, our farmers will never fail the nation in time of stress.

A tricky system has been used many times to more or less pull the wool over the eyes of the farmers; the current year is compared with the year previous, or the year before that, to show how the revenue or the profit or commerce has increased. The government never compares the better year with the worse, but always the worse with the better. Then they say, "Things are improving. You go ahead and rely on us to see that you get what you deserve." That has been the system used right along. There is only one reason why our farmers will not accept a negative answer from this or any other government until they get what they want and what they are entitled to, and that is the law of self-preservation. This nation is fighting Germany because of the same law; we must obey it or submit, or die. That is the only choice we can expect. This government should be proud and glad that our people in the west are not dead yet but are making themselves heard and are placing certain demands before the government, through their elected representatives. I think that this is a good sign. If we ever came to the time when our people would no longer demand or ask for anything, it would be a sign that we had reached the end and that there was no future before us.

I beseech the government to consider our farmers, our workers, the real pillars of our nation. Give them what they deserve; then, believe me, these farmers will not refuse to produce. Give them five per cent over the cost of production and they will be only too glad to carry on. And let us have no more deals in which we squander and waste three-quarters of a million dollars in buying a dead investment while the farmers really need money and would at least give some return on the investment.

UNITED CANADA

House of Commons, 25 November 1940

MR. ANTHONY HLYNKA (Vegreville): Mr. Speaker, since the outbreak of the present war the problem of Canadian unity has been a subject of many discussions, but in my opinion it still remains a topic which warrants further consideration on our part at this time.

The mover of the address in reply to the speech from the throne (Mr. Claxton), the hon. member for Selkirk (Mr. Thorson), and more particularly the hon. member for Bellechasse (Mr. Picard), have made brief references to the part which Canadians of non-Anglo-Saxon origin play in our national life. I propose to discuss, further, other important phases of this subject which so far have hardly been mentioned.

There are two prevalent views on this subject of Canadian unity. There are those who feel that there is greater unity in Canada to-day than there has ever been before, and there are also those who view the whole situation with suspicion and doubt. I am inclined to agree, at least in part, with the former, that the present war has unified our people more than ever before. Nevertheless there are some prevalent viewpoints which in my opinion deserve the immediate attention of this house, and the sooner the situation is remedied, the better it shall be for all concerned.

Sir Norman Angell, world-renowned analyst of national and international affairs, has recently discussed, in his two articles published in the *Financial Post*, some of the reasons why he thinks Hitler has been successful in overrunning several European countries. He maintains that Hitler has used the age-old weapon of "divide and conquer" in the most masterly and subtle way. In the first place, he used this weapon to get control of Germany. He then proceeded to unify his own forces at home, and at the same time set out to create disunity and distrust among the democratic countries of the world. Having done that, he concentrated upon dividing the people internally, in countries he set out to conquer, by cleverly scheming and creating class and racial disharmony. One has little choice but to agree with Sir Norman's analysis in the light of what has happened in Europe. Alas, the unscrupulous fifth-column tactics are too well known as an integral part of the blitzkrieg machine which is threatening to destroy the very existence of our democratic institutions in the world. Let us make sure, then, Mr. Speaker, that there is no room in Canada for those who would seek to create disunity among our people by playing upon racial differences or racial superiority in our midst.

It is a well-recognized fact that there exists a greater unity to-day among all the peoples of the British commonwealth of nations than there has ever existed in the entire history of the British people. Since 1931, when by the Statute of Westminster all the British dominions were granted equal sovereign rights, united only by their common allegiance to the crown, and each functioning as an independent unit, the bonds of unity have strengthened among all the dominions. They are now united on a voluntary basis. The British commonwealth of nations to-day is the greatest democratic unit in existence. This has been made possible only by the wise and tolerant British colonial policy towards its people of many racial origins and creeds. The British people to-day constitute, chiefly for this reason, one of the greatest powers the world has ever seen.

But our responsibility lies specifically here within Canada – we are assembled here for that purpose. The question before us is, how can we give maximum aid to Britain and at the same time be well prepared for our own home defence? At the moment I shall not discuss the material side of the question, because that has well been done by others on previous occasions. My chief purpose to-night is to discuss the question of our Canadian unity.

I believe we are all of opinion that Canada must be united to the utmost if she is to be effective in her aid to Britain and if she is to be prepared for her own home defence. The people within the borders of Canada must assume equal responsibilities as well as share equal rights and privileges. We must have only one purpose in mind; that is victory. In answer to all agents of disunity, let me say that we must eradicate all possibilities of disharmony and check all those influences which tend to cause disunion and build racial barriers within Canada. Then, and only then, will Canada be looked upon as a powerful nation.

But to our regret, Mr. Speaker, we find that certain individuals who hold responsible positions in our public life make loose and ill-advised statements which may easily be misconstrued and made use of as the basis or cause for disunity.

In the first place, let me make a passing reference to the rather loose statement made by the Conservative leader in the British Columbia legislature. While speaking in the debate on the address in reply to the speech from the throne he said, as reported in the Edmonton *Journal* of November 1:

> Planning for the period of readjustment which will follow the war and a vigorous stand against the "furtherance of foreign language or foreign creed in this country" were urged in the provincial legislature Thursday by R. L. Maitland, K.C., leader of the Conservative opposition.

And further it reads:

> Mr. Maitland deplored the existence of foreign language schools in Canada....

There may be several interpretations of what the hon. gentleman had in mind, but my chief objection is to the fact that utterances of this kind throw an unfair suspicion upon our loyal Canadian citizens who happen not to be of Anglo-Saxon extraction. This may and does create disunity at a time when unity is most imperative.

Secondly, I should like to refer to an item appearing in the Edmonton *Bulletin*, in its issue of November 4. I quote:

> With the stress of war causing a widening of activities in the force, 500 new constables are being enrolled by the R.C.M.P. throughout the dominion.
>
> Because of rigid requirements in the way of both mental and physical qualifications, few as yet have been accepted.
>
> Applicants must be single of British racial origin.

Here again, the meaning of the words "of British racial origin" is vague. When interpreted broadly, it would appear to mean that any person born in any British dominion is eligible for enrolment, be he of Anglo-Saxon or any other racial extraction. But interpreted in a narrower sense, it would simply rule out the eligibility of all those not of Anglo-Saxon origin. Unfortunately, this narrower interpretation is being used by minor officials for the purpose of racial discrimination. I suggest that in future when the government is putting out circulars of this type, that a more specific choice of words be made.

Lastly, I should like to draw the attention of the house to a much more serious statement which appeared in the Saskatoon *Star-Phoenix* of October 8. Mr. G. W. Parker, relief officer of Saskatoon, commenting on the administration of relief, is reported to have made this assertion. I quote in part:

> There should be two scales of relief, one for central Europeans and one for "white people."

This, I submit, Mr. Speaker, is a vile form of racial discrimination. I challenge the authority upon which Mr. Parker bases his classification of people, in saying that central Europeans do not belong to the white race. I also question the mentality of those who would propose a higher scale of relief for one group of our citizens and a lower scale for another.

Probably the most notorious example of this same attitude of racial discrimination as well as higher and lower rations is exemplified in Hitlerian philosophy. We all know what that attitude of mind has brought upon us; let us, then, not have anything to do with it in Canada. No one who takes the attitude that this man does is fit to hold public office. In our country, where approximately half the population is of non-Anglo-Saxon extraction, ideas of this kind and at this time of national crisis should not be tolerated. It is about time some of our public men realized that they are nothing more than public servants hired to serve the people. I suggest that the defence of Canada regulations should also be made to apply to individuals who deliberately make malicious statements which cause dissension among our people.

I am happy, however, to be able to reply to the above and other would-be critics, on the authority of some of our eminent public men. Fortunately the great majority of our public men are much more broad-minded. It is gratifying to find that sincere efforts are being made by this government to bring about among all our people, of whatever racial origin they may be, a better understanding and singleness of purpose.

Some members on this side of the house have criticized the bureau of public information for being too partisan. I think that criticism is well founded. But so far as unity of our people of different racial origins is concerned, I believe that this bureau is rendering an invaluable service by publishing from time to time translations of articles appearing in the non-English press in Canada. I do not know of a better way of passing on to our Canadian public material which appears in Ukrainian, Czech, German and other publications. It helps to clear up a great deal of misunderstanding which may exist with regard to the stand these groups have taken in connection with the war. It is to be hoped that in future the press will take a greater advantage of this fine service.

I have not the time to quote many of these translations; let it suffice to give the house one short extract. But before doing so, let me quote the head-note by the director of public information, Mr. G. H. Lash, introducing one of these articles:

> Note to editors: In view of the misunderstanding which seems to exist in some parts of Canada respecting the attitude of the foreign-speaking sections of our population towards Canada's war effort and our war aims, the following translation of an editorial which appeared ... in the German language newspaper *Der Nordwesten* is interesting. Nobody recognizes better than myself how precious newspaper space is these days, but if you could find room to reprint or to comment upon this editorial and others which I hope to send you from time to time from other foreign-language newspapers of Canada I think you would be making a fine contribution towards the development of national unity.

The following quotation from the above-mentioned newspaper was translated and reprinted in the circular of public information in the issue of October 10:

> The war has created the spirit of unity among Canadians of every race and creed such as this country has not known. The full meaning of our Canadian citizenship is better understood, and if there be the few who do not value its privileges, it must be apparent to them that this land has no place for them.
>
> The people of Canada of whatever racial origin have one supreme duty – the winning of the war, and to that end there must be a complete unity in our land, and a determination to give and to sacrifice. And from the grave situation which has been thrust upon us by those who would destroy our way of life, we shall emerge a better people and a greater Canada.

That, Mr. Speaker, is a sample of material which is being translated and reprinted in these circulars. From that I would judge there is a good will on the part of all our Canadian citizens, regardless of racial origin, towards a common understanding and national unity.

While discussing the subject of Canadian unity, I feel that I would not be doing justice to the topic if I did not refer to Doctor Watson Kirkconnell, who is undoubtedly Canada's greatest authority on our population of non-Anglo-Saxon extraction. Doctor Kirkconnell has been for many years a keen student of all our racial groups. It is only to be regretted that this government has not, as far as I know, used Doctor Kirkconnell's exceptional talent in the interest of our national unity. I would recommend to hon. members to read, for example, Doctor Kirkconnell's recent booklet, entitled "The Canadian Ukrainians and the War." It is well worth reading.

Here is an interesting extract from the London *Free Press* reprinted in the Ottawa *Citizen* of October 31, regarding Doctor Kirkconnell's contribution. To me it is an encouraging bit of information.

> According to Doctor Watson Kirkconnell of McMaster University, who is Canada's greatest authority on our foreign population, Herr Hitler has done more than any other man to draw Canada together

and to unite the dominion. Despite intensive propaganda which was carried on in Canada by Berlin, Moscow and Rome, Doctor Kirkconnell says that more than ninety-eight per cent of the peoples of alien birth are loyal to Canada today, and are enthusiastically lined up behind the British effort....

In most cases the Nazis overran their home countries, while they realize that the freedom and liberty which they came to this country to seek will be lost if Hitler wins. Doctor Kirkconnell gave as one example the Ukrainians. He pointed out that in Saskatchewan they form ten per cent of the population, yet over ten per cent of the enlistments in that province are from peoples of Ukrainian stock. The war has brought English and French closer together, and it is optimistic to learn that it is making for national unity among those who are not of French or Anglo-Saxon origin.

In closing, may I sum up the whole problem of our national unity by quoting from one of Canada's greatest statesmen, who was a friend of all the Canadian people. He worked hard for Canadian unity and was a man who understood even the simplest soul in our land. I speak of Lord Tweedsmuir.

While addressing a large Ukrainian gathering of 1,500 people on September 21, 1936, at Fraserwood, Manitoba, Lord Tweedsmuir spoke in such a way that even to this day those who heard him hold sacred the ideas he expressed. On that happy occasion the hon. member for Selkirk (Mr. Thorson) was present. I crave the indulgence of hon. members while I read a part of that great statesman's short message. I would suggest that they follow this masterpiece. Many hon. members find themselves at a loss at times, when they have to address a gathering of people of some other racial extraction. This is a wonderful example of an address to such a gathering, and is one of the most interesting short speeches I have ever read. These were the words uttered by Lord Tweedsmuir:

> I thank you most warmly for the way you have received me today. I do not think that anywhere I have gone in Canada I have been welcomed with a more beautiful ceremony; your escort, your national ceremony of presenting me with bread and salt, and if I

may be allowed to say so the beautiful and well chosen words of your address.

I realize that my welcome is due to the fact that I represent your king, and it will be my pleasure to convey to the king the cordial greetings of the Ukrainian people in Canada.

I am very happy to be among you to-day. I am among people who have behind them a long historical tradition, for it was your race which for centuries held the south eastern gate of Europe against the attacks from the east. I can well imagine that this country is home to you, for these wide prairies are very like the great plains of south eastern Europe from which you came. During my tour of the prairies I have come across many of your people, and I am glad to see that in a short time you have come to be a vital element in the Canadian nation. You played your part in the great war. To-day I find your sons in the permanent and non-permanent militia.

Wherever I go I hear high praise of your industry and hardihood and enterprise even under the most difficult conditions. You have become good Canadians. Every Briton and especially every Scotsman must believe that the strongest nations are those that are made up of different racial elements. The Ukrainian element is a very valuable element to our new Canada. I wish to say one thing to you. You have accepted the duties and loyalties as you have acquired the privileges of Canadian citizens, but I want you also to remember your old Ukrainian traditions – your beautiful handicrafts, your folk songs and your folk legends. I do not believe that any people can be strong unless they remember and keep in touch with all their past. Your traditions are all valuable contributions toward our Canadian culture which cannot be a copy of any old thing – it must be a new thing created by the contribution of all the elements that make up a nation.

That was the outlook of a great man who understood the people. I think it would be worth while to compare utterances such as I quoted in the first part of my address with the sentiments to which I have just referred.

Let me say, then, that in this crucial and historic moment every Canadian, whatever may be his racial origin, must hold dear the principles for which the British flag stands, namely liberty, without which there is no true life; justice, so essential to all people, and fair play, which makes life worth living. In the name of all these things, Mr. Speaker, let us unite and work in harmony for the good of Canada and a brighter future for all our Canadian people, regardless of racial origin.

Mr. W. A. TUCKER (Rosthern): First of all, Mr. Speaker, I should like to extend my congratulations to the young member (Mr. Hlynka) who has just taken his seat. As a Canadian of British origin I should like to express my support and appreciation of what he has just said and what he represents to Canadian life to-day. I have been told by people who accompanied their majesties across Canada that the most moving episode of the whole trip was the welcome they received at Melville, where practically everyone was of other than French or English-speaking origin. I suppose those of Polish, Ukrainian and German origin predominated, and I am told that there the outpouring of affection for the head of our country and our commonwealth was such that it moved even the most staid and cynical newspaperman. Many people had come there, after a journey of perhaps a day, to look at their sovereign, and it was said that there was such an evident spirit of affection that among those humble people many had tears in their eyes that they should have the privilege of meeting their king and queen.

Then we hear of such utterances of racial hatred and discrimination as were quoted by the hon. member for Vegreville. We try to think those who are guilty of these things are endeavouring to be good citizens. The gentleman, Mr. Parker, mentioned by the hon. member is a returned soldier who served in the last war. I am certain he wants to be a good citizen and do his best for Canada, but I am at a loss to understand the psychology of such a man. Here are people who have left their own country, who glory in the freedom they find here, who intend to live and die in Canada, who expect to bring up their children to be good Canadian citizens, who to-day in Saskatchewan are enlisting for the defence of their country to a greater extent than might be expected from the portion of population they represent.

In fact, of the first two young men from my constituency to give their lives in this war in the service of their country, in the sinking of the *Fraser*, one was of Ukrainian origin. Then, in almost the same issue of the newspaper that announced his death, we had the statement referring to these people of Ukrainian origin as not being "white." That Ukrainian mother laid her most precious possession upon the altar of freedom; then, after making that sacrifice she had to hear that statement made by a fellow-Canadian of British origin. It was cruel. So with all my heart I support what the hon. member for Vegreville has said tonight; that sort of thing should have no place in Canadian public life.

Mr. ROBERT FAIR (Battle River), November 26, 1940: Last night we heard an able address from the hon. member for Vegreville (Mr. Hlynka), who spoke on behalf of the Ukrainians and other minorities in Canada. Those who were not here to listen to his speech would, I suggest, do well to read it in *Hansard*. Knowing the Ukrainians as I do, and having the honour to represent quite a number of them, I compliment the hon. member upon his address in their behalf, and I add my own words to his. The Ukrainians are misunderstood to a great extent simply because people do not take the trouble to find out anything about them. I have been a neighbour to Ukrainians for a number of years and I have also gone through districts in which there were few people but Ukrainians. It is true that the older people who came from the old land and slaved to make millionaires of some people in Canada, do not speak English as well as some of the rest of us do, but that is no fault whatever of theirs. I can imagine several members of this house going to a foreign country and trying late in life to learn the language.

With regard to the young Ukrainians, those in school, university or business, I can say that we of the English-speaking and French-speaking races have nothing at all on them. They are pretty intelligent and industrious. Moreover, as far as I have been able to find out, they are honest, which is one of the main things, I believe, in getting along.

WHAT PRICE FREEDOM?

Ukrainian Weekly, 11 March 1944

— By Anthony Hlynka
Member of Canadian Parliament

AN ADDRESS DELIVERED AT THE U.N.A. GOLDEN JUBILEE CONCERT AT CARNEGIE HALL, NEW YORK CITY, SUNDAY, MARCH 5, 1944

Mr. Chairman, Honored Guests, and Our American Friends:

Tonight you are commemorating the fiftieth anniversary of the founding of our organization – the Ukrainian National Association. From your Canadian friends, I bring you greetings, and sincere wishes for your continued success. May I say, also, that I am fully conscious of the honour accorded to me in being invited to address you briefly on this memorable occasion.

In the course of the past fifty years, your organization has attained signal success. The Ukrainian National Association is unquestionably the largest Ukrainian institution on this continent. That in itself is a unique achievement! I hasten to convey to you, therefore, my highest admiration of your outstanding success.

"What Price Freedom?" is the subject of my address.

The people of the world are interested, above all else, in three major objectives, namely: freedom, economic security, and a just and lasting peace. And without freedom and economic security, there can be no lasting peace. That is axiomatic.

The Supreme Challenge Today

It is not an accident, Mr. Chairman, that within one generation the world has found itself in two of the greatest cataclysms ever recorded in history. At the termination of the last war, the statesmen of the day failed to make certain that the world was purged of all wickedness, and that the resurrection of evil was rendered impossible. President

Wilson endeavoured at that time to incorporate into his Fourteen Points a vision of sovereignty (and sovereign equality) for all peoples and all nations. This proposal, however, was never realized for lack of its universal application. The result was that the principle of sovereignty did not become the basis of world society. Twenty years later the world was again plunged into a still more demoniac conflict. The flower of world's manhood is once again being sacrificed for the same purpose and the same cause. And unless every democratic-minded citizen does his utmost to make certain that after the present war is won, that freedom, economic security and a lasting peace are assured, we may again find ourselves helpless to avert a third world conflagration within our lifetime, and perhaps one of still greater proportions. That problem presents to us the supreme challenge of the present day.

Canadians of Ukrainian origin, and I am certain Americans of Ukrainian origin, consider it their prime duty to discharge their full responsibilities of citizenship to their respective countries, in peace, and in war, and generally to make their maximum contribution to the well-being of their nations. I am positive that they will never fail their countries in this respect.

Our Debt to Ukraine

However, we all feel that we owe a debt to our kinsmen in the Old Homeland. We have endeavoured to repay this debt to them by interpreting to our fellow citizens the history and aspirations of the Ukrainian people in Europe, a people whose millions have paid the supreme sacrifice in the last, as well as in the present, world conflict. Ukrainians have always fought heroically for freedom. Yet this freedom was to them denied! Cognizant of this fact we feel that we owe our kinsmen at least a sympathetic understanding. This we shall continue to extend to them until they shall have become free and a self-governing nation among the free nations of the world. We owe them this consideration, not only because we are of the same blood, but we also consider it proper to be concerned with the fate of any fifty-million nation deprived of its freedom and enslaved by aggression and tyranny. This is but an humanitarian consideration.

Ukrainians Entitled to Freedom

The will to freedom is inherent in every human being. The will to be free rises from the deepest instincts and emotions of mankind. It springs from the yearning of men who struggle to be free from foreign domination to govern themselves. All nations aspire to freedom so that they may accomplish their great mission in contributing their share to the advancement of world culture and civilization. And that is the only way in which they can fulfil the purpose for which they were placed upon this earth by the Great Creator. The indisputable fact is that freedom has been achieved and safeguarded only by the price of blood. The Ukrainian people have paid that price many times over, but, unfortunately, they still remain submerged and enslaved. What is the price of freedom, then, to the Ukrainian people?!

History has recorded indelibly that both the last and the present war involved Ukrainian land and its people. The world knows that some of the fiercest battles of both wars were fought on Ukrainian soil; that Kiev and Kharkiv, two historic capital cities of Ukraine, changed hands more times than have any other two cities in the world during the last and the present war. And the world knows, too, that the "scorched-earth policy" was applied with the utmost severity to Ukrainian territory.

Unfortunately, it has not been the policy of nations to recognize any rights of subjugated peoples, unless it were directly or indirectly in their interest so to do. That is precisely one of the reasons why the world has not had a lasting peace! But what of the future? Will the right be recognized as right, and the wrong be recognized as wrong, irrespective of where it is found? For eventually there must evolve a moral code to be applied equally to all – and, if there is not, then might, aggression and covetousness will continue to rule the world.

Of late we have heard much of "liberations," "federation," and many other platitudinous offers called by other than their own names. To my mind, no nation is ever liberated by a mere change of masters, as the dominated people remain slaves.

What then of "federations"? Once again there cannot be a true federation effected between separate peoples unless both signatories enter the federation as sovereign units, possessing equal rights. As there cannot be an amicable partnership between a master and a slave, so there cannot be a true federation between a dominating power and a subservient people. Consequently, the talk of federations is nothing but a sham.

I said at the outset that one of the objectives of the people of the world is a lasting peace. At the present time there are three distinct proposals being advanced with a view to gaining this end.

Three Proposals on Securing Peace

One is the proposal of world police force. It is based upon the principle that each unit-nation forfeit a part of its sovereignty to a central world authority. This world authority, they say, would work in the interests of world peace and security. It is evident, however, that if this scheme were adopted the principle of sovereignty and national freedom would be ceded. Personally, I am of the opinion that there is no likelihood that this scheme will meet with much success in the immediate future.

Another proposal is that of the Big Power politics, and what is sometimes termed "the spheres of influence" scheme. The immediate probability is that this proposal is most likely to succeed. If it does, it would simply mean that many of the small sovereign nations – and peoples who are aspiring to sovereignty – would be swallowed by the few big powers.

A further and third proposal is diametrically opposite to the first. It is based on the principle of sovereignty and self-government. This proposal is receiving its strongest support from peoples who have been wronged, and also from individuals with foresight and vision. Under this scheme each nation would be free to forge its own destiny. The former president of the United States, Mr. Herbert Hoover, is among the most prominent advocates of this proposal. And may I say that practically every small nation, whose freedom is threatened by the Big Power politics, favours this proposal as the basis of postwar peace. If this proposal were adopted, the world structure would then be based on Christian principles of the sovereignty of nations and of freedom of the individual, which is a direct opposite to all forms of totalitarian philosophy.

But while we are deeply concerned with the establishment of world peace, after the present war is won, I seriously suggest that there is a strong likelihood that there may not be a peace conference, in the usually accepted term, following the end of hostilities. On the contrary, there are indications that the war may end in a state of military occupations. A scramble of the Big Powers for greater spheres of influence would commence. The power using the best strategy would seize upon the opportunity to acquire new territory. Already moves have been made in that direction by the Russian realists.

Interpretations of the "16 Soviet Republics" Move

Russia, approving of the Atlantic Charter, which incorporates in part at least the principle of sovereignty of nations, has recently amended the Soviet Constitution, granting the sovereign rights, so called, to each and every republic within the Soviet Union. Some hold that this announcement on the part of our allied friends, the Russians, was a strategic move on the chess-board of world political diplomacy. At any rate, the move has left the commentators speechless. There was, however, one interpretation placed upon this move by some of the leading thinkers to the effect that in the political sense this move may lead to a continuation of a certain type of Russian imperialism, and that in the cultural sense it may become a long-range panslavist movement. But, whatever the correct interpretation may be, the announcement of the amended constitution is most significant. The true picture of passing events, however, now somewhat obscure, will eventually be revealed to us with the inevitable march of time.

Ladies and Gentlemen, my conviction is, that the two great nations in the world today who are outstanding in their recognition of sovereign peoples, and of peoples who are aspiring to sovereignty, are the countries to which you and I belong. I speak of the British Commonwealth of Nations, of which my own beloved Canada is a partner, and our good neighbour, your glorious democracy – the United States of America.

In this brief message to you tonight, I have endeavoured only to focus your attention upon a few of the important problems facing the world today.

May I now wish your organization, and your two publications, "Svoboda" and the "Ukrainian Weekly," an even greater success in the next fifty years than that which you have attained up to the present. May our great, common ideal of freedom, economic security and a just and lasting peace be speedily realized. And may I wish you, also, that instead of a humble personage like myself, you will welcome on your next historic occasion, a special guest, the Prime Minister of a Free, United, and Self-Governing Ukrainian Republic.

FARMERS' PROBLEMS

House of Commons, 23 May 1944

...I should like to say a word about beef marketing and the embargo placed upon the movement of beef to the United States. Not long ago I had an opportunity of visiting our good neighbours to the south, and not once during my four days' stay there did I see beef on the menus of the restaurants. Yet this afternoon the hon. member for Lethbridge and the minister were matching arguments as to the true situation concerning beef. When the minister and his department found that they were unable to market all the beef produced, surely they could have made arrangements within twenty-four hours to sell to the United States what beef they could not otherwise dispose of.

The farmers of Ontario were calling mass meetings and getting together from one end of the province to the other, sending resolutions to this government to lift this particular restriction so that they could sell their beef to the people in the United States who needed it at that time. But no action was taken. Our people were told to take their cattle back home when they brought them to the market. That sort of situation cannot possibly be justified. Surely we should have taken advantage of every opportunity to sell what we had to sell, and the people of this country are in a position to produce more if more is required.

The Minister of Agriculture said that he was unable to forecast what was going to happen in the future, that everything depended on the law of supply and demand. That is an old story, Mr. Chairman, and it will not stand the test now. In the first place our people must have all the food they require, and our farmers are ready to produce all the food that our people can consume. But in order that the farmers may buy the commodities which they need in order to get along, they must be able to sell some of their surplus products to other countries. That subject has been discussed by members of this group on many occasions. The government has always maintained that unless we are able to export our surplus products to other countries, then our own people in Canada must go hungry because we shall have no money. After this war we must get down to brass tacks and assure the people of Canada that they will never, never go hungry again because we can produce all the foodstuffs that we need and still have a surplus to export to other nations. That is the first thing we must ensure. Second, we must be ready to exchange our surpluses with other nations. This talk that goes on from time to time to the effect that everything must be based on gold or some other fictitious basis will not hold water after this war. Mr. Wilson, when he was speaking to one of these gentlemen, was given a plain indication of what might be expected. He was told: "We will buy all the bacon and cheese and wheat you want to sell to us, provided that you buy a like amount of British products in return." We must recognize the fact that exchange of goods is the basis of all trade. To repeat, we must first of all produce to satisfy the needs of our own people. Second, we must export our surpluses in exchange for the goods we need. If the minister can assure our people of those two things, this committee and the people of Canada will not blame him for the difficulties that may arise.

DISPLACED PERSONS *in* EUROPE

House of Commons, 26 September 1945

MR. ANTHONY HLYNKA (Vegreville): Mr. Speaker, during the course of the past twelve days we have had the privilege of listening to some very fine contributions to this debate, dealing with the problems mentioned in the speech from the throne. The most important and immediate problems, of course, are those which have arisen directly as a result of the war. Our domestic problems should be less difficult of solution, particularly in view of our fortunate geographic position, since Canadian soil has not been ravaged by war. But in wartorn Europe the problems of providing food, clothing, shelter and medical supplies, finding refuge for millions of displaced persons and their rehabilitation, are matters of great magnitude and extreme urgency. It is my firm conviction that on humanitarian grounds alone we have a moral responsibility to those unhappy people, particularly when we consider the tremendous sacrifices and limitless contributions they made to the winning of the war. It is true that the lion's share of this gigantic task is being discharged, and with some success, by such official organizations as UNRRA, intergovernmental committees, the International Red Cross and its auxiliaries, and so on. However, I am more concerned with that phase of the problem which extends beyond the scope of officialdom but which is by no means less deserving of the most sympathetic and humanitarian consideration.

Before proceeding further I should like to say that I have nothing but the highest admiration for the organizations to which I have referred and for the work they are doing with the limited resources which have been placed at their disposal for such a colossal task. I believe, nevertheless, that we have fallen short in our humanitarian response to that other phase of this gigantic problem which, as I have said, extends beyond the jurisdiction of the organizations I have mentioned. I would refer to the situation which exists in regions where complications have arisen due to racial or political differences.

In order to alleviate the situation with respect to food, clothing and other supplies in regions where complications do exist I should like to make the suggestion that societies, private individuals and relatives of displaced persons be permitted to make direct gifts to those needy people so that all such articles may be received by those for whom they are intended. Under the present arrangement all articles of food, clothing and so on are collected into a common pool and distributed in the various zones by local officials and agencies as they see fit. Should the suggestion of direct gifts be adopted I am certain that additional aid would be forthcoming, both from those who are interested in their own relatives and from many other public-spirited individuals and societies on this continent.

Speaking in this house on March 26, 1945, in a debate on the San Francisco conference, I suggested then that there was a great need for some mechanism to be devised whereby stateless peoples and persons would be provided with the means of voicing their own opinions on their own behalf, when and if they consider themselves not represented by the various de facto governments. To-day, in the light of what is taking place in the Soviet sphere, I am convinced more than ever that there has become a still greater need for the setting up of such mechanism. For it is quite obvious that any problem which involves millions of people cannot and must not be lightly dismissed or brushed aside. To substantiate my contention that the magnitude of this problem has reached serious proportions, may I quote from an editorial which appeared in the Ottawa *Evening Citizen* of September 15, 1945, under the heading "Estonian Odyssey." The editorial says:

> A small Canadian press item from London tells of the setting out in a 37-foot sailing yacht of a group of sixteen Estonian refugees from the west coast of Scotland. The destination of these seven men, five women and four children is the United States. Three times already the small craft has set out, but it is in an earnest of the determination of the group not to return to their native land that a fourth attempt is now being made to reach the new world in the hope of a new life.
>
> The desire to go far from their own land will surely raise problems on this side of the Atlantic if they complete their desperate

voyage. It emphasizes the plight of many thousands of what are now known as displaced persons.

Such lands as Estonia and Latvia, and other territories in Europe where governments have changed, inevitably leave numbers of former residents unwilling to return to their former homes. In the case of the Estonian group they are unwilling to return to the land which is now incorporated under the Soviet Union.

It will take a great deal of wisdom and understanding to deal with this class of refugee. The war has been fought in the great cause of freedom. It would be a negation of that struggle to be a party of the unwilling return of such refugees or other displaced persons – they include victims of nazi forced labour from Poland and even Russia – to former homelands. The United Nations, particularly the big three, have a test of their ideas in stern realities to face.

I have other reports describing in the most pathetic and desperate terms the fate of these homeless millions. Here is another extract found in the Czech press service bulletin of June 28, 1945. This bulletin is published in London, England. The article is entitled "News From the Crucified Continent," and the subheading reads, "Be Communist or Perish." It states:

> According to information received from Trieste, the western allies are forcing large numbers of people who escaped the wrath of Tito communists to return to the parts they ran away from. Thousands of Croats and Slovenes who sought refuge in the British-American zone in Karinthia, have been handed over to Tito. They were stripped naked and executed by the deadly fire of machine guns. The Bishop of Lubljanja, together with 161 Slovenian priests and clerics, made their way into the American zone beseeching protection. It has not yet been decided whether they will be given up to Tito or not.
>
> There is silence over these horrors in the press of the Christian civilized countries in the west. It seems almost as if a decision has been taken that the peoples of the European continent must be communist, or else perish.

It will readily be seen, Mr. Speaker, that the two quotations which I have cited reveal the desperate situation which faces so many freedom-loving people of the world. I may say further that the fate of the continent of Europe is in the hands of the English-speaking nations – Canada included.

According to the figures of the international labor office there are no less than 40 million displaced persons as a result of the war. A good number of these persons will return to their former homes of their own free will, but in the case of what I call "stateless persons" the word repatriation has a different meaning. To them it means penal servitude, concentration camps, or, to use the favourite Soviet term, liquidation. This group of stateless people comprise several millions of Ukrainians, Jews, Czechs, Slovaks, Estonians, Latvians, Lithuanians, Finns, Poles and others, and the most tragic and ironic thing of all is that this group is made up of persons who hold democratic views, and, as the quotation says, democracies are forcing them to become communist or perish.

I find brief reference to this subject of repatriation in the British *Hansard*, for August 20, 1945, wherein Hon. Ernest Bevin, Secretary of State for Foreign Affairs in the British government, asserts "that over 600,000 (sic) Russians," as he calls them, "have been transported from the British zone to the east," and, "that it was expected that by autumn only 645,000 will be left, of whom 500,000 will be 'Poles.'"

During the past several weeks desperate letters, messages and pleas have been reaching many of our Canadian homes, and we have read press dispatches to the same effect, that the group of displaced persons who are found in American and British zones are being repatriated by force to their former homes. Many of these displaced persons commit suicide rather than return under the Soviets. Still others go so far as to resist the British and American military police in self-defence, and we learn from the latest reports that the situation is growing worse. In dealing with this question I should like to ask: Is repatriation by force a solution to the problem, and is it in conformity with the principles proclaimed in the Atlantic charter and later endorsed at Yalta, namely: "the right of all peoples to choose the form of government under which they will live," and also "afford the assurance that all the men in all the lands may live out their lives in freedom from fear and want?"

Representations have been made to me, Mr. Speaker, by many of our Canadian veterans of world war II, who have met many of these displaced persons and who have personal knowledge of the situation as it exists with respect to the question of repatriation; and being of Ukrainian origin themselves, they asked me to plead the cause of these unfortunate people, among whom there are many Ukrainians. In addition to this I have been receiving letters and telegrams almost daily from all parts of Canada, sent by Ukrainian church bodies and other Canadian-Ukrainian organizations, requesting that I bring this matter to the attention of the Canadian government and to the attention of this democratic tribunal.

I should like, therefore, on behalf of Ukrainian refugees who are involved in this repatriation, and on behalf of others, to submit a plea to the Canadian government to transmit through its high offices to the British and United States governments an appeal to cease forceful repatriation of displaced persons, and in addition to give sympathetic consideration of the following specific requests:

1. That permission be granted to representatives of Ukrainian relief committees to visit various camps and districts where Ukrainian refugees are found. These representatives are to act on instructions of the British and United States commanders in their respective zones.
2. That where the number of Ukrainian refugees warrants it, they be organized or granted permission to organize themselves into Ukrainian refugee camps, and that they be permitted to organize their own welfare committees. If this were done, all material aid meant for Ukrainians would be more likely to reach them.
3. That radio news and information broadcasts – now being transmitted to Europe in many languages, but not in Ukrainian – be also given in the Ukrainian language. For at present all authoritative information is broadcast in languages which are not adequately understood by Ukrainian people.
4. That British and United States military governments alone

issue and announce statements of policy in regard to problems respecting refugees, instead of permitting Russian and other representatives to confuse the Ukrainian refugees.
5. That permission be granted to Ukrainian refugees to edit, print and distribute a "news letter" in the Ukrainian language for the benefit of Ukrainian refugees, as is being done in Russian, Polish and a few other languages.

From the five specific requests which I have just placed before the government and this honourable house it will be quite evident that not only do Ukrainians share the unfortunate fate of a refugee life, but they also have been overlooked in respect to the privileges granted to Polish, Russian and other refugees. It is in the light of all these cruel and horrible conditions and because of the tragic fate of the Ukrainian refugees that I make this plea.

In conclusion, I should like to read an extract from Mr. Churchill's speech which he delivered in the British House of Commons on August 16, 1945 and which is recorded in the British *Hansard* of that date. This extract describes a scene which appears in the tragic world drama of to-day and which I could not even hope to describe in my own inadequate words. Mr. Churchill said:

> It is not impossible that tragedy on a prodigious scale is imposing itself behind the iron curtain which at present divides Europe in twain....
>
> I cannot conceive that the elements for a new conflict exist in the Balkans to-day.... Nevertheless not many members of the new House of Commons will be content with the new situation prevailing in those mountainous, turbulent, ill-organized and war-like regions ... for almost everywhere communist forces have obtained, or are in process of obtaining, dictatorial powers.... We must know where we stand, and we must make clear where we stand in these affairs of the Balkans and of eastern Europe, and indeed of any country which comes into this field.
>
> Our idea is government of the people, by the people, for the people – the people being free without duress to express, by secret ballot without intimidation, their deep-seated wish as to the form

and conditions under which they are to live. At present ... a family is gathered around the fireside to enjoy the scanty fruits of their toil and to recruit their exhausted strength by the little food that they have been able to gather.... Suddenly there is a knock at the door and a heavily armed policeman appears.... It may be that the father or son, or a friend sitting in the cottage, is called out and taken off into the dark, and no one knows whether he will ever come back again, or what his fate has been. All they know is that they had better not inquire. There are millions of humble homes in Europe at the moment, in Poland, in Czechoslovakia, in Austria, in Hungary, in Yugoslavia, in Romania, in Bulgaria – where this fear is the main preoccupation of the family life.... "Freedom from fear" – but this has been interpreted as if it were only freedom from fear of invasion from a foreign country ... but that is not the fear of the ordinary family in Europe to-night. Their fear is the policeman's knock.... It is for the life and liberty of the individual, for the fundamental rights of man, now menaced and precarious in so many lands that peoples tremble.

... Democracy is now on trial as it never was before, and in those islands we must uphold it, as we upheld it in the dark days of 1940 and 1941, with all our hearts, with all our vigilance and with all our enduring and inexhaustible strength.

Yes, democracy is on trial. No atheistic philosophy of force, torture and extermination shall ever restore the God-given democratic right to humanity unless the surviving democracies write a new chapter of history founded on Christian principles.

Mr. W. A. TUCKER (Rosthern): There is another matter with which I should like to deal shortly, the question of foreign policy. I realize that the situation to-day is a delicate one, and I do not want to say anything that might make it more difficult. However, there are certain things I feel should be said on the floor of this free parliament. First, I do not think the council of foreign ministers representing the five great powers has any right to try to settle the future peace treaties of this world. I know it will be said that the council will just make suggestions, but the suggestions they finally make will lack only formal ratification because the smaller countries will not be able to change them very much if the council has reached agreement.

Canada, Australia, New Zealand, South Africa and the other united nations have played a sufficiently great part in winning the victory which has been ours to have the right to have some real and effective say in the settlement of the terms of peace. Further, the present policy is not working out to advantage, because I find the following which appeared in the *Daily Herald*:

> We repeat our calm conviction that the international situation is more than alarming; it is becoming desperate.

And the following is from the Manchester *Guardian*:

> Would it not be best if all were to return to the principles of the Atlantic charter which states that the powers (it was endorsed by Russia) seek no aggrandizement territorial or otherwise?

Mr. SMITH (Calgary West): Is that the *Herald* of Calgary or London?

Mr. TUCKER: The London *Daily Herald*. I quoted that for the benefit of my hon. friends of the C.C.F. over there. In regard to this whole question of foreign policy, I realize that there seems to be a feeling on the part of the English-speaking world that there is such a passionate desire for the world peace that they are determined to let no disagreement creep into the discussions of the future settlement of world affairs. Because of our reluctance to express disapproval of some of the aspects of Soviet policy, the Soviet leaders are coming to think, I am sure, that they can make demands that they otherwise would not make, that the governments of the free countries of the world will give way for them, or, if they do not give way, sufficient public opinion will develop to force them to give way.

Mr. FULTON: Apparently the hon. member holds the view that Canada should have an opportunity to have her voice heard. I should like him to explain why this government did not see that this country was represented at the conference that is now going on.

Mr. TUCKER: If my hon. friend knew what was going on, I believe he would find that great pressure was exerted to have the various nations of the British commonwealth represented at these peace discussions. But just as in the past times the Soviet objected to the British commonwealth having more than one vote, I think my hon. friend will find that there was objection to the British commonwealth being represented by several votes. My hon. friend has no right to jump to conclusions. I do not think he would suggest that the British government, which I am sure would like to have Canada represented there and have her fair say, would not want that to be done. I think when the record of this thing comes to be written it will be found that the British government was anxious to have the dominions represented there on an equal basis with themselves, but they had to take the five-power conference or nothing. It is very easy for my hon. friends to suggest that the Prime Minister (Mr. Mackenzie King) should have gone over there, but as I read over the dispatches he was asked to go over there and sit in the background and have the British representatives speak for all the nations of the commonwealth.

Canada Has Right to be Heard

So far as I am concerned, Canada has a right to be represented in the councils of the nations of the world in her own right as a nation, and not to be represented by anybody else. If my hon. friend wishes to have Canada speak through another nation, I believe he does not represent the best thought of the Canadian people.

I was going on to say that I think the present situation is a dangerous one. It leads to claims being made that otherwise would not be made.

Mr. JACKMAN: What does Mr. Bevin say?

Mr. TUCKER: I have read the debates in the British House of Commons and know what Mr. Bevin said. I think my hon. friend cannot have read it or he would not be asking that question. The fact remains that it is a dangerous situation, and the sooner we make it very plain to the Soviets that we believe just as much in freedom and liberty now as we did when the Atlantic charter was signed, the better it will be for the world peace.

The Problem of Displaced Ukrainians

That brings me to another question, and here I should like to associate myself with an hon. member of this house who is other than of British or French origin. I am glad to see him in this house representing one of the important elements of our population, the population of Ukrainian origin. He had every right to get up and show that he felt for his own flesh and blood who he fears and believes are suffering on the continent of Europe. I put it to those of English, Scotch, Irish or French origin, if according to all the news they could get, their own people on the continent of Europe were being crucified, we would, I am sure have heard more from them than what the hon. member for Vegreville (Mr. Hlynka) said in his most moderate speech.

What is the situation now before the Big Five conference? The west Ukraine comprises a large part of the Ukrainian population of Europe. The granting of the Soviet western boundary at the so-called Curzon line included the Ukrainians in the west Ukraine. At the Yalta conference it was claimed that these people thereby became Russian citizens. Russia claimed that it was agreed that they would be surrendered to the Soviet authorities. Mr. Churchill insisted that the Poles in that area should not be forcibly repatriated, that they should have the right not to be sent back to their homeland and that if necessary they would be granted the protection of the status of a British subject. Incidentally, Mr. Speaker, when I heard that, it made me proud to belong to the British commonwealth of nations.

An hon. MEMBER: The Conservative Party.

Mr. TUCKER: My hon. friend says: "the Conservative party." I say that it was the people of Canada of all parties who made the great record of Canada in the past six years. Mr. Churchill, at the request of these beset Poles, said that they should have the mantle of British citizenship thrown around them, which was a great compliment to the British commonwealth at least.

But what of the Ukrainians? They were claimed to be Russians, and to-day the demand is that they be forcibly repatriated from the British and American zones in which they are to-day to the number of about one million. When attempts are made to carry out these orders, these unfortunate people, we are told, commit suicide or forcibly resist being handed over to the Soviet authorities. The Ukrainian committee in the

United States has addressed a moving appeal to the president of that country to save their kith and kin in Europe from being forcibly repatriated to the Soviet. The Ukrainian committee of Canada has made a submission to our government, from which I quote two sentences:

> We have received information from Europe to the effect that the Soviet Union has demanded the repatriation of those Ukrainian refugees who came from the now Soviet occupied territories east of the Curzon line. In the name of humanity we appeal to the government of Canada to do whatever may be possible to prevent such deportations to the Soviet territories.

What is the situation of these people? We know that in the west Ukraine there were thousands of people who looked to the end of this war to bring them a free Ukraine. They wanted their freedom. They spoke for it and they worked for it. They were against being in the Soviet, and they were against communism – their preachers, their doctors, teachers, leading authors and writers – and for that reason they have been marked down, not as anti-communist but as fascist; for in Europe there is a tendency to say that if a man is against communism or in any way against being incorporated in the Soviet, he is fascist or pro-nazi. I would say to the members of this house that we do not want communism in this country – or most of us do not; we do not want to be incorporated in the Soviet Union, and we would not like it if we were called fascist for that reason. In the hearts of these Ukrainians there beats the love of liberty and the love of country just the same as in the hearts of Canadians, but they are branded as anti-Soviet, and we are told that for that reason they fear to be handed over to the Soviet authorities. They fear what is going to happen to them. Somebody might say: You do not know what is going to happen to them over there. But to use the words of Mr. Churchill, nobody knows what is happening behind the iron curtain that divides Europe to-day, and if the Soviet authorities are not willing to let the representatives of our people and the representatives of the press come in to see what is happening over there, have we any right to doubt these people when they say they fear what is going to happen to them when they are forcibly repatriated?

And so, Mr. Speaker, I would urge this upon the government with all the feeling I possess: Do not let our Canadian troops have anything to do with forcing these people into the hands of those who they fear are going to liquidate them. Surely our great contribution to the fight for freedom was not made to have our troops in any way forcibly repatriate these people. Let them have the same protection as has been freely granted to the Polish people. I honour the representatives of Great Britain and the United States, at the Council of Foreign Ministers, who, we are told in press dispatches, are to-day resisting the demands of Mr. Molotov that these people be handed over.

Once more I see the British people and the people of the United States standing on guard for freedom and liberty, and I am sure that, our government has been making representations to the British government of approval of that policy.

I hope that this debate may be soon concluded so that we can send our own Prime Minister over there to add the voice and support of Canada to the conscience of the world in bringing to pass an era of freedom and liberty which alone will only begin to justify the tremendous sacrifices that have been made to render it possible.

THE PROBLEM *of* UKRAINIAN DISPLACED PERSONS

New Pathway, 12 January 1946

FROM AN ADDRESS DELIVERED BY ANTHONY HLYNKA, M.P., AT A CONCERT HELD IN THE MASONIC TEMPLE SCOTTISH RITE CATHEDRAL, AT DETROIT, MICHIGAN, ON SUNDAY, DECEMBER 16, 1945, AT 2:30 P.M.

It is certainly an honour and a privilege to have this opportunity of addressing such a distinguished audience in the city of Detroit. Although this is my first visit to your great city, I know I can surely say I have many close friends in the audience here this afternoon. I need hardly emphasize the fact that I am most happy to renew many of my former acquaintances, of Detroit and Windsor, and, of course, I am most eager to meet many others, should I be offered the opportunity.

I should like to say also that I am greatly indebted, indeed, to the Executive of your "Dumka" choir for extending an invitation to me to be present with you on this occasion.

May I, first of all, pay a sincere and well-deserved tribute to the work of the "Dumka" choir, which seems to have become almost legendary. For more than twenty years it has delighted hundreds of audiences with its magnificent performances, a record perhaps unequalled by any other choir on this continent.

I know, too, Mr. Chairman, that you and the audience here this afternoon will agree with me when I say that the fame and success of "Dumka" is largely due to its talented and inspiring leader, Mr. Atamanetz. I have had the good fortune of listening to this choir on several occasions, and always I was entranced by their splendid singing, and inspired by the skill and artistic ability of its conductor. He throws his very soul into his work and through his appreciation of the real depth and extraordinary beauty of Ukrainian songs, he is a worthy interpreter of the finest gifts of art as expressed in the music of the Ukraine.

Today we again heard this choir perform, and as I was listening to it, I was filled with pride that I myself am of Ukrainian origin. I was also proud that the Ukrainian people have such a great treasure to offer the world. It goes without saying that this culture, these spiritual qualities, should be preserved. And may I add, that a people who, in these and other respects, have made such a rich contribution to the world, should also be preserved and be given the opportunity to develop further their God-given talents. To the achievement of that end, "Dumka" is making a noble contribution. It is my sincere hope and desire that this choir may continue its great work; that it may remain the ambassador of Ukrainian culture for many, many years to come.

Unfortunately, Mr. Chairman, despite the magnificent contribution of Ukrainian people to world culture, as was so well expressed here this afternoon by the artists, millions of freedom-loving Ukrainians in Europe today face the great tragedy of their history. This, Mr. Chairman, brings me to the topic of my address.

But before dealing with what I intend to say, may I reflect for a moment on the conditions under which Canadian and United States citizens have lived during the past five years, the conditions under which we live at present, and those under which we are likely to live in the immediate future.

I am conscious of the fact that I am speaking now to an audience of Americans and Canadians who have generously contributed to the forging of weapons of war. I am conscious of the fact also that there are persons in this audience whose loved ones have paid the supreme sacrifice on the far-flung battlefields of the world – they died that democracy and freedom may live! I know, too, that there are many young men and women in this audience who have served in the Armed Forces of our respective countries and who were fortunate enough to return home. At the same time, let me say this: that we on this continent are the most fortunate people on earth!

We must remember that not a single bomb fell on our land. We know that not a single home was destroyed by explosion or fire resulting from the war. We know too, that not a single acre of land was scorched. We were not dispossessed of anything by force. Parents and children were not separated. We had not experienced the horrors of murder and suffering. We were not exposed to cold, hunger and disease, and not one family remained without a roof over their heads. Above all – we saved our freedom! ....

IMMIGRATION

The Second Ukrainian Canadian Congress, 5 June 1946

Mr. Chairman, Rev. Fathers, Distinguished Guests, and Worthy Delegates:

To Canadians of Ukrainian origin the question of immigration at this time is undoubtedly of greater concern than any other immediate problem. In my judgment there are five main reasons for this:

1. As a result of World War II, and owing to present day political conditions in Europe, several hundred thousand Ukrainians have found themselves outside the boundaries of their historic lands.
2. There is hardly a Canadian family of Ukrainian origin which has not one or more close relatives in the displaced persons' camps. It is only natural, therefore, that they should be keenly concerned about those dear to them.
3. From the Canadian point of view, Canadians of Ukrainian origin consider it to be in Canada's interest that a number of these people should be accepted as immigrants and be given the opportunity to become Canadian citizens.
4. Apart from any question of blood ties, it is the humanitarian and Christian duty of Canadians to extend a helping hand to these unfortunate, homeless, stateless and suffering people.
5. The displaced persons are a direct responsibility of the United Nations. Canada, being a member of the United Nations and a signatory of the United Nations Charter, should assume a share of the responsibility in an effort to solve this gigantic problem.

The Problem of Displaced Persons and Refugees

Never before in the history of mankind have people had to endure such suffering, and on so large a scale, as that which has been the lot of the displaced persons since the conclusion of the Second Great War. At the conclusion of hostilities a year ago, no fewer than 40 million people had been uprooted from their homes. The great majority of these have been transferred to various regions for permanent settlement. The remainder, comprising more than six million persons, for one reason or other did not wish to be returned to their former homelands, controlled and dominated as they are by foreign powers. Scattered as they were, across the continent of Europe, some of them lived in displaced persons' camps; others lived as best they could and wherever they could. Nearly five million of them have been forcibly sent back, and close to two million have remained in the displaced persons centres scattered over Central and Western Europe – most of them in the American and British-occupied zones of Germany.

UNRRA and Other Organizations Temporarily Provide for Displaced Persons in Camps

The DP's who find themselves in displaced persons' camps are fed, clothed, and housed by UNRRA and are assisted by the Red Cross and other welfare organizations. This arrangement, however, is of necessity only temporary; therefore, it is imperative that a permanent solution to the problem be found. This can be done only by seeking for these people a permanent home in the democracies of the world, preferably in the English-speaking countries. It is in the hope of solving this problem that citizens of Canada have been making impassioned appeals to the Canadian Government to allow a considerable number of these people to enter Canada as immigrants.

Why Are There Displaced Persons, and Who Are They?

In the course of the war, and as a direct result of the policies of totalitarian states, millions of people were uprooted from the centuries-old homes of their forefathers. One group was sent into German-controlled territories as forced labour. A second group consists of persons who, on racial, political or religious grounds, were thrown into concentration camps and persecuted by both Nazi and Communist dictatorships. A third group consisting of men, women, and children, sought refuge outside their own devastated countries and experienced untold misery and horrible persecutions during the Nazi-Soviet occupation of their countries during the period from September, 1939, to June 22, 1941. The fourth group consists of prisoners of war. The fifth comprises all others who have been evicted from their homes by invading armies or forces of occupation. Clearly, all these victims have chosen to remain on the west side of the iron curtain in the hope that some day they will find new homes where they may live as free people.

Why DP's Refuse to Go Back

The Western Powers are now becoming more and more strongly convinced that displaced persons have valid reasons for refusing to return to Soviet-controlled territories. There are no less than five important reasons for this:

First, because they are democratic-minded people in the Western sense of the word, as they wish to live their lives as free men. They hate dictatorship in all its forms.

Second, because they are deeply religious, and there is no freedom of worship in the Communist-controlled territories. This has been amply demonstrated by the disbandment of the Ukrainian Greek-Catholic Church, by the imprisonment and murder of many Ukrainian clergy, and by the persecution of the Ukrainian Greek-Orthodox Church.

Third, because under Communist dictatorship, individual and national freedom is impossible either in the economic or in the political sense.

Fourth, because of the constant fear of N.K.V.D. (the notorious Russian Secret Police).

Fifth, because those who were forcibly sent back were to be returned to their former homes, but were sent East as far as Siberia. They were "repatriated" not to the Ukraine, but to Russia. Ukrainian lands on which Ukrainians have lived for more than a thousand years are now being populated by Russian and Mongolian peoples.... In fact, a policy of dispersion, and not one of reassembling, has been adopted by the Soviet Government in the Ukraine. The number of Ukrainians in the Ukraine has dropped by two-thirds.

Kin of Canadians of Ukrainian Origin

Of particular concern to Canadians of Ukrainian origin are, of course, several hundred thousands of Ukrainians who remain in Central and Western Europe and who live in D.P. camps. These people are their very kith and kin. The heart-rending plight of Ukrainians naturally concerns many Canadian citizens of Ukrainian origin. The Ukrainian people today are living through the most tragic period of their history. It is for these reasons that for more than a year, Canadians of Ukrainian origin have been urging the Canadian authorities that a generous number of Ukrainian displaced persons be accepted as immigrants.

Contribution of Canadians of Ukrainian Origin to the Development of Canada and the Part They Played in Canada's War Effort

It is reasonable to assume that before any country decides to receive immigrants it must make certain that they will make good citizens. In support of prospective Ukrainian immigrants I can do no better than to make a brief reference to the contribution made by former Ukrainian immigrants to the development and upbuilding of this country, and the manner in which they acquitted themselves in a time of crisis – during the last war.

As an outstanding contribution made by Ukrainians to the development of this country I need but mention the complete transformation of much of the western Canadian wilderness by the first Ukrainian settlers into some of our most productive areas. Virtually with bare hands, they cleared thousands upon thousands of acres, which today, blossom with wheat, barley, rye and many varieties of vegetables. They built homes, fences, and roads. They erected schools, churches and community halls. In touring Western Canada today, one finds that some of the most exemplary communities are those settled by Ukrainians. By their industry and their devotion to Canada, and by their sons' sacrifices in World War II, and by their love of the land, Ukrainians have proven themselves excellent citizens.

Ukrainian Canadian workers in the various industries have earned for themselves the envy of all. They are resourceful, reliable, and conscientious.

Ukrainian Canadian students have also set a high record. Their scholastic achievements have been of the first order. Canadians of Ukrainian origin are well represented in practically every field of endeavour, and they are acquitting themselves very well, indeed.

Canadians of Ukrainian origin have made remarkable progress in the short period of fifty-five years. I refer to it as a short period, for I have the honour to represent the constituency in which the first Ukrainian settler chose to live. He is Wasyl Eleniak, still living on his original homestead at Chipman, Alberta. Canadians of Ukrainian origin love their land, as is evidenced by the fact that 76.76 per cent of all Ukrainian Canadians in the three Prairie Provinces live in the rural areas, and only 23.24 per cent in urban areas. In a word, they have done exceptionally well, and their success may be considered a criterion of their adaptability, their industry, and their loyalty.

Does Canada Need New Settlers?

I realize that what I have said thus far does not necessarily establish the fact that Canada needs immigration. I have described the plight of displaced persons, explained who they are, pointed out that they have relatives in Canada, shown that Canadians of Ukrainian origin have done well, and indicated that Canadians of Ukrainian origin would like to see a generous number of their people admitted to Canada. But I must show that Canada needs immigration. I should like, therefore, to give what I consider to be sound reasons in favour of immigration to Canada.

1. In the first place, it must be obvious to all Canadians, and especially to those charged with the responsibility of steering the course of Canada's destiny, that Canada must increase her population if she is to play an important role in world affairs, if she is to hold her important position in the councils of nations, and if she is to be of much assistance to the British Commonwealth of Nations. No one will

argue, I am sure, that it is easy for Canada to play an important part in all these matters with only 12 million people. Our limited population inevitably consigns us to the group of third rate powers, in spite of our assertions that we are a foremost world power.

2. Not only are we conscious of our shortcomings in International Affairs, but with our sparsely populated country we cannot hope to be a prosperous nation and build a stable national economy. Let me explain what I have in mind: Canada needs markets in which to sell her goods. The surest and most stable market is always the home market. But, as we know, our Canadian market is so limited that the cost of every production must of necessity be higher than it should be. Then, too, the heavy burden of taxation, freight rates and other costs fall on a small portion of our population. It is a known fact that certain settlements in Western Canada have been refused rail branch transportation services because the population is too small to pay the costs of building and maintaining the branch lines. The result is that Canadians in these settlements must either abandon productive areas or carry on by transporting their products by trucks and teams. The answer is, of course, more settlers.

3. Then I might mention the cultural loss which Canada suffers because of her small population. It is a well known fact that Canadian creative works in music and literature are lost to Canada because of the more attractive market in the United States. Moreover, Canada has been a very heavy loser of intellectual peoples, because of the more lucrative positions and opportunities available to them in the United States. Our small population makes it necessary for us to operate everything on a small scale, consequently there are fewer opportunities in this country. Salaries, too, in the United States are much higher.

Let me read to you from an item headed "Southward Trek," which appeared in "Time" magazine of April 1, 1946:

> In 14 U.S. consulates, from Halifax to Vancouver, hard-pressed clerks interviewed Canadians, laboriously filled out long forms, took finger-prints of prospective new Americans. Last week consular officials paused to look at the record. In the last six months of 1945 they had okayed permanent visas for 8,767 Canadians. If the

present pressure continues, 20,000 Canadians will migrate to U.S. in 1945–46 fiscal year.

What worried Canadian authorities most was the sharp increase in the number of visas issued to top-class citizens. Visas for professional, clerical and other white-collar categories have shown the biggest rise of any group – 2,332 issued in the last six months of 1945, compared with 1,770 in the year 1944–45.

For Canada this posed a major problem. The Dominion had lost one-sixth of her population to the U.S. before 1930.

I am sure it is the unanimous opinion of all Canadians that such losses of our best and ablest young people are serious, indeed. Persons who are born, raised, and educated in Canada and who show great promise, are forced to leave for more attractive fields, never to return. This subject has, on many occasions, been discussed in the House of Commons. When the Ministers were asked why the Canadian government did not raise the pay of able young men rather than lose them to the United States, the answer invariably was that with our small population Canada could not afford to pay the high salaries which are offered in the United States. Also we must not forget that there are tens of thousands of Canadians with the best qualifications who are struggling on small salaries, but who remain in Canada because of family ties or for other reasons.

During the 80 years, from 1851 to 1931, Canada lost 6,110,000 people to the United States. At the present time Canada has a golden opportunity to remedy this situation by accepting a goodly number of new immigrants who would be forever grateful to her for adopting them as her citizens.

4. There may be those who would argue that the best policy for Canada is to depend on her own natural increase of population. But the projected calculations indicate that, if immigration were not allowed, the increase in our population would be only three million in the next 45 years. That means that by 1990, if unaided by immigration, Canada's total population would amount to 15,000,000. And from 1990 on, according to the calculations of the Dominion Bureau of Statistics, our population would decline in numbers. In studying

these figures one cannot help but feel disturbed about the future of this country.

5. I now come to the study of projected population in Europe. In my opinion Canada would be well advised to consider these figures when deciding upon her immigration policy.

In a book entitled *The Future Populations of Europe and the Soviet Union*, prepared by several men, among whom was Professor Frank W. Notestein, and published in 1944 by the League of Nations, we find the following interesting table on page 134:

Men 15–34 Years of Age (a Source of Military Manpower) in the Ten Most Populated Countries of Europe (in Millions)

Country	1940	1955	1970
U.S.S.R.	30.1	36.9	43.3
Germany	11.3	10.9	9.9
United Kingdom	7.6	6.9	5.7
Italy	7.4	8.2	7.4
France	6.0	6.1	4.8
Poland	6.1	7.0	6.3
Spain	4.3	4.8	4.1
Romania	3.4	4.3	4.2
Czechoslovakia	2.6	2.5	1.9
Yugoslavia	2.6	3.3	3.2

Commenting on this chart, the author of the book states that, "By 1970 the U.S.S.R., in its 1937 boundaries, will have as large a source of primary military manpower as Germany, the United Kingdom, Italy, France, Poland, Spain and Romania combined, these being seven European countries with the greatest forces of manpower outside the Soviet Union."

It will be realized, of course, that this chart did not take account of the losses in the war recently concluded. But when we consider the territories annexed to the Soviet Union during the war, it would be reasonable to assume that the Soviet Union is likely to have a larger primary source of manpower of military age than the combined total of the other nine countries mentioned in the chart.

In addition to this tremendously large population of the present Russian Empire, we took a hand in assisting the Soviets in forcing a few more millions to leave Central and Western Europe. The people pleaded with us to allow them to remain until they could find permanent homes elsewhere, but in spite of their pleadings we shipped them back because we were afraid we would have too many people on our hands. Russia, on the other hand, was not afraid to take them, even by force, having in mind the plan of populating and developing her northern regions, particularly Siberia, which is not far from Alaska.

6. One other reason why it is in Canada's interest to accept a good number of European immigrants has to do with the existing trends and projected calculations of population trends in the United Kingdom. Only recently an exhaustive research was undertaken by three outstanding authorities on population in the United Kingdom. It was found that the present birth rate in the United Kingdom was 20 per cent below replacement level. It was found, too, that the gravity of population was tending toward old age groups, which was another disturbing factor. It appeared from the figures that if the present trend continued, the burden of maintaining social services would fall on the shoulders of a shrinking producing class, resulting in a burdensome taxation and a general decrease in the standard of living. In view of these facts Canada would be wise if she decided on a generous immigration policy, and, while admitting immigrants from the United Kingdom, she should also admit a considerable number of people from Central and Western Europe.

Canada's Christian and Humanitarian Obligations

Having pointed out why it is in the interests of Canada to increase her population, by immigration, I should now like to state that Canada, with her vast expanses of land and with her unlimited natural resources, has also an inviolable humanitarian and Christian obligation toward displaced persons and refugees, particularly in view of the fact that Canada has not suffered the destruction and the ravages of war and that we are in a position to help. I know that, to those who have no relatives among the starving and the homeless, it is difficult to grasp the magnitude and urgency of the problem. The colossal figures of the loss of life cannot sum up the tragedy, for, the larger the figures the less impressive they seem, as, by their very immensity, they appear unbelievable. The horrifying facts are, however, that even in the course of the past twenty minutes or so, while I have been addressing this distinguished audience, somewhere, hundreds of people have died from starvation and lack of proper care and hospitalization. In the name of humanity and of Christianity, let us exert all our power in an effort to heal the wounds of those suffering people.

DP's Are a World Responsibility Also

Lastly, I wish to refer to the question of displaced persons as a responsibility of the United Nations. In this connection it should suffice to recall to this Congress but one declaration of the United Nations Organization, which states that they (the United Nations) "reaffirm faith in fundamental human rights, in the dignity and worth of the human person, in the equal rights of men and women and of nations, large and small."

As a member nation of the United Nations Organization, Canada can use her influence in asking an all-out effort on the part of UNO and its member nations in the matter of satisfactory solution of the displaced persons problem.

What Has Canada Done in the Matter of Immigration?

And finally, I should like to give a brief account of what Canada has done, up to this time, in the matter of immigration. As we all know, no Ukrainian immigrants were admitted to Canada during the six-year period of the war. In the course of the past year, however, that is, since the conclusion of the war, I know of one Ukrainian displaced person who was admitted to Canada for permanent residence. To say the least, this total exclusion of Ukrainian immigrants had a disheartening effect on Canadians of Ukrainian origin. But we all realized that Canada's service personnel and their dependents had to be brought back first. Other Canadians took the same view. In the past several months, however, Canadians of various racial stocks, aided by numerous organizations and prominent public men, applied considerable pressure on the government urging the government to open Canada's gates to relatives of Canadians, as a first step, and later, to permit a more general immigration. As a result of this pressure, Hon. Mr. J. A. Glen, Minister of Mines and Resources, who has jurisdiction over immigration matters, on Wednesday, May 29, 1946, made a statement in the House of Commons, in behalf of the Government, announcing a temporary short-term measure by passing Order-in-Council 2071, dated 28th of May, 1946, which provides for the admission to Canada of persons who fall into the following classifications. Here I quote the Minister's own words:

> "The father or mother, the unmarried son or daughter, eighteen years or over, the unmarried brother or sister, the orphan nephew or niece, under sixteen years of age, of any person legally admitted to, and resident in, Canada who is in a position to receive and care for such relative. The term 'orphan' means a child bereaved of both parents."

The Minister added also that a provision has been made by Order-in-Council P.C. 2070, dated May 28, 1946, "to permit of the acceptance of a travel document establishing the identity of the holder in the case of an immigrant who has been displaced from his country of origin as a result of the war and is not in possession of a valid passport."

I am sure that Canadians of Ukrainian origin received the Minister's announcement with deep satisfaction and much enthusiasm. Already I have received scores of letters and telegrams from Canadians of Ukrainian origin requesting assistance in bringing their relatives to Canada immediately. But I am afraid that the Press did not explain clearly enough an important reservation which the Minister made in the latter part of his statement. On reading Hansard carefully I note that he stated that (and I use the Minister's own words) "it undoubtedly will be the end of the present year before accommodation will be available for the ordinary traveler." This simply means that it will be another six or seven months from now before proper immigration machinery is set up and transportation is made available for relatives of Canadians who come under the Order-in-Council to which I referred.

In view of the Minister's announcement and in view of the fact that this is only a temporary measure, I would urge it upon this Congress and upon all branches of the Ukrainian Canadian Committee, throughout Canada, to write the Minister expressing appreciation to him and to the Government for the step already taken; at the same time to make a further plea to the Government to extend the provisions of the Order-in-Council, as soon as transportation facilities become available and as soon as proper machinery for handling immigration is set up for the admission to Canada of a generous number of Ukrainian displaced persons so that they may share with us the bounty of this land and enjoy the freedoms which are ours.

* * *

Herewith ended the afternoon session of the second day of the deliberations of the Congress, 6:15 p.m.

1947–48 BUDGET *and the* CANADIAN FARMER

House of Commons, 27 May 1947

Mr. ANTHONY HLYNKA (Vegreville): Mr. Speaker, on his first budget speech the Minister of Finance (Mr. Abbott) has been showered with bouquets from all sides of the house. The kind references to the minister are a good indication of the esteem in which he is held by members of all parties. These references may be taken as a recognition also of the minister's all-around ability. I too should like to join with those who have already congratulated the minister on the delivery of his first budget speech in the house. I should like to add, however, that along with their congratulations hon. members should have also expressed sympathy for the minister in his present position because, as he no doubt knows, he is now the chief target on the government side not only for members of this house but for the Canadian people generally. It is my view that if the minister does become the subject of bombardment from this side of the house it will not be as a result of any weakness on his part but because he has allowed himself to become the spokesman of the old debt-creating system which belongs to the sixteenth-century but persists in running Canada's financial policy in the twentieth century.

Whatever the outcome of my forecast may be, I would in all sincerity suggest to the minister that he request the leader of the house to place him on the front benches, as near to the Social Credit group as possible, so that it may be easier for us to get at him. The present seat which the minister occupies may be convenient for him as he appears to be well shielded, but that seat is definitely inconvenient for the opposition members. What I am saying bears out the contention of the Social Credit members that it does not matter how able or how popular a member may be before he is appointed a minister of finance; he is bound to fail because he is given an impossible task, that of operating a money system which cannot distribute to the Canadian people the goods and services which they require. So we sympathize with the Minister of Finance, but we sympathize even more with the Canadian people....

UKRAINIAN CHRISTMAS

Station CFRN, Toronto, 5 January 1948

In English:
Good evening ladies and gentlemen:
I am grateful to the owner and management of the Broadcasting Station CFRN for kindly consenting to my speaking in the Ukrainian language on this occasion. To many of my Ukrainian listeners tomorrow evening is Christmas Eve. I am sure that my friends of Anglo-Saxon stock will be glad to have me deliver this Christmas message in Ukrainian.

In Ukrainian:
Christ is born:
The whole Christian world observes Christmas once a year. On this day, in all parts of the world, hundreds of millions of people observe this great holiday. It is on this occasion that Christians wish each other a merry Christmas. It is on this occasion they wish each other all well.

But that is not the only reason why we observe Christmas. The chief purpose is to dedicate ourselves to the teachings of Christ and the principles of Christianity – to be practicing Christians for our own good, for the good of our families, for the good of our people, and to live a Christian life with other people and other nations.

However, when we look with sober eyes upon the present world, we see lack of fairness, lack of sincerity, lack of human kindness, and a lack of respect for Christian principles. More than ever before, we see today a lack of those spiritual virtues that raise human beings above ordinary beasts. Truly, perhaps the entire human history has never recorded a period comparable to the present one, when there is such a crying need to bring humanity back to Christianity – to practicing Christianity, and to arouse them to defend the Christian concepts of life.

We are all familiar with the history of the past eight or ten years. Millions of people died on the battlefields. They died because there were too many in the upper crusts who forgot, ignored, and even laughed at the very mention of Christian principles. Some of these leaders took it upon themselves to subordinate to their egotistical appetites and ambitions everything and everybody. They did not believe in God. They considered themselves supreme and in their quest for power and more power they trampled with their boots over millions of innocent people. They found sadistic pleasure in spilling human blood and in celebrating their triumphs over the defenceless and homeless people. In them and over them ruled Antichrist.

It was expected that after the armed conflict peace would come. But although the armed conflict is over, and some regard the past two and a half years as a period of peace, the fact remains that the fight for Christian principles is continuing. This conflict is not subsiding, but its flames are reaching farther and farther. For this reason Christmas this year should offer an opportunity to us to strengthen our belief in Christian principles, in the first place, within ourselves, and secondly, truly to become Christian soldiers on the moral front and to exert every effort in the task of saving the ignorant who are falling prey before the onslaught of Evil. In the past this task was left to those preaching the Gospel from the pulpits and to other church leaders, but we have arrived at a point when all Christians must stand shoulder-to-shoulder in defence of the highest moral values: namely, freedom of the individual, freedom of peoples and nations, and freedom of the Gospel of Christ.

Tomorrow evening, that is on the 6th of January, a large section of Canadians of Ukrainian origin will observe Christmas Eve. One section has already observed Christmas Eve on the 24th of December. But since this is my only opportunity to speak on this subject, my words tonight are meant for all Canadians of Ukrainian origin who are listening to this programme.

I know that during Christmas Canadians of Ukrainian origin in Alberta will not only observe Christmas in their traditional way and with their families together, but the thoughts of many Canadians of Ukrainian origin will be cast beyond the seas where their kin is found. I know, too, that many of those who have no close relatives in Europe will also feel a deep sympathy for the unfortunate people of their origin who have remained in the war-torn lands. For it could not have been the desire of the Creator that millions of Ukrainians should be slaves or wander from country to country as displaced persons. In a Christian world there should also be a place for Ukrainians where they could live out their lives. But at present Ukrainians cannot celebrate their Christmas as happily and amid such abundance as we have in Canada. This we must always keep in mind.

Yes, about 300,000 Ukrainians will be celebrating their third Christmas in displaced persons' camps in Germany, in Italy, and in Austria. We know that their Christmas could not be a happy one. They will not have the variety of twelve Ukrainian dishes on Christmas. Whole families will not sit at tables for there are no whole Ukrainian families in Europe. Those who will sit at the tables will just be skeletons of one time happy families. These people have lived so long under subsistence level and in shabby clothes that there is little hope left in them for a better future. These people will sit around small tables accommodated in old German or Italian garages, in old German or Italian stables, in old German or Italian military barracks. Small children will not get candy and oranges for Christmas. Their food will be plain, monotonous, and rationed. And what about the other Ukrainians who were not accepted in the D.P. camps? They will inevitably spend their Christmas in old German or Italian chicken-coops, beside a flickering light and with little or no heat in their hovels. Let us, then, compare our Christmas with theirs and is it not possible to share a little of our abundance with those who have none, so they would know that we thought of them on Christmas and that we really believe in Christian principles and are willing to help those who need the assistance the most.

We must never forget that it is only a matter of their misfortune that these people find themselves in Europe and not in Canada, and it is only our fortune that we are in Canada and have not remained in Europe and occupy the camps in which they find themselves. If the positions were reversed, what would be our wish? Would we not expect them to remember us?

It will be a year tomorrow that I spent my Christmas Eve in the Ukrainian displaced persons' camp at Regensburg, in the U.S. zone of Germany. I was a guest at a Christmas Eve dinner in this camp. There were about 150 in the dining hall. Camp directors, two priests, leaders of the camp, and I were seated at the head table. The people of the camp were saving food for weeks to make this a memorable occasion. When food was served I could not eat. I felt that I would be depriving the unhappy children of their share of food. Directly opposite our table there were seated Ukrainian orphans who did not have a relative in the whole world. Their parents were killed by those who had no use for Christianity. The children were watching me quietly and listened to speeches to determine who I was, and whether I would arrange for their admission to Canada.

After dinner, more than three thousand DPs lined up along the corridors to wish me a merry Christmas, and hundreds came to me and asked me to bring their wishes to their relatives in Canada and the U.S.A.

I can never forget that Christmas Eve. From my visits of the camps I brought with me several mental pictures which I will never forget. I will never forget thousands of Ukrainians in whose eyes and faces I saw pleadings to help them. I will never forget their workshops which were the pride not only of the DPs, but also of the camp directors. I will never forget a number of horses that DPs brought with them from their former homes. They held such great affection for these animals! And I will never, never forget the church symbols which I saw in their camp churches with the inscription "O God, Listen to Our Prayers." Yes, that prayer is dear not only to the DPs, but also to the whole Ukrainian people.

On the occasion of Christmas it is also customary to wish people a happy and prosperous New Year, which follows Christmas a few days later. But many are wondering if the dark clouds have disappeared which hung over the world during the war. Canadians and Canadians of Ukrainian origin should at this time make certain important resolutions for the New Year. Among others, we should resolve to consolidate the world by beginning to work on ourselves and place greater emphasis on the moral values of life. As always, it will be to the advantage of Canadians of Ukrainian origin to stand on guard for Canada not only in the physical sense, but to stand on guard for

Canada also in the moral sense, on the moral front, so as not to allow the negative elements to weaken Canada from within.

Canadians of Ukrainian origin who believe in Christian principles had reason in the past to be proud of their record as citizens of Canada. They had reason to pride themselves in the way in which they discharged their duties as citizens. But Canadians of Ukrainian origin had not been too forward in taking advantage of their privileges. One of the New Year's resolutions should be, therefore, to place more emphasis on asking for the privileges which are rightly theirs. As an example: Why not request the Canadian government to admit a number of Ukrainian orphans to Canada? To help these children is not only a humanitarian, but also a Christian duty of the Canadian government. I believe that Canadians of Ukrainian origin have earned over the past half-a-century a fair consideration of such requests. We must remember that it is in the interest of a democratic form of government for people to avail themselves of the opportunities and to take advantage of their privileges. For if some people do not take advantage of their privileges, someone else will and such a state is not healthy to a democracy. For in a democracy equal treatment of all is one of the principles.

I now wish to extend best wishes to my constituents and also to all others who are listening to this message, and I wish all of you to spend your Christmas in a truly Christian spirit and I wish everyone a prosperous New Year.

This is Anthony Hlynka saying: Christ is born.

DISPLACED PERSONS and REFUGEES

House of Commons, 31 May 1948

MR. ANTHONY HLYNKA (Vegreville): ...This is the seventh time in the last three years that I have risen to discuss the problem of displaced persons and refugees. I do so, knowing that displaced persons, in their present position, cannot speak for themselves. In one month from now the present session will likely be concluded and up to this time in this session but few references have been made to this tragic and extremely important problem. I desire, therefore, to take this opportunity to review in a sort of documentary way the displaced persons problem under the heading, "What have the democratic nations done to solve the displaced persons problem?"

First I wish to deal with repatriation. From the D-day landing in Normandy in May, 1944 to the present time the policy of the West has been the repatriation of displaced persons to their places of origin. That was the policy of UNRRA and it is now the policy of the preparatory commission of the IRO.

* * *

Four methods have been used to carry out the repatriation programs of UNRRA and IRO. The first method was that of forced repatriation. For more than a year following the end of the war in Europe, repatriation was carried out by every means, including the use of force. Persons who were born citizens and actually present within the boundaries of the territories held by Soviet Russia on September 1, 1939 were forcibly repatriated in accordance with the terms of the ill-omened Yalta agreement to which the United States and the U.S.S.R. were signatories. Many persons who came from territories which, following World War II, were annexed to the U.S.S.R. were also forcibly repatriated. This is what *Life* magazine had to say on this matter in its editorial in the issue of September 29, 1947:

The first thing that happened to them in the hectic hours after V-E day was that, where-ever they found themselves, outside the Soviet zones, masses of them were herded by British and American troops back over into the Russian side of the line ... several millions of people who had been pulled out of Russia and Russian occupied territory and who now didn't want to go back went back whether they wanted to or not. And quite a few went back tied up in ropes, delivered like African slaves in the black-birding days.... The more loath a non-returner is to return, the more eager the Soviet Union is for his return. You can guess why. Let loose in the capitalist world, he would not serve as a very good propagandist for communism. In short, these people are "not displaced persons." They are, in the simplest terms, political refugees. They are refugees from communism.... If the American people and their representatives were agents of the Kremlin, they could have scarcely done more to deliver these refugees to the assassin and slave master.

After a year of this bloody business, which is so vividly described in the editorial just quoted, the west discovered that most displaced persons would rather commit suicide than return to their places of origin. Many actually committed suicide; but finally the horrible tragedy stirred the conscience of true Christians in the United Kingdom, the United States, Canada, France and above all in the Vatican, and as a result appeals were made to the British and United States governments to terminate the policy of forced repatriation. Consequently, forced repatration was largely discontinued, except for three classes of persons, namely only those persons who were both citizens of and actually domiciled within the territories held by Soviet Russia on September 1, 1939: that is, (1) those who were captured in German uniforms; (2) those who were members of the armed forces on or about June 22, 1941, and were not subsequently discharged therefrom; (3) those who, on the basis of responsible evidence, have been found to be collaborators with the enemy, having voluntarily rendered aid and comfort to the enemy.

Although the terms to which I have just referred lend themselves to various interpretations, nevertheless the amended directives were an improvement over the previous vicious terms to which the West agreed at Yalta on February 11, 1945.

The second method which was used in repatriating a large number of defenceless and unfortunate DPs was a practice privately arranged between the U.S.S.R. repatriation officers and some camp and area directors. Under this scheme the director would be conveniently absent from the camp when the Soviet repatriation teams called. With the use of firearms the Soviet officers would round up a number of DPs and load them on trucks, and that would be the last anyone would see or hear of them. This kidnapping method of repatriation was employed until about a year and a half ago.

The third method followed in the matter of repatriation is still being used to this very day. Under this scheme the Soviet repatriation personnel are granted permission to carry on in camps what is called an "educational campaign." This is done by means of the distribution of literature depicting the "happy life" under communism. The moving-picture technique is also being used. Following the showing of a movie, or an educational program, appeals are made to DPs by Soviet officers to return to their places of origin. In the past, Soviet repatriation officers have been assisted in this work by UNRRA officials, while at the present time the IRO personnel are under obligation to render such assistance. However, this system of repatriation brought disappointing results, and for that reason still another system was initiated two years ago and is still being used.

The fourth system is called "voluntary repatriation by incentive." The nations of the West adopted this system as a face-saving scheme. However, in the net result this operation is very much similar to forced repatriation. Under this method of repatriation, food rations are reduced considerably below the number of calories required by a normal person. The second step of this softening-up process as used in certain areas is the transfer of DPs from camp to camp several times during the year. Orders are issued to move the occupants from one camp to another, in order to break their morale. Following such food reductions and camp movements, extra rations of food and better clothing are offered those who volunteer to be repatriated.

* * *

The reason I have emphasized this particular point is that there is a moral principle involved and to show also to what lengths the nations of the West have gone in appeasing the evil totalitarian regimes even at the cost of suffering, and life itself, on the part of the defenceless DPs. To me, that has only one meaning: namely, a new form of slave trade in the twentieth century. It is obvious that such anti-Christian treatment of people does not belong to the western world, nor can such treatment be reconciled with our concept of civilization. The use of bread as a bait in forcing starving, broken-down, unfortunate and defenceless Christians into the clutches of tyrannical and atheistic regimes will remain a hideous blot on the conscience of the West for generations to come. It is barbarism, regardless in what clothes of respectability it may be garbed.

The second phase of the DP problem with which I propose to deal has to do with the care and maintenance of displaced persons. It has been the responsibility of UNRRA and now it is the responsibility of the preparatory commission of IRO to provide displaced persons with living accommodation, food, clothing, hospital and medical care.

* * *

I have already stated that both UNRRA and the preparatory commission of IRO deserve credit for much of what they have done. In this connection I should like to pay a sincere tribute to a large number of conscientious men and women who served with UNRRA, and I should like to pay an equally sincere tribute to the conscientious workers who are now serving with the preparatory commission of IRO. During my tour of displaced persons' camps a year ago, I personally met many of them. Of the majority of UNRRA and IRO personnel, I will say that they are persons who have devoted themselves to a humanitarian and Christian task. But I must also make reference to a small number of former UNRRA personnel, and the same would apply to IRO personnel, occupying strategic positions, who looked for their directions to Moscow and not London or Washington. It was on account of the infiltration of these persons into the service of UNRRA at all levels that UNRRA fell into disrepute and finally had to be absorbed by the preparatory commission of IRO. It is regrettable that a small number of Soviet sympathizers succeeded in changing the UNRRA into a repatriation organization and also into a Soviet propaganda agency.

Many directives which originated in UNRRA offices have been of the most vicious type. Under these directives, the people in the camps were screened and re-screened. They were moved from camp to camp. Camp publications were suspended. Newspapers published in the democratic countries of the west, in the languages in which DPs could read, were not allowed in the camps. Anyone failing to produce sufficient identification cards was refused acceptance into the camp. This further reduced the ration of camp occupants, because they had to share their food with those living outside of camps. The facts are that a large number of genuine DPs have not received and are not at present receiving any assistance. This assistance was refused to them, while they would have been entitled to it under a more humane set-up.

Before leaving this point I should like to put on record a decision which was made by the preparatory commission conference of IRO and which appeared in a statement issued to the press on October 15, 1947. Included in the list of classes of persons to whom IRO is forbidden to give any assistance is found the following clause:

> Persons who, since the end of hostilities, have become leaders of movements hostile to the governments of their country of origin.

May I ask: To which governments have the leaders of displaced persons been hostile? Obviously to the communist governments in the totalitarian countries. It follows therefore, in fact, that this IRO resolution prohibits displaced persons from opposing communist regimes. I leave that statement to hon. members to ponder over.

I now come to the third phase of my discussion: namely, the one on emigration. Millions of people having been repatriated and some thousands having been settled in the various countries of the world, in January, 1948, there still remained in the camps, supervised by the preparatory commission of IRO, 626,200 DPs. An additional 79,200 receive care and maintenance from sources other than the preparatory commission of IRO. A further 846,500 DPs of various classifications do not receive care or maintenance from any organization. The net total of all DPs is, therefore, 1,551,900. Of the last group mentioned, only a portion will qualify for emigration. For practical purposes a figure of 750,000 is the immediate concern of the countries that signed the IRO charter.

* * *

Keeping these people in the camps is costly, in spite of the fact that many of them live on a below-subsistence level, and to continue keeping them in the camps will not solve the displaced persons problem. The obvious thing to do is to resettle them in various countries that will accept them. The task of resettling this remaining number of DP's was commenced about a year and a half ago by the intergovernmental committee on refugees. The work of IGCR has, however, been taken over by the preparatory commission of IRO, together with the responsibilities which were formerly carried by UNRRA: namely, those in connection with the caring for the DPs.

The preparatory commission of IRO has in the past few months made a beginning in what may be considered an ultimate solution of the problem. It is a source of satisfaction to know that in the course of the past year or so a number of DPs have emigrated to the United Kingdom, Belgium, Holland, France, Canada, the United States of America, Australia, South Africa, Switzerland, Guatemala, Argentina, Brazil, Bolivia, Chile, Columbia, Ecuador, Paraguay, Peru and Venezuela. The last nine countries mentioned have agreed to admit refugees and immigrants in considerable numbers, under mass settlement agreements, or as individual migrants. The United Kingdom, although in a weak economic position, is leading all countries in accepting the DPs. The South American countries have made offers to accept large numbers of DPs, but climate and settlement conditions in some of these countries are not entirely suitable. In a press report from Lake Success, of May 12, this is what appeared in the newspapers of May 13, 1948:

> Guatemala offered to accept 50,000 European refugees, but on closer inspection the offer looked more like the harsh indenture contract.... For five years DPs accepting the Guatemalan government's

offer would have to work in clearing and farming the remote Ixican valley at a wage of 16 cents a day. There would be guards to see they did not escape to commercial centres.

Thus far the United States of America made no special provision for admitting DPs. It has, however, admitted a number of DPs under the existing United States regulations, under a quota system. I notice in the press that the United States is now considering legislation which, if adopted, would provide for the acceptance of a substantial number of DPs over and above the quotas provided for under the immigration act.

Canada has made a beginning in accepting DP settlers. According to the statement included in the proceedings of the committee on immigration and labour of April 28, 1948, out of a total of 16,010 DPs who arrived in Canada up to April 26, 1948, 10,336 were workers brought over by various industrial firms through the Department of Labour. Of the remaining number, 5,168 were relatives of Canadians. I need hardly comment on the number admitted, except to say that it is also in Canada's interest to help in the solution of the displaced persons problem. At least one of the many considerations is that it is in the interest of the West to remove the DPs from Germany and Austria as early as possible and before the peace treaties are signed.

* * *

In spite of the fact, however, that a certain number of DPs have been accepted by various countries, the problem of displaced persons has merely been touched.

* * *

Mr. Speaker, in order that Canada do her share in the solution of this problem, I wish to submit to the house and the government the following ten points for sympathetic consideration:

1. In view of the fact that the majority of those already admitted have been brought to work in the mines, forests, and factories, I suggest that a land settlement scheme be worked out with the provinces and that a generous number of displaced persons be admitted to settle on the land. I have in mind that Canadian-born young people are

not likely to go into new settlements to start from scratch for, as we know, many of our young people are moving into the cities, and as our manufacturing industry expands they are being absorbed by the industries. In view of this fact, we would be advised to admit a generous number of displaced persons families, and other immigrants, to open up and develop the unsettled areas, particularly in the four western provinces. The statement is often made by those who are prejudiced against immigration or by those who do not know better that there is no arable land left for new settlements, and therefore the possibilities of further land settlements are discounted. I have here a table based on a study giving the figures of land settlement possibilities in Canada. This study gives the number of farm units, each capable of supporting an average family-unit of five persons. The farm units may be anywhere from a few acres to as many as 200 acres, depending on the type of soil and other conditions.

* * *

On the basis of these figures, an average family of five persons may make a comfortable living on each farm unit. Multiplying the farm units by five will give us the number of persons that can be supported in the proposed settlements. According to these figures, therefore, Manitoba can settle an additional 29,680 persons; Saskatchewan an additional 105,120; Alberta an additional 363,155; and British Columbia an additional 233,780; or a total of 731,735 persons in the four western provinces. So much for land settlement possibilities.

2. Relax excessive health standards which were presumably set for the pre-war period and which do not take into account the human consideration that should enter into our dealing with these stateless people who are the victims of war and communism. The only life they have known in the past nine years was six years in the actual theatre of war and now three years in the camps. Official preparatory commission IRO figures show that in the British zone of Germany hospitalization of camp population is 2.8 percent; in the United States zone of Germany the population of hospitalized cases is 2.25 percent; in the French zone of Germany the population of hospitalized displaced persons is 2.4 percent. These percentages are in excess of the

normal rate, which is generally considered to be two percent. But there are many reasons for this higher than normal percentage:

(a) Lack of facilities for the sick in the camps;
(b) Not sufficient fuel in sick bays;
(c) Under-nourishment and lack of varieties of food;
(d) Lack of fresh air due to over-crowding;
(e) Many camp occupants spend a number of years in German and Soviet concentration camps;
(f) Psychological factor of hopelessness as to the future.

At any rate, the rejections by selection immigration missions, which are from twenty to fifty-six percent, are excessive, if the element of humanity enters into the picture at all. Under a much less exacting health combination than that of any other country, of the 30,500 DPs that the United Kingdom accepted to November 30, 1947, only ninety refugees were returned to the camps.

Rejections on the following grounds should be reconsidered:

(a) DPs who are slightly underweight are not accepted, even though under the existing conditions it is impossible for them to gain in weight, but a few weeks in a new country and some additional food would solve the problem for the underweight;
(b) A person minus a finger or two is now rejected;
(c) A person with a natural mole on the body is rejected;
(d) Persons fifty years and over are not readily accepted, although of the total D.P. population in the camps only 12.9 percent are over forty-five years of age;
(e) Endemic goitre which is due to local conditions of the water in certain countries, such as Austria and southern Germany, causes rejection, although the fitness of the person is not affected by it, and this condition could easily be remedied, especially upon removal from the region;
(f) Mild cases of heart ailments without decompensation, and otherwise fit in every way, have been rejected;
(g) Persons with healed minimal tubercular lesions which have

been healed for some years are condemned as unfit, those who cannot produce a five-year test of cure. This test for cure is normally impossible for DPs to furnish.

The exacting health requirements break up families or discourage them from accepting emigration. Consideration should therefore be given to the relaxation of health standards for persons who are members of a family unit in order that the stronger members of the family may assist a weaker member and the skill of one member balance a lack of skill in others.

3. Extend the regulations to include not only immediate relatives, but also cousins, nephews, nieces, uncles and aunts.

4. Give sympathetic consideration to applications made by Canadians who are in a position to guarantee employment and support to DPs regardless of profession, occupation, or age.

5. Accept a number of people of cultured talents and professions. Among the DPs there are many top-ranking artists.

6. Make provision for the acceptance of a number of specialists in the various fields. The British government has already accepted a number of such specialists and has granted to them the right to practice their professions, provided that they can produce evidence that they are qualified.

7. I would suggest that the government should accept a number of intellectuals who have lived under communism for twenty-five years but escaped, in order that they may tell Canadians the truth about communism. Why the government has not done this up to this time I cannot understand.

8. Arrangements should be made by the immigration missions to process entire families at the same time as the breadwinner. At present, in some instances, examination of all members of the same family is not made at the same time, and the result is that the family unit is broken up or the examined members of the family refuse to leave.

9. Make provision for allowing a certain number of orphan DP children. Representations have been made to the department to allow a number of DP children to enter Canada; but, for instance, not a single Ukrainian child has been allowed to enter Canada up to

this time. Many well-to-do persons are anxious to adopt DP orphans. If organizations or private citizens desire to accept the guarantee for these children, why not improve their lot, or are we still thinking that by repatriating them we may gain the good will of the communist regimes?

10. My last point has to do with the matter of correct information with respect to procedures and certain decisions in connection with immigration matters. For instance, the preparatory commission of IRO issued a statement on January 5, 1948, regarding transportation grants to group movement of immigrants and also individual immigrants. The people, however, do not know about this decision, and yet it is extremely important to those who cannot afford to pay transportation costs for their relatives.

* * *

Finally, I wish to conclude with a short quotation from *Life* magazine on the point, political asylum to stateless persons:

> We used to have in this country, and in those of our real allies, a great tradition of political asylum. The communist Trotsky, for one, was very happy to flee to New York from czarist Russia. But get this for a switch: Nowadays the Soviet Union recognizes no right of asylum – its own escapees being branded as traitors and eligible for death – except to those "friends of the working class" who may have to scuttle back to the U.S.S.R. from abroad.... Ever since we have had a government, we have, like all the rest of the world's free lands, offered a haven for oppressed or political fugitives. Has our national memory lapsed? If we took in all the present European crop, Jews and non-Jews, it would increase our population by less than one per cent. And who knows by what amount it would increase our democratic beacon light in an ever-darkening world?
>
> Can any nation say it was not enriched by those to whom it afforded hospitality? Can any say it was not impoverished by those who fled?
>
> We have the example to set in providing asylum for some part of these million fugitives from communism. Literally and piously,

for God's sake let us get these people out of their cages. And let us bring in those who wish to come to us.

I hope and pray, Mr. Speaker, that Canada will also establish the principle of providing asylum to those needing it who believe in democracy and God....

CANADA

Station CFRN, Toronto, 28 September 1948

In this opening program I consider it proper to say something about Canada.

To Canadians, the word "Canada" should mean much more than a large part of the North American continent, inhabited by 13 million people. It should mean even more than all Canada's physical wealth in the form of almost unlimited natural resources, such as our vast grainfields, our mines, our lakes, our forests, and Canada's superb scenic beauty. When we speak of Canada, we also mean far more than the productive capacity of the Canadian people. Canada means even more than an overall high standard of living compared to that of almost any other country in the world. All these things are important, but they are but a portion of Canada's wealth which offers unlimited opportunities to Canadians and which is also of inestimable value to the world. Truly, the meaning of the word "Canada" challenges the imagination at description.

Complementary to her physical wealth, there is also a moral and spiritual side to Canada: Canada is a nation! Canada is a free nation. Canada is a democratic nation. And above all – Canada is a Christian nation.

In order that Canada may remain free and democratic, our citizens must become conscious of the meaning expressed in the words: "Eternal vigilance is the price of freedom."

In order that Canada may remain Christian, the recent inroads of materialistic thinking must be forced back into their own sphere and Christian morality must reclaim the minds, the hearts, and the spirit of Canadians.

In spite of the fact, that Canada is still a very young nation, she is fast developing a distinctive national spirit, a distinctive national consciousness, a distinctive national culture and traditions, and she is becoming conscious of her own national pride. It should be obvious to all that more and more effort should be exerted in further strengthening and developing these essential characteristics of Canada.

However, Canada is also a member of the British Commonwealth of Nations. The British Commonwealth is an association of free sovereign nations. It is the greatest and the most effective democratic organization the world has ever known. The underlying principle of the British Commonwealth is freedom and mutual advantage. Canada's membership in this organization entitles Canadians to the benefits which have accrued to the British people over centuries of progress. Canada should prize her position within the great Commonwealth, and thus she will continue to enjoy the common benefits.

Then, too, it is from the British people that Canada inherited her form of government, her basic laws, and her institutions. These are indeed a priceless heritage!

For our population, traditions, and culture, Canada has drawn chiefly upon two European peoples, the British and the French, but notable contributions have also been made and continued to be made by many other Canadians of various stocks, such as those of Ukrainian origin who made this program possible.

I know that most Canadians sincerely appreciate the cultural and other contributions which are being made by peoples who came from the far lands. A good number of outstanding Canadians who made a study of the cultural wealth of the various racial groups insist that not only should these ethnic groups be allowed to retain their cultures and traditions, but that they should be encouraged to retain what is best in the cultures and traditions of their former homelands. Indeed, Canada has much to gain from such rich cultural contributions, and this without much effort or monetary cost on the part of the Canadian people. Those who guide the building of a still greater Canada recognize this fact more and more....

THE PRESENT POSITION *of* AGRICULTURE *and* ITS OUTLOOK *for the* FUTURE

House of Commons, 7 March 1949

...I wish to turn now to another subject for a few moments. I want to deal with the government's taxation policy as it is applied to farmers in western Canada. May I say at the outset that the government's handling of farm income taxation is the worst bungle imaginable. Not only does the taxation department lack any clear-cut, well defined income taxation policy, but the handling of assessments is so muddled and confused that something must be done about it without delay.

In the first place, in order not to lose votes in 1940, the government did not tell the farmers that they were expected to file income tax returns from 1941 on. Nor were the farmers told that they should have kept account books showing their expenses and their income. At that time the majority of farmers were in debt, and not even a thought entered their minds that the government might some day send out assessors and ask for a detailed accounting.

Five years passed, and again the government did not say a word. The election of 1945 took place, and there was still not a word by the government about the filing of income tax returns. Immediately after the 1945 election, however, the government sent out a crew of assessors to check on the farmers. As if from the blue sky, farmers were told that they should have kept account books, and that they should have filed income tax returns. In view of the fact that the farmers did not keep any record of their incomes and their expenses, the government proceeded to assess the farmers on what is called the "net worth" system. Under this system the farmer is forced to accept the arbitrary assessment of the assessor. Further, the farmer is considered guilty of failing to file his returns, and he pays a penalty for each year plus interest up to the date on which the penalty is paid. In addition to that, if the assessor decides that the farmer should have paid, let us say, $100 as income tax for 1941, the farmer must also pay interest on that amount from 1941 until the date when the indebtedness is paid in full. The farmer pays similar penalties and interest for every year for which he is found to owe money.

The farmer can argue and protest, but the assessor's estimate of the cost of farm produce consumed by the farmer is also arbitrarily fixed. Then, too, if the farmer could not sell his 1942 wheat crop, let us say, because of quotas at that time, and he sold it in 1944, he is taxed on both crops in 1944 unless he can prove that he did not voluntarily carry over his 1942 crop, but sold it at the first opportunity. These are only a few of the injustices imposed upon the farmers of the prairie provinces. In northern Alberta the farmers are simply terrorized by the taxing authorities.

I should now like to put on the record a sample of what the taxing authorities of this government are doing in Alberta. Here it is:

> Department of National Revenue
> Taxation Division
> Tower Building, Edmonton
> December 1, 1948.
>
> Dear Sir:
>
> Your letter dated November 27, 1948, is acknowledged. You will recall that on the 18th of March, 1948, you called in person at our office regarding your income tax returns which were filed at this office. At that time explanations were submitted by you to the effect that as the net income earned from your position as agent for the Imperial Oil Limited was not sufficient for your personal living expenses, it was necessary for you to supplement this income with income earned from card playing. As this form of income is considered taxable $1,500 was added to other income for the years 1945 and 1946. If there is any further information required please do not hesitate to get in touch with us and we shall endeavour to explain everything to your satisfaction.
>
> Yours faithfully,
> H.E. Boulay,
> For Director of Income Tax.

May I point out that this young man – I did not put his name on the record for obvious reasons – served in the army during the recent war. What is more, he gave me his word that he never plays cards. The young man explained that the income tax official in this case got away from the serious subject and asked what the people did out in the country for past-time during evenings. The young man replied that there were many things they could do. The income tax official suggested cards. The young man agreed that some people did entertain themselves by playing cards. The conversation ended there, but in a few days the young man received the letter I just read. This sort of thing, Mr. Speaker, is scandalous and outrageous.

To complete the case I want to say that, following receipt of the letter which I quoted, the young man called at the income tax office again and explained that a mistake must have been made in regard to his assessment, as he never played cards. He was told then that if he was not satisfied he could appeal to Ottawa. Two or three weeks later he received this short letter:

> Department of National Revenue
> Taxation Division
> Tower Building, Edmonton
> February 18, 1949
> Final Notice
> Re: 1945–46 income tax arrears, $631.26
>
> Dear Sir:
>
> As payment has not been received on the above mentioned tax, it is the intention of the department to institute legal proceedings unless the amount is paid within ten days of receipt of this letter.
>
> This may be through the exchequer court or by way of garnishee to your employer.
>
> Yours faithfully,
> H. A. MacDonald,
> For Director of Income Tax

And the letter was registered. I need only add, Mr. Speaker, that under the law the padding of accounts by any person is a criminal offence. I say, the same law should apply to the padding of assessment accounts by income tax officials.

EMPIRE DAY

Station CFRN, Toronto, 24 May 1949

In the modern sense, the Empire Day or Victoria Day may also be called the British Commonwealth of Nations Day. But whatever its name, to 500 million people living within the Commonwealth, the 24th day of May represents more than a historical tradition.

For many generations the British Commonwealth of Nations has led the world in the extent of its territory, in population, and in world influence. However, the real greatness of the Commonwealth lies in the moral field. The most significant feature of the Commonwealth is the fact that its organization is based on the principle of free association of peoples and nations in many parts of the world. Each and every member-nation enjoys equal rights and equal privileges within the Commonwealth. Each and every member-nation recognizes the Crown as the symbol of unity of the Commonwealth. And all the member-nations of the Commonwealth have a common purpose and a common understanding of the democratic principles. There is no other political organization in the world today, nor has there ever been one, which could in any way be compared to that of the British Commonwealth.

Perhaps never in our history had we more reason for rejoicing than we have this very day. There are two main reasons for this. First, the British Commonwealth of Nations (and that includes Canada) has successfully weathered the recent war without losing any of its freedoms. Second, in spite of the dark forces of evil which aim at the destruction of the Commonwealth, it has withstood the severe tests and remains united. For this, we owe a prayerful thanks to the Almighty for His guidance and care.

The most recent test which the British Commonwealth of Nations faced took place at the Commonwealth Conference held in London, England in the latter part of April this year. The conference was attended by prime ministers of all the member-nations of the Commonwealth. It was an extremely important conference, as the main subject of discussion was the revision of the political basis which would be acceptable to all the members of the Commonwealth and to the Republic of India. There was the danger that if India withdrew from the Commonwealth, Pakistan and Ceylon would probably have done so also, and South Africa might have gone, too. Those who follow the present world situation may well imagine what would have been the result. It was in the face of this danger that millions of the commonwealth people were breathlessly awaiting the outcome of the conference.

Then, on Wednesday, April 27th, the governments of the Commonwealth countries received the message that the government of India has agreed to continue her membership in the Commonwealth and that she accepted His Majesty the King as the symbol of free association of its independent member nations and as such the head of the Commonwealth. Consequently, all the members of the British Commonwealth remain united to freely continue cooperating in the pursuit of peace, liberty, and progress.

When this message was read in the Canadian Parliament, the Commons' members rose instantly to their feet and sang "God Save the King" as I have never heard them sing it before. On this occasion, in the hearts of the members of that assembly the anthem struck deeper chords than it does under ordinary circumstances. The mood of the House revealed that the members realized the full meaning of the British Commonwealth unity. I am certain that in all the far-flung corners of the British Commonwealth, millions of people of many races and many creeds received the same message in a similar mood and with similar understanding.

At this point I should like to make a particular reference to Canadians of various racial origins. I have often stated that the diversity in the composition of Canada's population may be a source of strength rather than a source of weakness if used wisely. Let me but mention on behalf of Canadians of Ukrainian origin the pride they share in the fact that the unity of the Commonwealth remains unbroken and strong. The program to which you are listening now is an attempt on the part of Canadians of Ukrainian origin at an expression of Empire Day rejoicing.

Canadians of Ukrainian origin feel that they owe a debt of gratitude to the Empire and to Canada. In the past half century or more, the Canadian people accepted many settlers from many lands. They offered them a home and a country. The Canadian people accepted these settlers into their communities. They accepted them as citizens, with equal rights and equal duties. In short, all of us have become one family called the Canadian Nation. And today I am certain that there are no regrets on either side.

Again, following the recent war, it was chiefly the countries of the Commonwealth that came to the rescue of the unfortunate, the homeless, and the stateless people of Europe. The Commonwealth countries played a prominent part in the setting up and in the financing of various relief organizations. And in the past three or four years, the Commonwealth countries accepted a fair number of displaced persons and refugees. In the last four years the United Kingdom is by her generosity again leading the world in accepting the largest number of stateless people, and that in spite of the overcrowded conditions of the island and the shortage of food. Canada and Australia have also made a good start on that direction. And it is in appreciation of the generous and humanitarian attitude of the Canadian and Empire people that this program is being given tonight. My information is that a good portion of this program is being contributed by the newly arrived Ukrainian displaced persons. On their behalf, I wish to express thanks to the Canadian people and to all those who made their coming to Canada possible.

Yes, the British Commonwealth of Nations is the most effective international organization the world has ever known. It is in the Commonwealth countries that freedom of speech, freedom of worship, freedom from fear, and freedom of choice are practised. It is in the Commonwealth countries that a true political democracy is practised. It is in the British Commonwealth countries that the Christian principles are observed. In order that all these freedoms may be preserved and extended, it is in our interest that the bond of unity among the British Commonwealth nations should be strengthened more than ever before.

It is proper and fitting, therefore, that on the 24th day of May, the people of the Commonwealth countries should rededicate themselves to the lofty principles upon which the British Commonwealth stands.

HLYNKA in HANSARD

The following list, taken from Hansard, shows the extent of Hlynka's participation in the House of Commons.

Nineteenth Parliament, First Session, 1940
    Advertising, large-scale, taxation 1305
    Budget, 1305–07
    House rentals in war time, qu., 2401
    Unemployment relief bill, 518, 987–89
    United Farmers of Alberta, res. On additional payment for 1939 crop, 518

Nineteenth Parliament, Second Session, 1940–42
    Address in reply, 378–82
    Annie Rubelietz, petitions for commutation of death sentence, 15
    Budget, 2679–85
    Bureau of information, translations of articles, 380–81
    Census enumerators, 3898–99
    Defence of Canada regulations, M. (Mr. Mackenzie King) for committee, 1213
    Farmers, suggested assistance for, 2684–85
    Military training, position of only son required by parents for spring work, 1571
    Naturalization of relief recipients, 3908
    Racial barriers, attempts to build in Canada, 379–80
    Racial origin of officers and men enlisted for active service, qu., 454
    Trade and Commerce estimates, 3898–99
    Ukrainian organizations, reference of Mrs. Nielsen, 1213

Nineteenth Parliament, Third Session, 1942
    Address in reply, 229–35
    Budget, 3896–3900
    Canadian Wheat Board bill, 1331–36

Dominion Loans, financing, 845

Foreign relations policy, 230–32

National sovereignty, Atlantic charter, 231

Tire rationing, clergymen, qu., 1315

Ukrainian independent state, 231–35

Nineteenth Parliament, Fourth Session, 1943–1944

Address in reply, 520–22

British Commonwealth of Nations, 521

Budget, 1559–63

Dictatorial bureaucracy, 837

Farm debt in western provinces, 836–37

Farm labour, shortage of, 1563

    M. (Mr. Pouliot), 3295–96

Farmers' Creditors Arrangement bill, 5059–61

Farmers, eight freedoms for, 1560

Live stock, grading, 1562

Man power

    Regulations and farm labour, 1655–56

    Shortage, M. (Mr. Pouliot) 3295–96

Marketing of western grain crop, 1654–56

Mortgage companies, tenancy in land passing to, 1561

Naturalization requirements, 5343–44

Naval services estimates, 3434–35

Old age pensions, 837, 996–97

Post-war reconstruction, 522

    Appointment of committee, 834–38

Royal Canadian Navy, 3434–35

Social security, M. for appointment of committee, 995–99

Soldiers, foreclosure of lands, 1563

War appropriation bill, 3434–35

Western grain crop, marketing, 1654–56

Nineteenth Parliament, Fifth Session, 1944
    Address in reply, 282–86
    Agriculture estimates, 3128–29, 3189–90
    Bank Act Amendment bill, 2810–12
    Censorship regulations, 2865–66
    Civil aviation, 2194–97
    Committee on cooperation in Canadian citizenship, 2395–2423
    Defence of Canada Regulations committee, M. (Mr. St. Laurent), 631
    Farm improvement loans bill, 3674–75
    Farm labour, postponements, 2534–35
    Farm ownership and mortgages, 284–85
    Foreign languages, banning from air, 2873
    Kirkconnell, Professor Watson, work of, 2416–23
    Loan of $1,000,000,000 bill, 1673
    Man power situation, 2534–35
    National selective service, 2534–35
    National war service estimates, 2399–2423, 2865–73
    Old age pensions, 3523–27
    Packing industry, price spreads, 3189–90
    Post-war reconstruction, 282–83
    War appropriation bill, 2194–97, 2399–2423, 2534–35, 2865–73, 3128–29, 3189–90, 3523–27

Twentieth Parliament, First Session, 1945
    Address in reply, 384–87
    Bretton Woods agreements bill, 3112–15, 3122–23
    Emergency powers bill, 2928–31
    Housing bill, 1498–99
    Immigration, 3528–30
    Income war tax bill, 2751–52
    International monetary fund, 3112–15, 3122–23
    National housing bill, 1498–99
    Post office estimates, 2817
    Ukrainians, repatriation of, 3717–18

War expenditures bill, 1743

Twentieth Parliament, Second Session, 1946
    Address in reply, 224–31
    Bread rationing in Britain, 3578–79
    British food mission, failure of, 3577–78
    Budget, 3575–80
    Canadian citizenship bill, 589–91, 1141–42, 1200–08, 1591
    Canadian Soviet Friendship League, meetings in research council building, return ordered, 4639
    Cooperative taxation, 4063–65
    Displaced persons in Europe, 224–31
    Farm implements, prices, M. (Mr. Bracken) 883–84
    Farmers, income tax, 3576–78
    Income war tax bill, 4063–64
    Pension Act Amendment, 4161
    Ukrainians, problem of, 225–31
    Wheat agreement with Britain, 3578–80

Twentieth Parliament, Third Session, 1947
    Address in reply, 1229
    Budget, 3474–78
    Diplomatic service, 5102–05
    Displaced persons brought by industrialists, M. (Mr. Coldwell), 3679–82
    External affairs estimates, 5102–05
    Farmers, delegations to government, with fourteen recommendations, 3475–77
    Foreign policy, 1502–05
    Freight rates, Social Credit stand on, 1229
    Immigration of, displaced persons, 2735–39, 3679–82, 5431–35, 5444–49
    Income tax, comparison of payments in Canada and United States, 3477
    International organizations and global philosophy, 3853–54
    LaGuardia, former Mayor, reference to, 5434, 5447–49, 5492–93
    Mines and resources estimates, 5431–35, 5444–49, 5492–93
    National defence estimates, 5295–96

Old age pensions bill, 4594–4600

Polish girls, brought in by Mr. Dionne (Beauce) for spinning mills, 3679–82

Prairie farm assistance bill, 3822–54

Ukrainians

    Admission of to Canada, 5432–35, 5444–49

    Displaced camps in, forcible deportation to Russia, 5444

Visiting forces bill, 3851–54

World youth festival, Prague, Canadian delegation, 5434–35, 5444

Twentieth Parliament, Fourth Session, 1947–8

Agriculture estimates, 4279, 4518–19, 4529–30

Alberta Farmers' Union, grain non-delivery strike, 287–88

Canadian citizens in Soviet controlled territory, repatriation of, 5615–16

Canadian newspapers fight against communism, 3555

Citizenship registration branch, 5053–54

Communist party, strength of in various countries, 3554–55

Controls, position of Social Credit party, 285–86

Displaced persons

    Health requirements for entry to Canada, 5812–16

    Refugees and, problem of, admission to Canada, 4567–75

External affairs estimates, 3551–56, 5615–21, 6197–98

Farmers

    Income tax, 5925, 6031

    Selling land to oil companies, on royalty basis, income tax, 4859, 5708

Foreign policy, 3551–56

Freight rates, increase

    Amendment (Mr. Coldwell), 2932–34

    M. (Mr. Coldwell), 2631–34

Human rights and fundamental freedoms, M. (Mr. Ilsley), for appointment of committee, 2883–86

Illustration stations, grants to, 4279, 4518–19

Immigrants, transportation arrangements, 6198

Income tax bill, 5708–18

Income War Tax Act Amendment bill, 4859

Land settlement scheme for displaced persons, suggested, 4571–73
Live stock and feed grain prices, 286–87
Married men with families in Europe, income tax, 5718
Mines and resources estimates, 5812–17
National revenue estimates, 5925, 6031
Osborne, John Robert, award of V.C. to posthumously, 2885
Ruthenian Catholic Mission bill, 4269–70
Secretary of state estimates, 5053–54
Transitional measures bill, 2242
Transitional Measures Act 1947, M. (Mr. Ilsley), 285–88
Veterinary surgeons from Europe, employment of, 4529–30
Wheat prices, difference between British and world price, 286

Twentieth Parliament, Fifth Session, 1949
Address in reply, 1213–16
Agricultural conditions, 1213–16
Farmers, income tax, 1215–16
National Anthem, adoption of "O, Canada", (Mr. Côté, Matapedia-Matane), 2164–67

Twenty-first Parliament, First Session, 1949
Hlynka, Mr. Anthony, former member for Vegreville, communist campaign to defeat, 364–65, 1423

part IV

HLYNKA AS PORTRAYED IN THE CANADIAN PRESS

PARLIAMENT

— By Ian Sclanders
Ottawa Journal, 26 November 1940

...First there was Anthony H. Hlynka, New Democracy member from Vegreville, Alberta, a riding where more than half the population is of foreign racial origin.

Of Ukrainian stock, Mr. Hlynka is getting a little bit tired of the way his constituents are regarded in certain quarters. He figures that as loyal Canadians, they ought to be given their due as such, no matter what country their ancestors came from. And he strongly objects to statements like one attributed by the press to a fellow called Parker, who is relief officer at Saskatoon. Parker was reported to have said that Canada ought to have two scales of relief, one for "white" persons and another (obviously lower, in his view) for Central Europeans.

The Vegreville member is one of the youngest members of Commons, just 33. He prints a periodical in Alberta which circulates largely among the foreign population and often has editorials on the meaning and responsibility of citizenship. He's a pleasant chap and he speaks effectively and – unlike some politicians we know – he admires newspapermen. But then, he's a newspaperman himself.

UKRAINIAN CALLS FOR UNITY

—— *By Austin F. Cross*
Montreal Star, 26 November 1940

An impassioned appeal to forget racial prejudice and to get together to win the war was voiced by Anthony Hlynka, young Ukrainian Canadian from Vegreville, who did not say a word about his Social Credit affiliations, but who talked of freedom and justice to be found only under the Union Jack.

Anthony Hlynka, Social Credit, Vegreville, spoke purely of racial programs, and his fine, clear presentation of the loyalty of people of non-Anglo-Saxon origin got him good reception. He spoke with some heat about a certain Mr. Parker of Saskatoon, who had something to do with relief, and who prescribed one form of relief for Central Europeans, and a better standard for what he called "white people."

"The term 'white people' was in quotations," said Mr. Hlynka, "I challenge the mentality of one who would in this country, at this time, ask for one scale for Anglo-Saxons, and one for Central Europeans."

At this time, when national unity was so important, this racial cry was a bad thing, he said. In Saskatchewan, half the people were of non-Anglo-Saxon origin. Of Saskatchewan's population, 10 per cent are Ukrainian, but more than 10 per cent of the enlistments are Ukrainian.

The young Ukrainian publisher spoke with some feeling about a speech the late Lord Tweedsmuir made, when he told them that he was proud of them as Canadians, but urged them never to forget they were Ukrainians, because of the traditions of that race.

"I call for justice, for fair play, in a time like this," he concluded, "Let us unite under the British flag, which stands for freedom, and fight for a common cause, regardless of racial rights."

UKRAINIAN HALL DEDICATED to FURTHERING WAR EFFORT

Toronto Evening Telegram, 17 March 1941

FEDERATION VICE-PRESIDENT PREDICTS DOOM OF STALIN, HITLER AND DUCE – OPENING FETE

Ukrainian people throughout Canada, regardless of their racial origin, must realize the importance of carrying on with their efforts to aid Canada in her war effort, Anthony H. Hlynka, only Ukrainian member in the House of Commons, stated Saturday night before a large audience at 300 Bathurst street.

The occasion was the opening of the building by the Ukrainian National Federation. M. Topolnitsky presided.

Mr. Hlynka pointed out that in Canada there was no nation as loyal as the Ukrainian people. They were proud of their war work, he stated, and had nothing to hide.

M. Sharik, vice-president of the Ukrainian National Federation, told the audience that the Bathurst street hall was being opened to help Canada in her war effort. Ukrainians have given a great percentage of their men in helping Canada and the British Empire.

Doing Everything

"We are now able," he said, "to have a chance of working for the common task of Britain and the Ukraine in this hall. We'll educate our children to work for Canada and its welfare, and we'll show our fellow Ukrainians how much we think of liberty. The Ukrainian National Federation is doing everything that Canada needs and wants."

He predicted the deaths of Stalin, Hitler and Mussolini, and stated that the cause of freedom would prevail. He asked that a one-minute silence be observed for those who died for the British Empire.

Other speakers were N. Romaniuk, Rev. P. Kamanecky, Col. Webster, Mrs. S. Sawchuk and W. Hirniak.

The concert was one of the most ambitious given this season by the Ukrainian people. Equipment in the hall is excellent and added greatly to the program, especially the dancing.

Effective Program

A choir and string orchestra were under the direction of Dr. J. Kozaruk. "O Canada" was sung with great fervour, and the rest of the choral music was made up of Ukrainian songs. The men's section was particularly effective throughout. The orchestra was composed of 20 young people, and their music, typically Ukrainian, was well received.

Dancing, under the direction of J. Kozak, was splendid. Mr. Kozak and nine-year old Olga Gural gave a breath-taking interpretation of a sword dance which brought an encore.

Others assisting in the variety programs were Olga Hawreliuk, soprano soloist, who was accompanied at the piano by Theodora Humeniuk; a violin solo by Miss M. Jaworska; a vocal trio, in which Miss I. Lazar and her two brothers, Nick and Eugene, took part, and a baritone solo by N. Lazar. All gave excellent work and were well received.

UKRAINIANS IN CANADA INSIST MOTHER COUNTRY REMAIN as INDEPENDENT

— By J. H. Fisher, Staff Writer
Toronto Telegram, 23 May 1941

WESTERN M.P.'S TELL MR. KING PEOPLE DISAPPROVE PLAN FOR LINK-UP WITH POLAND

Ottawa, May 23 – An independent Ukrainian state in a free, reconstructed Europe is the hope of this race, a deputation of western M.P.'s informed Prime Minister W. L. Mackenzie King yesterday when they presented a memorandum on the subject prepared by the Ukrainian Canadian committee which represents all Ukrainian organizations in Canada.

Heading the delegation was the Ukrainian-born Anthony Hlynka, who represents the riding of Vegreville in the House of Commons. With him were three other members. J. T. Thorson, Walter Tucker and Robert Fair, in whose ridings on the prairies there are numbers of residents of Ukrainian descent.

The memorandum, signed by Dr. W. Kusknir, president, and J. W. Arsenych secretary of the Ukrainian Canadian committee, was read by Mr. Hlynka. It recalled that during his recent visit to Canada, General Wladislaw Sikorski, premier of the Polish government-in-exile, made a declaration that it is proposed after the war to set up a Polish-Czechoslovak federation with a population of 50,000,000.

Oppose Sikorski Plan

In this memorandum it was stated that the combined population of Poles, Czechs and Slovaks does not exceed 35,000,000, hence it may be assumed that General Sikorski proposed the inclusion within the boundaries of the new Polish-Czechoslovak state a substantial part of western Ukrainian territories adjoining the ethnographical boundaries of the Polish and Czech peoples.

"The incorporation of such Ukrainian territories within Poland or Czechoslovakia or the Polish-Czechoslovak federation, without the express will and collaboration of the Ukrainians, will be strongly opposed by the Ukrainians and will remain a source of constant troubles and painful misunderstandings dangerous to European peace," the memorandum stated. "The declaration above referred to contemplating such incorporation of Ukrainian territories within the Polish-Czechoslovak federation is contrary to the basic principles and efforts of His Majesty's Government directed against all forms of aggression."

Fight for Freedom

"The Ukrainian Canadians respectfully submit to His Majesty's Government that in the plans of the reconstruction of Europe, evolved by the democracies under the leadership of the British Commonwealth of Nations, the claims of the Ukrainian people to an independent free state in a free Europe should not be disregarded and that the Ukrainian question should be included in any just and permanent settlement of Europe...."

Praises Loyalty

Mr. King gave the delegation a courteous hearing and mentioned their loyalty to the British cause at the present time. If he were so fortunate as to be a participant in a peace conference he would bear in mind the representations of the committee, he said.

Mr. Hlynka, in speaking for his people, said they will do their part in Canada as Canadians. "Facts speak about their efforts louder than I can. Let me say, however, that when this war is won by the Allies, Ukrainians will make sure their deeds shall be recorded among those worthy of praise and pride. We feel that sooner or later the fate of Ukrainians in Europe will be closely connected with that of the British people. I have in mind not only the setting up of an independent Ukrainian state, but also keeping it independent and its people free."

Referring to Gen. Sikorski's statement, Mr. Hlynka said that planning a federation of people which would include Ukrainians, without consulting their opinion, is not in keeping with the democratic principles which we are fighting to preserve....

Mackenzie King noted in his diary: "Thursday, May 22, 1941. Later, I received a delegation of 3 M.P.s: Thorson, Tucker and Fair and Mr. Hlynka who presented a petition on behalf of the Ukrainians urging that when the war was over, we should see that they were not made part of a federation which included Poland but were made free and independent state. I told them that I would be the happiest man alive if I could believe that within the next few years, there was going to be a single free independent state in Europe. I was not sure we would ever see anything of the kind in the way of a return to old boundaries and countries, and freedom as it was after the last war. That their petition showed how remote people of this country were from realizing what the real situation is like. The most I could promise was to put the petition away and take it out if occasion afforded later on." <http://king.collectionscanada.ca/EN/default.asp>

ONLY UKRAINIAN MEMBER IS PROUD OF COUNTRYMEN HERE

Timmins Press, 26 June 1941

URGES GREATER UNITY AND UNDERSTANDING AMONG UKRAINIAN-CANADIANS AND OTHER SECTIONS OF POPULATION; VISITING IN NORTH

Only Ukrainian member of the House of Commons, Anthony H. Hlynka, of Vegreville, Alta., paid his first visit among his fellow-countrymen in Timmins, Wednesday.

"I am very pleased with the conduct of Northern Ontario's Ukrainian-Canadians in the Dominion's war effort," Mr. Hlynka told The Press in an interview. He arrived in Timmins Wednesday after brief speaking engagements in Sudbury and Kirkland Lake.

Finds Prosperity

Discussing his observations during his short visit in the North, the member marvelled at the prosperity which Ukrainian-Canadians enjoy in this section of the country.

"They seem to be making a real 'go' of it," he commented.

Mr. Hlynka described himself as the "connecting link" between the large Ukrainian population of Canada and the English-speaking sections of the nation. One of the youngest members of the House of Commons at 34, he is a native of the Ukraine but a real citizen of Canada. He arrived in this country when he was slightly less than three years of age and received his entire education and training in the Dominion.

Unity Essential

"Since my entry into the political field, I have been urging greater unity between the Ukrainian-Canadians and the other groups in Canada. I feel that it is essential if we are to build a great nation."

Mr. Hlynka pleaded for a greater understanding between Ukrainian-Canadians and other nationalities.

"The Ukrainians should not be treated as persons who are here to gather what they can and then leave the country. Every one of them is eager to become a real citizen. They are here to stay, to build homes and to do their part in developing the Dominion."

During his short visit to the North, Mr. Hlynka reported that he had noted a better understanding here between Ukrainian-Canadians and other sections of the population.

"The North's example in this regard is a lesson in the principles of unity which should be applied to all parts of the Dominion."

Mr. Hlynka left Timmins Thursday afternoon, planning a hasty visit to other sections of Ontario before returning for a between-sessions stay in his own constituency.

BIOGRAPHY: ANTHONY HLYNKA

New World Illustrated, November 1941

Born in the Ukraine, at 34 member of the Federal House, proves Canada to be land of opportunity and democracy

Definite of purpose, dynamic of personality and unshakable in his determination to follow the path upon which he has set his feet, Anthony H. Hlynka, only Ukrainian member of the House of Commons and probably the only Ukrainian in the entire world free to discuss the problems of his people publicly, gives the impression that he can shoulder his task with ease and thoroughness.

His job, he feels, is to bring closer unity and understanding between the Anglo-Saxon world and the Ukrainian Canadians. No small job when one considers that there are 300,000 Ukrainians in Canada and that, apart from his own constituents in the riding of Vegreville, which he represents, he is in constant touch by means of speaking tours all over the Dominion, and by a voluminous correspondence which exceeds that of any other member of the House, with a good proportion of Ukrainians outside his own "fold."

A biographical sketch of Mr. Hlynka's life since he arrived in this country in 1909 at the tender age of two and a half years sounds like a genuine "success story." Coming straight to Alberta with his parents, he spent his first years on a western Canadian farm where he divided his time between helping on the farm and attending public school.

At 15 he came to Edmonton and for the next six years spent his winters going to high school, and his summers working in a brickyard. In addition to this strenuous programme, he taught English two or three times a week to his fellow Ukrainians.

Nor was this all. For Mr. Hlynka, sure of the path in life he meant to follow, started his speaking career at the age of 16 when he became president of the high school students' union. After leaving high school he sold insurance for a short time, utilizing the money he earned to buy books which he studies endlessly.

Journalism was the next step towards public life and from the years 1935 to 1940 he published *The Call*, a magazine written in both Ukrainian and English and designed to bring about greater unity between his fellow-countrymen and those of the land of his birth. During the same period he published a newspaper, *Social Credit*, in Ukrainian.

His first definite link with political life came when he started working for the Aberhart government in 1938, in the bureau of information as a translator and interpreter. At the same time he made an exhaustive study of his native language and wrote articles.

It was in the general election of 1940 that Mr. Hlynka took the plunge into real political life. Constantly in demand as a public speaker, he was asked to run as a New Democracy member, and was elected in the Vegreville constituency with a clear majority.

Dark, thick-set, and with a look of unwavering determination, Anthony Hlynka makes an instant impression of courage and clear purpose. Ask him a question and it is answered with the promptness of one whose opinion is definite and unswerving. But modesty is another attribute of this rising young politician who claims earnestly that "my success is due to my fellow Ukrainians. Perhaps I understand them better than most members do their people, but I am just one man with thousands behind me."

Hobbies? – clippings from newspapers on social, economic and political problems. But study is one of his main occupations in his spare time, and his books include works on philosophy, psychology, history, literature and writing. In fact, the ultimate aim of this "new Canadian" is to be a writer and he has already started work in that direction.

It hasn't all been study though, and Mr. Hlynka has found time to take part in sports which have helped to build up a sturdy frame. He has played on both rugby and soccer teams and is a devotee of tennis. He hasn't found time to get married though.

His convictions are sure. As a member for an almost entirely agricultural riding, he is convinced that farming must be placed on a paying basis with a different machinery for paying debts and a reduction in interest rates. He believes that as far as strikes are concerned it takes two to make a quarrel, and that a board of conciliation which includes in its personnel one or two members for each political group is essential to bring about cessation of strikes and a better understanding between labour and capital. He believes in total war effort for Canada – and he means total.

But above all his firmest conviction is the part his country and his countrymen will pay in the future of the world. "In Canada we will never flinch in our loyalty. We will stand beside the British people, for we believe that the future fate of the Anglo-Saxon world will be closely linked with that of the Ukrainian people. It is my sincere hope and belief that Ukraine will, after this war, become an independent state."

DEFINITE PLAN of FREEDOM URGED

Windsor Daily Star, 2 February 1942

M.P. Born in Ukraine Wants Assurance to Occupied Areas

OTTAWA, Feb. 3 – Ukrainian-born Anthony Hlynka, Social Credit member for Vegreville, last night called upon the democracies to announce a definite plan of freedom for peoples now subjugated. He stated such a program would give inspiration to those concerned, and might conceivably help shorten the war.

Wants Detailed Proposals

Obviously thinking mainly of his native Ukraine, now the battle-front in Southeastern Europe, Mr. Hlynka referred to the Atlantic Charter and saw in there hope, but not in a sufficiently definite form.

"Should not democracies, of imperative necessity, formulate a more definite and detailed set of proposals which will give the needed promise of release to all people under the domination of aggressive nations? Should not our proposals be more positive, more dynamic, so they may add more inspiration to the explosive force of the temporarily subdued peoples? I suggest that in this manner we should change the whole course of the war very much in our favour.

"It can well be assumed that the Axis powers are bound to offer some enticing formula to subdued nations for the express purpose of giving themselves a breathing spell before they begin tightening the reins on the unfortunate countries. Germany is already trying desperately to consolidate her position in the overrun regions.

"The Allies should take upon themselves to become the guardians of sovereign ideals and sovereign nations. Can we not promise all of them their national sovereignty, which would be in accordance with the Atlantic Charter, and which would make a revolutionary rebellion on their part worth while? It would be an inspiration and a challenge to them. There is no stronger force than that manifest in defence of personal and national existence."

As to why Canadians should be interested in an independent Ukraine, Mr. Hlynka spoke of the number of those of this origin in Canada, the number of them who have enlisted, the heroic contribution of Ukrainians on the battlefields of Europe, and because Canadians believe in the rights of others. But, above all, he claimed an independent Ukraine necessary as a balance for Britain in Europe after the war.

There are about 50,000,000 Ukrainians in the world, and they are the third largest group in Europe and ninth in the world. Though eleven new states were created after the last war, Ukraine was not one of them, though it was an independent state for a couple of years, then being divided between Russia, Poland, Romania and Czecho-Slovakia.

Russia's Position

As to Russia, an ally, with the largest portion of Ukraine within her pre-war boundaries, Mr. Hlynka said: "Let me remind members the Soviet Government favours the proposals embodied in the Atlantic Charter. In addition, Article 17 of the Soviet Union Constitution of 1936 says that 'each Union Republic is reserved the right freely to secede from the U.S.S.R.' This should be sufficient assurance that the Soviet Union would be inclined to favour a recognition of the principle of the sovereignty of nations."

He suggested Ukrainian committees be allowed to join with governments-in-exile in planning for the post-war Europe. "The stability of Europe and of the world can be achieved only on a basis of universal justice. The European madhouse will remain a madhouse until Europe is reconstructed with freedom written into every word of its constitution."

ANTHONY H. HLYNKA DECLARES: *for* MORE DEFINITE PRONOUNCEMENT *of* PEACE AIMS

Edmonton Bulletin, 3 February 1942

VEGREVILLE M.P. URGES PARLIAMENT TO CONSIDER NATION'S POST-WAR ROLE

Ukrainians this year are celebrating the fiftieth year of their coming to Canada. Mr. Anthony Hlynka, member of parliament for Vegreville, Alta., last night in the House of Commons made a noteworthy contribution to the records of parliament in his speech during debate on the address in reply to the speech from the throne. A Ukrainian-Canadian is privileged to speak on behalf of the people from which he comes, even in the most critical of times, living proof of Democracy within the British Commonwealth of Nations. *The Edmonton Bulletin* considers it proper at this time to reproduce in full Mr. Hlynka's speech coming as it does from one of the sons of Canadian Ukrainians representing them in the Canadian parliament. – EDITOR

OTTAWA, Feb. 3. – Speaking in the House of Commons Monday night during debate on the address in reply to the speech from the throne, Anthony Hlynka, member for Vegreville, Alta., urged parliament to study the role Canada may play in settling world affairs after the war. World problems are the problems of Canada, Mr. Hlynka said. He also urged a more definite pronouncement of peace aims. Mr. Hlynka's speech follows:

Mr. Speaker, during the past two sessions of the present parliament our task has been directed toward a solution of the problems which confront us in our national life, particularly those which arise in a maximum effort in the prosecution of the war. Considerable progress has been made in this initial period, but no effort could have been too great while the destiny of free peoples was at stake. From now on, and until a decisive victory is ultimately won, both on the battlefields and at the peace conferences, not only must we further mobilize, equip and maintain our armed forces as our chief contribution to the cause of freedom, but we must of necessity go beyond this primary requisite.

We must not only win the war, but we must also make certain that we shall win the peace. To achieve less would be to fail in the trust bestowed upon us, the sacred privilege of delivering to future generations the hard-won liberties of our forefathers. It is our duty, therefore, to study and prevent the weaknesses and recurring dangers of past adjustments ... of world problems which gave rise to the present world conflagration. This should be one of our many immediate concerns.

Present Problems

I believe, Mr. Speaker, that hon. members will agree with me when I say that we are faced today with problems of first magnitude. Many of these problems have arisen with the present conflict, but multitudes of them find root in the past. We cannot, therefore, shirk responsibility in the solution of this chaotic state of affairs. World problems are our problems; for they have either a direct or an indirect bearing upon our national life – yes, even upon our individual lives.

We must necessarily realize that it is not the war alone that we are fighting today; we find ourselves also in the grip of two of the greatest revolutions of all time. Nationally we are fighting a war; internally and internationally we are engaged in two prodigious revolutions – one economic, one political. We are therefore, endeavouring to survive one of the most critical and dangerous of transitional periods.

Let us, then, examine the role that we Canadians are playing in this struggle, and let us envision the role that Canada is destined to play in the future. We are now in the third year of war. To what extent have we crystallized our view on Canada's foreign policy? What plans are we prepared to advance or adopt as the basis for post-war reorganization and reconstruction of the world? How many hours have we devoted in this chamber to the discussion of this problem during the last two years? If none, why not? Can we afford to be caught unprepared in this respect? For, as we know, this war will also end sooner or later as all other wars are supposed to have ended.

Canada's Position

Now, when we consider the position that Canada occupies among the nations of the world at this time, it does seem that we have underestimated her importance. As a matter of fact, until recently Canada's position was unique in that it was second only to that of Great Britain; indeed in many respects, even with the entry of the United States into the conflict, Canada still remains a number one ally of Great Britain. I say this with all due respect and consideration to the material aid given to Great Britain by our good neighbour directly to the south of us, and with all due respect and consideration to the entry of the Soviet Union into this conflict on our side.

To amplify my statement: Canada's strategic position makes her the logical mediator between Great Britain and the United States. Her geographical location makes her an ideal arsenal for the turning out of tools of war for the allies. She is admirably situated for the training fields of the empire forces, and especially for the empire air training plan. And lastly, because of her limitless potential natural resources and her rich wheat fields, she will undoubtedly be the key to post-war reconstruction of Britain. It is only fitting, therefore, that Canada's foreign policy should be commensurate with her important position.

It is gratifying indeed to find that the broad principles which are intended as the basis for post-war reorganization of the world have been enunciated. I refer, of course, to the world's men of destiny – Prime Minister of Great Britain, Mr. Churchill, and the President of the United States, Mr. Roosevelt. I am more than pleased, Mr. Speaker, to hear reference made to the Atlantic Charter in the speech from the throne.

Four Freedoms

Then again, there are the four great human freedoms proclaimed by the President of the United States – freedom of speech and expression, freedom of every person to worship God in his own way, freedom from want and freedom from fear.

These declarations deserve all the acclaim they have already received from all parts of the world, particularly for their universality and noble purpose. We, of course, welcome and accept these principles, just as we had accepted the fourteen points of Wilson after the last war.

We may at least be proud of the fact that the democratic world recognizes that world stability and enduring peace can be achieved only on the basis of freedom for all peoples capable of shaping and directing their own destinies.

Further, in his address on January 6, 1941, President Roosevelt had this to say on the subject:

"No lasting peace can be bought at the expense of other peoples' freedom."

Again, in his speech delivered at the annual dinner of the White House Correspondents' Association, he said:

"Humanity will never permanently accept a system imposed by conquest and based on slavery."

To my mind, Mr. Speaker, not only are these statements true, but they are expressions of foresight and vision. We can no longer tolerate a short sighted plan or settlement. There must be built a new world citadel of freedom and civilization. If we ever hope to have stability and enduring peace, the principle of freedom must constantly be kept in mind and incorporated into the post-war settlement. If this basis is ignored, let us then not expect a peaceful world in the immediate future; the lives spent in this and the last war will have been given in vain.

Should Be Definite

Let us look a step further. Should not the democracies of imperative necessity formulate a more definite and detailed set of proposals which will give the needed promise of release to all peoples under the domination of aggressor nations? Should not our proposals be more positive, more dynamic, so that they may add more inspiration to the explosive force of the temporarily subdued peoples, I venture to suggest that in this manner we would change the whole course of the war in our favour.

I make this observation because it can well be assumed that the Axis powers are bound to offer some enticing formula to subdued nations for the express purpose of giving themselves a breathing moment before they begin tightening the reins on those unfortunate countries. Germany is already trying desperately to consolidate her position in the overrun regions.

She is organizing these areas into zones which are to operate in complete subordination to her, and she is totally ignoring all racial and ethnographic lines. It is a sort of forced federal union. It would mean an eventual and permanent enslavement of millions of people. It would become a new and horrible prison of nations.

Stand for Sovereignty

In view of this increasingly dangerous threat, the Allies should, therefore, take it upon themselves to become the guardians of sovereign ideals and sovereign nations. Can we not promise all of them their national sovereignty which would be in accordance with the spirit of the Atlantic Charter, and which would make a revolutionary rebellion on their part worth while? It would be an inspiration and a challenge to them. For, as we know, there is no stronger force and incentive than that manifest in the defence of personal and national existence.

I cannot, therefore, emphasize too strongly the immediate need on the part of democracies to make known their foreign policy in as complete and definite form as time and conditions permit. The issues at stake are too important for us not to make use of the incentive of confidence in the future – instead of vague hopes and wishful thinking.

Allow me now to draw your attention to the three items relevant to national sovereignty as outlined in the Atlantic Charter. They are 2, 3 and 6. Here is what they say:

> "Second, they desire to see no territorial changes that do not accord with the freely expressed wishes of the people concerned.

"Third, they respect the right of all peoples to choose the form of government under which they will live; and they wish to see sovereign rights and self-government restored to those who have been forcibly deprived of them.

"Sixth, after the final destruction of the Nazi tyranny, they hope to see established a peace which will afford to all nations the means of dwelling in safety within their own boundaries, and which will afford assurance that all men in all the lands may live out their lives in freedom from fear and want."

These three points, Mr. Speaker, deal generally with the phase of the problem which I am discussing. They read well, but I found numerous interpretations of them. One outstanding United States publication interprets the Atlantic Charter as being opposed to the setting up of any new organisms. Of course, much depends on how the word "new" is interpreted. But are we to understand that nations who were not fortunate enough to liberate themselves during the last war shall remain in bondage? More clarification of this point is definitely needed. Then, again, the Charter was interpreted as favouring the federal union proposals.

Personally I fail to find in the document any trace of expression of these views. As a matter of fact, I find that the Charter upholds the sovereignty of all peoples in accordance with their expressed will, which is definitely contrary to ideas propounded by federal unionists.

Ukrainian Question

From what I have said thus far, it is evident that this question of foreign relations policy is an extremely broad one in scope. I wish, therefore, to confine my following remarks specifically to the discussion of a Ukrainian independent state and its importance to the British commonwealth of nations.

The question may arise in the minds of some hon. members as to why should we Canadians be interested in an independent Ukrainian state in Europe. Is it because Ukrainian-Canadians constitute a large group of our citizens, and we owe them that courtesy?

Is it because they are so generously enlisting in great numbers in the Canadian armed forces and are ready to give their lives for Canada? Is it because of the heroic contribution of Ukrainians on the battlefields of the Ukraine against Germany? Or, is it because it is in the very blood of the English-speaking people always to stand up for the rights of others as well as their own?

Yes, Mr. Speaker, but there is a much more important reason than those I have already given.

Independent State

Above all, a Ukrainian independent state in eastern Europe would be important to the British commonwealth of nations and the United States as a balance of power. I venture to suggest that not in a distant future the British people and the principles for which they stand will be more closely associated with the Ukrainians than they have ever been before.

Furthermore, Ukraine is important because of the extent of its territory, the richness of its natural resources, the size of its population, and its strategic position with reference to the Black Sea, the Dardanelles, Iran, Iraq, the Persian Gulf and India. Professor G. W. Simpson, of Saskatchewan University, has this to say in his "Atlas of History and Geography of the Ukraine":

> "Thus the Ukraine constitutes a wide assembling place which could be used either by ambitious dictators as the starting point for sweeping military conquest, or by wise statesmen as a strong wedge-like area of defence which would stabilize all these regions tributary to the Black Sea."

Consequently, Mr. Speaker, it is definitely contrary to the interests of Britain to permit Germany to take and hold the Ukraine and exploit its people and its resources for aggrandizement and greater power. Again, it would not be in the best interests of Britain to see any other power ... holding this strategic position in Europe.

Finally, a division of the territory after the fashion of the divisions made after the last war would only complicate the problems of Europe, and the dangerous situation would remain unchanged. Hence the problem of a Ukrainian independent state in eastern Europe is of extreme importance to the British commonwealth of nations and to the stability of the world at the present time.

British Publication

I have before me a handbook prepared under the authority of the Historic Section of the British Foreign Office, entitled "The Ukraine," the topic which I propose to discuss briefly. This booklet is numbered 52 of the series of such authoritative information prepared and collected for the sole purpose of having it available for those who were to participate in peace conferences. It may be observed from the series number that there must have been at least 51 others of the kind, dealing with various important problems.

This booklet contains information having to do with physical geography, political history, social and political conditions, and much other useful material. One cannot help but admire the British for their thoroughness in dealing with important matters such as these; on the other hand the total lack of similar preparation on our part in Canada stands out in striking contrast.

True, many Canadians show a keen interest in the Ukrainian problem. Many of them seek information on the subject, but it is essential that they obtain their information from authoritative and unbiased sources. All those interested in the subject must remember that there is a great deal of distorted information emanating from people who are not totally disinterested in the possession and the control of the Ukraine.

This information is usually disseminated with the purpose of obliterating the authenticity of the ethnological and ethnographical existence of the Ukrainian people. For example, any aspiration manifested by Ukrainians looking to freedom and independence in their own native land is immediately given the interpretation of being instigated by an enemy of the British. This method of propaganda is by no means new, but unless one guards against such sources of information he may be hopelessly misled.

Authoritative Sources

For the benefit of those who may be interested in the subject I wish to place on record just a few authoritative sources of information: "Ukraine, an Atlas of Its History and Geography," by G. W. Simpson, professor of European History, University of Saskatchewan, published in 1941; "History of the Ukraine," by D. Doroshenko, professor of Prague and Warsaw universities, which was edited by Professor Simpson, and published in 1939. The third and perhaps the most comprehensive study is "A History of Ukraine," by Michael Hrushevsky, one of the world's outstanding historians. This book was edited by O. J. Frederiksen, professor of History at Miami University, and published by Yale University Press in 1941.

May I now give this house, so far as my humble ability will permit, the fundamental facts concerning Ukraine and the Ukrainian people. First let me deal with the land they inhabit and claim.

Geography of Ukraine

Ukraine is a vast rich territory lying in the southeastern corner of Europe on the threshold of Asia, immediately north of the Black Sea. It is the second largest ethnographic territory in Europe and fourteenth largest in the world. This territory comprises 362,200 square miles.

Immediately prior to the last world war the whole Ukraine was held by Russia and Austro-Hungary.

By 1923 the Ukraine was dismembered and divided among the four neighbouring nations. The largest portion, comprising 298,610 square miles and containing 35,026,000 Ukrainians, called the Great Ukraine, was assigned to Russia and was incorporated as one of the republics of the Soviet Union. The western Ukraine, comprising 51,042 square miles and containing 7,500,000 Ukrainians, was made a Polish "protectorate." The provinces of Bessarabia and Bukovina, comprising 6,795 square miles and containing 1,500,000 Ukrainians, were placed under Romanian rule, while Carpatho-Ukraine, comprising 5,753 square miles and containing 600,000 Ukrainians, was assigned to Czechoslovakia.

At the moment almost the entire territory has become the battlefield of the German and the Soviet Union forces. It has been for many months and still is being torn by destructive forces of war, and the Ukrainian people are undergoing the cruelest ordeal of their history. In addition to this tragic fate that befell the Ukrainian people, the scorched earth policy of the Soviet government was mainly applied to the Ukraine. The land which is capable of providing freedom and life to its people has brought nothing but extreme tragedy with slavery and death.

Wealth of Ukraine

To one who has not the facts about the Ukraine it may seem confusing why so many nations are forever determined to grab a piece of this land for themselves. The answer is that it is one of the richest regions in the entire world. Ukraine is often referred to as "the granary of Europe." More than that. Her mineral deposits are the envy of all her good neighbours. The 1932 Encyclopedia Americana points out that in 1928–29 Ukraine supplied the Soviet Union with 80 per cent of its coal, 60 per cent of its iron, 95 per cent of its manganese, 80 per cent of its sugar, the bulk of its wheat, vast quantities of mercury, copper and gold. The striking fact is that its rightful owners share little in this wealth.

There are now in the neighbourhood of 50 million Ukrainians in the world. Numerically they are the third largest group in Europe and ninth largest in the world. They first appeared in history in the fourth century. My time will not permit me to deal with the ethnology and the general characteristics of the people at this time; suffice it to say that C. S. Coon, Professor of Anthropology at Harvard University, states in his book, "Races of Europe," that Ukrainians are a distinct and separate people.

Perhaps the greatest contribution made by Ukrainians to the world was that of staving off the Asiatic hordes for many centuries from invading Europe. That is what Lord Tweedsmuir meant when he said on September 21, 1936, at Fraserwood, Manitoba, "for it was your race which for centuries held the south-eastern gate of Europe against the attacks from the east."

Christian Gateway

Again, it was through Kiev, the capital of the Ukraine, that Christianity was introduced into eastern Europe in 988 A.D. Let me mention one or two other contributions in art, music and literature. Alexander Archipenko, one of the world's foremost contemporary sculptors, now living in the United States, is a Ukrainian. The immortal Tschaikowsky, in the field of music, was of Ukrainian origin. Taras Shevchenko, the Robert Burns of the Slavic races, was a Ukrainian. These are but a few indications of Ukrainian contributions to the world.

When national states were established after the last world war it was held that the basis accepted was not some remote appeal to historic claims, but rather a clear and unmistakable determination of the people to rule themselves. With regard to historic claims of many peoples, some, like Finland, had not known complete political independence for many centuries; some, like Estonia, had never known political independence in the modern sense of the word.

The Ukraine, however, has had a continuous historic tradition extending back for over a thousand years, and three times, at least, this tradition incorporated itself in terms of political independence. First, there was the Kievan State, existing from the ninth to the middle of fourteenth century; then the Cossack State, established in 1648, which lasted to the middle of the eighteenth century, and, lastly, the United Ukrainian Republic of 1918–23.

Kievan State

At the time when Alfred the Great of England was attempting to maintain his Saxon state against the Danes, the ancestors of the Ukrainian people were establishing a large and flourishing kingdom with its centre at Kiev. This Kievan state, with its Slav-Byzantine culture, was the outstanding political state in Eastern Europe at that time. It is the fountainhead of the Ukrainian historical tradition. When it disintegrated into principalities and suffered the devastating blow of the Tartar invasion its traditions lived on in the southern principalities, particularly in the western Ukraine. Although western Ukraine fell to Poland and the other principalities to Lithuania which was later joined to Poland, the ancient Ukrainian laws, customs and language persisted and developed.

Cossack State

Again, when Oliver Cromwell in England, in the seventeenth century, was striking a mighty blow for that liberty which we are today defending, Bohdan Khmelnitsky created on the basis of Ukrainian tradition a free and independent Cossack state. Unfortunately, Khmelnitsky had not the advantage of a sea wall, which Cromwell enjoyed, and the state which he had erected was torn between Poland and the rising state of Muscovy which was then becoming the modern empire of Russia. So firmly entrenched, however, were the institutions of self-government in the Ukraine, that it was more than a hundred years after the death of Khmelnitsky, in the latter half of the eighteenth century, before the imperialist regime could root out the last remnants of these institutions of self-government.

But the love of freedom which is an undying part of the human spirit was again awakened in the nineteenth century among the Ukrainian people as well as among the Czechs, the Poles and others who had been suppressed.

United Republic

Finally, in the first World War, when the Russian empire fell from its ruins for the third time in the history of the Ukrainian people, there emerged a Ukrainian independent state, proclaimed on January 22, 1918. Nine months later the Austro-Hungarian empire fell, and from its remnants there was created the Western Ukrainian National Republic, proclaimed on the first day of November, 1918, ten days before the Armistice. These two Ukrainian areas were proclaimed united on January 22, 1919, forming a United Ukrainian Republic.

The Ukrainian patriots fought desperately to defend this state, so that they might live as free people among other nations of the world. They lost this freedom, and one element in their misfortune was the fact that their cause was so gravely misunderstood and misrepresented.

By 1923 the Ukrainians found themselves divided among four states, as I have already pointed out.

It seemed that it was the original intention of the Paris peace conference to give the Ukrainians the right of self-determination in the western Ukraine. In 1923, however, the Council of Ambassadors granted to Poland the title to this area, on the distinct understanding that she would eventually grant autonomy to this part of the Ukraine under the stipulated clauses of the Minorities treaty of 1919. Finally, in 1934, however, Poland formally repudiated this obligation.

Last Settlement

The results of these minorities treaties present many interesting angles. It may be granted that it was not easy to divide the territory in question into national states, since there were many conflicting claims; but, allowing even for that, all were not treated with equal consideration. For instance, in the territorial revision after the last war some eleven states were created that were not on the map in 1914. Some of these were: Poland, with some 20 millions of people; Yugoslavia, with about 15 millions; Finland, with 3,600,000; Lithuania, with 2,500,000; Latvia, with 2,000,000, and Esthonia, 1,100,000. I strongly uphold the granting of sovereign rights to all these nations, because I am a firm believer in the sovereign rights of all peoples in accordance with their will. It does seem inconsistent, however, that Ukrainians, with over 40 millions at that time, came out of the struggle empty-handed, in spite of the fact that they had been an historic unit in the past. Were not the Ukrainians entitled to the same privilege as others? If not, why not?

Another error in the settlement arose out of the fact that minorities created by this division constituted a dangerously high percentage. According to Mr. C. A. Macartney, a recognized authority on European affairs, in Czechoslovakia 33 per cent were other than Czechs or Slovaks; in Poland over 25 per cent were non-Polish; in Romania over 25 per cent were other than Romanians. The important question is, can we afford to ignore racial lines in the future?

Present Position

The present collapse of the state structure in Europe has again involved the Ukrainian people, along with other peoples, in the utmost misery and desolation at the hands of aggressor nations. The Ukrainians have again joined hands with other liberty-loving peoples in a fight for freedom. In Carpatho-Ukraine they fought against the axis partner, Hungary, in 1938. In western Ukraine and Poland they fought against Germany in 1939, and they are now fighting against Germany with the Soviet Union forces.

Ukrainians have fought for their freedom throughout their long and unhappy history. They fight for it now, and they will continue to fight for it until they are free. Ukrainians believe that they are just as much entitled to their sovereign rights as any other people are; they wish to contribute their maximum share to the culture and civilization of the world. This will be possible only through the restoration of their own independence. A nation can give its best only when it is free from bondage. These are the tenets of the Atlantic Charter; these are the tenets of Christian civilization.

It may be pointed out by some that there appear to be two obstacles in the way of realization of Ukrainian sovereignty. In the first place it may be suggested that after this war there will be no sovereign states; that some sort of federal union will take their place. Personally I do not believe that the British people would favour any plan that would require the forfeiture of their sovereignty. If they did, they would not be fighting this war.

Relations with Soviet

The second obstacle which may be suggested is one with reference to the Soviet Union. It may be said that since the Soviet Union is our ally in this war, any suggestion of an independent Ukraine might endanger our relations with the Soviet Union. Let me remind hon. members that, according to press reports, the Soviet government favours the proposals embodied in the Atlantic charter. That this is so, was indicated by the British Foreign Secretary, Mr. Eden, after his recent return from Moscow. In addition to that, article 17 of the Soviet Union constitution (1936) says that "Each union republic is reserved the right freely to secede from the U.S.S.R." This should be sufficient assurance that the Soviet Union would be inclined to favour a recognition of the principle of the sovereignty of nations.

Asks Representation

In conclusion, Mr. Speaker, may I be permitted to leave with the house the following suggestion. In view of the fact that all the subdued countries that had been sovereign nations prior to this war are now privileged to form their provisional governments in exile in order that they may carry on the work in the interests of their respective peoples, and in view of the fact that Ukrainians, who form a larger group than any of these, have not now that privilege simply because they were not an independent nation immediately prior to the war, I humbly submit that steps should be taken by the allied governments to make it possible for the Ukrainians to be represented at the various conferences now being held from time to time. In Great Britain, the United States and Canada, there are in existence United Ukrainian committees, whose primary object is to assist the governments, in Britain, the United States and Canada in the successful prosecution of the war. I do suggest, if I may, sir, that since all the allied nations are fighting for a common cause of freedom, that Ukrainian committees to which I have referred be also invited to delegate their representative or representatives to express the view of 50 million Ukrainian people at conferences held by the allied nations.

I believe I have sufficiently pointed out that the stability of Europe and of the world can be achieved only on the basis of universal justice. The European madhouse will remain a madhouse until Europe is reconstructed with freedom written into every word of its constitution. When that is done we may expect a lasting peace.

ASKS CANADA HELP UKRAINE REGAIN HER INDEPENDENCE

—— By J. H. Fisher, Staff Writer
Toronto Evening Telegram, 3 February 1942

ALBERTA M.P. TELLS HOUSE BRITAIN CAN'T AFFORD TO PERMIT NAZIS TO HOLD TERRITORY

Ottawa, Feb. 3 – The right of the Ukrainian race to establish a sovereign state in Europe following the war was lucidly argued by Anthony Hlynka of Vegreville, Alta., in the House of Commons last night.

When this youthful son of the Western Ukraine, who has learned the English language so well that he speaks it without accent, had finished his speech his colleagues had an appreciation of the long history of this race and the importance of the rich territories it has occupied in Central Europe.

Mr. Hlynka's address was instructive in its substance and at the end he had one proposal to make, as follows:

> "In view of the fact that all the conquered countries who had been sovereign nations prior to this war are now privileged to form their provisional governments in exile in order that they may carry on in the interests of their respective peoples, and in view of the fact that Ukrainians, who form a larger group than any of these, have not now that privilege simply because they were not an independent nation prior to this war, I submit that steps should be taken by the allied governments to make it possible for the Ukrainians to be represented at the various conferences now being held from time to time.

Of Interest to Canada

> "In Great Britain, the U. S. and Canada, there are in existence United Ukrainian committees whose primary object is to assist the governments of these countries in the successful prosecution of the war. I suggest since all the allied nations are fighting for the cause of freedom that the Ukrainian committees to which I have referred be also invited to delegate their representative or representatives to express the view of 50,000,000 Ukrainians at conferences held by the allied nations."

There are reasons for Canada favouring a Ukrainian independent state in Europe, Mr. Hlynka argued. There are many Ukrainians in this country; they are enlisting in large numbers, but above all a free, Ukrainian state in Eastern Europe would contribute an important political balance to that continent.

With its rich resources, the large population and its strategic position, it is definitely contrary to British interests to permit Germany to hold the Ukraine, said the speaker. "It would not be in the best interests of Britain to see any other power enslave the Ukrainian people, and with the use of their territory and natural resources, become a dominant power holding this strategic position in Eastern Europe."

Expects Russia's Support

Mr. Hlynka did not shut his eyes to the fact that Russia had been in possession of the major part of the Ukraine. He expressed the opinion "that the Soviet Union would be inclined to favour recognition of the principle of the sovereignty of nations."

After giving some background on the Ukraine and pointing out that the Ukrainians numerically form the third largest group in Europe, he said: "The present collapse of the state structure in Europe has again involved the Ukrainian people, along with other peoples, in the utmost misery and desolation at the hands of aggressor nations," continued Mr. Hlynka. "The Ukrainians have again joined hands with other liberty-loving peoples in a fight for freedom. In Carpatho-Ukraine they fought against the Axis partner, Hungary, in 1938; in Western Ukraine and Poland they fought against Germany in 1939, and now they are fighting against Germany with the Soviet Union forces.

"Ukrainians have fought for freedom throughout their long and unhappy history. They fight for it now. They believe they are just as much entitled to their sovereign rights as any other people are. They wish to contribute their maximum share to the culture and civilization of the world. This will be possible only through the restoration of their own independence," Mr. Hlynka declared.

A PECULIAR SPEECH

Toronto Daily Star, 7 February 1942

In the Dominion House of Commons last week, Mr. Anthony Hlynka, M.P., asked the Canadian government to help establish an independent Ukrainian state in Europe. He thought it would be right meanwhile that committees of Ukrainians who were organized for this purpose in Britain and on this continent should be represented among the governments-in-exile. He included the people in Soviet Ukraine as among the "conquered" and suggested that the Soviet federal government be asked to return sovereign rights to its Ukrainian republic.

The fact is that autonomy of the Soviet republics is clearly granted in the constitution of the Union. The government of the Ukrainian republic has the right to pass a law at any time to secede from the federal body. That it has not done so to date is doubtless because the people in that province have not desired it. It is significant that there were few if any fifth columnists waiting to help the Nazis when they shot their way into the Ukraine, nor have the Ukrainians in Russia been known to reach out for anyone's aid to break away from the Soviet Union. On the contrary, the Ukraine has contributed troops, workers, wealth, technicians, great military leaders such as Marshal Timoshenko, for the defence of the entire Union, the Ukraine included. The United Ukrainian organization, referred to by Mr. Hlynka, which is a group outside of Russia, has looked to the Nazis who promised to "liberate" the Soviet Ukraine. Recently the Nazis announced they intend to make the Soviet Ukraine part of eastern Germany.

The Ukrainian republic in present-day Russia has the same status as a province in Canada or a state in the U.S.A. – except that by the Soviet constitution it is specifically declared that any republic now in the Union may vote itself out. It would sound strange indeed for a Nova Scotian to stand up in the Russian parliament asking that Nova Scotia be helped to become an independent state in America.

Concerning the Ukraine, the practiced policy of the Soviet federal government has been to encourage and aid the maintenance of their language and culture. According to objective reports, the Ukrainians in Russia have achieved remarkable progress in economic, cultural and other fields. This is a tribute to the splendid character and ability of the people of course, and it is testimony also to the opportunities they have had as members of the federation of Soviet Republics.

LETTER TO THE EDITOR

Toronto Evening Telegram, 16 February 1942

Sir:
The *Toronto Star* refused to print the following letter in answer to its editorial appearing in February 7 issue, under the caption "A Peculiar Speech." Would your paper oblige me in printing my reply in your columns? *The Evening Telegram* has in the past endeavoured to be fair to all Canadians; I am, therefore, sending a copy of my letter to you. I may say that the only other newspaper besides the *Star* which chose to attack my speech was the *Canadian Tribune*.

The Editor,
Toronto Star,
Toronto, Ontario.

Sir:
Your editorial appearing in the last Saturday's issue (Feb. 7) under the caption "A Peculiar Speech" attributes to me several statements which cannot be found in my speech delivered in the House of Commons, Monday, February 2nd. I should not like to think that it could be the practice of your paper to deliberately misrepresent those whom you choose to criticize. I, therefore, kindly request that you print this letter in one of the immediate issues of the *Star*.

No statement of mine can be found in my speech asking "the Canadian Government help establish a Ukrainian state in Europe," as attributed to me by your editorial. I did, however, endeavour to point out that it should be in the interest of the Allied Nations to see to it that Ukrainians be granted the same privileges and sovereign rights as are being granted other peoples in accordance with the principles embodied in the Atlantic Charter. I ask, could any request be fairer than that?

Your editorial states further: "He thought that it would be right meanwhile that Committees of Ukrainians who were organized for this purpose in Britain and on this continent should be represented among the governments-in exile." Here again, I said: "In Britain, the United States and Canada there are in existence United Ukrainian Committees, whose primary object is to assist the governments in Britain, the United States and Canada in the successful prosecution of the war." And further I said: "I so suggest, if I may, sir, that since all the allied nations are fighting for a common cause of freedom that Ukrainian Committees be also invited to delegate their representative or representatives to express the view of 50 million Ukrainian people, at conferences held by the allied nations." Again I ask, is that an unreasonable request?

Finally, your editorial says: "The United Ukrainian organization, referred to by Mr. Hlynka, which is a group outside of Russia, has looked to the Nazis who promised to 'liberate' the Soviet Ukraine." This statement deserves nothing but resentment by all the Ukrainian organizations and myself personally.

In the first place, there is no Ukrainian organization in Canada which is looking to the Nazis to be liberated. Secondly, I did not refer to any Ukrainian organization in my speech whatsoever. I did refer, again, to the United Ukrainian committees in Britain, the United States and Canada, which are organized for the purpose of assisting their respective countries in the successful prosecution of the war, and which include many prominent personages of high standing in these countries. The Ukrainian Canadian Committee to which I had referred is composed of representatives of all the Canadian Ukrainian organizations (with the exception of the Communists) and among its honorary members you will find such names as Hon. J. T. Thorson, Minister of National War services, Hon. Arthur W. Roebuck, M.P. and others.

After all, Mr. Editor, about half the total of our Canadian population is not of Anglo-Saxon extraction; nevertheless they are good and loyal Canadians, and it will just not do to slur them every time we think we have an excuse to do so. We must live and work together, and it is most imperative at all times that we treat them as Canadians.

Anything short of this is a disservice to Canada and her present war effort.

The last impression that your article seems to convey is that I should not have spoken on this subject. Reading your editorial I am convinced more than ever before that it should be brought up more often. Besides, Members on both sides of the House have been constantly asking me to give the House some information about the Ukraine and the Ukrainian people, about whom they have heard and read so much since Ukraine became the battlefield of the present war. I obliged them, and wish to express my pride in being privileged to do so under our democratic form of government. Would not the worthy Editor speak of the people from which he comes the same as I have done, particularly when these people are contributing so much to the allied cause?

Yours,

Anthony H. Hlynka, M.P. for Vegreville.

House of Commons, Ottawa.

GROUP of UKRAINIAN CRITICS COMMUNIST, M.P. CHARGES

By J. H. Fisher, Staff Writer
Toronto Evening Telegram, 21 February 1942

VEGREVILLE MEMBER SAYS TORONTO COUNCIL DOES NOT REPRESENT MAJORITY OF COUNTRYMEN

Ottawa, Feb. 21 – Following upon a recent speech in the House of Commons by Anthony Hlynka of Vegreville in which he outlined the aspirations of the Ukrainian people in Europe after the war, the National Council of the Ukrainian Association to Aid the Fatherland, 274 College street, Toronto, has issued to all M.P.'s a circular which is critical of Mr. Hlynka's remarks.

In it, the National Council of the Ukrainian Association asserts that Mr. Hlynka's speech "constitutes a plan for the creation of a Quisling government which corresponds to the desire of Fuehrer Hitler and his Axis partners."

Mr. Hlynka, in an interview has replied to this criticism. He says that members of the National Council, which is criticizing him, were adherents of the Communist doctrines and that they do not speak for the majority of Canadians of Ukrainian extraction.

"In order that we may be able to understand better the two prevalent views which exist, it is necessary to know something about the aims of the two groups," said Mr. Hlynka. "There is the United Ukrainian-Canadian Committee which is composed of representatives of all the smaller Ukrainian organizations, and it represents over 80 per cent of all the organized Ukrainians in Canada. This committee was organized for the purpose of assisting the Canadian government in its prosecution of the war more effectively.

Was Communist Group

"The other, a much smaller group, was originally the Communist group. It is the same group, under a new name, which is taking exception to the ideas expressed in my speech. They believe that the whole Ukrainian territory should belong to the Soviet Union. On the other hand, I believe that Ukrainians in Europe should be a free nation after the war. I believe in sovereignty for European nations, including Poland, Yugoslavia, Russia, Latvia, the Ukraine and others. I maintain that the basis for the lasting peace is freedom of nations in accordance with items 3, 2 and 6 of the Atlantic Charter. They claim on the other hand, that Ukrainians should not aspire to their nationhood as that would be against the principles of the Atlantic Charter.

"I, for one, believe that the 'Council' is entitled to its opinion as I am to mine, and we should be grateful to the democratic way of life, which permits us to have our own opinions. But this council takes it upon itself to attribute to me and the Ukrainian-Canadian Committee all sorts of motives which they hope would not meet with the approval of public opinion. My answer to that is the very speech which they criticize.

Committee Aids Canada

"The same 'Council' charges that Ukrainian-Canadian Committee has not contributed much to the aid of the Soviet Union. That, of course is true. The Canadian-Ukrainian Committee has chosen to aid Canada instead. The British Commonwealth of Nations and the Soviet Union are allies in this war, and surely no one should criticize Ukrainian-Canadians for aiding Canada instead of the Soviet Union. But this, again, is a matter of choice.

"With reference to the Ukrainian-Canadian Committee, I must say that I cannot speak on their behalf as I am not a member of that committee, and, further, I believe that its executive is capable of making their own statements. I have not collaborated with the members of the committee, or anyone else for that matter, prior to the delivering of my speech, and, therefore, I can speak only for myself. But judging from the press reports and the letters I receive from all the organizations including church organizations, I am happy to say that I am receiving whole-hearted endorsation of the stand I took.

"One word more to draw your attention to the fact that this circular does not make a single reference to the vigorous attack I made in my speech against the Nazi tyranny and its proposed 'new order,' which aims to abolish all nations in Europe and is already dividing the over-run regions into zones, ignoring all racial and ethnographic lines. One wonders why the circular omitted that part of my speech."

CROWDED THEATRE HEARS UKRAINIAN M.P.

Sudbury Daily Star, 23 March 1942

Tells of Many Compatriots in Canadian Army

Enlistment of Ukrainian Canadians in the active army is, in proportion to their population, second to none in all Canada, declared Anthony Hlynka, M.P. for Vegreville, Alberta, who was guest speaker at the Ukrainian Canadian Committee's concert at the Grand Theatre Sunday night on behalf of the Kinsmen's Milk for Britain Fund and the British War Victims Fund.

The lone representative of Ukrainian Canadians in the House of Commons expressed his pride at living in Canada and added that there was no better place in which to live than under the British flag where democratic principles gave such freedom to the people to conduct their lives after a manner which would be of most benefit to themselves and their country. He stated that Canadians need have no fear of the loyalty of the Ukrainian Canadians to Canada and then referred to the large enlistment of Ukrainian Canadians in the army. He challenged anyone to look up the records at Ottawa should they doubt that Ukrainian Canadians are second to no group, in proportion to their numbers in Canada, in enlisting to defend Canada.

Free Speech Thrills

The Vegreville member of parliament told of addressing the House of Commons recently in which speech he told of the feelings of the Ukrainian Canadians. At the close of the address, he stated, he was given much applause by the members of the House of Commons. This gave him great satisfaction, he stated, since such freedom of expression would not be allowed in a dictator country. "There was no one with a gun behind my back to tell me what I could not say, as would be in the case in a dictator country," he said.

The theatre was filled to overflowing and it is estimated that more than 900 people were in attendance. Over 300 people were unable to gain admittance. As far back as last Tuesday, sufficient tickets had been sold to fill the theatre....

"The King" in Ukrainian

The program opened with the singing of "O Canada" and was closed with the singing of "God Save the King" in the Ukrainian language. It was a large and appreciative audience which applauded the musicians and dancers, dressed in colourful Ukrainian costumes....

The guest speaker of the evening, Anthony Hlynka, M.P., of Vegreville, was introduced by Chairman Martin Keaney. Mr. Keaney stated the Vegreville member was not yet 35 years of age but he had made a name for himself on the floor of the House of Commons.

"Having a moral significance, gatherings such as this one should take place at this time in every city in the Dominion," said Mr. Hlynka.

"Tonight the world finds itself in perhaps the darkest hour in all human history," said the guest speaker. "Every one of us must realize the seriousness of the situation. We must each get down to business and do our part.

"We were disarmed mentally and physically after the last war. Yet, today, those very nations which were lulling us to sleep are the ones that are striking the mightiest blows at us at the present time.

"We have in Canada the man-power and the natural resources. As yet, we have been unable to get things properly organized to strike at the enemy.

Must Work Together

"The power of a nation is not in accordance with its population but in its ability to work together. We must learn to work together in Canada. All the enemy offers is slavery and we want none of that in Canada.

"The fight today is not that of democracies against dictators, as is commonly imagined. We must realize we are now fighting for our very self-preservation.

"I think that all Canadian members of parliament should be out 24 hours a day, travelling the length and breadth of Canada, if necessary, to make the people of Canada realize the things they should realize.

"Each of us must not adopt the attitude of 'Let George do it' in our war effort. We must all feel we are the ones to do our duty and not the other fellows."

The guest speaker expressed his pleasure on the apparent success of the concert. He extended his thanks to the Anglo-Saxons and then French-Canadians who had co-operated with the Ukrainian Canadians in making the concert a success. The co-operation of others was heartening to the Ukrainian Canadians, the speaker stated. He pointed out that there never need be any doubt about the loyalty to Canada of the Ukrainian Canadians.

"I assure you," concluded Mr. Hlynka, "that the Ukrainian Canadians will never take second place to any group in their loyalty to Canada, now or ever."

END of RACE PREJUDICE
FORESEEN by ALBERTA M.P.

The Toronto Telegram, 15 April 1942

Canadian, Regardless of Origin, Will Be
Considered Canadian, Says A. H. Hlynka

Predicting that the day is not far off when racial prejudices will be overthrown, and every Canadian, regardless of his origin, will be considered a Canadian, Anthony H. Hlynka, M.P., for Vegreville, Alberta, last night addressed the annual graduation banquet of the Ukrainian Students' Club of the University of Toronto.

"If we intend to make any head-way in Canada, all such prejudices must be thrown aside," he said. "I am quite sure that the time will come when the people in the Dominion will discover more about each other. It is the duty of your graduates to see that things move in this direction. Work hard, create goodwill, and cultivate many friendships."

Mr. Hlynka shared the opinion that young people starting in life now will become leaders in the many communities throughout the length and breadth of Canada, and suggested that they prepare themselves for the task.

Youth's Role Great

"The future world will be in the hands of aggressive young leaders," he continued. "Youth is playing the greatest role in the war, and there is no reason why they should not play an even greater part in the post-war period."

Mr. Hlynka stated that he felt that the blitz period was over and that the struggle will now be a hard and grinding one. The war may spread to greater areas, he said, and stressed the fact that the United Nations will have to take an offensive.

"So far," he said, "we have only been defending ourselves and mobilizing our human and material resources. Our cause cannot lose, because we are fighting for freedom of nations and individuals."

The Vegreville M.P. paid a glowing tribute to the first settlers who came to Canada from the Ukraine. He said that the progress the Ukrainian people made in Canada in a comparatively short period of time was nothing short of a marvel. They have, he said, proven themselves worthy Canadian citizens in every field of endeavour.

MR. HLYNKA WILL VOTE "YES"

The Vegreville Observer, 27 April 1942

Sir:

My attention has been directed to your editorial of April 1st, questioning my attitude in the forthcoming plebiscite. If my reply has been delayed it is because of the demands on my services which made it necessary for me to remain in Ottawa instead of enjoying the privilege of an Easter recess at home and but for an urgent call to the bedside of my aged father, I would not have rushed home now for this brief spell.

I welcome the *Observer*'s invitation to make my views known to those of my constituents who may share your editorial views on my duty in the forthcoming plebiscite.

My stand is perfectly straightforward and it occasions me no embarrassment to declare it without equivocation. The plebiscite does not, or should not, involve any partisan political considerations and any attempt to represent it in that light would be most unfortunate – a view in which I gather you, sir, will readily concur.

In the first place, we have to be clear in our minds on the nature of the plebiscite. Its purpose is to relieve the Government Members of "any obligation arising out of any commitment restricting the method of raising men for military service." That applies to Government Members. No obligation or commitment is involved or implied as far as the New Democracy Members are concerned. I was elected by the Vegreville constituency on the clear-cut policy of a total war effort, with the greatest possible equalization of sacrifice and the conscription of the monetary system taking precedence over the conscription of manpower.

The New Democracy Group has taken that stand consistently since the outbreak of the war. That is our mandate and the forthcoming plebiscite will not relieve us of that commitment, nor indeed, are we seeking to be relieved from it. Events subsequent to the last election have proved the inherent rightness of that stand.

The government has made it clear that even if it receives an overwhelming "yes" vote, as seems probable, it has no intention of changing its present policy either regarding conscription for overseas service or anything else for that matter, unless circumstances compel it to change its views. The Prime Minister has stated that the issue is not conscription in the plebiscite....

Therefore, however the people vote, they will be voting in favour of the government's policy being continued. A "yes" vote will merely relieve the government of its obligation arising out of its self-imposed commitment not to conscript men for overseas service....

EDITORIAL

The Winnipeg Free Press, 29 April 1942

While the other three Winnipeg constituencies piled up substantial majorities for the affirmative vote in Monday's plebiscite, North Winnipeg ran far behind. Only two polls in the whole city returned negative majorities. Both were in North Winnipeg, at 1578 Arlington Street and 599 Aberdeen Avenue. Some very sobering conclusions can be drawn from the reaction of 6,983 North Winnipeggers to the government's request for release from its pledges. They went to the polls with their eyes wide open and voted against total war.

One of Canada's most cosmopolitan constituencies, Winnipeg North contains large numbers of Canadians whose origin is Anglo-Saxon, Jewish, German, Ukrainian, Polish and Hungarian, to name only a few. These people have for years tended to confine themselves to several rather easily defined areas. Point Douglas is predominantly Ukrainian, of whom two-thirds are usually considered pro-Communist and one-third Ukrainian Nationalist. The Jewish people are in the majority in the area bounded by Main Street, McGregor Street, the Canadian Pacific Railway and Mountain Avenue. The northwest corner of this district is largely German and Ukrainian, and these people dominate the area west of McGregor Street.

Elmwood is largely Anglo-Saxon, except in the east and where there is a German and Ukrainian settlement. Anglo-Saxons and Jews are settled east of Main Street north of St. John's and around St. John's Technical High School.

In the Jewish district and in Elmwood, the affirmative vote carried with majorities up to ten and twelve to one. In Point Douglas a strenuous campaign for the affirmative vote was run. Yet it is apparent from the returns that the Ukrainian Nationalists came out in force to vote No. The heaviest No vote in the city was cast at Hallet Street. This was 250 votes, while the affirmative vote at the same poll got 607.

In the rest of the constituency the No vote probably averaged about 40 to the poll. But in the Ukrainian-German district in the north and west of the area it jumped above the hundred mark. Indeed, there were 28 polls in the Ukrainian-German area where in each more than 100 votes were cast against releasing the government from its pledges.

Among many of the German people it can be taken for granted that the votes they cast in the negative were votes for Hitler. These people are still Nazis at heart. They do not want Canada to win the war. The same will be true of a number of the Ukrainian votes. They are obsessed with a phobia where Russia is concerned. Anybody who fights Stalin is their friend. Apparently they don't want Canada to help Russia, so they voted No in the plebiscite.

All this means of course that the German-Ukrainians in Winnipeg North have been the victims of some very bad leadership. They would have accepted the glorious chance the plebiscite gave them to express their solidarity with the rest of Canada. They refused. They voted against an all-out Canadian war effort because they knew it would help beat Hitler. The plebiscite has shown us that Winnipeg has a large number of potential fifth columnists loose in the North End. Unless steps are taken to counteract the pro-Hitler leadership of these foreign groups, there will be trouble ahead. What is apparently needed there is some effective democratic education. Many Canadians of German and Ukrainian origin will have to be shown that this war is just as much in their interest as it is in anyone else's. If they can be made to see this and to return to democracy instead of Nazism, all will be well.

PARLIAMENTARY PERSONALITIES: ANTHONY HLYNKA, SOCIAL CREDIT, VEGREVILLE, ALBERTA

— By Austin F. Cross
Canadian Business, March 1943

In many ways one of the most remarkable men in the House of Commons is Anthony Hlynka, Social Credit member of Parliament for Vegreville, Alberta. Mr. Hlynka believes he is the only Ukrainian-born person sitting in any democratic assembly in the world. He smiles sometimes as he says: "So I can speak for 50,000,000 Ukrainians throughout the world every time I make a speech." It is a tribute to the democratic system that a so-called foreign-born lad could, at the age of 33, reach the Canadian Parliament, and it is a tribute also to the aggressive young man himself.

Hlynka was born in the western Ukraine in 1907, the son of Harry Hlynka and Katherine Krywaniuk. He came to Canada with his parents in 1910 and settled on a homestead farm. But the prairie, while satisfying enough, is a country of wide horizons and on one of the horizons was the city of Edmonton. There he went to attend high school, and later a technical school.

The contact with Canadian-born lads gave him the idea that this was a land of great opportunity, if only one were smart enough to grasp it when it came along. The trick in getting on a freight train is to wait until the caboose comes by, then grab it. If you grab too soon you get sucked under the train; if you grab too late, you fall flat on your face. Hlynka did not miss the caboose.

The fact that he espoused Social Credit should not be held against him by stern easterners. In the era in which he grew up, if young, impressionable Anthony were not attracted to Aberhartiana, he would have been less than normal. It seems to me, however, that Hlynka is not one of its most ardent apostles. Believe in it he certainly does, though as a realist who notes Social Credit's standing outside the province he probably has a few reservations. He does not soap-box all over the place for the Douglas Doctrine as do some of his fellows on Parliamentary Hill.

It was when Hlynka started working his way through college that he began thinking about politics. Six long, weary, dusty summers he worked in a brickyard, and he learned more than brick-making. Later he laboured on the railways, never a genteel job at best. Hlynka, having got his education the hard way, set out to instruct others and for a while taught English to foreign language groups.

Then he got the idea that the best way to get his ideas across to other people was to be a publisher. From 1935 to 1940 he was publisher and editor of a magazine named *The Call*, written both in Ukrainian and English, and of another bi-weekly sheet. After he had been in the publishing business for five years he decided, at the ripe old age on 33, that he could make the grade in politics.

Running as a New Democracy candidate, which was the label temporarily adopted by the S.C.'s, he beat the Liberal, a Progressive and a C.C.F. candidate handily and walked into the Commons, there to be assigned a back seat.

Hlynka is six feet tall, rosy-cheeked, and has a heart-shaped face and other typically Ukrainian features. He is so broad-shouldered that a football coach would look on him as a great middle wing gone to waste because he never played with any varsity team.

If you sound him out on his views, you will find him a firm believer in Canada's standing on her own feet. But at the same time he hastens to point out that he ardently advocates British ideals. He has said that Canada should be drawn closer to Britain than any other country, because, as he told *Canadian Business*, "We have received so much from Britain in our culture, traditions, and centuries of statecraft experience." He also believes that Canada has so far gained more from Britain than Britain has from Canada.

"In a word," he told me, "I believe that Canada's ideal position is to remain within the pattern of the British Commonwealth of Nations."

No one doubts that he is a typical Canadian. The Toronto *Telegram*, not always eager to endorse our foreign-born, said, through its gifted parliamentary correspondent, J. H. Fisher: "Born in the Ukraine, and brought to Canada as a child, Anthony Hlynka's perfect English is a tribute to the Canadian school system and to the assimilating qualities of some of the European stocks."

As for his own people, 50,000,000 strong in Central and Eastern Europe, he believes he owes a debt to them, and he asks for them as he does for himself, liberty and freedom. That seems to him a reasonable request. Hlynka's speech on this problem given in the House of Commons last winter was reprinted in booklet form and circulated to thousands of Ukrainians in United States.

Hlynka is anxious about the youth of this country, and wants to see Canada give them a better chance from now on. He also wants to see the racial question tackled properly. He believes too little attention has been paid to it.

What are his views on Social Credit? He says that it is misunderstood by many and condemned by those who never have studied it.

"I do not believe, however, in uprooting everything that has been built up over centuries, but rather in remedying the faulty parts of our social and economic system." That does not sound too radical.

Hlynka, being young and fancy-free, gets around in the geographical sense. He is in Vancouver one day, Vegreville the next....

URGE UKRAINIANS BOOST ENLISTMENTS to FORCES and FURTHER WAR DRIVES

Toronto Evening Telegram, 17 March 1943

Freedom For 50 Millions in Europe Sought by Anthony Hlynka, M.P., at Convention

A resolution urging that all members and supporters increase the enlistments in all the services of Canada's armed forces to the maximum, and assist Canada still more in her campaigns such as Victory Loan, sale of War Savings Certificates and the Red Cross was adopted last night at the conclusion of the sixth annual provincial convention of the Ukrainian National Federation of Canada, held in Toronto.

The resolution concluded with an appeal for co-operation among the various groups of Canadian citizens.

The convention met on Friday at 300 Bathurst Street, where about 60 out-of-town delegates were present.

Principal speaker at the rally was Anthony Hlynka, M.P. for Vegreville, Alta., who spoke Saturday night to a crowded hall.

"The four aims of the convention," Mr. Hlynka said, "were, firstly, that as Canadian citizens they should take a responsible part in fighting for the victory of the Allies and simultaneously for the freedom of the Ukrainians; secondly, that as Canadian citizens they are interested in a post-war world, and if it is not organized as it should be, we will have died in vain.

Want Lasting Peace

"We must organize a world order for lasting peace to prevent the tragedy of the present war. We must put every ounce into an effort to educate every national and political group in Canada towards this objective. We must mobilize all our energy and resources that all our boys will come back from overseas victorious and to ensure peace and freedom to all nations.

"Thirdly," said Mr. Hlynka, "there are the social and economic aims. Some groups in the past have claimed that they alone were interested in the fate of the worker, and that other organizations did not stress the social and economic problems of the common man. But today all groups, including the Ukrainian Committee, raise this problem.

"Our fourth problem is organizational. Nobody has to be ashamed of the work done by this organization during the past ten years. No nation can live without freedom. If the Ukrainian people in Europe do not obtain freedom and liberty, all their traditions and culture will be lost.

"In Western Canada there is hardly a Ukrainian family which has not given a son or a father to the Armed Forces of Canada, because they believe in the Atlantic Charter. But when the Ukrainians, as a nation of 50,000,000, ask for freedom, no one is prepared to offer it to them.

"We, as Canadians, have a double mission to perform. We would be worth not one red penny as Canadians in an Anglo-Saxon world, if we did not ask for the freedom of our brothers. We would not be honourable if we forget our forefathers who fought for our freedom. We owe a debt to our forefathers, and I am not ashamed to state this on any platform or even in Dominion Parliament.

First Duty

"Our first great duty is Canada and the successful prosecution of this war. Our people came to Canada with bare hands and now have freedom and liberty and are willing to fulfill their duties.

"Did you ever hear of the great sacrifices of the Ukrainians in Europe?" Mr. Hlynka asked. "No. Did you ever hear any newspaper state that the Ukrainian boys in Western Canada have the highest percentage of numbers enlisting with the armed forces? The record of this war does not give a full picture of the work and the sacrifice of our people in Canada.

"Why did we come to Canada? The search for freedom compelled our forefathers to leave their native land. Having attained this freedom, we are in a position to ask for the liberty of those who are still in bondage.

Mr. Hlynka told the delegates that they should support that part of the Anglo-Saxon press which interpreted the Ukrainian movements truly.

"Best reports are given by the *Toronto Evening Telegram*. The *Telegram* studies our problems and is interested in our cause."

CHARGES PEOPLE *to* THROW WHOLE EFFORT *into* WAR

Sudbury Daily Star, 24 March 1943

Only Ukrainian M.P. Speaks in City

Sudbury's Ukrainian-Canadians were urged to throw their full weight behind the national war effort by Anthony H. Hlynka, only Canadian member of parliament of Ukrainian extraction. The member for Vegreville, Alberta, was the guest speaker at a meeting held in the Ukrainian Hall on Sunday night.

Pointing to his unique position in the House of Commons, he reminded a large audience that he was probably the only Ukrainian-Canadian in the entire world free to discuss the problems of his people publicly.

"That is possible only under the British flag, in time of war," he declared. "Regardless of what complications arise, either here or beyond the seas, we will never flinch in our loyalty to Canada. We will stand beside the British people, for we believe that the future fate of the Anglo-Saxon world will be closely linked with that of the Ukrainian people. The Ukrainians are undoubtedly one of the strongest people, potentially in Europe.

Must Look to Future

"Not only must we win the war, we must plan for the future of the post-war world.

"In this regard, I am working hard for unity among Ukrainian groups in this country, and for unity among the Canadian people, regardless of racial extraction. Unity has been my theme for years. I have always believed that only through it can be built a great Canada and a great Canadian nation. With unity, there is no doubt who will win this war."

Ukrainian-Canadians, he stated, are helping Canada by enlisting in the fighting services, by industrial labour, and by serving unflinchingly wherever they have been stationed.

INDEPENDENT UKRAINIAN STATE IS URGED in BRIEF to OTTAWA

Winnipeg Free Press, 31 March 1943

The setting up of an independent Ukrainian state in Europe, under the terms of the Atlantic Charter, has been advocated in a brief submitted to Prime Minister W. L. Mackenzie King by the Ukrainian Canadian committee. The brief was drawn up in Winnipeg and is signed by Rev. Dr. W. Kushnir, president; Rev. S. W. Sawchuk, vice-president; W. Swystun, vice-president; J. W. Arsenych, secretary; A. Malofie, treasurer, and S. Chwaliboga, financial secretary. The text of the submission follows:

The Ukrainian Canadian committee beg to present to His Majesty's government their views regarding the future eastern boundary of Poland, believing that such views may be helpful in the framing of a Canadian policy in external affairs and in the consolidating of our war effort.

We believe that the winning of this war in a military sense is the first and immediate task of all Canadians to which every other activity and interest must be subordinated. Discussions regarding the details of post-war settlements and boundaries which tend to produce differences of opinion ought to be postponed. We, therefore, view with apprehension the thesis advanced by the Polish government regarding the future eastern boundary of Poland, which advocates that such a boundary should pass through the centre of the ethnic territories inhabited by Ukrainians.

Facts and Principles

We hold the following facts and principles to be indisputable:

1. Whenever the Ukrainian people have had a chance to express freely their wishes they have shown their desire for their

sovereign rights and self-government. This was particularly manifest at the end of the last war.

2. The Atlantic Charter clearly and unmistakably lays down as a principle the right of a people to determine their political destiny. The Allied nations have made this principle the basis of their present war objective.
3. The Ukrainian people desire unity. They believe that whatever form the post-war settlement takes it should result in the final political unification of the territories inhabited by Ukrainians.
4. The Ukrainian people desire equality of treatment. They believe that in the post-war settlement their claims to an independent free state in a free Europe should not be disregarded and that the Ukrainian question should be included in any just and permanent settlement of Europe.

Therefore, the Ukrainian Canadian committee representing Canadians of Ukrainian origin believe it is a duty which they owe to their kinsmen to bring these facts and principles to the attention of His Majesty's government, and also a duty which they owe to Canada, in order that the war effort based on clear and accepted principles may receive the greatest support from all Canadian citizens, the submission states.

Following the formal submission, the brief contains an appendix in which some of the historical facts of the Ukraine are summarized.

UKRAINIANS PLAY BIG ROLE in CANADIAN WAR FORCES

Toronto Evening Telegram, 3 April 1943

Virtually Every Family is Represented in Armed Services, Says Anthony Hlynka, M.P.

"Nearly every Ukrainian home out west has given one or more of its members to one of three services of the fighting forces," said Anthony Hlynka, Social Credit member of Parliament, in an interview today.

Son of a Ukrainian farmer the young, Slavic-looking M.P. represents farmers of his western province of Alberta in the federal government. Dark, broad-shouldered and slow-speaking, he seems to have more the calm of the wide acres of the prairies than the hectic hurry of political endeavour about him.

He measures his words as gravely as he might have measured his furrows, and sucks at his pipe as contemplatively during an interview as he might have while astride a fence by a green spring field.

Anthony Hlynka's parents came to Canada from western Ukraine when he was two and a half years old. They have since then homesteaded in the west, bringing up a family of three sons and five daughters, now all of them part of the Canadian pattern.

Varied Experience

Young Anthony grew up close to land, was the president of the Student Union at his school, loved to speak and began making public lectures at the age of 16. Since then he worked at a brickyard for six years, he taught English to new Canadians, has sold insurance, published a paper, worked on the railroad and the farm.

Now, a member of Parliament at the age of 35 he says with amused pride: "I surely came up the hard way. I feel I am close to people, and I am proud of that, for all I am or will ever be is directly due to everyone I meet."

"Canada must never permit poverty, debt and privation of the prewar days to return," he said gravely. "Conditions have been far from satisfactory as far as farmers are concerned in the prairie provinces, though these have, at the moment, somewhat improved."

Urges Economic Change

"The present temporary prosperity brought about by the war is something that cannot be lasting in the west unless certain fundamental adjustments and changes are made in our economy affecting our farmers who, after all, constitute one-third of our total population."

He is slow to speak about himself, or his ideas, or his opinions. But he speaks eagerly of his people, the 400,000 Ukrainians now living in Canada.

"The Ukrainians first settled out west 51 years ago," he says, relating the story as though it was some ancient saga. "They came in batches of 40 or more. They cleared the lands, established their homes, had families and assimilated a new way of life. In a short while they have educated us – their children – so that now there is a class of professional men and women in the ranks of Ukrainians. My two brothers are both in scientific research; there are doctors, lawyers, writers among men whose fathers came from little houses in old Ukraine."

Anthony Hlynka came to Toronto from Ottawa yesterday to speak at a Ukrainian celebration held at Massey Hall. He expects to return to the capital today.

EXTRACT FROM MACLEAN'S MAGAZINE

1 August 1943

Extract from a speech by Anthony Hlynka, member for Vegreville, in the House of Commons, Ottawa, 1943.

To me, the British crown is the heart and symbol of the British Commonwealth of free and sovereign people. To me, the British crown is the symbol of unity and the heritage of British ideals for more than a thousand years. More than that, we should prize our position within the Commonwealth because we are the benefactors in all and everything that has been achieved over centuries of progress.

VEGREVILLE'S M.P. MARRIED *in* TORONTO

Vegreville Observer, 1 December 1943

Announcement is made of the marriage of Anthony Hlynka, member of the House of Commons for Vegreville, to Miss Stephanie Chole, daughter of Mr. and Mrs. John Chole of Toronto. The event took place on Saturday, November 27th, at Josaphat's Ukrainian Church, Toronto.

Among the guests at the wedding was Hon. John Bracken, Progressive leader, who extended congratulations to the bride and groom.

In case his constituents have forgotten it, the *Observer* would remind them that Mr. Hlynka belongs to the New Democracy party, erstwhile Social Crediters.

The report of the wedding also states that Mr. and Mrs. Hlynka will reside in Ottawa during parliamentary sessions and in Vegreville between times. Fine; they will be welcomed here.

Mr. Hlynka's constituents will gladly unite in wishing him and his bride every happiness. ...

The wedding of Anthony Hlynka and Stephanie Chole

HLYNKA WORRIES ABOUT UKRAINE

Toronto Evening Telegram, 27 March 1945

OTTAWA. – Anthony Hlynka (S.C. – Vegreville) said Monday night in the commons he was in complete agreement with the sending of a delegation to San Francisco, but could not give advance approval to any scheme. He spoke as the world security debate continued.

"The concept of sovereignty, in my opinion, is still the only real security for freedom so long as more powerful nations retain their own sovereignty," said Mr. Hlynka.

All parties in parliament except Social Credit were ready to surrender Canadian sovereignty to the new organization and perhaps to the Big Three.

People Losing Power?

He wondered if power "is slipping out of the hands of the people" and if that was the reason sovereignty was to be surrendered now when it was not proposed in the League of Nations.

Mr. Hlynka said the British Commonwealth was the closest example of an ideal world organization one could find.

The commonwealth and the U.S. were privileged to be the great democratic leaders today. The age demanded that they assure not only their own continued existence, but also that of other countries who fought by their side.

Mr. Hlynka said a great debt was owed to Russia for the part she played in the war, but he could not agree that "Russia alone saved us."

Thought Not True

Such a statement "was not entirely true," he said. It should not be forgotten that a great debt was owed by the United Nations to many countries which still had not their full liberties, for example the Ukraine.

The Ukrainian people had made great sacrifices and they were silent partners throughout the war. There were other subjugated nations which should be given a chance to present their cases at all international conferences such as the forthcoming one at San Francisco.

He suggested that Ukrainian societies in Canada and the U.S. should be invited to the conference to present the case of the Ukrainian people who now were unable to present their own.

He did not believe the Russian delegation would present the Ukrainian problem as it should be presented.

People desire peace only to the extent that it is consistent with freedom. There could be no peace while there were submerged nations fighting for their self-preservation.

EDITORIAL

Edmonton Journal, 28 March 1945

The Editor,
Edmonton Journal,
Edmonton, Alta.

Dear Sir:

In the March 28th issue of your paper there appears an editorial entitled "Mr. Hlynka's Outrageous Proposal." This editorial criticises me for the speech I made in the House of Commons on March 26th last when I spoke in the debate on the San Francisco Conference. May I be privileged to make a reply.

I suggested in my speech that submerged nations be enabled to make their representations at world peace conferences. I suggested, too, that the Ukrainian people, who are the most numerous in Europe without self-government, be accorded the same privilege.

The *Journal* strongly objects to this proposal and says: "If anything of this kind were attempted, the successful outcome of the conference would be seriously endangered." May I point out two facts in this connection.

During the debate on the San Francisco Conference, Russo-Polish relations were discussed quite extensively. Several members on the both sides of the House pleaded the Polish case. No one suggested that their speeches "seriously endangered the outcome of the conference." Why should any suggestion on my part concerning freedom for the Ukrainian people endanger the outcome of the conference?

The most striking part of the editorial is this: "The Ukraine has long been part of her (Russia's) territory and she would have as much right to resent having its future discussed as the people of the United States would have to object consideration being given to whether or not Texas should have been or should continue to be included in the American union." It is beyond comprehension that this parallel is drawn. The Ukrainian people have their own language, history, traditions and culture. They are a distinct people who, in the course of more than a thousand years, have had their sovereignty and self-government time and again, and have always asserted their desire to be free.

To say that because a large portion of the Ukraine was dominated by force for some time, the solution to the problem is to place the whole of the Ukraine under the occupation of the dominating power, is contrary to logic.

The editorial also says that "it would seem to the impartial observer that dissention among the Ukrainians only exists outside of the Ukrainian Republic and that it only exists here in Canada because it is carefully cultivated by interested persons who would receive short shrift from their fellow Ukrainians in the Soviet Union if they were to attempt such tactics in their native land as they do here in Canada."

The facts are that the overwhelming majority of Canadians of Ukrainian origin are not communists, and the overwhelming majority of the Ukrainians in the Ukraine are not communists. The non-communist Ukrainians have always aspired to sovereignty, as it is not natural for any people to resign themselves to submission to any foreign power.

Certainly, any one should realize that a people, once under the domination of a totalitarian government, are not free to plead their own case.

I have always contended that the principle of sovereignty and self-government must be made to apply to all peoples if we are to achieve a lasting peace.

Yours truly,
Anthony Hlynka, M.P.

House of Commons,
Ottawa, Canada.

VEGREVILLE M.P. THANKS HIS ELECTORS

The Tofield Mercury, July 12, 1945

To the Electors of the Vegreville Federal Consitituency:

It is with a deep sense of gratitude that I wish to thank my electors for the splendid support they have given me at the polls on June 11th. May I also thank those who in so many ways have contributed so generously to our success. I know, too, that many of my supporters worked hard to give me such a large majority. I thank them sincerely for all they have done.

Especially do I wish to mention my supporters in the Armed Services, both overseas and in Canada, who have given me the largest share of the service votes from the Vegreville consituency, and who believed in my sincerity. A young airman, formerly of Lavoy, Alberta, had this to say in his recent letter to me:

> Here in the United Kingdom awaiting repatriation after nearly five and a half years of service overseas.
>
> I sincerely believe that you will work hard for us young lads, who have given our all, and endeavour to give us a chance to start anew to get adjusted to civil life.

Truly, not only will I work hard for the "young lads who have given their all," but I will do my utmost in urging the Government to stand by our young lads as loyally and as devotedly as the young lads stood by Canada.

As for my electors at home, I desire to say that when I was first elected to the Canadian House of Commons in 1940, it was then that I fully realized the responsibility with which my constituents entrusted me. I resolved then to work in the best interests of my constituency and in the best interests of Canada. This I have have tried to do in my humble way and will continue to do – with faith in the people I represent and with faith in the great future of Canada.

Anthony Hlynka,
Member of Parliament for Vegreville.

HLYNKA URGES STOP PRESSURE ON REPATRIATES

The Canadian Press, 25 September 1945

OTTAWA, Sept. 25. – (CP) – Anthony Hlynka, Social Credit member for the Alberta constituency of Vegreville, yesterday asked the government to urge British and American officials to halt the forced repatriation of displaced persons in Europe.

Speaking during continued throne speech debate, Mr. Hlynka, son of a Ukrainian immigrant, said reports from Europe indicated that displaced persons from the Russian sphere of occupation were being forced by the democracies "to become communist or perish."

Prefer Die First

"Many of these displaced persons commit suicide rather than return under the Soviets," said Mr. Hlynka. "Still others go so far as to resist the British and American military police in self-defence, and we learn from the latest reports that the situation is growing worse."

He made a particular plea on behalf of Ukrainian refugees in Europe and asked that representatives of the Ukrainian relief committee be allowed to visit camps where such refugees were held. He asked that European news broadcasts also be made in Ukrainian and that the refugees be allowed to publish a Ukrainian newsletter.

He asked that societies, private citizens and relatives of displaced persons be allowed to send food, clothing and other supplies direct to refugees in regions where complications have arisen due to racial or political differences.

SOCRED M.P. SLAMS REDS

Windsor Star, 26 September 1945

ALBERTA MEMBER SPEAKS IN DETROIT

Soviet agents are circulating through the British and American zones of occupation in Europe, using force in some cases to get Ukrainians to return to the Soviet-dominated Ukraine, Anthony Hlynka, Social Credit M.P. for Vegreville, Alberta, declared yesterday, addressing a large audience in the Masonic Temple auditorium at Detroit. The gathering in Detroit was to raise money for the Ukrainian War Relief Fund.

Depicts Plight

Declaring that the war had been fought to preserve liberty and to end tyranny, the speaker went on to depict the plight of millions of displaced persons in Europe, scattered through the areas under American and British occupation, who are in dire need of food, clothing, and most of all, protection against Soviet agents who would force them to return to the Ukraine.

Their objection to returning voluntarily to their homeland is that penal servitude, concentration camps, or death awaits them there, Mr. Hlynka said.

Referring to a letter he had received from a Ukrainian in Europe, Mr. Hlynka said: "The letter says that when the Russian officers were gathering Ukrainian refugees, an old Ukrainian peasant stepped forward and exclaimed, 'You come here to persuade us to return to our homeland? Whoever heard of a people sending agitators to persuade its people to return to it? Do you think we do not love our native land? When conditions are what they should be, we shall be glad to crawl on our knees, and with our last bit of strength, back home.'"

Quotes Article

Mr. Hlynka quoted from an article which Elma Birkett had written for the Weekly Review, an English publication: "Executions combined with mass deportations into the depths of the Soviet Union filled the whole population with terror. Many political leaders, essentially nationally and democratically minded, were deported into Asia and soon died in exile...."

Following the concert, a banquet in honour of Mr. and Mrs. Hlynka was held at the Ukrainian National Temple in Detroit.

HLYNKA PROTESTS MOVING UKRAINIANS

Windsor Star, 25 January 1946

TORONTO – Anthony Hlynka, Social Credit member of parliament for Vegreville, said Saturday he thought it "rather presumptuous" on the part of the Soviet Union to take it for granted that people who have come from territories annexed by the Soviet during the war would be handed over to Russia.

Mr. Hlynka, who arrived from Ottawa, was commenting on the news that 500,000 Ukrainians in British, American and French occupation zones in Germany may be deported to the Soviet Union. The stocky, vigorous Ukrainian-Canadian, who represents a large number of Ukrainians in northern Alberta, will plead for the cause of these European Ukrainians at a public meeting Monday sponsored by the Ukrainian-Canadian committee.

"The great majority of these persons have never been Russians or Soviet citizens, nor were their ancestors," said Mr. Hlynka. "It appears that at Yalta it was orally decreed that all those who were Soviet citizens up to 1939 would be returned to the Soviet Union, but at no time was there any agreement made … that persons who never were Soviet citizens would be handed over to Soviet authorities."

PROTESTS PATRIOT BETRAYAL to RUSSIAN PERSECUTION

Toronto Evening Telegram, 26 January 1946

ANTHONY HLYNKA, MP, TO PUT UKRAINIANS' CASE BEFORE TORONTO – HUNTED BY SOVIETS

Anthony Hlynka, Social Credit Member of Parliament for Vegreville, Alberta, tireless representative in the House for 400,000 Canadian Ukrainians, arrived in Toronto today.

Mr. Hlynka is here to put before the public the plight of nearly half a million Ukrainians in the British, American and French zones of occupation in Germany who are faced with the possibility of being deported to the Soviet Union. He will speak on that subject in Massey Hall tomorrow afternoon.

The meeting is under the sponsorship of the Ukrainian Canadian Committee, and Mayor Robert Saunders has been invited to be present. Music will be supplied by the very fine choir of the Ukrainian National Federation.

Driven to Hills

In an interview today, Mr. Hlynka said that in addition to those in camps in the occupational zones there are many thousands of Ukrainians hiding out in the hills and forests, living like animals, because they dare not enter the camps to face the possibility of being deported.

"The great majority of these 400,000 persons have never been Russian or Soviet citizens, nor were their ancestors," he said. "It appears that at Yalta it was orally decreed that all those who were Soviet citizens up to 1939 would be returned to the Soviet Union, but at no time was there any agreement made, or promise given, that persons who never were Soviet citizens would be handed over to the Soviet authorities."

Speaking with considerable emphasis, Mr. Hlynka stated that as yet the peace treaties have not been signed.

Soviet Presumption

"It is rather presumptuous on the part of the Soviet authorities to take it for granted that people who have come from territories annexed by the Soviet Union during the war would be handed over to them. It is assuming a little too much," he declared.

Born of Ukrainian parents, Mr. Hlynka came to Canada when he was two years of age. Stocky, square-shouldered and slow speaking, he has no trace of accent. He is dark-complexioned, and vigorous, and his life is devoted to the Ukrainian cause. He is the champion of the great number of Ukrainians in Canada, and he will fight to the last to see that justice is done to the hundreds of thousands of displaced Ukrainians in Western Europe.

He admitted that he had little time for relaxation. "I am kept pretty busy," he said. "Demands are reaching me from all over Canada – demands that something be done about the plight of Ukrainian displaced persons in Europe and demands from Ukrainians for entry into Canada."

After his engagement in the Massey Hall, Mr. Hlynka will return to Ottawa.

PEOPLE WEEP, RAISE $5,000 as HLYNKA PLEADS for REFUGEES

Toronto Evening Telegram, 28 January 1946

2500 PEOPLE GO TO HEAR SOCIAL CREDIT ORATOR

A tremendous and prolonged applause from a great audience in Massey Hall yesterday afternoon greeted the statement made by Anthony Hlynka, MP, that "The Evening Telegram has done more to bring about racial unity than any other newspaper in Canada."

Mr. Hlynka was addressing a crowded house on the political situation in Europe and the grievous position of Ukrainians who are gathered in the zones occupied by the British, French and American troops. There is the immediate possibility that these hundreds of thousands of people will be deported to the Soviet Union against their will.

"Canadians of Ukrainian origin in Toronto and Canada should appreciate the assistance they have been given by this great newspaper," he said.

Force for Unity

"The Evening Telegram has done more to unify the different racial groups than any other paper, helping them to mould their opinions and assisting them in their problems. We should indeed be grateful for the assistance of this great Canadian newspaper."

Mayor Robert Saunders welcomed Mr. Hlynka to the city and said that he believed he voiced the sentiments of the citizens of Toronto when he said that "we are definitely behind an effort on the part of your committee to assist your relatives still in the Old Land."

"We have fought a six years' war to bring freedom to the world," he said, "and men and women the world over should be able to choose their own form of government.

"It is our hope that millions of Ukrainians in Europe will have the privilege of forming their own government. We know the Ukrainians in Canada make wonderful citizens. They have brought to us many worthwhile traditions, and I am glad to be here with a member of Parliament who represents some of the thoughts of the Ukrainian people – one whose parents are Ukrainian; one who knows the democracy which sent him to parliament to represent the Ukrainian-Canadian citizens in the West."

Thousands in Misery

Mr. Hlynka spoke impassionedly for an hour about the displaced Ukrainian people of Europe. He told graphically of their misery. He told, not only of those 400,000 in the occupational zones, but of those additional thousands who are living out in the mountains and forests, practically starving, afraid to enter the occupational zone camps with their fellow-Ukrainians because of the fear that they might be deported to the Soviet Union; a fate so terrible that mass suicide is attempted in an effort to escape it.

Originally a nation of 45,000,000 in Europe, the Ukrainians are known to have lost at least 10,000,000 casualties in the war through fighting, famine and the deliberate effort of their enemies to exterminate a nation.

In addition, an unknown number of Ukrainians, which probably amounts to another 10,000,000, is at present unaccounted for. They have been chased from zone to zone, starved, murdered and carried off for forced labor in Siberia and parts of Europe under Soviet control.

Mr. Hlynka, who is Social Credit member for Vegreville, Alberta, spoke first in faultless English, and then in Ukrainian. He is a master of both and dislikes the microphone....

When he had finished his address a collection was taken to aid the unfortunate people in Europe, and in 15 minutes $5,000, much of it in bills, was poured on the platform. Many of those who rushed forward with their money had tears streaming down their cheeks.

Appeal to Mr. King

At the conclusion of the meeting, the following resolution, in part, was sent to Prime Minister Mackenzie King:

"We Canadian citizens of Ukrainian origin, to the number of 2,500 assembled this 27th day of January, 1946, in Massey Hall, Toronto, respectfully submit the following request to the end that on behalf of the Canadian Government he communicate it to the government of the United Kingdom; that the order issued by Senior Army Headquarters in the British Occupational Zone with regard to Ukrainian displaced persons be reviewed in the light of its discrimination against Ukrainian people, and its denial of the most elementary human rights; and that the necessary instructions be issued for the immediate revocation of the order; that all necessary food, clothing, and medical supplies be permitted entry into Ukrainian Displaced Persons' Camps."

'CROSS TOWN WITH CROSS

Ottawa Evening Citizen, 20 March 1946

A COLUMN OF CHATTER ABOUT THIS AND THAT IN AND AROUND OTTAWA BY THE *EVENING CITIZEN*'S AUSTIN F. CROSS.

A lady keeps phoning me, wanting to urge me that I expose these spy suspects as being non-Canadians. Now I quite agree that in this particular instance, some of those arraigned in court are foreign-born. But I do not see why we should condemn those of foreign birth as a whole, because of the alleged excesses of a few Kremlin stooges.

Having taught school among the Ukrainians in the West, having in another country school (Rosefield S.D. No. 3884, Saskatchewan) been "Schullehrer" to a mixed assortment of Russian-Germans, Austro-Germans, Poles, Norwegians and other combinations, I retain, a full quarter century later, a profound respect for the children of foreign-born people. Indeed, that respect has been heightened by a constant perusal of the casualty lists, the lads whose names end in chenko, chuk, and ski, have proved they can die for Canada just like the Smiths, Jones, and the Macdonalds.

* * *

I recall with particular distaste the remark of a Western bishop, who should have known better, when he referred to our new Canadians as "Garlic-smelling Continentals." It was pretty small potatoes for a man in so exalted a position, and surely couldn't have done his church any good. Well, I feel this lady who calls me is in the same category.

I'll take a foreigner any day to a renegade Englishman, and I'll take a good Bohunk to a degenerate Canadian. I'll back foreign members of parliament like Anthony Hlynka and Frank Jaenicke and Dave Croll against a lot of other solid citizens you and I know.

There'll never be a great Canada as long as we have super-patriots trying to jump on anybody with a foreign name. This woman who considers it her duty to phone me, to attempt to straighten me out, and to correct *The Evening Citizen*, who urges me to attempt the role of the anti-Semite, has a lot to answer for, and so have some of her sisters. Canada's big enough for anybody and everybody who wants to be a Canadian.

Because a very insignificant number of people – perhaps only a fraction of one per cent – chose to act the knave, if not worse, there seems to be no reason why we should condemn all our foreign born. Let's have no more letters and phone calls appealing to race and religion. That way lies bigotry and bloodshed; by hounding anybody with a strange name, we turn back the clock, we about-face and start marching toward the Dark Ages.

WARNS AGAINST FIFTH COLUMN WORK of REDS

Sudbury Star, 20 May 1946

A warning against the fifth-column activities of Communists in Canada was made by Anthony Hlynka, M.P. for Vegreville, Alta., addressing a meeting of the Ukrainian-Canadian Committee in the Ukrainian National Federation Hall Sunday afternoon. Mr. Hlynka stated that it was regrettable that more heed had not been taken to the continual warnings by Ukrainian-Canadian organizations of the existence of such subversive activities.

After paying special tribute to those Ukrainian-Canadians who served in the armed forces, and to those who worked on production lines and on farms, Mr. Hlynka expressed regret that despite this contribution, the Canadian government had so far failed to comply with the plea of Ukrainian-Canadians to grant permission for entry of their relatives who are among the displaced persons in camps throughout Europe.

Helped Win War

Echoing the words of Mr. Hlynka, Rev. Father M. Horoshko, parish priest of St. Mary's Ukrainian Church in Sudbury, stated his conviction that by their contribution his countrymen had won for themselves everlasting honour. Father Horoshko, recently discharged from the Canadian army, was the only Ukrainian Greek Catholic padre with the Canadian forces overseas. The ex-padre said that just as during the war, so in the future Canadians of Ukrainian origin will never shirk their responsibilities and duties as Canadians.

Mrs. Hlynka, wife of the visiting speaker, made a few brief remarks at the meeting, stressing more the human sympathy angle of the "tragic problem" of the homeless and stateless families who are in the displaced persons' camps. She graphically depicted the plight of orphaned children growing up without proper food or proper education, and appealed to the women of the organization to do everything in their power to make their pleas for immediate assistance heard.

ALL-CANADA UKRAINIAN CONGRESS an EYE-OPENER

Toronto Telegram, 7 June 1946

Canada needs more groups inspired by the moderation, fairness and commonsense shown by the All Canada Ukrainian Canadian Congress in session in Toronto this week. The Congress has been falsely denounced as fascist because it does not take orders from Moscow. It can easily refute the allegation by pointing to its loyal service to Canada when Stalin was acting as Hitler's other office boy.

The Congress, however, wastes little time answering fools according to their folly. It is often considered as a western product, because its first convention was held in Winnipeg, but it is continent-wide and is, as it proclaims itself, All Canada. Delegates have come from British Columbia, all the western provinces, and even Quebec. They have come without any wheedling for municipal or provincial grants. The three hundred delegates, or the organization appointing them, pay their own expenses.

Instead of poulticing an inferiority complex by wailing for legislation against racial discrimination, or braying for bi-lingualism, these Ukrainians settle with satisfaction into the duties of full Canadian citizenship. They know they are good Canadians and know others must eventually know it.

Instead of snarling like dogs in the manger against newcomers the Congress has taken the broad view that the best interests of Canada are also their interests and the interests of their friends abroad. They welcome newcomers. They were newcomers themselves, even more recently than the Great War. They know what it is to work hard, to live thriftily, and to succeed. Few of them have ever been on relief; not one per cent.

They came to Canada with college diplomas or calloused hands, their only capital brawn and brains. There were no remittance men among them. There is no Ukrainian equivalent for that term. They took the first job offered. For many it was dish washing. None washed dishes long. No race has made better progress in Canada in one generation than the Ukrainians. Boys who washed dishes for their first meal got jobs next day and now own cars, houses, farms, factories, businesses and bank accounts. Their children throng collegiate institutes and universities, and win scholarships and medals. They keep on working. Canada has no more industrious citizens than her Ukrainians.

Such guests at the Congress as Anthony Hlynka, M.P. for Vegreville, are grand advertisements of the value to Canada of second generation Ukrainians.

There are 305,000 of them now including the surviving first comers. They sent 40,000 men and women to the fighting services, without waiting to question whether this was a "phoney," "imperialistic," "capitalistic" or "democratic" war, or whether Yadko Jo, as they call Marshal Stalin, wanted them to. They knew whose liberties were at stake, viz., their own and our own, and they fought for them. When they came back from the war they went to work where they left off.

The Congress has naturally endorsed a broad immigration policy for "displaced persons," nightmare phrase of a nightmare peace in Europe. Many of the displaced are their own fathers, mothers, aunts, uncles, nieces and nephews, chained for seven years now behind the spreading iron curtain and menaced with slavery. They have homes for them here, and work for them, paid work, in their little stores, in their big factories, on their farms, in their professions. In a country with three jobs offering for every pair of hands these Ukrainians have no patience with the palaver that the first requirement regarding immigration must be that it shall not affect the stranglehold of Quebec on Canada and its government, and the second that it must not affect the security of entrenched organizations that will not work or let others work.

LAKEHEAD UKRAINIANS HEAR ANTHONY HLYNKA; M.P.

Port Arthur Chronicle, 8 June 1946

A meeting sponsored by the Fort William-Port Arthur branch of the Canadian Ukrainian Committee was held in the Lake Theatre, Fort William, Sunday afternoon with an attendance of 500. Anthony Hlynka, M.P. for Vegreville, Alberta, was guest speaker.

Mr. Hlynka spoke of the contribution of Canadians of Ukrainian origin to Canada's war effort and stated that so far as non-communist Canadian-Ukrainians are concerned Canada should never have any doubts as to their loyalty. Mr. Hlynka warned the audience of the necessity of combatting fifth column activities in this country, supporting his warning by quoting from the recent report of the Royal Commission on espionage in Canada.

Mr. Hlynka said he wished to remind Canadians that the Ukrainian Canadian organizations were the only ones that over a period of many years continually warned the Canadian people and the Government about fifth column activities of the Communists. It was regrettable, he said, that the authorities paid little heed to these warnings, but on the contrary did everything to please the Communists. The espionage probe vindicated the stand that patriotic and loyal Ukrainian-Canadians had taken.

Mr. Hlynka said he was proud of the war record of Canadians of Ukrainian origin. He paid tribute to the men and women who served in the Canadian armed forces. Virtually every Ukrainian family had had one or more members serving. An outstanding example was the family Strynadka of Rossburn, Man., whose eight sons joined. Two of these boys were killed in action and one wounded.

Not to Be Overlooked

The contribution made by Ukrainian workers, miners and farmers was also not to be overlooked. The total contribution of Canadians of

Ukrainian origin was such that they earned for themselves everlasting honour. Just as during the war, so in the future they will never shirk their responsibilities and duties as Canadians and would always defend the principles of freedom and democracy.

As an outstanding contribution made by Ukrainians to the development of this country, the speaker described how much of the western Canadian wilderness was transformed by the first Ukrainian settlers into some of our most productive areas. Virtually with bare hands these settlers cleared thousands upon thousands of acres which today blossom with wheat, barley, rye and all kinds of vegetation. They built homes, fences and roads. They erected schools, churches and community halls. In touring Western Canada today one found that some of the most exemplary communities were those settled by Ukrainians.

By their industry and devotion to Canada, by their sons' sacrifices in World War II and by their love of land, Ukrainians had proved excellent citizens. In 50 years they had made remarkable progress in all lines of endeavour.

On Immigration

To Canadians of Ukrainian origin Mr. Hlynka said that the question of immigration at this time was undoubtedly of great concern. He referred specifically to the several hundreds of thousands of displaced persons of Ukrainian origin. Never in the history of mankind had people had to endure such suffering and on so large a scale as that which has been the lot of the displaced persons since the conclusion of the Second World War. There was hardly a Canadian family of Ukrainian origin which had not one or more close relations in the displaced persons' camps.

Mr. Hlynka expressed regret that the Canadian Government had so far failed to comply with their plea to grant permission of entry of their relatives who are among the displaced persons. From the Canadian point of view Canadian Ukrainians consider it to be in Canada's interest that a number of these people should be accepted as immigrants and be given the opportunity to become Canadian citizens. Apart from any question of blood ties, it was the humanitarian and Christian duty of Canadians to extend a helping hand to these unfortunate homeless and stateless people.

Mr. Hlynka said the problem of the displaced people is a serious one and with the termination of U.N.R.R.A. this year the plight of these people would be a desperate one.

Resolution Passed

Following Mr. Hlynka's speech a resolution was unanimously passed urging the Canadian Government to initiate steps to (1) stop the forceful repatriation of Ukrainian refugees to the Soviet Union, (2) aid these people in settling in countries where they may live in peace, (3) set a precedent by opening the doors of immigration to these victims of war and oppression.

It was explained that the reason why Ukrainian displaced persons refuse to go back to their former homes are these:

(1) Because they are democratic-minded people in the western sense of the word and wish to live their lives as free men.
(2) They are deeply religious people and there is no freedom of worship in the communist controlled territories, as has been demonstrated by the disbandment of the Ukrainian Greek Catholic Church.
(3) Under Communist dictatorship, individual and national freedom is impossible, either in economic or the political sense.
(4) Because of the constant fear of the Russian secret police.
(5) Because those who were forcibly sent back were not returned to their homes but were sent to Siberia and other distant places.

During the meeting Mrs. A. Hlynka was presented with a corsage on behalf of the Canadian-Ukrainian Women's Committee and Organization of Ukrainian Women of Canada.

Alderman Dr. E. V. Anten of Port Arthur was chairman of the meeting. Other speakers were Rev. L. Soluhub, S. Kotyk, S. Borowetz and W. Kuzyk.

The sum of $486 was contributed by the audience toward the central executive of the Canadian Ukrainian Committee.

In the evening Mr. and Mrs. A. Hlynka were guests at a banquet sponsored by the Ukrainian National Organization in their hall on McKenzie Street.

SEES RED VOTING IMMIGRATION BAR

Montreal Herald, 24 March 1947

Anthony Hlynka, Social Credit M.P. for Vegreville, Alberta, speaking at Monument National hall, yesterday, said that a vote for a Communist in Montreal's Cartier riding would mean closing the door of Canada still tighter against immigration.

Speaking in Ukrainian, Mr. Hlynka, who has just returned from a three-month tour of displaced persons' camps in Europe, said many of the camp directors were paid Soviet agents who did everything possible short of actual physical force to make the D.P.'s return to Soviet dominated countries in Europe. Methods of mental torture used, he said, belong in the Middle Ages.

Mr. Hlynka said that he knew the population of Cartier riding was interested in immigration because many were of European origin and they wanted to see their relatives and friends come to Canada.

"It is imperative that this riding must not elect a Communist as that would have an adverse effect on public opinion as far as opening the doors to Jewish, Ukrainian and Polish peoples," he said.

"Fifth Column"

He declared that the Labour Progressive Party was not a Canadian political party, but an organized fifth column which follows the directives of a foreign power.

Mr. Hlynka made the tour of D.P. camps entirely at his own expense to obtain first hand information on the problem of these people. Of Ukrainian origin himself, he visited some 20 camps in the British and American zones which contained over 200,000 Ukrainian D.P.'s. He said there were easily another 100,000 Ukrainians in Germany who were foraging for themselves outside the camps. "I found that about 25 per cent of the camps were handled exceptionally well, 25 per cent fairly well, 25 per cent poorly and 25 were simply prisons," he stated.

Of the type of people in the camps, Mr. Hlynka declared they were the best cross section of Europeans that have ever been available for immigration. They were willing to put up with almost unspeakable conditions rather than be shipped under the rule of the communist dictatorship.

Mr. Hlynka's address was sponsored by the Montreal Branch of the Ukrainian Canadian Committee.

MP DESCRIBES PLIGHT *of* DISPLACED PERSONS

Winnipeg Free Press, 28 April 1947

Conditions under which Ukrainian displaced persons live in old German and Italian barracks, stables and garages, were described by Anthony Hlynka, M.P. for Vegreville, when he addressed about 1,500 Canadian Ukrainians in the Playhouse theatre, Sunday afternoon.

The meeting was sponsored by the Winnipeg branch of the Ukrainian Canadian Committee to mark the 30th anniversary of rebirth of the Ukrainian state. John Kereluk was chairman.

Following Mr. Hlynka's speech, more than $4,000 was collected from the audience in aid of displaced persons.

Pitiful Sight

"Children present the most pitiful sight, ragged, undernourished," Mr. Hlynka said. "I have been to several camps where the mothers of new born babies had not received any clothing for the infants whatsoever. These women cut up their worn old garments and wrapped their babies in them.

"When I asked one camp director why the people had not been given any clothing for more than six months, he told me that they gave clothes to the people who agreed to be returned to countries now annexed to the Soviet Union."

The shortages of accommodation, food and clothing do not worry the displaced persons as much as the fear that they may be shipped "under the rule of the Communist dictatorship," said Mr. Hlynka.

There is hardly a D.P. whose father, mother, brother or a sister has not been exiled into Siberia or murdered by the Communists.

"Displaced persons in the British and American zones are not allowed to receive newspapers from Canada, United Kingdom and the United States unless the newspaper is on an authorized list," he claimed. "Under this authorization only the Communist papers are approved by the Soviets."

Mental Torture

Mr. Hlynka agreed that physical force is now seldom used to repatriate D.P.'s "but the mental torture and other means which are used in about one-fourth of the camps belong to the middle ages."

"The treatment of D.P.'s is largely dependent on the character of camp leaders, and I found that 50 per cent of the camps were handled passably well, 25 per cent poorly, and 25 per cent were simply prisons."

He contended that D.P.'s are the best cross-section of European peoples that have ever been available for immigration and that Canada "is making a grave mistake in not taking a good number of D.P.'s immediately."

URGES CANADA to ACCEPT DESIRABLE EUROPEANS

Oshawa Daily Times Gazette, 5 May 1947

Anthony Hlynka, one of the youngest members of the House of Commons and Social Credit Representative for Vegreville, Alberta, spoke at a mass-rally of Ukrainians at the Ukrainian Hall, yesterday afternoon. The meeting was sponsored by the Oshawa Branch of the Ukrainian Canadian Committee, in commemoration of the formation of the first Ukrainian government after the World War of 1917, first time in over 100 years that all Ukrainians were united into a freedom-seeking nation.

Mr. Hlynka speaking on "Ukrainians in misplaced (sic) persons' camps, in British and American controlled zones of Europe," just recently returned from this area, after spending three months on a tour of the D.P.'s.

Immigration Policy Commended

He commented on the recent immigration policy, handed down by Prime Minister Mackenzie King, last Thursday in the House of Commons. He said it was satisfactory, but did not think, however, the government had done its best.

"The long range policy is inadequate," he said, "since, by the time it becomes effective, the best people will have gone elsewhere."

He suggested that Canada give visas to those D.P.'s that would be acceptable as immigrants, immediately. This would allow them to go to the Netherlands, France or Belgium, until such time as transportation to Canada could be provided. At the moment, he said, there is ample need for labour in these countries and they would be able to find work.

He told how pathetic it was, to see these displaced persons being shifted from camp to camp. Their children deprived of clothes and families separated, in an effort to break down their resistance. Camp directors told him that clothing was given to D.P.'s who agreed to return to countries annexed by the Soviet Union.

Mr. Hlynka stressed the fact that the people do not worry about the shortages and inadequate accommodations so much. "It's the fear that they may be shipped under the rule of a Communist dictatorship," he said.

"There is hardly a D.P. who has not had a father, mother, brother or sister exiled to Siberia, or murdered by the Communists," he said.

Refugees in the British and American zones, he said, were not allowed to receive newspapers from Canada, the United Kingdom, or the United States unless the publications were on an authorized list. Under "this authorization," he claimed, "only the Communist papers were approved."

He went on to say the Russians want these people in their zone of control and are using devious means to get them. He agreed that physical force is now seldom used to repatriate the D.P.'s to the Russian zone, "but," he said, "the mental torture and other means, which are used in about one-fourth of the camps, belong to the middle ages."

Should Be Accepted

"The English-speaking world and other Western Democracies have, for more than 30 years, asked the Central and Eastern European people to accept democracy and Christianity," he said, "but today, after they have given up practically all their earthly possessions in defending Christianity and democracy, they are told that we can't help them."

"I believe it is in our interests to accept our share of these people who desire to become Canadian citizens, rather than to meet some of them with bayonets in their hands, coming from the north and driven by a dictatorship."

He suggested that Canada should set up offices in Austria, Germany and Italy, give authorities the power to select and sort out the D.P.'s that would be acceptable to us.

"They are the best cross-section of European people," the member from Vegreville said, "that has yet been available for immigration. Canada is making a grave mistake in not taking a good number of them immediately."

He criticized the way in which, he said, the United States and British officials were allowing themselves to be pushed around in Europe, in the matter of displaced persons and commented on the fact that the Soviet had not given in on any of these matters as had the Western powers.

He urged the government to act quickly in implementing the announced policy of immigration.

HLYNKA ASKS IMMIGRATION RELAXATION

Windsor Star, 12 May 1947

Immediate admittance to Canada of relatives would not be difficult and would do much to solve the displaced persons problem, Anthony Hlynka, M.P., for Vegreville, Alta., said here in an address Sunday.

Appeasing Russia

"Canada's policy of high-sounding words and little action is merely further appeasement of Soviet Russia," the Alberta member declared. "While Canada's leaders are aware that this country could well absorb a goodly number of displaced persons – with desirable skills and talent – they do nothing about it but talk in general terms or vague promises.

"Meanwhile, the immigration missions from Argentina and Brazil are moving in on the scene and the higher skilled displaced persons are being selected for those countries. By the time Canada decides to do something, the best of these will be taken by other countries.

"From a purely defensive position alone, Canada needs these people," the Western M.P. declared in an interview prior to his address. "We need all the people we can get in Canada, especially people of this type. If trouble ever breaks out again, this country is in direct line of advance on the United States from the north.

"I do not advocate a wide open door policy at once, but Canada should accept relatives of people already well established here. There would be no problem of housing or any question of upsetting the Canadian economy. Later on, others could be permitted after careful selection had been made. Let Canada issue visas to these people. This would permit them to get out of the camps and get jobs in countries like France and Holland, who are ready to issue transit visas and provide jobs."

The plight of the majority of displaced persons is pitiable, he said. At least 100,000 are scattered outside the camps in the British zone alone – with no place to go and nothing to do – "just cast upon the German population," he explained.

"Let Canada make a statement on how many she is prepared to take – say 50,000. We have no ships at present, but we could examine and select and visa those whom we would like to see settle in this country. Even if it is two years before they could travel, we would still be greatly relieving the situation by giving them visas which would permit travel to countries outside the occupation zones."

Visited Europe

Mr. Hlynka spent three months in Europe from November to February last. He saw at first hand, under the protection of military permit, all the conditions of which he speaks. He spoke highly of the work of the Senate committee on immigration in arousing public opinion. He mentioned especially Senator Arthur Roebuck and Hon. Paul Martin as sympathetic to his suggestions. He credited Mr. Roebuck with doing "perhaps more than any other individual in Canada for the cause of the displaced persons."

He also praised highly the reports of government activities contained in *The Windsor Star*.

"The Star publishes one of the best reports from Parliament Hill. I read it regularly and thoroughly enjoy it."

Speaks in Ukrainian

The Kent Theatre, where Mr. Hlynka spoke Sunday afternoon, was filled to capacity. For almost three hours the visiting M.P. spoke in Ukrainian describing his three-month visit to Europe.

He paid tribute to the manner in which the English citizen is bearing up under "terrific difficulties." He brought his audience to tears on several occasions with descriptions of how privation and suffering have forced many D.P.'s to become exiles rather than return to what they fear may be a worse fate in their own lands. Many who heard him have close relatives in the D.P. camps, or scattered homeless across Europe.

The meeting was held under the auspices of the Ukrainian Canadian Committee organized during the war to aid Canada's war effort. At Sunday's meeting a collection was taken in aid of the refugees and $2,000 was gathered to help those who will be able to migrate to Canada and the U.S....

MERELY HALF OF CAMPS *for* DISPLACED PERSONS FOUND "FAIR *to* GOOD"

Toronto Telegram, 26 May 1947

Some Are Operated Without Humanity, Says Anthony Hlynka, MP, Returning From Tour

Only 50 per cent of the displaced persons' camps in Europe are operated on a basis which might be described as "fair to good," Anthony Hlynka, MP for Vegreville, Alta., told a large gathering of Ukrainians in Massey Hall yesterday.

Of the remainder about 25 per cent are operated poorly and 25 per cent are operated by persons without any conscience or humanity left in them, he declared. In some cases they are worse than prisons.

Mr. Hlynka and his wife recently made a three-month trip to Europe. One month was spent in touring the British and United States zones of Germany. The couple also visited Italy, France and London.

Main purpose in making the trip was to study the problem of the displaced persons from a first-hand point of view, collect important data and make recommendations to the various governments of democratic countries to accept displaced persons as immigrants.

If the people in these camps are allowed to remain there much longer most of them will suffer a serious breakdown, declared Mr. Hlynka.

"We must remember," he said, "that these people have lived through six years of most adverse war conditions, and they have now lived for more than two years in the camps which consist of old military barracks, stables and garages."

Economic conditions in the United States zones of Germany and Austria are better than those in the British zones, stated Mr. Hlynka. The British, however, seem to be handling the people much better, having had considerable experience in handling problems of this type in the past.

Food Lacking

In the British occupation zones the displaced persons obtain about one-third of the food required by working men, while in the United States zones they receive about one-half of what they require to be healthy, Mr. Hlynka added. Accommodation in the United States zones is not as overcrowded as that in the British zones.

Mr. Hlynka, in speaking of the children who are not living in the camps, said the lack of proper clothing presents a pitiful sight. Many of the children wore nothing but old rags which were stitched together into some resemblance of dresses and suits.

In the Russian zone displaced persons were not allowed to receive newspapers in their own language unless the paper was approved by the Soviet liaison officers. As a result the people have access only to the newspapers with a Communist ideology.

"I venture to say, however, that of all the displaced persons in the camps of the Ukrainian, Polish, Latvian, Lithuanian, Esthonian and Yugoslav origins, not one of them is a Communist," said Mr. Hlynka.

He explained that the reason for this was that there is hardly a person in the camps whose father, mother, sister, brother, husband, nephew or other relative has not been murdered by the Communists or exiled into the depths of Soviet Russia.

Deeds not Words

Referring to Canada's new immigration policy, announced by the Prime Minister on May 1, Mr. Hlynka said that the solution to the problem does not lie in high-sounding words, as these have not brought any relief to the displaced persons in the two years since the conclusion of the war.

"The fact remains that Canada has virtually done nothing toward the solution of the problem of the displaced person," he said. "There is only one exception, and that was the noble stand and worthy defence which your Hon. Paul Martin made at the United Nations Conference in New York last fall." ...

STRICTLY POLITICAL

— By Rodney Adamson, M.P., West York
The Toronto Star, 12 July 1947

The question of immigration has not received the attention it should have during this session of Parliament. As a matter of fact, it is what is known as a hot potato. Everybody gives general statements of the necessity for immigration, but when anybody does anything specific there are always a great many objections.

The action of Mr. Dionne, the Member of Parliament from Beauce, to bring in to Canada one hundred Polish girls from the displaced persons' camps in Germany was seized on by Mr. Coldwell and the CCF Party as an example of indentured labour, that is labour recruited outside Canada and brought in to work for a certain period under certain specified conditions or contracts signed outside Canada.

The debate took place on a motion by Mr. Coldwell to adjourn the House to discuss a matter of urgent public importance. The debate was an interesting one, and three Cabinet Ministers took part. The high point of the discussion was made by Mr. Anthony Hlynka, a Ukrainian member of the Social Credit Party for Vegreville in Alberta. Mr. Hlynka is probably more entitled to speak on the subject of displaced persons than any other member of the House of Commons as he and his wife have spent several months visiting these camps in person, both in Italy and in Northern Europe.

Mr. Hlynka pointed out that the food required for a normal man doing sedentary work was, in North America, some 2,500 to 3,000 calories a day. The target at the DP Camps aimed at by UNRRA was 1,550 calories a day, but that this had to be cut to about 1,000 a day, which was approximately one-third of the food a normal North American adult receives. Naturally the state of health is deplorable and the instance of TB, particularly amongst children, is extremely high. He stated that Mr. Dionne should not be condemned for bringing out these one hundred girls to work in his mills, but that he should be greatly complimented because he was the means of virtually saving their lives. I will quote one paragraph of Mr. Hlynka's speech:

> "It is in the interests of Great Britain; it is in the interests of the United States; it is in the interests of Canada to solve the displaced persons problem as quickly as possible. You cannot sign a peace with Austria and leave displaced persons there. You cannot sign a peace treaty with Germany and leave displaced persons there. The pre-war population of the United States zone of Germany, if my memory serves me correctly, was 13,000,000 people, but today, on account of the number of Germans who have been expelled from the territory held by Poland and Czechoslovakia, there are 18,000,000 people. That area simply cannot support that population."

All this shows how serious the feeding problem is and how the existence of these camps upset the whole economy of the world today. I think it is important that we in Canada should appreciate that this is our problem too.

As the debate wore on it was shown that the member for Beauce was not importing these people as indentured labour, but they were being paid at rates of pay in accordance with the Quebec laws and that they had neither made, nor had they been asked to make, any commitments with regard to paying their passage to Canada. This is covered by clause D of the agreement between the secretary, The Intergovernmental Committee on Refugees, 19 Hill Street, London, W 1, and the Dionne Spinning Mills Company. I quote the clause:

> "(d) No deduction from the wages will be made by the company for the cost of transportation of the worker from Germany to destination in Canada."

Despite the irregularity of the procedure, the net result is that one hundred human beings have been given a new start in life, and hope and freedom have been granted to those who were in despair.

BC CAN 'HANDLE' 230,000 IMMIGRANTS

The Vancouver News-Herald, 10 October 1947

A new estimate formed on the basis of unoccupied agricultural ground sets at 715,000 persons the minimum that should be accommodated as immigrants to western Canada.

This figure was revealed in Vancouver Thursday by Anthony Hlynka, M.P. for Vegreville, Alta., who is touring the country to "stir up public opinion" on behalf of hundreds of worthy displaced persons he saw in Europe, and thousands of Britons who want to come to Canada.

Based on unused but suitable land that is available to railroads, the figure for British Columbia is 46,000 families, with an average of five in a family – or 230,000 persons.

Govt. Does Nothing

This compares with 25,000 for Manitoba, 100,000 for Saskatchewan, and 350,000 for Alberta.

"Meanwhile, the government is doing nothing except talk," said Mr. Hlynka.

"We should have plans now to get the best of the British immigrants – people who are able to adjust themselves easily."

The M.P. has just made a prolonged tour of D.P. camps in Europe, and found cultured men and women in idleness.

Weak on Culture

"There are some fine people among the Ukrainians, Latvians, Poles and Yugoslavs," he said. "I met painters and artists who would be a credit to Canada. We would not be doing them a favour by letting them in, because Canada is not so strong on culture."

Mr. Hlynka says that public opinion will force the government to act, but hopes such action will not be too late.

"That doesn't mean that public opinion is always just and right, but, in this case, it will be forcing the government to do the right thing.

"At present, the department of immigration is a department of non-immigration.

"We can't keep this country empty and expect to be able to defend it, but too many Canadians seem to be quite indifferent to what is a major problem."

HLYNKA PRAISES THE STAR'S ANTI-COMMIE LEADERSHIP

→ *From the* Star's *Ottawa Bureau*
The Windsor Star, 4 May 1948

M.P. SHOWS ENLIGHTENMENT, STRONG EFFORT BY EVERYONE NEEDED TO PRESERVE FREEDOM

OTTAWA – Tribute to the *Windsor Star* for its part in stimulating a country-wide interest in the Communist problem was paid in the Commons last night by Anthony Hlynka, Social Credit, Vegreville, Alta.

Ukraine Native

Speaking in the foreign affairs debate, Mr. Hlynka, a native of Western Ukraine who came to Canada with his parents at the age of three, added his praise to that given previously by leaders and members of the various political parties.

The Alberta member referred to the series of articles carried by the *Star* which were made available to more than a score of other Canadian newspapers.

"If we had more newspapers taking that attitude I am sure Communism would not be as strong as it is today," he said.

Mr. Hlynka linked the *Windsor Star* with the *Toronto Evening Telegram*, one of the papers that carried the *Star*'s Communist exposé. The Toronto paper, he said, "has been working hard, has never given up" in its fight against Communism.

"I would couple with it the *Windsor Star*, a newspaper which has given good coverage of news which would enlighten the people as to what is going on," continued Mr. Hlynka. "I know there are other newspapers doing the same work, some in the United States and some in the United Kingdom, but the list is too long to mention this evening. I did want to pay tribute to these two newspapers, however, which have shown such leadership – the thing this country needs."

Effort by All Needed

The government and the people must realize, continued Mr. Hlynka, that in order to make sure Canadians shall not lose their freedom "the total effort in defence of our way of life must be greater than the total efforts exerted by totalitarian forces in their attempt to destroy our freedom." The external affairs minister, justice minister and defence minister "have lately made some very sound and sensible pronouncements with respect to Communism and Canada's defences."

HLYNKA ASKS D.P.'S USE IDLE FARMS

—— From the Star's *Ottawa Bureau*
The Windsor Daily Star, 1 June 1948

DOMINION-PROVINCIAL LAND SETTLEMENT URGED BY M.P.

OTTAWA – Development of a Dominion-provincial land settlement scheme so that Canada can accept a greater number of people from displaced persons' camps in Europe was suggested in the House of Commons yesterday by Anthony Hlynka, Social Credit, Vegreville, Alta.

Native of Ukraine

A native of Western Ukraine who came to Canada with his immigrant parents when he was three years of age, Mr. Hlynka expressed thanks of Canada on behalf of all displaced persons who have been admitted to Canada since the end of the war. He paid tribute to Canadian industrialists who have placed many of these people in employment.

However, though a certain number of displaced persons have been accepted by various governments, the problem has "merely been touched," said Mr. Hlynka. There are still more than 750,000 D.P.'s awaiting a chance to make a new start in some other country.

Since the majority of those already admitted to Canada are working in mines, forests and factories, the Alberta member suggested admission of a larger number to work on the land. According to a survey of the unoccupied agriculturally-usable land in the four western provinces, there could be settled some 731,735 persons.

Health Standards

Mr. Hlynka urged also a relaxation of health standards which are set for D.P. immigrants. Rejections by Canadian selection immigration missions vary from 20 to 56 percent, he said. Consideration should be given to lower health standards for members of a family unit in order that the stronger members may assist the weaker ones.

The Alberta member proposed also: Include the more distant relatives, such as cousins, nephews and nieces; consider applications by Canadians who are in a position to guarantee employment regardless of profession, occupation or age; accept a number of people of cultured talents and professions; admit a number of orphan D.P. children.

VOTERS of VEGREVILLE CONSTITUENCY!

The following anti-Hlynka political leaflet was circulated by the Labour-Progressive (Communist) party during the 1949 general election.

On Election Day, June 27th, you will need to make a choice.

On that day you will be marking your ballot for the man you want to represent you in the House of Commons for the next four years. You will be judged throughout the country by the man you choose.

Vegreville has not had a good name because of the man who has represented it in Ottawa. Anthony Hlynka is a reactionary, pro-fascist nationalist. His un-Canadian subversive activities need investigation. He boasts of bringing in the D.P.'s from Europe. Look around you and you'll see the kind he has brought in. Many are fugitives from justice, criminals fleeing the anger of the peoples of their homelands. Bringing in D.P.'s by the thousands only means that our own sons and daughters won't be able to get jobs. Already veterans of the First and Second World Wars have been deprived of jobs by D.P.'s. With the deepening of the economic crisis, D.P.'s also will find themselves in difficult circumstances. Who then will be to blame for the thousands of our unemployed sons and these same D.P.'s, if not Hlynka?

At the present time Hlynka is calling for a war against the Soviet Union, which would be a war against the Ukrainian people. But during the last war when our Ukrainian brothers and sisters were being massacred by the Germans, Hlynka opposed an all-out war effort! Hlynka is not interested in the welfare of the Ukrainian people; he is interested only in the propagation of fascist ideas which are against the best interests of both Ukrainian and Canadian people.

The Labour-Progressive Party calls on the people of Vegreville to defeat Anthony Hlynka on June 27th. Vote against him! Put him out of office! Send this war-mongering, pro-fascist back where he belongs!

When we call on you to kick out Hlynka this does not mean that in any way we support the Liberal government at Ottawa. This government has tied us to the U.S. Marshall Plan, and our farm export market has disappeared. They are driving our country down the disastrous road to war. They would have farmers' sons from Vegreville die in a war against their Ukrainian brothers in Europe, all for the glory of American dollars. The Liberal government policy is sending this country into another depression like that of the Hungry Thirties.

The Labour-Progressive Party is campaigning in every constituency for Peace, Democracy and Security. In Vegreville constituency we decided not to nominate a candidate in this election. We decided this because we do not want to split democratic opinion in the constituency as then Hlynka might get back in. We say to all voters in Vegreville: Stand united! Vote united! Defeat your main enemy – Hlynka!

We greet the decision of the CCF to also not contest this constituency. We urge all CCF supporters to actively campaign against Hlynka and to help defeat him.

VOTERS IN VEGREVILLE FEDERAL CONSTITUENCY:

GO TO THE POLLS ON MONDAY, JUNE 27TH, AND VOTE AGAINST HLYNKA!

– Labour-Progressive Party,
Vegreville Constituency Committee.

MP CLAIMS REDS' VOTE DEFEATED TONY HLYNKA

— By Frank Flaherty
Globe and Mail, Toronto, 3 October 1949

Ottawa, Oct. 2 (Staff). – Until one member of the House of Commons got angry at something said by another member, it was not generally known that communism scored one victory in the general election last June. Despite the fact the Reds failed to elect their leader, Tim Buck, in a powerful campaign in Toronto-Trinity, they did succeed in defeating Anthony Hlynka in Vegreville, Alberta. They had good reason for wanting to get Mr. Hlynka out of parliament, but until Hlynka's friend and former roommate, F. D. Shaw (SC, Red Deer), told the story in the House, it was not generally known how it was done.

Tony Hlynka, for the last nine years has been more than the member for Vegreville, more than a back-bencher in the Social Credit Party. He was the member-at-large for the Ukrainians in Canada, he was a spokesman for the Ukrainians in the Soviet Union with a platform from which his voice could echo around the world.

Canada's citizens of Ukrainian origin are sharply divided between left and right, between Communists who support the Soviet Government and try to push communism in Canada, and the majority who sympathize with the national aspirations of their homeland for independence from Russia, and who are strongly anti-Communist.

As a member of parliament, Tony Hlynka spoke out often for Ukrainians in the Old Country. He had contacts with Europe from which he drew information that he used against the Communists. He busied himself looking after the immigration and other problems of his people, no matter where they lived. He assisted in getting many Ukrainian displaced persons brought to Canada.

His position as a member of parliament was a source of pride to other Ukrainians in Canada, a constant counter to the arguments of the Communists that until there was a revolution Ukrainian-Canadians would never get a break in this capitalist country.

At the recent general election Vegreville elected John Decore, the Liberal candidate, with a vote of 8,872 votes to 7,115 for the Social Crediter Tony Hlynka.

That would have been that except for the fact that in his maiden speech Mr. Decore chose to do a little crowing about the inroads of the Liberal party made into Social Credit strength in Alberta. He twitted Social Credit Leader, Solon Low about a big gain in the Liberal vote in his constituency of Peace River.

Mr. Shaw thought Mr. Decore was the last man who should crow that way and said so as soon as he could get the floor. He said that in Vegreville in 1945 the Liberal candidate received 4,806 votes, the Communist candidate 3,372, and the CCF candidate 1,668. Mr. Hlynka received 7,146.

In 1949 it was a two-cornered fight. Hlynka received 31 votes less than he did in 1945. Mr. Decore got 4,066 votes more than the Liberal candidate in 1945.

Those votes did not represent an increase in Liberal strength, said Mr. Shaw. They represented a Communist gang-up behind the Liberal candidate to defeat Hlynka. The campaign was directed to that end. The Communists advised their supporters to vote for anyone but Hlynka, called him a Fascist tool and a Nazi, described his efforts to assist Ukrainians to come to Canada as bringing in the scum of Europe.

Mr. Shaw drew applause from the older members who knew Hlynka when he said that the former member was an arch-foe of Communism and totalitarianism in all its forms, an ardent supporter of Canada and the British Commonwealth.

He challenged Mr. Decore as the new member for Vegreville to take the same stand as his predecessor and try to equal Mr. Hlynka's record as a champion of Canadian democracy.

APPENDICES

Anthony Hlynka wrote several essays in Ukrainian that do not fit into the flow of the story but are of historical importance. Three of these translated essays are placed here. In addition a concise list of recommended readings of relevant literature is included.

1

THE HISTORICAL SIGNIFICANCE of UKRAINIAN GROUP SETTLEMENT in CANADA

Future Canadian historians and sociologists will one day thoroughly evaluate the real significance of group or bloc settlement of the first Ukrainian immigration to this country.[48] But even now [1950s] I believe that the practice of establishing pioneer settlements as blocs and colonies was a crucial factor in the lives of Ukrainian settlers of Western Canada. The importance of this practice has been perceived in two diametrically opposing views.

The popular view among the majority of Canadians – including government, academic, and political circles – is that bloc settlement of Ukrainians and other ethnic groups in Canada was a grave mistake on the part of Canada's leaders. These critics stress that this practice of unplanned settlement has a retarding effect on the process of Canadianization. Some even argue that bloc settlements place Canada in danger of fragmenting itself into ethnic ghettos. Their position, a correct one, is that in Canada all people should be Canadian. The problem is that, so far, not all Canadians agree on what exactly Canadianism is. In any event, the critics of bloc settlement point out that in districts where European immigrants settled among Anglo-Saxons, these newcomers learned English faster and entered into the mainstream of Canadian life sooner.

It is necessary to point out here that the French Canadians do not enter into this discussion. The French-Canadian society does not have a clear stand on the cultural rights of Canada's ethnic minorities. French Canadians do have certain historical and constitutional rights, which they defend vigorously.

Notwithstanding the negative opinion of the majority about bloc settlement, I am thoroughly convinced that bloc settlement, in fact, has hastened rather than retarded the process of Canadianization in the area of business, the professions, and politics by more than fifty years.

Before discussing examples that support my point of view, it is necessary to say a few words in defence of Canada's leaders of the past to whom is ascribed the mistake of unplanned settlement. My response to this criticism is as follows: in the circumstances of pioneer life in Western Canada, bloc settlement of the arriving settlers was the only viable alternative. One needs only to recall the fact that in those days in the northern half of Western Canada lay a wide belt of virgin but potentially arable land. In order to settle and cultivate this land, it was necessary to bring in suitable immigrants as quickly as possible. In 1891 there were less than five million people in Canada. By this time the source of British immigration, the mainstay of Canada's growth, had become depleted. In such circumstances, the Canadian government had no choice but to turn to other European countries for immigrants. As a result, Western Canada was settled in blocs by people from Central and Eastern Europe. It is well to remember that the northern prairies then were not as we know them today. They were covered with bush and forests. But setting aside geographic factors, we must not forget that the British, who had settled in the West, also wished to live among their own people. This was a natural thing to do. Therefore, negative criticism of the method of settlement of other ethnic groups in Canada has no basis.

All those who are interested in the life of Ukrainian Canadians know that the first Ukrainian settlers were almost exclusively farmers and labourers who earned their livelihood by demanding physical work. In the early days there were no Ukrainian businessmen, teachers, or other professionals. Ukrainians did not even participate in the political process except to be used as pawns by Canadian politicians. But due to the fact that they settled in blocs for mutual support, there soon emerged from among them people who took to the professions.

Those Ukrainians with talent for business established small businesses, learned rapidly, and became better businessmen with each year. Their numbers grew. However, it is well to remember that in those days Ukrainians could do business exclusively among people of their own origin. The mere fact that initially they lacked adequate knowledge of English meant that they could not have conducted their business activities in districts other than their own. Even in the

1940s, the majority of Ukrainian Canadian businessmen to a large extent still depended on the patronage of their fellow Ukrainians. However, there is an increasing number of Ukrainian businessmen who have successfully ventured beyond their communities into the Canadian mainstream. In any event, it was the bloc settlement of Ukrainians in Canada that first gave these entrepreneurs the opportunity to take to business at least twenty-five years sooner than it would have been possible otherwise. Therefore, it is clear that in the field of commerce, bloc settlement of Ukrainians hastened the process of Canadianization in the best interests of Ukrainian Canadians and Canada.

Let us look at the teaching profession in Canada. Here again bloc settlement played a major role. For the first teachers of Ukrainian origin the field of public education would have been closed or at best very limited. In view of the fact that the first immigrant teachers learned English only in their adult years, they had some difficulty in mastering the language. For this reason, it would have been difficult, if not impossible, to obtain teaching posts in the British or mixed districts. But these temporary linguistic obstacles did not stand in their way in Ukrainian districts. As a result, our first teachers not only were able to earn their livelihood and further their studies, they were also able to take an active part in community affairs of the various Ukrainian settlements. The work of the Ukrainian teachers left a positive influence on the children of the pioneers. Their community activism, without a doubt, benefited not only the Ukrainian districts but western Canada itself. The existence of bloc settlement allowed for a direct Ukrainian involvement in public education and this fact hastened integration or Canadianization of Ukrainian settlers.

In the area of professions – which includes doctors, dentists, lawyers, pharmacists, and others – members of the first generation of Ukrainian Canadian professionals began their careers as physical labourers, building railroads, or working in the mines. They were of strong will and determination and many entered teacher training programs in order to teach for several years in Ukrainian settlements. Having saved some money, they continued their studies, this time at the university level, until they obtained their professional diplomas. Here again bloc settlement contributed to the growth of professions among Ukrainians because without Ukrainian districts, our teachers would not have been able to have an opportunity to pursue higher education and move into professions.

But this is only part of the benefits that bloc settlement brought to the rise and growth of Ukrainian professionals. It is important to note that in the initial stages the professionals depended almost exclusively on the support of their Ukrainian community. Only in exceptional cases did a Ukrainian lawyer, doctor, dentist, or other professional get sufficient clientele from the general public.

In connection with this dependence of Ukrainians on Ukrainians, we can find numerous relevant examples. For instance, among the Canadian-born generation of Ukrainian students, there have been those who think that the Ukrainian language is unnecessary in their lives since we are all Canadians. But having completed their studies, they soon discovered that they did not have the support of the general public and that they were obliged to depend on their own people, whose language they had abandoned. They now struggle with broken Ukrainian. There is a lesson in their experience: that is, that one cannot escape from oneself. Nonetheless, it is heartening to note that relations among Canadians of various origins have been steadily improving, as these Canadians become responsible citizens without abandoning their heritage. The aim of this example is to stress once again the positive benefits of bloc settlement which gave Ukrainians the opportunity to become full participants in all aspects of Canadian life much sooner than it would have been otherwise. This breakthrough into full citizenship would have been very difficult, if not impossible, had they not lived in bloc settlement.

To be objective, I must mention that now there already are a number of Ukrainian professionals and specialists who have found acceptance in Canadian society and are totally independent of their fellow Ukrainian Canadians. In this category are chemists, engineers, accountants, and even some businessmen and manufacturers. They found acceptance and respect because of their exceptional talents and skills that equalled, and sometimes exceeded, those of others. Even though they are not dependent on Ukrainians, nonetheless, many of them have not alienated themselves from their own people but take an active role in the Ukrainian community.

In conclusion, let us look how bloc settlement allowed Ukrainians to become involved in Canadian politics. It is clear that so far, the participation and success of Ukrainian political candidates in local, provincial, and federal elections have depended almost exclusively on the support of Ukrainian bloc settlements. To date, there is only one example of a Ukrainian candidate winning a nomination in a constituency with a non-Ukrainian majority. This happened in East Edmonton in 1949, when Ambrose Holowach[49] obtained the official nomination of the Social Credit party. This was the first time in Canadian federal politics that a Ukrainian Canadian received the support of the majority of delegates among whom there was only a handful of Ukrainians. This event is also important because Holowach was the first Ukrainian to be nominated in an urban federal riding. Although this was a unique case, it does not mean that Ukrainian candidates do not find any support among the general public. But such support is limited. When looking at Canada as a whole, it is obvious that the main base of support for every federal and provincial candidate of Ukrainian origin has been the rural constituency with bloc settlement of Ukrainians. This means that without bloc settlement not one Ukrainian would have been elected either to the federal Parliament or to the provincial legislatures of Alberta, Saskatchewan, and Manitoba. As a result of bloc settlement, our people have been taking an active part in provincial politics since 1913 and in federal politics since 1926. Bloc settlement has played an important role in the process of Canadianization because it made it possible for Ukrainians to participate fully in the political life of this country.

I should point out that matters appear somewhat different in municipal politics. Here we do have examples of Ukrainians being elected to school boards and municipal councils with the support of the general public.

In the city of Port Arthur [now part of Thunder Bay], Ontario, its mayor, Dr. Edward Anton [Antochiw] was elected and re-elected several times. Statistics indicate that in 1941 Port Arthur had only 1,814 Ukrainians. Yet, Anton received more votes than any previous mayor of that city. However, so far the most important achievement in municipal politics was attained by Michael Starr [Starchevsky][50] who in 1949 was elected mayor of the city of Oshawa, Ontario, a city with a population of over 30,000. He was re-elected by acclamation. Obviously in these examples credit for success belongs to Anton and Starr but it also belongs to our fellow Canadians who supported the Ukrainian candidates.

Returning to the final appraisal of bloc settlement, I reiterate its positive impact on the various ethnic groups as well as on Canada. Every ethnic group may be compared to a family, one that grows and matures best together. In a good family, all members help one another mutually until each member ventures into the world. So too, bloc settlement has given Ukrainians and other ethnic groups the best opportunity to grow together and go out into the world.

If one were to pose the question "Which Ukrainian district leads in the achievements of Ukrainians in Canada?", the answer can only be, without a doubt, the Vegreville federal constituency in Alberta. This constituency has earned for itself first place, not only for having the largest number of Ukrainian settlers, but for its successes in every field, including politics. It therefore deserves special attention.

2

THE FEDERAL CONSTITUENCY of VEGREVILLE, ALBERTA (1940S)

The Vegreville constituency or riding in Alberta has had the most political significance for Ukrainian Canadians because this electoral district more than any other enabled Ukrainians to enter into Canadian politics. On 17 April 1913, the first Ukrainian Canadian, Andrew Shandro, was elected as a member to the Alberta provincial legislature. He was elected from the provincial riding of Whitford, then part of the Vegreville federal riding. Although the court nullified Shandro's victory for a breach of the Elections Act, he won the riding again on 15 March 1915. On 14 September 1926, Michael Luchkovich was elected the first Ukrainian Canadian as a member to the House of Commons. Since that time, with the exception of the years 1935–45, the Vegreville constituency has been represented in Ottawa by Canadians of Ukrainian origin.

The second federal constituency in Canada which, nineteen years later, followed the lead of Vegreville was Dauphin, Manitoba. Fred Zaplitny,[51] a young teacher, was elected in 1945 from this riding to the House of Commons. Unfortunately, because of narrow-minded politics played by some of our community "leaders," Ukrainian Canadians lost this riding in 1949.

For the political achievements of Ukrainians in Vegreville, we must, without a doubt, credit the concept of bloc settlement. Ukrainians came to Canada from different parts of their homeland, mainly from Halychyna (Galicia) and Bukovyna with a few who emigrated from Eastern Ukraine and Carpatho-Ukraine, and they soon found a common bond. The Vegreville federal riding is the only riding in Canada where the majority of voters are of Ukrainian origin. Of the total population, 70 per cent are Ukrainians; 6 per cent Romanians and Poles; 24 per cent Anglo-Saxons, Germans, Scandinavians, French, Finns and a few Chinese who are proprietors of restaurants, as well as some Japanese who farm in the district of Thorhild. In 1941 there were 48,546 people living in the riding.

The settlement in the Vegreville district began in the 1880s – that is, but a few years before the first Ukrainians arrived there. Before the arrival of the Ukrainian settlers, there were already small settlements in Vegreville, Tofield, Fort Saskatchewan, and Bruderheim. The first Ukrainian settlers in Canada began to colonize the lands around Bruderheim in 1892 and from this date to 1920, almost all of the arable land had been settled.

The Vegreville riding begins about twenty miles northeast of the capital city of Edmonton. The town is served by five railways. The first railway – connecting Edmonton, Mundare, Vegreville, and Lloydminster – was built in 1905. This C.N.R. line goes to Saskatoon. How the first Ukrainian settlers lived in the Vegreville district without this railway is hard to imagine. During this time, our settlers traveled many miles to Edmonton by oxen and those who settled even farther northeast found travel even more difficult. The second railway, completed in 1909, went from Edmonton to Tofield, then to Wainwright and Saskatoon. This railway line is used now by C.N.R. from coast to coast. With the building of the railway such towns as Bruderheim, Lamont, Chipman, and Mundare sprang up. One can imagine the joy of our farmers when they first saw the railway, which connected their primitive areas with the outside world.

However, these two railway lines solved only the transportation problems for those people who lived south of the North Saskatchewan River. It was in 1916 that transportation became available to the people who lived on the north banks of the river, for the Northern Alberta Railway was completed. It linked Edmonton, Opal, Egremont, Thorhild, and Lac le Biche. In 1919, the C.N.R. ran from Edmonton to Spedden, through Radway, Smoky Lake, and Vilna. Finally, in August 1929, the C.P.R. completed its line to the north of the river and connected Edmonton, Andrew, Willingdon, Two Hills, and Myrnam. With the arrival of more settlers to the district and the cultivation of the land, small towns began to flourish close to the railways. There are about thirty of them, the largest being Vegreville, with a population, in 1950, of 2,312.[52]

The second-largest settlement grew around Redwater. This came about because of the discovery of oil in this area. While in the first half of 1948 there were only about one hundred people living here, in 1950 the population exceeded that of Vegreville.

I wish to say something about the roads which serve the Vegreville riding, for roads in the farming districts are like windows to the world. The people of Vegreville, like farming communities throughout Canada, make use of three types of roads. First of all, there are the so-called "farmers' roads." These were built north/south about one mile apart, and the east/west roads were built two miles one from the other. In the beginning these roads were built by the farmers themselves, because when the farmers first settled in the new districts, there were not only no roads, there were few paths. But with the formation of the municipal districts, farmers, according to their means, began to build the first roads. First of all, they had to clear the forest with the help of oxen, horses, ploughs, and harrows, and then take the soil from the hills to fill the low areas. To be able to build roads over swamps, they had to use tree trunks, cover them with straw and then with earth. Such were the roads our farmers traveled and walked near and far, for many years. In time, the swamps dried up and municipalities bought or rented modern machinery and built and repaired the country roads. For a number of years now, the municipal roads have been built much more efficiently with modern machinery.

The second type of road consists of the so-called commercial roads. These roads connect the larger towns and are wider and higher than the ordinary roads. They are gravelled so that they could be used in all kinds of weather. The municipal and provincial governments pay the cost of building these roads. Today, there is a substantial number of these commercial roads in Alberta.

The third type of road is represented by the main provincial routes, the highways. To date, five such roads have been built in the Vegreville district, and have since become essential to the economic well-being of the district. The first two roads across the riding were built in the years 1925–1930: Highway No. 14, which links Edmonton, Cooking Lake, and Tofield, and Highway No. 15, which links Edmonton, Fort Saskatchewan, Bruderheim, Lamont,

Chipman, Mundare and Vegreville. A portion of the latter highway, from Edmonton to Fort Saskatchewan, was covered with asphalt in 1929.

In the years 1930–1931, Highway 16, which runs from Edmonton to Ross Creek, was built, and in 1940 it was extended to Vegreville. In the years 1949–1950 this entire highway was rebuilt and it now has been covered with asphalt.

The fourth main highway, No. 28, which runs through the riding to the north side of the river, was built in 1944–1945. This highway links Edmonton, Opal, Egremont, Radway, Smoky Lake, Vilna, and Spedden. On the north side of the river, our people often refer to it as "the Dmytro (Jim) Popil Highway," a former member of the provincial legislature representing Redwater riding, for it was he who worked the hardest to have this highway built by the provincial government.

The fifth highway, No. 45, runs from Fort Saskatchewan through Bruderheim and Willingdon to Two Hills and was built in 1948–1949. Our people call this the "Wasyl (Bill) Tomyn Highway" because it was through his great efforts that this highway was built.

But the picture of the Vegreville riding would not be complete if we did not mention its industry. The chief industry of Vegreville, as of Canada itself, is still farming, specifically the production of grain, meat, and dairy products. We call farming an industry because our farmers, with modern agricultural machinery, produce grain on a vast scale. This extensive production applies also to raising cattle, swine, and domestic fowl. In fact, to do justice in describing the achievements of our farmers, it would be necessary to write a separate book. We will, however, limit ourselves only to a brief overview.

Our farmers in Canada, on every count, are indeed worthy agriculturalists. When evaluating the farming industry in this country, we must acknowledge the fact that farmers of Ukrainian origin deserve first place. They are industrious, tenacious, steadfast, methodical, and totally committed to their farming. They produce food not only for Canadian consumption, but each year produce various commodities, valued in millions of dollars, for export.

To this general characterization, we can add that there are many farmers in Vegreville who have distinguished themselves with their talents for husbandry in the national arena. One of these exemplary farmers in Western Canada is Bill (Wasyl) Zazulia, who farms four miles northwest of the town of Willingdon, where he cultivates a beautiful experimental orchard. Thousands of Canadians and Americans visit him each year to take a look at his orchard.

Wasyl Zazulia began farming in 1926. In 1938, he began to cultivate, on six acres of land, 160 varieties of fruit trees: apple, plum, pear, nut, apricot, and crab apple. He also has twelve varieties of raspberries, fifty-five varieties of gooseberries, seven varieties of strawberries, four varieties of currants, and several varieties of cherries, and also grows decorative trees, shrubs, flowers, and grasses. His orchard is protected from wind and frost by rows of one thousand "Colorado" spruce trees. In the summer, Wasyl Zazulia's house is full of all kinds of flowers. Every guest who comes to visit his orchard always receives a bouquet of flowers, which best attests to the hospitality of this Ukrainian family. For us, the value of Zazulia's experimental orchard is twofold: he has elevated the good name of Ukrainian-Canadian farmers and, at the same time, has proved that it is possible to cultivate fruit trees successfully in the northern part of Alberta.

It is unnecessary to write much about the quality of the land in the Vegreville district as it is generally good and level. The larger portion of that land is the most fertile in Canada, although there are occasional sandy farms with small hills and some rocks. Today, there is not much land left that is not under cultivation in the Vegreville district.

The reason why our farmers settled on the best lands is rather interesting. During the early settlement in the northern half of Alberta, our fellow citizens of other origins chose the less wooded farms and Ukrainians, who arrived later, had to take the wooded areas. Having chosen the less wooded lands, our fellow citizens cultivated them with less difficulty and soon were able to reap the benefits from them. Ukrainians, on the other hand, having settled the forested areas, had to work very hard to uproot trees and clear the land. But soon it became evident that where there was forest, the land was more fertile and resistant to erosion. Thus by chance, Ukrainian settlers came out better than their neighbours as they and their children have benefited from the rich lands.

The second important industry in the Vegreville riding is the oil business. One of the biggest reservoirs of oil on the North American continent was discovered in the district of Redwater. To 15 February 1951, there are 775 oil wells with daily production of 45,000 barrels. Each week on average ten new wells are discovered. But only a portion of the wells is allowed to produce, because of the limits set by provincial law to insure future production.

It is not difficult to guess what economic significance this oil production will have for the district. The discovery of these rich oil wells has already brought huge benefits not only to the town of Redwater and the surrounding area, but also to the province and all of Canada. The district of Redwater is settled mainly by Ukrainians who also operate the majority of businesses.

The third industry in the riding is, so far, a small coal-mining enterprise. Several years ago two surface coal mines were opened in the district of Thorhild. These mines supply coal to nearby towns and farms and were discovered by the ingenious brothers, Michael and John Libych, and John Naruschetsky, all three Ukrainians.

Besides these three industries, a fair number of people in the district engage in a variety of businesses, services, and professions. In towns where the majority are of Ukrainian origin, almost all businesses have passed into their hands. It is interesting to note that in Alberta, and even in other parts of Canada, many small and medium-sized hotels are owned by Ukrainian Canadians. For instance, in the Vegreville district, twenty-three of twenty-six hotels are owned by Ukrainian businessmen.

Health care in the district has high priority. There are nine hospitals located in Vegreville, Lamont, Mundare, Two Hills, Willingdon, Radway, Smoky Lake, Vilna, and Tofield; there are seventeen doctors, six of whom are of Ukrainian origin; three dentists, one of whom is Ukrainian; and several pharmacists, three of whom are Ukrainian. In addition to these medical people, there is a respectable number of other professionals: eight lawyers, three of whom are sons of Ukrainian pioneers; six agronomists, all Ukrainian; and two veterinarians, both Ukrainian, who came to Canada as displaced persons after the Second World War.

Education also has been flourishing in the Vegreville district. There are 50 elementary public schools and 25 high schools. In the school year 1948–1949 there were 283 teachers, 215 of whom were of Ukrainian origin, which equals the percentage of voters of Ukrainian, Romanian, and Polish origins in the Vegreville riding.

It is characteristic of the Vegreville area that every town and almost every district has a community hall, where dances, concerts, public meetings, and lectures take place. Larger centres also have movie theatres. The Ukrainian character of the Vegreville district is defined in the best way possible, by churches built in the Byzantine style. There are the Ukrainian Catholic, Ukrainian Orthodox, as well as several Russian Orthodox and Presbyterian churches. The town of Mundare, a community of eight hundred, boasts a Ukrainian Catholic monastery built by the Order of Basilian Fathers in 1923, where young seminarians are trained for the priesthood. Affiliated with the monastery is an orphanage, where Ukrainian nuns take care of Ukrainian orphans.

Five newspapers are published in the Vegreville federal riding. The weekly *Vegreville Observer* has been published in Vegreville since March 1906. The owner and editor of this paper is A. L. Horton, a former teacher, who has been editing this weekly for forty-five years and last year celebrated his seventy-fourth birthday. In Tofield, the weekly *Tofield Mercury* is published; in Lamont, *Lamont Municipal and School Gazette*; in Fort Saskatchewan, a small newspaper, *Fort Saskatchewan News*, and a short time ago, a small newspaper began to appear in Redwater.

In Mundare a Ukrainian Catholic biweekly, *The Light* (*Svitlo*), was published from 1937 to 1949. Religious books were printed there as well. However, in autumn of 1949, the printing press and the publication *The Light* were moved to Toronto, Ontario.

There is also a national park in the riding. In 1906 the Canadian government reserved as a park 75.2 square miles near Lamont where there is a small forest, a lake, and some open land. The park is named Elk Island Park. Until recently, the biggest attraction in this park was the large herd of buffalo and a small number of elk, deer, and roe. For the past two or three years more and more people have been visiting the park. This popularity is due to the fact that after the end of the war in 1945, the federal department of natural resources, in an effort to make the various national parks more attractive, decided to build an historical museum in Elk Island Park. On 5 July 1950 the Minister of Natural Resources, R. H. Winters, gave an explanation in this matter, which we quote from the *Edmonton Bulletin*:

> The building will be a monument to the first Ukrainian settlers in this district of northern Alberta. The museum will comprise of three segments. The first building will be a replica of the home of the first Ukrainian settlers. Here will be displayed the various household tools which were once used by Ukrainians, as well as all other implements which they used to work on the farm. The second building will be modern and large. Here will be placed samples of plants and animals of this park. A public auditorium will also be included. The third section of the museum will be a replica of old Fort Victoria. The entire museum will be a memorial to honour and remember the life and career of Dr. A. E. Archer, pioneer doctor in northern Alberta, about whom Minister Winter said that he was "one of the most devoted humanitarians of his generation." (5 July 1950)

In accordance with the ministerial announcement, a replica of a Ukrainian pioneer home was built. It now remains to gather the appropriate furnishings that perhaps will be made in the near future. It is interesting to know what impression this house will make on the younger generation of Ukrainian Canadians and on tourists. Our fellow citizens erect monuments with a view to emphasizing the strength and spiritual greatness of past generations and never, even in the least way, do they give an impression of being poor, weak, or primitive. Therefore, while not casting doubts about the worthiness of the Ukrainian section of the museum, the committee of Ukrainian advisors, in my opinion, failed in its task. A representation of a contrast between a pioneer hut and a modern Ukrainian home would have clearly shown the progress that we made in Canada over the past sixty years. This would have made a strong impression on tourists and would have been a matter of pride and gratitude to Canada from the upcoming generations of Ukrainian Canadians. However, in connection with this suggestion, some may say the progress of Ukrainian Canadians is seen all around. But the clear evidence of the past and the present is the most convincing.

In regard to the Ukrainian section of the museum in Elk Island Park, it is necessary to make one more observation. Some Ukrainian people maintain that the government built the Ukrainian section of the museum to honour Ukrainian pioneers in Canada. Such an assumption is only partly true. Although it is true that the very building of the pioneer home is a monument to them, Minister Winters stated clearly that "the museum will be a memorial in honour and memory of the life and work of Dr. A. E. Archer." Therefore, it is not a monument in honour of Ukrainian pioneers.

In concluding this account of Vegreville, one cannot fail to mention one special achievement of this area. The one thing that stands above any other achievement of our people in Canada, and one that binds Ukrainian Canadians with their ancient Ukrainian traditions and talents of those remarkable Ukrainian ploughmen and cattlemen, is the recognition accorded Ukrainian Canadian producers at national and international grain and cattle exhibitions.

Canadian farmers from Alberta began to participate in world competitions and championships in the various species of grains as early as 1876. And from that time to 1937 on the list of those who won first place at the exhibits of grains, one can find only names of our fellow citizens. But in 1937, a momentous event occurred. That year, for the first time on the North American continent, Yuri [George] Topolnytsky from Andrew, Alberta won first prize for oats at the world exhibition of grains in Chicago, United States. From that time, his success has been emulated by many Ukrainian Canadians. One can add that almost all of them, with one or two exceptions, live in the Vegreville federal riding. Here again, we see additional benefits of bloc settlement of Ukrainian Canadians.

As has been said, Ukrainian pioneer farmers in Canada knew that they were good at agriculture. Their superior farming skills were recognized and acknowledged. Their sons, however, went a step further and gained for themselves official recognition for excellence in world competitions. Naturally, those taking part in such competitions are obliged to meet very high standards, which require hard work, perseverance, patience, and endurance. As it is, our Canadian-born young people are endowed by their fathers and grandfathers with those positive qualities of character.

During the war years, the world exhibitions of grains were stopped. In 1948, Alberta farmers again began to take part in these competitions. Once again Ukrainian-Canadian grain producers excelled as world champions. Thus the first prize winner for oats at the Chicago World Exhibition in 1948 was John T. Iliuk from the Hairy Hill district, who had arrived from Western Ukraine in 1925. In 1949, he again won first prize for oats and for barley, this time at the Toronto Exhibition, while S. H. Pawlowsky, from Vilna, received first prize for oats at Chicago. In 1950, Iliuk won his second world oats championship at the World Exhibition in Chicago.

Those who read of the achievements of Ukrainian Canadians at world exhibitions may come to the conclusion that either all lands in the Vegreville riding are exceptionally fertile, or that Ukrainian farmers meet with little competition. They are mistaken. The land on which Ukrainian Canadians produce grains that win world championships had been abandoned by our fellow citizens long ago, as they searched for better farm land in other districts. The district of Vilna-Spedden, where the Pawlowsky family farms, is a good example. The soil in this area is sandy with small rocks. The frost-free period is short and, as in other districts, drought often ruins crops. And yet, notwithstanding these hostile circumstances, the Pawlowsky family attained several world championships.

3

THE FIRST UKRAINIAN CANADIAN *in* PARLIAMENT: *Michael Luchkovich*

On the evening of 14 September 1926, the election headquarters of the United Farmers of Alberta (UFA) in the town of Vegreville was filled to capacity. Hundreds came into the hall, glanced at the number of votes written on the blackboard, and left. Everyone followed the results of the federal election that day. But as usual, the voters were especially interested in the election results in their own riding. This time the election in the Vegreville riding had overwhelming significance for all Ukrainian Canadians. This was the first time in the history of this country that a Canadian of Ukrainian origin was a candidate in the federal election. This was the first attempt of Ukrainian Canadians from a predominantly Ukrainian riding to open the door to the highest national tribunal – the Parliament of Canada.

The running account of ballot counting was conveyed to the election headquarters by telephone. Throughout the evening, the telephone rang every few minutes, and the committee members wrote the results on the blackboard. One column recorded the votes for Luchkovich and another column for J. S. McCallum, the candidate of the Liberal party. At that time there were only two candidates in the Vegreville riding.

The first news, coming mainly from towns, gave McCallum a lead over Luchkovich by several hundred votes. Understandably, such news did not please those present in the headquarters. And in the early hours of the evening, the majority of Luchkovich's supporters were beginning to lose hope for their candidate to win. However, between ten o'clock and midnight news began to trickle in from farming districts, where, with but a few exceptions, they gave Luchkovich the majority of votes. In any event, although not all farm polls could send the results to the headquarters that day, because in some places there were no telephones nearby, nevertheless, Luchkovich needed about three hundred votes to catch up to McCallum. This change in the number of votes also altered the mood not only of Luchkovich's supporters but also of his opponents. It was clear that Luchkovich had a realistic chance to be elected. On the third day after the election, when all votes were counted, it was announced that Luchkovich won by 728 votes.

The election of Luchkovich was an event about which the Canadian and Ukrainian press throughout Canada commented for several months. This was the first time a Canadian of Ukrainian origin had won a seat in the Canadian federal Parliament. While Luchkovich received sufficient support from non-Ukrainian districts, nevertheless his election signalled the beginning of the full participation of Ukrainians in our country's federal politics.

The success of Luchkovich in the 1926 election had very interesting origins that are worth recalling. When the federal election of 1926 was announced, Ukrainian Canadians were not really prepared to participate in Canadian federal politics. It is true that to this time Ukrainians already had two members in the Alberta provincial legislature, as well as two in the Manitoba legislature. But to succeed in federal politics, it was necessary for our people to take a much more active part in Canada's political parties than they had to date. Unfortunately, the number of Ukrainian Canadians who were familiar with the nature of federal politics was still limited. But regardless of these shortcomings, the biggest obstacle for Ukrainians wanting to enter into federal politics was the negative attitude of the two old Canadian parties. The Conservative and Liberal parties for many years managed their politics in such a discriminatory and manipulative manner that a potential Ukrainian candidate not only did not reach the stage of election, but was even unable to receive the nomination in these parties. It was only in 1935 that a Ukrainian, John Hnatyshyn, first received the official nomination from the Conservative party in the riding of Yorkton, Saskatchewan. John Decore won the Liberal party nomination in Vegreville in 1949.

In the 1920s, however, circumstances in Alberta were somewhat different. In this province, the Conservative party had never been elected as a provincial government and never had strong support in federal politics. The Liberal party was in power from the very beginning of the formation of this province: that is, from 1905 to 1921.

However, Albertans were dissatisfied with the Liberal party's rule and in 1921 the newly formed party, the United Farmers of Alberta (UFA), like a prairie fire decimated old parties and took power. Six months later, on 17 December 1921, the federal election took place, at which time ten members were elected to Ottawa from this party, which at the federal level called itself the Progressive party.

The UFA was in essence a protest party against the politics of both the Conservatives and Liberals. The prairie provinces, as well as all of Western Canada, believed that the old parties gave preferential treatment to the central provinces of Ontario and Quebec, where all manufacturing was concentrated, and where the majority of federal members were elected. Depending to a large extent on this protest and not on a "national" platform, such a movement could not spread throughout Canada. In any event, from this time on the old parties were forced to reckon with the demands of the farmers. It is for this reason that the farmers' political movement played an important role.

The federal riding of Vegreville was created in 1924. Its first federal member was A. M. Boutillier, who was elected in 1925. In this election nine members were elected from the Progressive Party and seven from other parties. Boutillier perhaps was more English than French, although he had a French name.

The federal Liberal government, elected in 1925, did not last long. In June 1926, on a vote of confidence, the opposition defeated the government by two votes, which forced it to resign. Then the Conservative opposition tried to form a government, hoping to get the support at least of a few Liberal members. But this plan was unsuccessful and a new general election was called for 14 September 1926.

While Vegreville was a newly created riding and its first Member of Parliament, A. M. Boutillier, represented it for less than a year, a radical idea began to circulate in Ukrainian communities: let us elect someone from among ourselves to the federal Parliament! And because the UFA, without a doubt, had the best chance in the Vegreville riding, and perhaps in all of Alberta, then naturally its members and supporters proposed that a candidate should come from this party. The idea of selecting a candidate of Ukrainian origin arose in the town of Vegreville, but soon reached other parts of the riding and grew with each day. Enthused with this possibility, people began thinking whom to propose as a candidate. Among the initiators who took this matter seriously were several schoolteachers, farmers, and businessmen. Among the teachers, the most active were O. Hryhorovych, Wolodymyr Kupchenko, who then was preparing to enter teachers' college, Wasyl Dorosh, and others. Among the Ukrainian businessmen who worked fervently in this cause we can mention Ilia Porayko, and among the farmers, John Kosiura and others.

It occurred to someone to approach Michael Luchkovich with the proposition. Luchkovich was teaching at the time in Bushland, north of the town of Ranfurley. His supporters believed that Luchkovich was the most suitable candidate. He was one of the most active Ukrainian Canadians in Alberta and played a leadership role in community affairs. In the first years, when the Michael Hrushevsky Institute,[53] a Ukrainian residential school, was founded in Edmonton, he became president of the student body. In those years we often came across the name of Luchkovich in connection with various lectures and resolutions of which he was the prime mover. Luchkovich spoke excellent English. He was born in Shamokin, Pennsylvania, U.S.A. and came to Canada in 1907. He began to learn Ukrainian only in Canada, while a student at the University of Manitoba in Winnipeg, where he obtained an Arts degree. Upon his arrival in Edmonton, he began to study law at the University of Alberta and taught school between semesters.

When the delegates approached Luchkovich with their proposition that he agree to stand as a candidate in the forthcoming nominating convention of the UFA party, he was so taken by surprise that he was unable to give his decision immediately. However, after a lengthy discussion, he made a positive decision.

The matter of nominating a candidate of Ukrainian origin was extremely difficult, because in those times there were only a very few Ukrainians in the riding who were members of any political party. And in order to nominate a Ukrainian as an official candidate of a political party, it was necessary to have at the convention a majority of delegates of that origin. As there was little time left before the convention, the committee of supporters of Luchkovich had to begin signing up Ukrainian members for the UFA party as soon as possible. This was in July when many of the farmers were busy haying, while others were clearing forests or working the land, and this posed difficulties for the organizers. In addition, the membership fee was three dollars and not every potential new member had ready cash, and the committee did not have any funds for that purpose. Therefore, in many instances, Luchkovich's supporters themselves had to cover the deficit in the member fund and to pay the cost of their travel. Nevertheless, this determination and dedication of a small group of people prevailed and a respectable number of Ukrainian delegates promised to come to the convention in the town of Andrew.

On the day of the convention, members of the committee worried that not enough Ukrainian delegates would appear because of the costs of travel and because very few owned their own cars. But the determined Ukrainian farmers got together with their neighbours and began arriving by wagon, buggies, and car before the designated hour. Farmers from farther districts set out at night to arrive on time.

After the opening of the convention and the adoption of formal resolutions, the nominations began. The first to be nominated was A. M. Boutillier. The names of Michael Luchkovich and Peter Miskiw followed. There were other nominations of Anglo-Canadians, but each of them stood, thanked the delegates and asked their supporters to vote for Boutillier. Thus, after the first count, Boutillier was in first place; Luchkovich, second; and Miskiw, third. But before distributing the final ballots, Luchkovich's supporters pleaded with Miskiw that he step aside in favour of Luchkovich. Finally, when Miskiw began to walk to the platform to withdraw his candidacy, supporters of Boutillier began to shout in order to prevent him from doing so. This so angered Miskiw that he was now determined at all cost to carry out his intention. Overcoming the shouting of his opponents, he reached the platform and announced that when supporters of Boutillier withdrew in his favour, he also withdraws and asks his supporters to back Luchkovich. The resignation of Miskiw and the thunderous applause of the Ukrainian delegates that followed was a dramatic moment which deeply stirred the Ukrainian delegates.

After counting the ballots, it was announced that Luchkovich was elected, with a small majority of votes, as the UFA candidate for the federal riding of Vegreville.

It has been said by the participants at the convention that some supporters of Boutillier were so incensed by the outcome of the nomination that they tore off their UFA tags in front of Luchkovich, threw them on the floor, and stomped on them. At that time there were some people who could not accept the idea that Ukrainian Canadians should have the same privileges as other Canadians who enjoy full rights as citizens, including the right of choosing from among themselves a candidate to represent them in Parliament. But such individuals were exceptions and the great majority of the UFA party members worked diligently on behalf of Luchkovich. For Ukrainians the election of Luchkovich was an achievement of momentous significance. This is why the majority of Ukrainian voters, regardless of their own political ideology, enthusiastically assisted the Luchkovich campaign right up to the election day.

To assess appropriately the achievements of a public figure, one must recognize not only his talents and character but also the circumstances under which he had to work. In this respect, the contributions of Luchkovich make him an historic Ukrainian-Canadian figure, as his achievements were truly great. 28 May 1929 was a day when Luchkovich's name attained great popularity among Ukrainian Canadians. On that memorable day he delivered a powerful speech in the House of Commons attacking the discriminatory treatment of Ukrainian settlers, a practice that was prevalent in some Anglo-Canadian circles. This important speech was prompted by a letter that had accidentally come into his hands. Written by Protestant Bishop George Lloyd to his clergy, the letter portrayed Ukrainians in very derogatory terms and called upon the clergy to protest further Ukrainian immigration to Canada. Among other things, Bishop Lloyd wrote:

> The Ottawa committee recommended to Parliament the non-renewal in its present form the existing railway's agreement, expiring in 1930. But why should this country be inflicted with another three years of these dirty, ignorant, garlic-smelling, unwanted

continentals as we have been in the last three years? Surely this country ought to be able to govern its railways rather than the railways demoralize our population.

Luchkovich built an effective speech around this letter and delivered it brilliantly in the House of Commons. The Canadian and American press publicized his speech widely, returning to it for several weeks in their editorials. For example, *Maclean's* magazine referred to Luchkovich as "one of the most talented orators in Parliament." The *Chicago Tribune* noted, "several weeks ago there occurred something of a sensation in the Canadian Parliament when Mr. Luchkovich delivered his reply to Bishop Lloyd of Saskatchewan." Without question this speech made Luchkovich a well-known and respected politician among Ukrainians throughout Canada and abroad.

Federal elections were held on 28 July 1930. This time it was much easier for Luchkovich. Although his Liberal opponent waged a strong campaign, Luchkovich won by 904 votes. During the second term, Luchkovich's accomplishments exceeded those of the first term. On 8 May 1931 he delivered the most powerful speech of his political career. This was his attack on the well-known and brutal Polish "pacification" of Western Ukraine. The speech made such a profound impact in Parliament that the then Conservative Prime Minister of Canada, R. B. Bennett, was obliged to speak twice on the subject of Polish–Ukrainian relations but without stating a clear position of his government. Ernest Lapointe, the future long-time Minister of Justice in the Liberal cabinet, spoke on behalf of the Liberal party. Among the leaders of the Canadian political parties, the most sympathetic stand toward Ukrainians was taken by J. S. Woodsworth, the distinguished labour leader and one of the founders of the Cooperative Commonwealth Federation (CCF). Eight other MPs, who perhaps wished to impress their Ukrainian voters, participated in the debate. The debate on Polish repression of Ukrainians lasted almost a full day. In reporting these proceedings, the *Edmonton Ukrainian News* called the debate a Ukrainian day in the Canadian parliament.

In September 1932 Luchkovich traveled to Europe. He was chosen as the only delegate of the Canadian branch of the Empire

Parliamentary Association to attend the international parliamentary conference in Bucharest, Romania. In view of the fact that elections were being held in Britain at that time, the British branch of the association authorized Luchkovich to represent it at the conference as well. It turned out that the only representative of the largest empire at that time to the international conference of parliamentarians was the son of Ukrainian immigrants from Bukovyna, Michael Luchkovich. He took advantage of his unique position to defend the rights of Ukrainian people who were repressed in their own native land. That defence represents one of Luchkovich's historical contributions to his people. In Bucharest he spoke on the subject of minority human and national rights. During an audience with the king of Romania, Luchkovich stated that the issue of national minorities was one of the most urgent problems in Europe. Such challenging statements made in Romania, a country whose police used harsh methods to suppress every manifestation of national aspirations of its Ukrainian minority, speak for themselves.

After the congress Luchkovich visited his ancestral homeland, Bukovyna. There he met with many prominent Ukrainians, such as the famous writer Ol'ha Kobylanska and the Bukovynian political leader Dr. W. Zalozetsky. He also addressed a public meeting and visited his family village of Berehomet.

From Bukovyna, Luchkovich traveled to the Polish-occupied Western Ukraine, where he was a guest of Metropolitan Andrei Sheptytsky, archbishop of the Ukrainian Greek-Catholic Church. During his stay in Lviv, Luchkovich met with a number of prominent Ukrainian community leaders, including Kost Levytsky, Milena Rudnytska,[54] and Ostap Lutsky. A banquet was held in his honour.

When Luchkovich returned to Canada, his status and popularity increased further. But this fact did not prevent a group of Ukrainian Liberals from the Ukrainian Self-Reliance League from plotting against him. While the majority of the Alberta USRL members were staunch supporters of Luchkovich, several of their ambitious leaders had their own agenda. In 1933 the Liberal party in Alberta launched a serious political campaign, taking advantage of the mistakes made by the provincial UFA government to defeat the provincial government and also to elect Liberals to the House of Commons. This campaign attracted a small number of Ukrainians who were motivated by political partisanship, which they assumed would bring them patronage, personal benefits, and honours. Luchkovich, of course, faithfully served all Ukrainian Canadians, regardless of their political or religious affiliation. However, disregarding his popularity and achievements, these Ukrainian Liberals saw Luchkovich as an obstacle to their own ambitions and decided to defeat him.

The campaign against Luchkovich was subversive and clever, designed not to antagonize his many supporters. The main argument of his opponents ran as follows: "Luchkovich is a good and capable MP and he does have many achievements. But it is most unfortunate that he is not from the right party. If he had been elected from the Liberal party, then he could have done so much more. But because he is a member of a small opposition faction, it is necessary to replace him with another MP of Ukrainian origin, one from the Liberal party." As this and other negative arguments circulated in the riding, some people began to waver in their support of Luchkovich. In addition, Canada's communists were also determined to defeat Luchkovich because he always had spoken on behalf of the Ukrainian nationalists. Thus Luchkovich found himself attacked from two sides, by the communists and by Ukrainian Liberals.

In the summer of 1934, the nominating convention of the Liberal party was held in the town of Willingdon. To the dismay of the Ukrainian Liberals, their candidate William Pidruchny of Vegreville was defeated by J. McCallum, who had been Luchkovich's opponent in 1926. The majority of Ukrainian Liberals were outraged with the outcome of the nominating convention and returned to support Luchkovich. But it was too late to correct the damage that they had inflicted with their foolish propaganda against him. Moreover, a new political movement, the Social Credit, was spreading so rapidly in Alberta that supporters of various political parties were joining the new party *en masse*. There was no doubt that Social Credit would win a respectable number of seats in the provincial legislature and could even elect some MPs to Ottawa if the party decided to participate in federal politics.

The UFA government of Alberta has had serious problems, particularly of a personal nature caused by the premier and some ministers. Furthermore, after fourteen years in power, the UFA lost its initiative and energy. When the provincial election was held on 22 August 1935, the Social Credit party won with 163,700 votes, while the Liberal party came second with less than 70,000 and the UFA trailed with only 33,063. Whereas before the election, the UFA had 36 members and the opposition had 27, now the Social Credit elected 56 members, the Liberals 5, the Conservatives 3, and the UFA had none.[55] This was the state of Alberta politics when the federal election was announced.

It should be noted that the nine UFA MPs, including Luchkovich, had officially adopted the name of the Canadian Commonwealth Federation (CCF) party, organized in 1932 and whose founder was J. S. Woodsworth. This party was based on principles of moderate socialism and was supported by organized labour.

The federal election was held on 14 October 1935 and not one UFA member was elected. Luchkovich[56] himself was defeated by Social Credit candidate William Hayhurst. In fact, of the seventeen MPs from Alberta, fifteen were Social Creditors, one Liberal, and one Conservative – R. B. Bennett, the defeated Prime Minister.

4

ADDITIONAL READINGS

There is a rich and comprehensive Ukrainian Canadian historical literature in the English language, thanks in part to the efforts of the Canadian Institute of Ukrainian Studies at the University of Alberta. The following studies are relevant to the Anthony Hlynka story:

William Darcovich and Paul Yuzyk, eds., *A Statistical Compendium on the Ukrainians in Canada, 1891–1976* (Ottawa, 1980).

Gerald Friesen, *The Canadian Prairies: A History* (Toronto, 1984).

C.W. Hobart et al., *Persistence and Change: A Study of Ukrainians in Alberta* (Edmonton, 1978).

Vladimir J. Kaye, *Early Ukrainian Settlements in Canada, 1893–1900* (Toronto, 1964).

John Kolasky, *The Shattered Illusion: The History of Ukrainian Pro-Communist Organizations in Canada* (Toronto, 1979).

Bohdan S. Kordan, *Canada and the Ukrainian Question, 1939–1945* (Kingston, 2001).

Peter Krawchuk, *Our History: The Ukrainian Labour-Farmer Movement in Canada* (Toronto, 1996).

Michael Luchkovich, *A Ukrainian Canadian in Parliament* (Toronto, 1965).

Lubomyr Luciuk and Stella Hryniuk, eds., *Canada's Ukrainians: Negotiating an Identity* (Toronto, 1991).

Manoly R. Lupul, ed. *A Heritage in Transition: Essays in the History of Ukrainians in Canada* (Toronto, 1982) and *Continuity and Change: The Cultural Life of Alberta's First Ukrainians* (Edmonton, 1988).

Orest T. Martynowych, *Ukrainians in Canada: The Formative Period, 1891–1924* (Edmonton, 1991).

Helen Potrebenko, *No Streets of Gold: A Social History of Ukrainians in Alberta* (Vancouver, 1977).

Thomas Prymak, *Maple Leaf and Trident: The Ukrainian Canadians during the Second World War* (Toronto, 1988).

Jaroslav Rozumnyj, ed., *New Soil – Old Roots* (Winnipeg, 1983).

Julian Stechishin, *A History of Ukrainian Settlement in Canada* (Saskatoon, 1992).

Frances Swyripa, *Ukrainian Canadians: A Survey of Their Portrayal in English-Language Works* (Edmonton, 1977) and Swyripa and John H. Thompson, eds., *Loyalties in Conflict: Ukrainians in Canada During the Great War* (Edmonton, 1983).

Ukrainian Association of Alberta, *Ukrainians in Alberta* (Edmonton, 1975).

Olha Woycenko, *The Ukrainians in Canada* (Ottawa-Winnipeg, 1967).

SPEECHES to VEGREVILLE RIDING

During the period of 1940–49, Anthony Hlynka gave 322 speeches throughout the Vegreville riding. They are listed as follows.

Location	No. of speeches	Location	No. of speeches
Andrew	10	Lavoy	3
Muendare	10	Peno	3
Radway	10	Ranfurly	3
Willingdon	10	Royal Park	3
Oleskiw	8	Tofield	3
Smoky Lake	8	Beaver Lake	2
St. Michael	8	Brody	2
Warspite	8	DesJarlais	2
Wostok	8	Great Bear Lake	2
Bellis	7	Highway	2
Bruderheim	7	Inland	2
Krakow	7	5Ispas	2
Vegreville	7	Cossack	2
Vilna	7	Lamont	2
Chipman	6	Moscow	2
Hairy Hill	6	North Bellis	2
Ministik	6	Opal	2
Redwater	6	Peremysl	2
Spedden	6	Shandro	2
Two Hills	6	Sprucefield	2
Weasel Creek	6	Stanislawiw	2
Egremont	5	Boian	1
Hilliard	5	Brookville	1
New Kiew	5	Brosseau, Lac.	1
Polos	5	Cadron	1
Plain Lake	5	Dalmuir	1
Podolia	5	East Gate	1
Ross Creek	5	Good Hope	1
Skaro	5	Green Lake	1
Borschiw	4	Hastings Lake	1
Delph	4	Kolomyia	1
Limestone	4	Lilyfield	1
Stry	4	Mackenzie	1
Thorhild	4	Molodyia	1
Warwick	4	Moose Hills	1
Waskatenau	4	Partridge Hill	1
Wasel	4	Prut	1
Barich	3	Sniatyn	1
Eldorena	3	Spring Creek	1
Holowaychuk	3	Star	1
Yaroslaw	3	Sunland	1
Josephburg	3	Ankas	1
Kahwin	3	Wahsteyo	1
Keyland	3	Whitford	1
		Total	322

NOTES

1. Metropolitan Andrei Sheptytsky (1865–1944) was archbishop of Lviv and head of the Ukrainian Greek Catholic church in Halychyna where he strongly defended Ukrainian religious and national interests against Polish and Soviet encroachments. Following his death in 1944, Soviet authorities abolished the Ukrainian Greek Catholic church by forcing it to "reunite" with the Russian Orthodox Church, to which it had never belonged. The Ukrainian church remained underground until its rebirth in 1989. In 1910 Sheptytsky had visited Ukrainian pioneer settlements in Canada and this led in 1912 to the appointment by the Vatican of the first Ukrainian Catholic bishop, Nykyta Budka, for Canada. A balanced discussion of Sheptytsky is presented by a symposium, Paul R. Magosci, ed., *Morality and Reality: the Life and Times of Andre Sheptyts'kyi* (Edmonton, 1989).

2. Basil Ladyka (1884–1956) succeeded the controversial Bishop Budka as primate of the Ukrainian Catholic church in 1929. He strengthened his church, which had been losing members to the rival Ukrainian Orthodox church, by integrating lay organizations into its activities. The influential Ukrainian Catholic Brotherhood was formed on his initiative.

3. Michael Pohorecky (1899–1964), a veteran of Ukraine's independence struggle, arrived in Canada in 1926. As long-time editor of *Novyi shliakh/New Pathway* (1930–1964), he became an ideologue of moderate nationalism as represented by the UNF. *New Pathway* was transferred to Winnipeg in 1942 and to Toronto in 1974 where it is still published as a bilingual weekly.

4. The Ukrainian Military Organization was a clandestine revolutionary organization formed in 1920 to continue the armed struggle for Ukrainian independence from Poland and Soviet Russia. In 1929 it submerged itself into the new Organization of Ukrainian Nationalists.

5. A detailed history of the Ukrainian National Federation, including its women's and youth wings, was produced by the organization to commemorate its fiftieth anniversary: *Na sliakhu do natsionalnoi iednosty, 1932–1982* (Toronto. 1982). There is a rich Ukrainian-language literature on the subject of Ukrainian nationalism. English-language studies, however, are in short supply. John Armstrong provides a balanced account of Ukrainian nationalism in his much-quoted *Ukrainian Nationalism*, 2nd ed. (Littleton, CO, 1980). See also Alexander Motyl, *The Turn to the Right: The Ideological Origins and Development of Ukrainian Nationalism, 1919–1929* (New York, 1980) and Paul R. Magosci, *The Roots of Ukrainian Nationalism: Galicia as Ukraine's Piedmont* (Toronto, 2003).

6. *Klych (The Call)* in its short life, 1935–1937, attempted to undermine the appeal of communism among the Ukrainian Canadian workers by exposing Soviet communism ("Moscovite Bolshevism") as a new form of Russian imperialism that brutally repressed Ukraine.

7. During the 1940 election, the King government promised that there would be no conscription. However, in 1942 the manpower shortage in Canada's armed forces obliged the government to hold a plebiscite by which Prime Minister King was released from his pledge of no conscription. Since a majority of French Canadians

voted against the plebiscite, a serious breach developed between English and French Canada.

8   Peter Lazarowich (1900–1983) was president of the Ukrainian Self-Reliance League and a key member of the executive (Consistory) of the Ukrainian Orthodox Church of Canada.

9   Dmytro Holubitsky was a well-known Alberta physician and a prominent supporter of Orthodox institutions.

10 Peter Zvarich (1877–1966) arrived in Canada in 1900 and became a successful businessman and entrepreneur. He is noted for his generous support of Ukrainian-Canadian cultural and educational institutions.

11 *Kanadiisky farmer (Canadian Farmer)* had the distinction of being the first Ukrainian-language newspaper in Canada (1903–1981). Originally published in Winnipeg with a subsidy from the Liberal party, *Canadian Farmer* promoted Canadian citizenship, firmly supported the Ukrainian Canadian Committee, and denounced communism. Its literary section provided opportunities for established and budding writers. In 1981 *Canadian Farmer* was amalgamated into *Ukrainian Voice*.

12 *Ukrainsky Robitnyk (Ukrainian Worker)* (1934–1956), despite its socialist name, promoted monarchist conservatism of the United Hetman Organization of Canada.

13 Although John Hnatyshyn (1907–1967) failed to get elected to Parliament, he remained active in the Progressive Conservative party and in 1959 was appointed senator by Prime Minister Diefenbaker. His son, Ramon, also a lawyer, represented Saskatoon in the House of Commons from 1974 to 1988 and served as Minister of Justice in the Mulroney government. In 1989 Ramon Hnatyshyn was appointed Governor General of Canada and in 1992 he became the first Western head of state to pay an official visit to the newly independent Ukraine, his ancestral homeland.

14 *Ukrainsky holos (Ukrainian Voice)* was established in Winnipeg in 1910 by Trident Press, a company of Ukrainian bilingual teachers, to raise self-esteem and pride in their community and heritage, to support the Orthodox church, and to promote education as key to success in Canada. With the organization of the powerful Ukrainian Self-Reliance League in 1927, the *Ukrainian Voice* became its organ. The USRL became an umbrella for the Ukrainian Women's Association, Ukrainian Canadian Youth Association, a network of National Homes, and four residential institutes. Once perhaps the most influential weekly in the Ukrainian Canadian community, the *Ukrainian Voice* remains as Canada's oldest active Ukrainian paper. See Oleh W. Gerus, "Consolidating the Community: The Ukrainian Self-Reliance League" in Lubomyr Luciuk and Stella Hryniuk, eds., *Canada's Ukrainians: Negotiating an Identity* (Toronto, 1991), 159–186.

15 John Danylchuk (1900–1942), a Saskatchewan-born writer-poet and a community activist in Winnipeg, edited the *Canadian Ukrainian Review*.

16 William Chumer (1882–1963) was one of the first Ukrainian teachers trained at the Ruthenian Training School in Winnipeg. He was one of the founders of the Ukrainian Pioneer Association of Alberta and author of one of the first historical accounts of the Ukrainian settlement of Western Canada, *Reflections about the Life of the First Ukrainian Settlers in Canada* (1942).

17 Myroslav Stechishin (1883–1947) was the oldest of the famous Ukrainian-born three brothers whose presence in Canada made a difference. As a long-time editor of the *Ukrainian Voice* and ideologue of the Ukrainian Self-Reliance League, he articulated the organization's philosophy of "self-reliance, self-respect, and

self-help." Michael Stechishin (1888–1964) was a Saskatchewan lawyer, writer, and one of the founders of the Ukrainian Orthodox church in Canada (1918). In 1949 Michael became the first Ukrainian in Canada to receive a judicial appointment. Julian Stechishin (1895–1971, also a lawyer, was best known as an educator in Saskatoon's Mohyla Institute and a historian of Ukrainian settlement of Canada. More importantly perhaps, he was married to Savella (1903–2002), an outstanding community activist, co-founder of the Ukrainian Museum of Canada in Saskatoon, newspaper columnist, and author of the internationally celebrated book on Ukrainian customs and traditions, *Traditional Ukrainian Cookery* (18 printings). Natalie Ostryzniuk, "Savella Stechishin, an Ethnocultural Feminist and Ukrainian Culture in Saskatchewan," *Saskatchewan History* 51, no. 2 (Fall 1999): 12–28.

18 Dmytro Gerych (1899–1971) was a Winnipeg notary public who organized a Ukrainian platoon in the Cameron's Highlanders Regiment and was active in the United Hetman Organization and municipal politics.

19 Theodore Datskiw (1888–1956), a university graduate, arrived in Canada in 1923. In Winnipeg he edited *Kanadiisky Farmer (Canadian Farmer)*, which promoted community solidarity around the UCC.

20 Nicholas Bachynsky (1887–1969) was a very successful Manitoba politician who arrived in Canada in 1906 and trained as a teacher. In 1922 he was elected to the Manitoba Legislature from the Liberal-Progressive party and was re-elected seven times. He served as House Speaker from 1949 to his retirement in 1958. He was a leading member of the USRL.

21 Taras Ferley (1882–1947) was a major community leader in the pioneer phase of the Ukrainian Canadian experience. A co-founder of the *Ukrainian Voice* and the Ukrainian National Home, in 1915 he became the first Ukrainian in Manitoba to be elected to the provincial legislature (Liberal/Gimli), where he staunchly but unsuccessfully defended the province's bilingual education system.

22 Isydore Hlynka (1909–1983) was a world-class research biochemist with the Grain Research Laboratory in Winnipeg and a prominent community leader. He was particularly active in the UCC, the Ukrainian Cultural and Educational Centre, St. Andrew's College, and the Shevchenko Foundation. Under the pen name of Ivan Harmata for twelve years he wrote a popular column in the *Ukrainian Voice* on Ukrainian Canadian issues, which later came out as a book, *The Other Canadians*.

23 By comparison, in 2003, an MP received $150,000 annually plus extensive support staff both in the House and at the constituency level. There was also a generous retirement pension. The prime minister's salary was $270,000.

24 Stephanie Hlynka (nee Chole) was born in Halychyna and came to Toronto in 1929 as a youngster. Trained as a legal secretary, she met Anthony in Toronto in 1940 and married him in 1943. During Hlynka's political career, she was his indispensable helpmate and travel companion. As she recalled:

> "After the sessions ended in Parliament, Anthony would travel throughout his riding giving an account of events that transpired in the House. His constituents, mainly agriculturalists, were well informed about issues, since they were directly affected by them. The Q and A periods were lively and interesting. His meetings were well attended as his constituents were eager to hear Anthony review the proceedings in the House, and they also came because they knew they would be entertained. Anthony was a great story teller."

Two years after Anthony's sudden death, Stephanie and her two children, Eugene and Gloria, moved from Edmonton back to Toronto where her family was, driving a vintage 1948 Dodge car. There Mrs. Hlynka first worked at Osgoode Hall Law School as the Dean's executive secretary and until her retirement in 1989, she served as executive secretary to the Chairman of the Ontario Law Reform Commission. She is in possession of Anthony's archives.

25 Solon Low (1900–1962) served in the Social Credit government of Alberta and in 1944 was elected leader of the federal Social Credit party. In the 1958 general election his party was wiped out by a Progressive Conservative landslide. However, the right-wing conservatism of the Social Credit and a sense of western alienation gave rise to the Reform party, which mutated into the Canadian Alliance, and after absorbing the Progressive Conservative party in 2003, became the new Conservative Party of Canada.

26 *Ukrainski Visti/Ukrainian News* (1929 to present) was originally published by the Edmonton eparchy of the Ukrainian Catholic Church and reflected developments in Western Canada. Since 1991 it has been national in scope and bilingual.

27 The Ukrainian Catholic Brotherhood of Canada (BUK), a national lay organization, was formed in 1932 to strengthen the Catholic church and its role in the community. BUK became the largest, though not the most dynamic, Ukrainian organization in Canada and was one of the founding members of the Ukrainian Canadian Congress.

28 The Ukrainian Canadian Committee (Congress) came into being on 7 November 1940 in Winnipeg. The founding members were the Ukrainian Catholic Brotherhood, the Ukrainian Self-Reliance League, the Ukrainian National Federation, the United Hetman Organization, and the League of Ukrainian Organizations. In 2004 the UCC had twenty-eight member organizations. For details and evaluation of the UCC, see Oleh W. Gerus, "The Ukrainian Canadian Committee" in Manoly R. Lupul, ed., *A Heritage in Transition: Essays in the History of Ukrainians in Canada* (Toronto, 1982), 195–214.

29 Ukrainian Canadian soldiers stationed in Great Britain during the Second World War in 1943 formed a social club, the Ukrainian Canadian Servicemen's Association (UCSA), which was maintained by the UCC and became involved with the postwar issue of repatriation and refugee relief. In June 1945 the returning members of the disbanded UCSA formed in Winnipeg a national organization, the Ukrainian Canadian Veteran's Association, which became a member of the UCC and of the Royal Canadian Legion.

30 Yuri Bozyk, ed., *Ukraine During World War II. History and Aftermath: A Symposium* (Edmonton, 1986) examines the Ukrainian experience in a main arena of the bloody Nazi-Soviet struggle. See also Karl C. Berkhoff, *Harvest of Despair: Life and Death in Ukraine under Nazi Rule* (Boston, 2004)

31 While a majority of Ukrainian Canadians retained their family names, thousands did change their surnames to escape prejudice or to be more readily acceptable to the Anglo-Canadian mainstream. Some names were merely translated (Chorney to Black/ Blackie or Kravets to Taylor), some were abbreviated and Anglicized (Kowalchuk to Coval or Cowell), and some were altered completely (Chykalenko to Noseworthy or Jurowsky to Smith). Luba Fedorkiw, "Ukrainian Surnames in Canada" (master's thesis, University of Manitoba, 1977).

32 Orest Zherebko (1887–1943) had the distinction of being the first Ukrainian to graduate from a Canadian university (BA Manitoba, 1913). He was involved in municipal politics in Saskatchewan and was elected to the legislature as a Liberal. He was also active in the fragmented Ukrainian community life, where he promoted unity.

33 The injustice of the internment of Ukrainians during World War I has been the outstanding grievance for the Ukrainian-Canadian community. Years of lobbying Ottawa by the UCC for redress and compensation have so far failed to bring this issue to closure, mainly because the government has been fearful of the consequences of its apology to the Ukrainians. See "Apology Fallout Feared: Ukrainian Redress for Internment Would Set Bad Precedent, Feds Advised." *The Winnipeg Free Press*, 22 December 2003. The subject of internment is discussed by Peter Melnycky, "The Internment of Ukrainians in Canada," in Frances Swyripa and John H. Thompson, eds., *Loyalties in Conflict* (Edmonton, 1983), 1–24; by Mark Minenko, "Without Just Cause: Canada's First National Internment Operations," in Luciuk and Hryniuk, eds., *Negotiating an Identity*, 288–303; and by Lubomyr Luciuk, *A Time for Atonement: Canada's First Internment Operations and the Ukrainian Canadians, 1914–1920* (Kingston, 1988).

34 Bohdan (Gordon) Panchuk (1915–1987) was a schoolteacher from Saskatchewan who served as a junior officer in the Royal Canadian Air Force. While stationed in Britain, Panchuk played a major part in founding the Ukrainian Canadian Servicemen's Association and later helped to organize the Central Relief Bureau. An energetic and egoistic activist, he tried to draw the attention of Canadian and British governments to the plight of the Ukrainian war refugees. Curiously, while Anthony Hlynka opened many diplomatic doors to Panchuk in London, Panchuk simply ignored Hlynka in his memoirs. Lubomyr Luciuk, ed., *Heroes of Their Day: The Reminiscences of Bohdan Panchuk* (Toronto, 1983).

35 The Reverend Dr. S. W. Sawchuk (1895–1983) was the principal personality in the organization and administration of the Ukrainian Greek Orthodox Church of Canada (1920–1950). During the war, he was vice-president of the newly created Ukrainian Canadian Committee (representing USRL) and a chaplain in Canada's military. He assisted a number of refugee Orthodox priests, including the Gerus family, to immigrate to Canada. For Sawchuk's part in the Ukrainian-Canadian experience, see Oleh W. Gerus, "The Reverend Semen Sawchuk and the Ukrainian Greek-Orthodox Church of Canada," *Journal of Ukrainian Studies* 16, nos. 1–2 (1991): 61–88.

36 Danylo Skoropadsky (1904–1971), an engineer by profession and a British resident, succeeded his father, General/Hetman Pavlo (d. 1945), who had ruled Ukraine in 1918, as head of the Ukrainian conservative-monarchist movement in the diaspora with links to Germany. He had toured Canada, 1937–38, as a guest of the United Hetman Organization of Canada.

37 Ann Crepleve was a Manitoba native who after her military service distinguished herself as director of the Ukrainian Canadian Relief Fund operations in Germany.

38 A Saskatchewan-born lawyer, Anthony Yaremovich served in the Canadian army and later on the executive of the UCC.

39 On the controversial subject of the Galicia division, see Wolf-Dietrich Heinke, *Ukrains'ka diviziia Halychyna* (Toronto-Paris, 1970); Basyl Dmytryshyn, "The SS Division 'Galicia': Its Genesis, Training, Development," *Nationalities Papers*, 21, no. 2 (1993): 53–73; Michael Logusz, *The Waffen-SS 14th Grenadier Division, 1943–1945* (Atglen, Pa, 1997); Taras Hunczak, *On the Horns of the Dilemma: The Story of the Ukrainian Division Halychyna* (Landham, MD, 2000); Wasyl Sirsky, "Why We Joined the Galicia Division," *New Pathway*, 10 May 2001. Wasyl Veryha, *Pid sontsem Italii* . (Toronto, 1984). Those veterans of the Galicia division who settled in Canada formed an association, the Brotherhood of the Veterans of the First Division of the Ukrainian National Army.

40 Although Argentina certainly did not accept millions of refugees, it did admit some six thousand Ukrainians, who joined the Ukrainian community there which dated from 1897. In the 1990s the overall Ukrainian-Argentinian population was estimated at 170,000–200,000. See Oleh W. Gerus, "Ukrainians in Argentina: A Canadian Perspective," *Journal of Ukrainian Studies* 2, no. 2 (1986): 3–18.

41 Father Dr. Wasyl Kushnir (1983–1979) of Winnipeg was a major force in the Ukrainian-Catholic as well as in the general Ukrainian community in Canada. As the first president of the UCC, he conducted an early but inconclusive tour of the DP camps in Germany. For a sympathetic biography, see Oleksander Baran, *Pratsia dlia tserkvy i narodu: zhyttia i dialnist o. Dr. Wasylia Kushnira* (Winnipeg, 1995).

42 Stanley (Yaroslav) Frolick (1920–1988) was an Alberta-born and European-educated community activist who served in the British intelligence during the war and later was involved with refugee relief and Ukrainian nationalist politics. Back in Canada, he practised law in Toronto and helped found the Canadian League for the Liberation of Ukraine.

43 Dmytro Dontsov (1883–1973) was a prominent political journalist and theorist who began as a Marxist and ended as the leading ideologue of the Ukrainian anti-democratic ultra-nationalism – that is, of the Bandera faction of the OUN. In 1947 he emigrated from Germany to Montreal, where he lectured at the University of Montreal.

44 Yevhen Onatsky (1894–1979) was a Ukrainian civic leader, journalist, and scholar who represented the Organization of Ukrainian Nationalists in Italy in the interwar period. In 1947 he immigrated to Argentina where he played a leading part in the Ukrainian community consolidation process. Among his many notable publications, the four-volume "little" Ukrainian encyclopaedia has been the most useful.

45 Yevhen Konovalets (1891–1938) was one of the major participants in Ukraine's unsuccessful struggle for independence, 1917–1919, as commander of the regiment the "Sich Riflemen" (Sichovi striltsi). In the interwar period, he headed the underground Ukrainian Military Organization and later the powerful Organization of Ukrainian Nationalists that waged political and armed struggle against Soviet and Polish occupation of Ukraine. Konovalets visited Canada, promoting the ideology of the OUN and fundraising. He was assassinated in 1938 in Rotterdam, Holland by a Soviet agent. His death led to a split in the OUN between moderates and hardliners.

46 Archbishop Mstyslav Skrypnyk (1895–1993), a former Ukrainian politician in Poland, was a member of the hierarchy of the revived Ukrainian Autocephalous Orthodox Church (UAOC), which had left Ukraine in 1944 to escape from communism. In 1947 Archbishop Skrypnyk was elected primate of the Ukrainian Greek Orthodox Church of Canada but in 1950 he assumed leadership in the American sister church. As head of the UAOC in the diaspora, he strove for the consolidation of Ukrainian Orthodoxy outside of Ukraine. In 1990, on the eve of the collapse of the Soviet Union and Ukraine's independence, a church council in Kyiv elected the elderly but still feisty Skrypnyk as the first Patriarch of the reborn Ukrainian Orthodox church in Ukraine. The much sought-after church unity, however, has so far failed to materialize, as the post-Soviet Ukraine has had three feuding Orthodox jurisdictions. See Oleh W. Gerus, "Church Politics in Contemporary Ukraine," *The Ukrainian Quarterly* 52, no. 1 (1996): 32–49 and "The Ukrainian Orthodox Disunity in a Historical Context," *The Ukrainian Quarterly* 53, no.4 (1997): 301–22.

47 Peter Savaryn (1926-) is a distinguished Ukrainian Canadian who immigrated to Canada in 1949 and in 1956 graduated from the University of Alberta with a law degree. He became actively involved in politics with the Progressive Conservative party of Alberta, and when that party came to power in 1971, Savaryn used his influence to establish Ukrainian-English bilingual schools and the Canadian Institute of Ukrainian Studies. He served as Chancellor of the University of Alberta and as president of the World Congress of Free Ukrainians.

48 A good examination of the subject of bloc settlement is presented by Orest T. Martynowych, *The Ukrainian Bloc Settlement in East Central Alberta: A History. Historical Site Service*, Occasional Paper No. 10 (Edmonton, 1985) and John C. Lehr, "The Government and the Immigration: Perspectives on the Ukrainian Bloc Settlement in the Canadian West." *Canadian Ethnic Studies* 9, no. 2 (1977): 42–55.

49 Ambrose Holowach was an accomplished pianist who had studied in Vienna in the 1930s. He was elected a Social Credit MP from Edmonton in 1953 and re-elected in 1957 but defeated in the 1958 Diefenbaker sweep. From 1959 to 1971 he served in the Alberta provincial legislature, and he was appointed to the Social Credit cabinet, the first Ukrainian-Canadian to hold such a post. For more detail on Ukrainian-Canadian politicians, see Senator Paul Yuzyk, "The Political Achievements of Ukrainians in Canada (1891–1981)," *The Ukrainian Historian* 1, no. 79 (1982–83): 79–91.

50 Michael Starr [Starchevsky] was Progressive-Conservative MP for the Oshawa constituency from 1952 to 1968. He served as Minister of Labour in the Diefenbaker cabinet (1958–1963); he was the first Ukrainian cabinet minister in the federal government of Canada.

51 Fred Zaplitny (1913–1964), a Manitoba native and a teacher by profession, was first elected in 1945 and again in 1953 from the CCF party. He supported Hlynka on Ukrainian issues.

52 In 2001 the population of Vegreville stood at 5,337. Since 1978 the town has been best known as the site of the world's largest *pysanka*, the Ukrainian Easter egg.

53 Named after Ukraine's foremost historian, the Michael Hrushevsky Institute was established in Edmonton in 1918 as a student residence and became a centre of Ukrainian political and cultural life. In 1944 it was renamed the St. John's Institute and it has been an integral part of the Ukrainian Self-Reliance League and its family of institutes, which include the Mohyla Institute in Saskatoon, St. Andrew's College in Winnipeg, and St. Vladimir Institute in Toronto. *Ukrainski visti/Ukrainian News* (1929 to present) was originally published by the Edmonton eparchy of the Ukrainian Catholic church and reflected developments in Western Canada. Since 1991 it has been national in scope and bilingual.

54 Milena Rudnytska (1892–1976) was a journalist and one of the leading activists and organizers of the women's movement in Western Ukraine in the interwar period. Elected to the Polish parliament, she articulated Ukrainian grievances before the League of Nations.

55 The Social Credit party dominated Alberta politics until 1971, when the Progressive Conservatives took power and have held it since. For insights into the origins of Social Credit, see Lewis H. Thomas, ed., *William Aberhart and Social Credit in Alberta* (Toronto, 1977), Albert Finkel, *The Social Credit Phenomenon* (Toronto, 1989); and Davis E. Elliot, ed., *Aberhart: Outpourings and Replies* (Calgary, 1991).

56 Following his political defeat, Michael Luchkovich (1892–1973) turned to literature, translating a number of Ukrainian books, such as Ilia Kiriak's *Sons of the Soil*, into English. His memoirs appeared in 1965 as *A Ukrainian in Canadian Parliament*.

Anthony Hlynka Portrait. (Arthur Roy / Library and Archives Canada / PA-047172)

www.ingramcontent.com/pod-product-compliance
Lightning Source LLC
Chambersburg PA
CBHW052053300426
44117CB00013B/2113